A CENTURY OF BRITISH BREWERS
1890 to 1990

by
Norman Barber

A Brewery History Society Publication

FOREWORD

It is with great pleasure that I put pen to paper to write this foreword to Norman Barber's magnum opus. Not least because it means that the task of my colleagues and I on the BHS Publishing Committee is almost at an end .... until the next book that is!

I have known Norman for many years now and during that time he has been tirelessly amassing data on past and present brewers with the sole intention of making the information available to the rest of us. For this we all owe him a great debt of gratitude. A quiet, almost shy man, he must nevertheless stand as a giant in the eyes of all those with an interest in the history of British Brewing.

Norman has brewed this book for your pleasure and enjoyment, we have nurtured it to a peak of condition that you may now tap the cask and drink your fill of brewery history.

Cheers!

Peter Moynihan

Peter Moynihan
Publishing Committee
Brewery History Society

INTRODUCTION

This development of my previous work "Where Have All The Breweries Gone?" has been prompted by a number of factors. Firstly, the book has inspired a steady flow of feedback over the ten years since its publication, for which I am grateful. The publication of Manfred Friedrich's Gazetteer, compiled from directory listings, posed as many questions as it answered and this itself prompted much further research. The growing number of local and county brewery histories being published has pointed out the errors and omissions in my original work. Finally, there has been a huge increase in the number of small scale brewers entering the industry. My cut-off date of 1990 has necessarily meant that recent developments in the latter field are not recorded herein, but this matter will be dealt with in a forthcoming BHS publication.

As before, the brewers are listed alphabetically for each location in current county order. Ireland, both north and south, has been included for the first time as have home-brew houses. Where little or no information is known, a date in brackets indicates the last directory listing. Four indexes are included enabling reference by county, town, brewery name or brewer's name.

A work of this size can never be complete or 100% accurate and I make no such claims for this volume. Pages have been provided at the back of the book for your own notes but please remember that if you have any further information which augments or contradicts any entry then I would be pleased to hear from you.

NORMAN BARBER

ACKNOWLEDGEMENTS

My thanks are due to a great many people, among whom must be especially mentioned are:- The Brewers and Licensed Retailers Association, John Arguile (Derbyshire), Denis McAllister (Durham), Martyn Cornell (Hertfordshire), Philip Eley (Hampshire), John Barnes (Sussex), Peter Moynihan (Kent), Andrew Davison (Norfolk), John Strange (Shropshire), Thomas Halpin (Ireland) and Tim Richards (New Breweries). The photographs were supplied by Ian Peaty, beer labels by Mike Jones and Chris Pearce, and old advertisements by Andrew Cunningham. Special thanks go to the BHS editorial team, especially Ken Smith, without whose tireless work this volume would not have been possible.

Photographic Illustrations

The Whitbread Archive; The Brewery History Society Archive; Ian Peaty Collection; McEwans Brewery; Paul Wregglesworth; Wrexham Lager Brewery; Everard's Brewery; Ludlow Museum & Tourist Board; Carlsberg, Tetley.

CONTENTS

Banwell

Castle, Sons & Woods. In 1859 the Banwell paper mill was converted into a brewery. Offered for sale April 1905 and was bought by Henry King with 18 public houses. The brewery was sold to the Bristol water undertaking April 1909.

Purrett & George (1892)

Bath

Bath Brewery Ltd, *13 Westgate Street.* Registered June 1889 to acquire 6 breweries in the area. Acquired by Bristol Brewery Georges & Co.Ltd 1923 with 40 tied houses and brewing ceased.

George Biggs & Sons, *Crown Brewery, 4 New Orchard Street.* Acquired by Bristol Brewery Georges & Co.Ltd 1924 with 3 public houses.

English Lager Beer Brewery Ltd, *Batheaston.* Registered 11th January 1890. Voluntary winding up 9th August 1893.

Corn Street Brewery, *1 Corn Street.* Brewing plant offered for auction 20th March 1891 by order of Frome United Breweries Ltd. Public house closed 1911.

William Howland, *Bear Brewery, Wells Road.* Also owned other pubs in Bath including the Beaufort Arms, Princes Street. Owned by Russells by 1924. Brewing ceased c.1902. The Bear brewhouse was destroyed in an air raid when owned by Ushers Wiltshire Brewery.

Pearce, Reynolds, Withers & Co.Ltd, *County Brewery, Batheaston.* Registered December 1904 to amalgamate 6 breweries with 38 tied houses in the district. Brewery and 23 houses offered for sale 1911 and were bought by the Bath Brewery Ltd.

Thomas Stride, *Albion Brewery, Bird in Hand, 8 Corn Street.* The Stride family operated breweries and pubs in Bath from the 1870s until 1988. The plant at the Bird in Hand was offered for auction July 18th 1915. Also brewed at the Burnt House Brewery, Odd Down, until the brewhouse was converted into a skittle-alley. Also at the Red Lion, Odd Down and the Three Cups, Walcot Street.

Sumsions Brewery, *The Bacchus, 22 Corn Street.* Founded 1882. Ceased brewing 1933. See also:- The Castle & Ball Brewery Ltd, Bristol.

Reginald C.Withers, *Ram Brewery, Claverton Street.* Home brew house acquired by Usher's Wiltshire Brewery Ltd August 1948.

William R. Withers, *Long Acre Brewery, London Road.* Home brew house bought by Wadworth & Co.Ltd 1956. Brewhouse demolished 1968/69.

Other Breweries

Albert Ash, *16 Old Orchard Street* (1914)
Joseph John Baker, *10 Avon Street* (1921)
Albert Bevan, *George & Dragon, Batheaston* (1900)
John Biggs, *Avondale Brewery, Batheaston* (1900)
Dinah Cottrell, *50 Rivers Street* (1930)
Albert Dabner, *4 Trim Street* (1914)
Alfred Dowding, *Lower Borough Walls* (1923)
James Dury, *10 Widcomb Parade* (1914)
John Alfred Garner, *6 Southgate* (1923)
Mr Harding, *Bell Brewery Co, Bell Inn, 1 Cornwell Buildings, Walcot Street* (1907)
Albert Charles Harding, *Claverton Brewery, Widcombe* (1892)
Clara Elizabeth Haskins, *12 Green Street* (1923)
Lansdown Brewery, *Ballance Street* (1969)
George McFarale, *Bathampton* (1923)
George Morris, *Lamb Brewery, Stall Street* (1895)
Edward Palliser, *Railway Brewery, 28 Lower Wells Road* (1928)
Louisa Phipps, *Cleveland Brewery, Sydney Wharf* (1926)
Henry D.Pointing, *Pointings Brewery, Weston* (1926)
J.Rawlings & Sons, *Devonshire Brewery, Wells Road* (1914)
Joseph George Reynolds, *27 Kingmead Street* (1921)
Walter George Reynolds, *37 St.James Parade* (1921)
Charles Wilfred Rossiter, *10/11 Abbey Green* (1935)
William Henry Rossiter, *Royal Oak Brewery, 8/10 Summerlay Place* (1946)
Eliza Shackell, *32 Bathwick Street* (1926)
William Henry Swaffield, *11 Newark Street* (1921)
James Vezey, *Batheaston* (1921)
Jane Mary Walter, *Trinity Brewery, 49 James Street* (1898)
William Charles Wyatt, *Lyncombe Brewery, 40 Claverton Street* (1914)

Bitton

D.W.Perrett & Son, *Springfield Brewery* (1930)
Smith & Hawkins, *Bitton Brewery* (1895)

Bristol

Ashton Gate Brewery Co.Ltd, *Ashton Gate, Bedminster.* Registered 1865 to acquire the business of the late Thomas Baynton. Name changed to Hardwick & Co.Ltd 1868 and back to the original title 1883. Acquired by Bristol Brewery Georges & Co.Ltd 1931 and was closed.

Bell (Bristol) Brewery Co.Ltd, *Bell Inn, 1 Gloucester Lane.* Registered May 1908 to acquire W.H.& Charles Winstone. Voluntary liquidation 1st May 1923.

Frederick William Bennett & Sons Ltd, *288 Hotwell Road* (1928)

Bond's (Bristol) Brewery Ltd, *Redcross Brewery, Redcross Street.* Registered October 1890. Closed 1904 and was bought by the Ashton Gate Brewery Co.Ltd 1911.

Brewer's Droop, *36 Gloucester Road.* Founded 1990. Still brewing 1990.

Bristol Brewery Georges & Co.Ltd, *Old Porter Brewery, Bath Street.* Founded c.1730. Registered February 1888. Acquired by Courage, Barclay & Co.Ltd 1961 with 1,459 tied houses. Brewery still in operation 1990.

Bristol United Breweries Ltd, *Lewins Mead Brewery.* Registered 24th July 1889 to acquire: Bowley & Bristow, St.Paul's Brewery; Bishop & Butt Ltd, Redcliffe Mead Brewery; J.H.Lockley & Sons, Lewins Mead Brewery and M.Reynolds & Co, Imperial Brewery, Bedminster. Acquired by Bristol Brewery Georges & Co.Ltd 1956 with about 600 public houses. Used as a sugar factory until 1966.

Castle & Ball Brewery Ltd, *Lower Castle Street.* Registered February 1902 to carry on the business of Miss A.E.Sumsion. One tied house, the Bacchus, Lower Castle Street. Offered for auction 1920 and was wound up in 1921. See also:- Sumsion's Brewery, Bath.

Michael Clune, *Old Market Brewery, Old Market Street.* Acquired by the Ashton Gate Brewery Co.Ltd May 1911.

Dunn & Patterson, *Horfield.* A new brewery founded October 1984. Closed in the same year.

Fleece & Firkin, *Old Wool Hall, 12 St.Thomas Street.* Home brew house founded by David Bruce, March 1982. Acquired by Halls (Oxford & West) August 1983 and is still brewing 1990.

Charles Garton & Co, *Easton Road, Lawrence Hill.* Acquired by the Anglo-Bavarian Brewery Co.Ltd 1898.

Robert Heal Goodenough, *34 Paul Street, Kingsdown.* Acquired by Fussell & Sons Ltd of Rode, Somerset December 1929 with one tied house.

Robert Isles Hewett, *Kingsdown Brewery, Montague Place.* Acquired by Starkey, Knight & Co.Ltd 1893.

R.W.Miller & Co.Ltd, *48 Stokes Croft.* Registered December 1893. Acquired by Bristol Brewery Georges & Co.Ltd 1911 with 48 public houses.

W.J.Rogers Ltd, *Jacob Street.* Founded 1845. Registered July 1894 with 25 tied houses. Acquired by H.& G.Simonds Ltd 1935 and brewing ceased 1952.

Smiles Brewing Co, *Colston Yard, 6/10 Upper Maudlin Street.* Founded by John Payne, March 1977 at Bell's Diner, York Road, Montpelier, brewing only for the restaurant. Moved to the above address 1978 and the name was changed as above 1981. Still brewing 1990 with 3 public houses.

Daniel Sykes & Co.Ltd, *Redcliffe Brewery, 107 Redcliffe Street.* Registered March 1889. Merged with Bristol United Breweries Ltd in 1897 and closed in 1898.

J.& T.Usher Ltd, *New City Brewery, River Street, Horfield Road.* Registered June 1896. New brewery built 1901. Acquired by W.J.Rogers Ltd 1922 with about 40 tied houses and was closed.

Other Breweries

Arthur Herbert Ansell, *83 Stapleton Road* (1914)
Auty & Co, *Lion Brewery, Church Road* (1914)
Caroline Daws, *690 Fishponds* (1923)
L.Dudley-Smith, (1920)
Gibbins Brothers, *133 St.Michael's Hill* (1890)
Hill & Sons, *70 Redcliffe Street* (1890)
William Samuel Horner, *Newfoundland Street Brewery* (1892)
Frederick Walter Hunt, *438/440 Stapleton Road* (1906)
Richard Jones & Co, *Sussex Street, St.Philip's* (1890)
Le Bozec Brothers, *Spread Eagle Brewery, Bread Street* (1890)
Richard Lewis & Co, *Cathay Brewery* (1890)
James Milford, *Trout Inn, Cherry Lane* (1892)
Augustus John O'Callaghan, *23 Milk Street* (1920)
Henry William Stokes, *Hallen* (1902)
George Henry Watts, *11 Narrow Plain* (1914)
Oliver William Wiltshire & Co, *Redcross Street* (1906)

Butcombe

Butcombe Brewery, *Rusling House*. Founded September 1978 by Simon Whitmore. Still in operation 1990 with 3 public houses.

Chipping Sodbury

Albert Henry Vizard (1914)

Clutton

North Somerset Brewery Co.Ltd, Founded by Richard Lewis in 1877. Registered as above in September 1894 to acquire R.Lewis, Clutton, and John Thatcher, Radford Brewery, Timsbury. Dissolved October 1897 but brewing may have continued until January 1914 when 7 public houses were sold.

Doynton

William Hendy (1921)

Freshford

Frederick Power, *Freshford Brewery*. Closed 1895. Brewery converted into an Architect's office 1964. The buildings are early Victorian and later.

Great Badminton

Joseph Davies, *Portcullis Brewery* (1902)

Hanham

Robert Francis Nurse (1935)

Kenn

Kingston Seymour Brewery Co.Ltd, *Kenn Brewery*. Private company registered 21st March 1932 to acquire the business of A.E.Edwards. Later moved to Clevedon and was possibly known as the North Somerset Brewery Co.Ltd. Closed before 1939.

Marshfield

Sarah Jane Billett, *King's Arms* (1906)
William Davis (1920)

Midsomer Norton

Welton Breweries Ltd, *Welton*. Registered 1896 as Thatcher's Breweries Ltd to amalgamate: George Henry Thatcher, North Brewery and John Thatcher, Radford Brewery. Merged with the Welton Old Brewery Co.Ltd 1901. The name was changed as above December 1906. About 100 public houses were sold to Bristol Brewery Georges & Co.Ltd 1918. Voluntary liquidation 12th March 1919 and was wound up 3rd May 1920.

Welton Old Brewery Co.Ltd, *Welton*. Registered 1891 to acquire the business of William James Thatcher and Henry James. Merged with Thatcher's Breweries Ltd March 1901.

Nailsea

Hall's Nailsea Brewery, *Southfield Industrial Estate*. Moved from the concern below 1984 and brewing ceased October 1985 when Dennis Jacobs retired.
Nailsea Brewery, *Southfield Road*. Set up April 1980 by Dennis Jacobs and Roy Savage. Acquired by Hall's (Oxford & West) 1984 and brewing was transferred to the above.
Edgar Thatcher & Co, *Heath Brewery*. Acquired by Bristol Brewery Georges & Co.Ltd 1917 with 5 tied houses.

Oakhill

Beacon Brewery, *High Street*. Founded April 1981 by Gerry Watts in the former Oakhill Brewery Co.Ltd premises. Ceased brewing March 1983 and was succeeded by the concern below.
Oakhill Brewery, *The Old Brewery, High Street*. Founded 1984 by Reginald Keevil in succession to the Beacon Brewery with Gerry Watts as brewer. Still operating 1990.
Oakhill Brewery Co.Ltd, *High Street*. Founded 1767. Registered March 1889 to acquire Jillard, Spencer & Co. for £180,000. Acquired by Bristol United Breweries Ltd 1925 and brewing ceased 1938. Used as a store by Courage until partly demolished 1959. Maltings continued by Courages.

Oldbury on Severn

Bland's Brewery, *Cider Mill*. Founded June 1980 by Vernon Bland. Brewing ceased later in 1980.

Old Sodbury

James Mason Perrett & Sons, *Hill House Brewery*. Brewing ceased 1921 but business continued as wine & spirit merchants until 1930.

Pill

Thomas & Sons, *Lodway Brewery*. Founded before 1877. Acquired by Bristol Brewery Georges & Co.Ltd 1917 with 39 public houses and the brewery was sold.

Radstock

Coombs' Breweries Ltd, *Bell Hotel*. Founded by 1884. Registered 1894 as Coombs' Clandown & Radstock Breweries & Hotels Co.Ltd to acquire the businesses of George Coombs & Co, Clandown Brewery and Joseph Coombs, Radstock Brewery. Name changed as above 1914. Acquired by the Oakhill Brewery Co.Ltd November 1922 and brewing ceased. Wound up August 1926.

South Stoke

Ernest A.James, *South Stoke Brewery* (1906)

Temple Cloud

Mendip United Brewery Ltd, *1 Shadows Factory, Eastcourt Road*. Founded by Roger Walkey as the Mendip Brewing Co.Ltd June 1978. Renamed as above 1982. Ceased brewing 1984.

Westerleigh

Charles Weeks (1902)

Weston-super-Mare

Purrett & Co, *Worle* (1906)

Wickwar

John Arnold & Sons, *High Street*. Founded 1877. Acquired by Bristol Brewery Georges & Co.Ltd December 1917 with 40 public houses and closed.

Arnold, Perrett & Co.Ltd, *High Street*. Founded 1820. Registered June 1886 to acquire Arnold & Co,and E.& B.Trimmer of Gloucester as Arnold & Co.Ltd. Name changed as above 1887 when H.& A.Perrett of Wotton-under-Edge was acquired with 325 tied houses. 40 public houses sold to Bristol Brewery Georges & Co.Ltd 1917. Merged with the Cheltenham Original Brewery Co.Ltd 1924 and brewing ceased. Premises used as a cider factory until 1969/70. Buildings are extant.

Wickwar Brewing Co. Founded 1990 by Ray Penny and Brian Rides in former Arnold, Perrett & Co.Ltd premises.

Ampthill

Morris & Co. (Ampthill) Ltd, *Ampthill Brewery, Bedford Street.* Brewery in existence 1738. Sold by the Morris family to John Thomas Green 1880 but carried on as Morris & Co. Registered 1906. Acquired by J.W.Green Ltd 1926 with 72 tied houses and closed.

Bedford

Frederick Charles Fuller & Son, *Lurke Street.* Founded 1819. Acquired by Charles Wells Ltd 1935.

Higgins & Sons Ltd, *Castle Brewery, Castle Lane.* Founded 1837. Registered 1902. Acquired by Wells & Winch Ltd 1928 with 55 public houses.

George Hopper & Son, *39 Midland Road* (1914)

Thomas Jarvis & Co, *Phoenix Brewery, 71 Midland Road.* Founded 1869. Acquired by Charles Wells Ltd 1923.

Newland & Nash Ltd, *Steam Brewery, Lurke Street.* Founded 1783 when Peregrine Nash acquired Robert Bell's brewhouse, St.Mary Street. Lurke Street brewery built 1875. Registered 1890 to acquire Newland & Co. and G.P.Nash & Son who had amalgamated in 1890. Acquired by Wells & Winch Ltd 1922 with 75 tied houses.

Charles Wells Ltd, *Eagle Brewery, Havelock Street.* Original brewery in Horne Lane built 1818/36 and was acquired by Charles Wells 1875. Registered 1910. New brewery as above opened 1976. Still independent 1990.

Biggleswade

Wells & Winch Ltd, *High Street.* Founded by Samuel Wells 1764. Registered April 1899 with 264 tied houses. Acquired by Greene King & Sons 1961 with 287 public houses. Still brewing 1990 as Greene King (Biggleswade) Ltd.

Cardington

Cardington Brewery Co.Ltd. Registered 1884 to acquire Charles Hickman. Acquired by the Nottingham Brewery Ltd 1897.

Dunstable

Benjamin Bennett, exors of, *North-Western Brewery, High Street.* Formerly a partner in the Bedford Road Brewery, Luton 1864-70. Also brewed at Harpenden 1874-93 and Redbourn 1882-97. Acquired by Mann, Crossman & Paulin Ltd 1938 with 59 tied houses. Brewery demolished 1971.

Daniel Costin, *106 West Street* (1910)

Cutler & Henceman, *Upper Houghton Brewery.* Acquired by Benjamin Bennett 1887.

Elstow

Henry Tucker (1920)

Henlow

John Holden, *Henlow Brewery.* Acquired by Wells & Winch Ltd with 10 public houses 1900.

Kempston

Joseph Ellison (1920)

Leighton Buzzard

Ashdown Brothers, *High Street.* Brewing ceased 1918 and was demolished 1920.

Linslade Brewery Co.Ltd. Registered May 1904 to acquire G.J.Monson & Co, and the breweries at Linslade and Wing Road, Leighton Buzzard. Dissolved 20th November 1908.

James Alfred Springham, *Lake Street* (1921)

Luton

Coney Hall Brewery, *Metralite House, Dudley Street.* Founded by Robin Yates to provide work for unemployed post graduates. Closed 1982.

Flower's Breweries Ltd, *Phoenix Brewery, Park Street West.* Founded 1857. Registered September 1897 as J.W.Green Ltd. The name was changed as above 1954 when Flower & Sons Ltd of Stratford-on-Avon were acquired. Acquired by

Whitbread & Co.Ltd 1961. The Phoenix Brewery was closed 1969 when Whitbread's giant new brewery was opened at Luton. This in turn being closed in 1984.

Luton Brewery Co.Ltd, *Bedford Road Brewery.* Founded 1767. Registered 1874 to acquire the business of T.Sworder with 90 public houses. Acquired by J.W.Green Ltd 1898.

Charles John Rosson, junior, *High Town Road* (1892)

Potton

Potton Brewery Co, *King Street.* Acquired by Newland & Nash Ltd of Bedford 1921 and was closed.

Alfred Richardson, *Sun Street* (1892)

Sandy

William Brooke, *High Street* (1898)

Shefford

Banks & Taylor Brewery Ltd, *St.Francis Way, Shefford Industrial Park, Ampthill Road.* Founded by Martin Ayres and Mike Desquesnes August 1982. Now own 12 public houses. Still in operation 1990.

Shefford Brewery Co, *Clifton Road* (1906)

Stotfold

Flitton's Brewery Ltd, *Stotfold Brewery.* Founded by 1877. Private company registered July 1937. Acquired by Whitbread & Co.Ltd June 1948 and was closed.

Toddington

Toddington Brewery Ltd. Registered February 1900 to acquire the business of Thomas George Green. Ceased trading 31st December 1902.

Turvey

Three Fyshes, *Bridge Street.* Home brew house which began brewing Christmas 1987. Still in operation in 1990.

Aldermaston

William Jeffreys Strange & Sons Ltd. Founded 1770 and was bought by Thomas Strange 1833. Acquired by Strong & Co.Ltd 1945 and was transferred to their subsidiary Wethered & Sons Ltd in 1949.

Ashbury

Thomas James Carter (1910)

Bracknell

A.L.S.Sellon & Co. Acquired by Fuller, Story & Co.Ltd 1906.

Cippenham near Slough

Stallion Ales, *Long Barn public house, Cippenham Lane.* Home brew house founded by Maureen Hurst and Ken Jones March 1983. Brewery closed August 1985 and plant moved to Helland, Cornwall where Stallion Ales are now brewed.

Harwell

George Day (1930)
J.Stanley
C.Greenwood (1939)

Hungerford

Tom E.Crook, *High Street* (1920)

Elisha Love, *Crown Brewery, High Street.* Offered for auction 1900.

John Platt & Son, *Manor Brewery, High Street.* Acquired by the South Berkshire Brewery Co.Ltd 1910.

Maidenhead

Fuller, Story & Co.Ltd, *Bell Brewery, King Street.* Acquired by Nicholson & Sons Ltd 1921.

Philip Sidney Langton, *Market Street.* Acquired by Nicholson & Sons Ltd 1906.

Nicholson & Sons Ltd, *High Street.* Founded by William Nicholson 1840. Acquired by Courage, Barclay and Co.Ltd 1959.

Newbury

J.Adnams & Son, *Eagle Brewery, Broadway, Speenhamland*. Founded 1809. Acquired by H.& G.Simonds Ltd 1936 with 3 public houses.

J.Emery, *Diamond Brewery, Cheap Street*. Acquired by the South Berkshire Brewery Co.Ltd 1900.

Herbert John Finn & Co, *Phoenix Brewery, Bartholomew Street*. Founded by 1842. Acquired by Usher's Wiltshire Brewery Ltd 1925 with 21 tied houses.

Newbury Brewery Co.Ltd, *Castle Brewery, 25/27 Northbrook Street*. Founded 1608. Registered September 1890 to acquire F.F.Somerset & Co. Acquired by H.& G.Simonds Ltd 1930.

Ernest Edward Palmer, *Donnington*. Acquired by Usher's Wiltshire Brewery Ltd 1922.

South Berkshire Brewery Co.Ltd, *Atlas Brewery, 17 Bartholomew Street*. Registered 1897 as Hawkins & Parfitt, South Berkshire Brewery Co.Ltd to amalgamate: Edmund Parfitt, Atlas Brewery and Thomas Edward Hawkins & Co, West Mills Brewery. Name changed as above April 1913. Acquired by H.& G.Simonds Ltd October 1920 with 150/200 public houses. West Mills Brewery closed 1920 and Atlas Brewery 7th September 1930.

Westcombe & Son, *St.Nicholas Brewery, 11a Bartholomew Street*. Acquired by Hawkins & Parfitt 1902.

Reading

Henry Bird, *Weldale Brewery, 17 Caversham Road*. Acquired by Wethered & Sons Ltd 1913 with 9 tied houses.

Blandy, Hawkins & Co, *Castle Brewery, 16 Bridge Street*. Founded 1698. Acquired by Hawkins & Parfitt, South Berkshire Brewery Co.Ltd 1910 and brewing ceased 1920.

William James Justins-Brinn, *Truro Brewery, 46/48 Castle Street*. Acquired by Fergusons Ltd 1900 with 30 public houses.

Dowsett Brothers, *46/47 Broad Street*. Brewery auctioned June 1906.

Dymore Brown & Sons Ltd, *Royal Albert Brewery, 16/18 Queen's Road*. Founded 1820. Registered May 1902 to acquire James Dymore & Son. Acquired by Morland & Co.Ltd 1927 and brewing ceased.

Fergusons Ltd, *Angel Brewery, 116/117 Broad Street*. Registered 1899. Brewing ceased 1914 and beer was supplied by Morland & Co.Ltd who gained control in 1943 and amalgamated them with Dymore Brown & Sons Ltd.

Robert Hewitt & Son, *Victoria Brewery, Chain Street*. Acquired by H.& G.Simonds Ltd 1900.

S.H.Higgs Ltd, *Lion Brewery, 20 Castle Street*. Operated by George Moore until 1877 when it was acquired by Samuel Higgs. Acquired by Wethered & Sons Ltd 1953, then a subsidiary of Strong & Co.Ltd and the business was transferred to the Marlow Brewery.

William Newell, *Mitre Brewery, 47 West Street* (1900)

Walter Julian Pain, *Britannia Brewery, 54/56 Caversham Road*. Acquired by Ind Coope Ltd 1896.

H.& G.Simonds Ltd, *Bridge Street*. Founded 1768. Registered November 1885. Acquired by Courage, Barclay & Co.Ltd 1960. Brewing ceased 1979 and brewery demolished 1983.

William Sims & Son, *Lion Brewery, Hosier Street*. Founded by 1864. Brewery and 16 tied houses offered for auction 10th March 1890.

Stratfield Mortimer

Headington & Sons, *Cooper's Hall Brewery*. Acquired by the Watlington Brewery Co.Ltd 1900.

Theale

Blatch's Theale Brewery Ltd, *High Street*. Founded by 1830 and acquired by the Blatch family 1854. Private company registered May 1938. Acquired by Ind Coope (Oxford & West) Ltd 1965 and brewing ceased.

Twyford

Ernest G.Ford (1898)

Waltham St.Lawrence

H.Hewitt & Co.Ltd, *Southlake Street*. Founded before 1842. Registered 1900. Merged with Dymore Brown & Sons Ltd 1925 and closed.

Windsor

Burge & Co.Ltd, *49/51 Victoria Street*. Founded before 1840. Registered 1920. Acquired by Meux's Brewery Co.Ltd October 1931 and brewing ceased 1932. Brewery site sold 1935.

John Canning & Sons, *Royal Brewery, 45 Peascod Street*. Founded before 1850. Acquired by Noakes & Co.Ltd 1921 who then transferred their brewing from Bermonsey to Windsor.

Nevile Reid & Co.Ltd, *Windsor Brewery, Thames Street*. Founded c.1810 by Nevile Reid of Meux Reid & Co. Registered 1915. Acquired by Noakes & Co.Ltd 1918 with 140 tied houses. Brewing ceased 1930.

Winkfield

Old Hatchet Inn, *Woodsman Brewery, North Ascot*. Home brew house founded April 1983 by landlord, Terry Wing. Ceased brewing 1984.

Wokingham

Baker, Powell & Co, *13 Broad Street*. Acquired by Brakspear & Sons Ltd 1913 with 9 public houses.

Headington & Son, *Wellington Brewery, 23 Denmark Street*. Acquired by Ashby's Staines Brewery Ltd June 1920 with 5 tied houses.

Broughton

Broughton Brewery Ltd. Founded by David Younger & James Collins 1979. Still in operation 1990.

Coldstream

Coldstream Brewery Co.Ltd, *Market Square.* Founded 1820. Originally known as J.& A.Davidson

(Coldstream) Ltd. Name changed as above 1922. Offered for sale 12th June 1913 with 5 public houses. Acquired by Vaux & Associated Breweries Ltd November 1943.

Innerleithen

Traquair House. Peter Maxwell Stuart, Laird of Traquair, renovated the ancient brewhouse in 1965 after 200 years of disuse. Still brewing 1990.

Jedburgh

David Keddie, *Friars Burn Brewery, High Street* (1910)

Melrose

Simson & McPherson Ltd, *Abbey Brewery.* See also:- Edinburgh.

Amersham

W.& G.Weller, *Amersham Brewery, Church Street.* Acquired by Benskin's Watford Brewery Ltd 1929 with 142 tied houses.

Aston Clinton

Walter H.Pullen. Acquired by Benskin's Watford Brewery Ltd December 1915 with at least 3 public houses.

Aylesbury

Aylesbury Brewery Co.Ltd, *Walton Brewery, Walton Street.* Registered 1895 to acquire Parrott, Walker & Co. Brewing ceased in 1937 as it was found to be more economical to buy beer. Acquired by Allied Breweries Ltd 1972. Used as regional offices until *c.*1989.

Samuel Gulliver & Co, *Kingsbury Square* (1892)

John Hamblen, *23 Castle Street* (1922)

Richard Jenkinson, *Chiltern Brewery, Burnham Farm, Nash Lee Road, Terrick.* Founded August 1980 in converted farm buildings. Offered for sale in 1987.

Bierton

Eagle Brewery Co.Ltd (1892)

Buckingham

Frank Higgens & Co.Ltd, *Swan Brewery, Market Square/West Street.* Registered November 1894. Acquired by the Aylesbury Brewery Co.Ltd 1896. Brewery was still standing 1983 as a garage.

Burnham

A.Terry & Co, *Burnham Brewery.* Acquired by Fuller, Story & Co.Ltd of Maidenhead September 1905.

Chesham

Chesham & Brackley Breweries Ltd, *Hempstead Road & Brackley, Northants.* Chesham brewery founded *c.*1841. Registered 1895 as the Chesham Brewery Ltd to acquire the business of T.& J.Nash. Name changed 1946 when they merged with Hopcraft & Norris Ltd of Brackley. Acquired by Taylor,

Walker & Co.Ltd 1956. Brewing ceased at Chesham 1957 and Brackley 1959. Properties transferred to Benskin's Watford Brewery Ltd 1962.

Sarah How & Sons, *Church Street.* Founded 1871. Acquired by the Chesham Brewery Ltd 1899.

Dagnall

James Batchelar, *Dagnall Brewery.* Acquired by Fuller, Smith & Turner of London 1897 with 24 public houses and was sold again to Locke & Smith of Berkhamsted *c.*1905 and was for sale again 1913 but no buyer was found.

Walter S.Mott, *Three Counties Brewery.* Bankrupt and for sale 5th September 1904 but was withdrawn at £1,475. Offered for auction again 14th October 1914 with 21 public houses.

Fenny Stratford

Bletchley Breweries Ltd, *High Street.* Registered 1896 to acquire the brewery of Edmund Holdon. Acquired by the Aylesbury Brewery Co.Ltd 1899 with 9 public houses. Premises later used by Cave's Solid Beer Brewery.

Haddenham

James Wilson (1898)

High Wycombe

Henry J.Grant, *83a Easton Street.* Previously under the name of Francis W.Allard, who had been brewer to Leadbetter & Bird and had set up in business for himself after the merger with Wheeler & Co. Closed 1914.

Leadbetter & Bird, *Frogmoor Brewery.* Merged with Wheeler & Co. 1898 to form Wheeler's Wycombe Breweries Ltd.

Wheeler's Wycombe Breweries Ltd, *Easton Street.* Founded in late 18th century as Biddle & King. Registered July 1898 to merge Wheeler & Co. & Leadbetter & Bird. Acquired by Ashby's Staines Brewery Ltd October 1929 with 148 tied houses and brewing ceased 1931.

Ivinghoe

Roberts & Wilson Ltd, *Ivinghoe Brewery.* Founded 1766 by Thomas Meacher. Registered 1915. Acquired by Benskin's Watford Brewery Ltd 1927 and brewing ceased.

The Lee

Carr's Ales, *Gate Public House, Swan Bottom.* Home brew house founded February 1981. Ceased brewing 1985.

Linslade

Linslade Brewery Co.Ltd. Registered May 1904 to acquire breweries in Leighton Buzzard and Linslade. Dissolved November 1908.

Marlow

Thomas Wethered & Sons Ltd, *Marlow Brewery, High Street.* Founded 1798. Registered March 1899. Acquired by Strong & Co.Ltd 1949 with 236 tied houses. Brewery ceased in operation 1991 as Whitbread Wethereds Ltd.

Marsh Gibbon

Phillips Brewing Co, *Greyhound Brewery, Greyhound Inn.* Home brew house founded February 1981. Ceased brewing December 1985 and brewery moved to Hundred House Inn, Norton, Telford, Shropshire.

Newport Pagnell

Newport Pagnell Brewery Co.Ltd. Registered 1899 to acquire F.Allfrey & W.G.Lovell. Acquired by Charles Wells Ltd 1919 and ceased to brew. Brewery still standing 1983 as an agricultural machinery depot.

Barham

Mrs M.Hufford (1910)

Bourn

Mrs Jane Miller (1910)

Brampton

Henry Crawley (1898)
George Green (1898)

Brinkley

Charles J.Riches (1892)

Broughton

Henry Onyett (1892)

Buckden

A.S.Thackray. Acquired by Wells & Winch Ltd *c.*1900.

Cambridge

Ancient Druids Public House, *Napier Street, Grafton Centre.* Home brew house founded by Charles Wells Ltd December 1984. Still brewing 1990.

William Henry Apthorpe, junior, *Albion Brewery, 15/17 Coronation Street.* Founded 1868. Acquired by Lacon & Co.Ltd 1896 with over 50 tied houses and was closed in 1965 and was later demolished.

Warman & Co.Ltd, *Cannon Brewery, 50 High Street.* Acquired by the Aylesbury Brewery Co.Ltd September 1909. Still standing 1983 behind the Cannon Hotel.

Olney

Hipwell & Co, *High Street & Kettering, Northants.* Acquired by Phipps & Co.Ltd of Northampton 1920.

Princes Risborough

Thomas Parsons, *Lion Brewery, Market Place.* Offered for auction 20th January 1899 with 80 public houses and was bought by the Welch Ale Brewery Ltd March 1900. Sold to the Aylesbury Brewery Co.Ltd 1920.

Rowsham near Aylesbury

John W.Gurney. Brewing ceased *c.*1939 and was converted into a private house.

Sherington

Oldham & Co. (1898)

CAMBRIDGESHIRE

Bailey & Tebbutt Ltd, *Panton Brewery, Panton Street.* Founded 1869 by Charles Lloyd Davis and was acquired by B.W.Beales in 1887. Became Bailey & Tebbutt in 1897. Private company registered March 1918. Acquired by Greene King & Sons 1925. Brewing ceased 1957 and the brewery was demolished 1969.

William Brewty, *1 Earl Street.* Founded by 1864. Brewing ceased *c.*1890.

Francis George Bullock, *Priory Brewery, Newmarket Road.* Founded by 1866. Bought by Charles Armstrong of the Star Brewery (Cambridge) Ltd in 1891 with 6 public houses.

Albert Alexander Burns, *Great Northern Hotel, Station Road/Hills Road.* Closed *c.*1907.

William Henry Cawthorne, *Rhadegund Brewery, 9 James Street.* Merged with F.J.Swann 1904 and traded as Cawthorne & Swann until 1909. Acquired by Bailey & Tebbutt 1911.

Walter Dagnall, *Blackbirds Public House, East Road.* Home brew house. Ceased brewing 1896.

Dale & Co.Ltd, *Gwydir Street.* Founded by Frederick Dale at the British Queen, Histon Road 1898 and the Gwydir Street brewery built 1902. Acquired by Whitbread and Co.Ltd 1955 and brewing ceased 1958. Brewery still standing in 1990 as an Antiques Centre.

Louisa Edwards, *Rabbit Brewery, Gold Street.* Founded by John Nightingale in 1864. Acquired by Bailey & Tebbutt 1911 but the 12 or so public houses were retained by Louisa Edwards until sold to Greene King & Sons 1925. Brewery later used by Wood & Sons as a mineral water factory.

A.G.Ekin, *Magdalene Street.* Founded 1780 by William Ekin. Known as William Ekin & Son in the 1860s. Acquired by P.L.Hudson of Pampisford 1888 with about 12 tied houses. Registered as Hudson's (Cambridge & Pampisford) Breweries Ltd May 1892. Acquired by Wells & Winch Ltd 1931 with 62 public houses.

Frederick Freeman & Son, *Sovereign Brewery, Gold Street.* Founded by 1856 and acquired by Freeman by 1874. Acquired by the Star Brewery (Cambridge) Ltd 1903 with at least 16 tied houses.

Stantonbury

P.Williams (1898)

Wendover

Joseph S.Holland, *Red Lion, High Street.* J.S.Holland as well as being the tenant of the Red Lion also owned the Wendover Brewery and its tap, the King's Head and at least one other public house. Brewing ceased *c.*1914.

Winslow

William Samuel Neal, *Market Square* (1925)

Woburn Sands

Down & Needham, *High Street* (1898)

Wooburn Green

Thomas Williams & Co.Ltd, *Royal Stag Brewery.* Registered June 1891. Acquired by Wethered & Sons Ltd October 1927 with 35 tied houses.

George Gibson, *Victoria Brewery, Albert (later Napier) Street.* Brewery built by William Henry Apthorpe senior *c.*1830 and acquired by Gibson 1881. Bought by the Star Brewery (Cambridge) Ltd *c.*1891. Demolished 1983.

George Gilbert, *26 Ainsworth Street* (*c.*1884-95)

William Hewitt, *British Queen, Histon Road.* Home brew house 1891-98. Later occupied by Frederick Dale.

Robert Brassey Jones, *Alma Brewery, Norwich Street.* Founded 1835. Bought by Jones 1900. Public houses sold to the Star Brewery (Cambridge) Ltd 1909 and brewery leased by Warwicks & Richardsons Ltd, who bought it in 1911. Sold to Tollemache 1926 and was leased by CAMRA Investments 1982. Still standing in 1990.

William Edward Pegg, *Benet Brewery, Newmarket Road.* Founded by Jacob Warwicker by 1829 and leased to Henry Pegg 1858. Brewing possibly ceased by 1922 and certainly by 1929 when bought by Fremlins Ltd for use as a store.

William Potts, *Anchor Brewery, Quayside.* Founded by 1830 and acquired by Potts *c.*1855. Acquired by the Star Brewery (Cambridge) Ltd 1895 with about 12 public houses and closed 1902.

George Powter, *Gardener's Arms, 118 Newmarket Road* (1904-10)

James Callan Preston, *Spring Brewery, Chesterton Road.* Founded *c.*1855 by James Dyson. Acquired by Preston 1880. Acquired by Lacons 1896 and closed.

John Read, *Victoria Brewery, Victoria Road* (1874-96)

Robinson & Tebbutt, *Granta Brewery, Newnham.* Founded in 1865 by H.Andrews. Partnership of F.K.Robinson & H.H.Tebbutt dissolved 23rd February 1897 and became Bailey & Tebbutt. Business transferred to the Panton Brewery and Granta Brewery closed and demolished.

George Scales, exors of, *Cambridge Brewery, 7 King Street.* Founded by 1857. Acquired by Barclay, Perkins & Co.Ltd 1926 with 13 tied houses and was closed. Premises sold to Wells & Winch Ltd 1928. Brewery converted 1979 into a new bar for the Cambridge Arms and the former brewery made the theme of the bar.

T.W.Scruby, *Bird Bolt, 61 Newmarket Road* (1890-1901)

Star Brewery (Cambridge) Ltd, *13 Newmarket Road.* Founded *c.*1822 by James P.Twiss. Bought by Frederick Bailey 1839 and registered as Frederick Bailey & Co.Ltd 1884 and sold to Charles Armstrong April 1889. Registered as above 18th November 1891 to acquire the Star Brewery and the adjacent Priory Brewery with 106 public houses. Acquired by Tollemache's Breweries Ltd 1934 with 119 tied houses. Brewing ceased 1972 and was demolished 1981/82.

Edwin William Swann, *Windmill Brewery, Russell Street.* Founded by 1860. Closed *c.*1896 and public houses sold to Lacon & Co.Ltd.

Frederick J.Swann, *Rodney Brewery, 94/95 East Road.* Merged with W.H.Cawthorne 1904 and brewing was concentrated at the Rhadegund Brewery. Public houses sold to Lacons.

Alexander Frederick Tooth, *Castle Brewery, Castle Street.* Founded by 1851. By 1874 was Wootten & Mann, King's Head Brewery and was acquired by Tooth 1894 and renamed the Castle Brewery. Acquired by Phillips of Royston 1899 and brewing ceased. In 1900 Hudson's Cambridge & Pampisford Breweries were using it as a store.

William Towler, *exors of, Shakespeare Brewery, 14 Newmarket Road.* Founded by 1837 and acquired by Towler 1861. Offered for auction 31st July 1897 with 20 public houses and the brewery was bought by Lacons and closed.

Wesson's Brewery Ltd, *47 Fitzroy Street.* Owned by Thomas Wesson before 1864. Registered February 1900. Voluntary liquidation 7th May 1913. Bought by Bailey & Tebbutt 1914. Wound up 21st January 1914.

Benjamin Worboys, *Globe Brewery, Newmarket Road.* Founded 1865. Globe Brewery closed 1901 but also listed at 5 Newmarket Road until 1907 and the Prince of Wales Brewery, 1 Church Street 1892-96.

Robert Worboys, *Cooper's Arms, 40 City Road.* Home brew house (1887-1913)

Worboys & Jarman Ltd, *Sturton Brewery, Sturton Street.* Founded 1874. Registered May 1909 as W.Worboys Ltd. Registered as above February 1913 when they merged with Jarman & Co. of Meldreth. Receiver appointed May 1915 and was dissolved July 1923. Premises at Cambridge and Meldreth occupied by Barclay, Perkins 1915 and bought by them September 1920. Public houses sold to Wells & Winch Ltd 1938.

Catworth

Charles Peacock (1910)

Chatteris

R.J.& C.T.Lindsell & Son, *High Street.* Founded before 1839 and acquired by Thomas Lindsell by 1851. Acquired by Marshall Brothers (Huntingdon) Ltd 1932 to form part of Huntingdon Breweries Ltd. Used in the late 1980s as an insulation factory. Brewery still standing 1990.

Charles Porter, *High Street* (1921)

Cottenham

Ebenezer Chivers, *Black Horse Brewery* (1906)
Holben's Brewery (1898)
Annie Peck (1910)

Dullingham

Henry Moore (1898)

Earith

James Bidwell, *Earith Brewery.* Acquired by William Cutlack of Littleport 1897.

Eaton Socon

Eaton Bedfordshire Brewery Co.Ltd. Registered September 1901 as the Eaton Socon Brewery Co.Ltd to acquire the business of E.A.Dalby. 12 public houses for auction 1901 and was dissolved 9th September 1904. New company registered as above April 1902 to acquire the brewery and 6 tied houses. Voluntary liquidation October 1903.

Ely

Arthur & Bertram Hall Ltd, *Forehill Brewery, Forehill.* Founded by 1894. Merged with Cutlack & Harlock Ltd September 1930 to form Hall, Cutlack & Harlock Ltd which merged with Huntingdon Breweries Ltd June 1950 to form East Anglian Breweries Ltd who were acquired by Steward & Patteson Ltd 1960. Forehill Brewery closed early 1969.

Frank L.Harlock, *Quay Brewery.* Founded 1771. Merged with William Cutlack of Littleport June 1907 to form Cutlack & Harlock Ltd. Brewing ceased 1930.

T.H.Legge & Co, *Market Street.* Acquired by Cutlack & Harlock Ltd 1910.

George Parker (1910)

Richard Porter & Sons, *Eagle Brewery, Cambridge Road.* Acquired by Morgan's Brewery Co.Ltd 1900.

Fenstanton

Henry Jeffrey Burt, *Fenstanton Brewery.* Founded by 1880 as Robert Odams & Sons. Offered for auction with 29 public houses 15th September 1894 and bought by Burt. Acquired by the Star Brewery (Cambridge) Ltd March 1901 with 54 tied houses.

Fulbourn

Daniel Herbert Miller, *Fulbourn Brewery* (1895)

Godmanchester

William Baxter & Son. Acquired by H.J.Burt, February 1898.

Great Staughton

William Henry Murfin, *Robin Hood Brewery* (1900)

Hamerton

Robert Murphy (1935)

Hemingford Grey

Thomas Knights & Sons. Brewing ceased *c.*1910 but business continued as maltsters until at least 1939.

Huntingdon

Thomas George Hearn, *73 High Street* (1923)

Jenkins & Jones Ltd, *Falcon Brewery, High Street.* Founded 1844. Registered 1898. Acquired by Marshall Brothers October 1932 and closed.

Marshall Brothers (Huntingdon) Ltd, *123 High Street.* Registered 1910. In 1932 took over Jenkins & Jones Ltd & R.J.& C.T.Lindsell & Son of Chatteris to form Huntingdon Breweries Ltd which merged with Hall, Cutlack & Harlock Ltd of Ely 1950 to form East Anglian Breweries Ltd. Brewing ceased at Huntingdon 1951.

Benjamin S.Murphy, *Hartford* (1898)

Landbeach

Frederick Webb (1910)

Linton

George William Grayston, *Three Tuns Brewery* (1910)

John Siggs. Brewery with flour mill attached offered for auction 23rd January 1919.

Little Shelford

Arthur Austin, *West End Brewery* (1895)

Littleport

William Cutlack, *Littleport Brewery*. Merged with Frank L.Harlock of Ely June 1907 to form Cutlack & Harlock Ltd and brewing ceased.
William Henry Rains, *Victoria Brewery* (1910)

March

Frederick Grounds, *High Street* (1900)
Ambrose Ogden & Sons, *Sun Brewery, High Street*. Founded 1800. Acquired by Greene King & Sons November 1930 with 40 public houses.
Wright Brothers, *High Street* (1892)

Meldreth

Jarman & Co, *Golden Ale Brewery*. Merged with W.Worboys Ltd of Cambridge February 1913 to form Worboys & Jarman Ltd.

Milton

Thomas William Essex, *Milton Brewery* (1921)

Needingworth

R.Sandifer & Sons. Acquired by H.J.Burt of Fenstanton 1897.

Orwell

P.A.Meyer. Acquired by J.& J.E.Phillips of Royston 1897.

Pampisford

Philip Llewellyn Hudson, *Pampisford Brewery*. Founded 1840. Merged with Ekin's Brewery, Cambridge 1892 to form Hudson's (Cambridge & Pampisford) Breweries Ltd.

Peterborough

Herbert Charles Calcutt, *49 Palmerston Road, Woodston* (1906)
Cutlack & Co.Ltd, *Phoenix Brewery, Priestgate*. Founded before 1865. Registered 5th October 1896 to acquire exors of C.Cutlack with 23 tied houses. William Cutlack of Littleport was the majority shareholder. Acquired by Cutlack & Harlock Ltd March 1917 and brewing ceased in 1923.
Home Brewery Acquired by Warwicks & Richardsons Ltd 1897.
Aubrey C.E.Malden, *Palmerston Brewery* (1920)
Thomas Stones, *Monument Street*. Acquired by Cutlack & Co.Ltd 1898.

Ramsey

Edward V.Sewell (1906)

St.Ives

How & Son, *Wellington Street* (1906)
James William Knights, *West End Brewery* (1911)
Reginald Martin Osborne, *Broadway*. Public houses sold to Marshall Brothers (Huntingdon) Ltd 1919.

St.Neots

Day & Son, *Priory Brewery, Priory Lane & New Street*. Founded before 1780 and acquired by John Day 1814. Offered for auction October 1919 with 61 tied houses after the death of Frank Day, the last of the family. Brewery and 42 houses bought by Wells & Winch Ltd for £40,000. Shortly afterwards half of the houses were sold to Charles Wells Ltd. Brewery still standing.
James Paine Brewery Ltd, *John Bull Brewery, Market Square*. Founded 1831 when James Paine acquired the brewery site. Registered as Paine & Co.Ltd July 1896. Acquired by a group of travel agents 1982, with 20 public houses and renamed as above. Acquired by Tollemache & Cobbold Breweries Ltd 1987 with 24 public houses.

Soham

Treadway & Percy, *Churchgate Street*. Brewery and 21 tied houses offered for auction 16th July 1921 but withdrawn at £19,000 and bought by Cutlack & Harlock Ltd March 1922. Ceased brewing 1926.

Stapleford

Walter Finch (1895)

Stretham

Holland E.Porter, *Spring Brewery* (1926)
Savidge & Co, *Stretham Brewery*. Receiver appointed 29th January 1897.

Sutton

Joseph Randall (1921)

Swavesey

Hawkes & Son (1906)

Wansford

George Earys (1892)

Warboys

S. Fyson & Sons (1917)
Thomas Piggott. Brewery and 7 public houses offered for auction 23rd August 1908.

Waterbeach

Sarah Froment (1910)

Whittlesey

George Coxell, *High Causeway* (1920)
William Farrington (1921)
Charles Henry Hawkes, *Station Road* (1920)
Samuel Howitt, *Whitmore Street* (1920)
John Thomas Phillips, *Nelson Brewery* (1898)
Herbert Reynolds, *Church Street* (1926)
William Henry Roberts, *Whitmore Street* (1923)

Whittlesford

Arthur Douglas & Son (1910)
Saunders & Co, *Steam Brewery*. Oliver St.John trading as Saunders & Co. Also at Great and Little Shelford. Receiving order made January 1894.

Willingham

Tobias Norris (1906)

Wisbech

Elgood & Sons Ltd, *North Brink Brewery*. Founded 1795. Registered 1906. Still brewing independently 1990 with 55 public houses.
Goulder Gray, *18 Albion Place*. Receiver appointed August 1897.
Mill's Brewery (Wisbech) Ltd, *Union Brewery, Nene Parade*. Registered August 1923. Acquired by Hall, Cutlack & Harlock Ltd 1938 and was closed. Brewery demolished and a police station built on the site.
Oak Brewery Ltd, *Leverington Road*. Originally known as Yates Brothers. Acquired by the Abington Brewery Co.Ltd of Northampton 1946. 23 public houses sold to Lacon & Co.Ltd June 1964.
Phillips & Co, *Elm Road Brewery, 4 Bridge Street*. Founded by Charles W.Exley in 1902 sold to Henry T.Herbert in 1906. Acquired by Phillips in 1910. Branch at Downham Market, Norfolk. Partly destroyed by fire 1911 but some remains still visible.
Alma Woods & Co, *Standard Brewery, Upper Hill Street* (1922)

Yaxley

William Rose (1898)

Alloa

Archibald Arrol & Sons Ltd, *Alloa Brewery.* Founded 1810 and was acquired by Archibald Arrol 1866. Registered May 1895 to amalgamate Walter & Archibald Arrol with J.Meikle and William Turnbull, both of Newcastle-upon-Tyne. Acquired by Samuel Allsopp Ltd 1930. Later traded as Ind Coope Alloa Brewery Ltd but is now known as the Alloa Brewery Co.Ltd. Still brewing 1990.

Blair & Co.(Alloa) Ltd, *Townhead Brewery.* Founded by Alexander Blair 1853. Registered 1883 as Blair & Co. of Alloa Ltd. Went into voluntary liquidation and a new company of the same name was registered on 10th June 1896. Voluntary liquidation January 1936 and was re-registered as above in the same year. Acquired by George Younger & Sons Ltd 1959 with 20 tied houses and was closed. Now demolished.

James Calder & Co.(Brewers) Ltd, *Shore Brewery.* Brewery built 1816 by John McNellan and was acquired by James Calder in 1862. Registered 1905 as James Calder & Co.(Alloa) Ltd. Re-registered as above in 1920. Brewing ceased in 1921 and beer was supplied by Arrols until 1951 when John Jeffrey & Co.Ltd brewed for them after the conversion of the Alloa Brewery into a lager only plant. Acquired by Northern Breweries of Great Britain Ltd 1960. The original Shore Brewery has been demolished.

Robert Henderson & Co.Ltd, *Mill Brewery.* Founded c.1804 and was leased by Robert Henderson in 1871. Registered 1909. Acquired by James Calder in 1944.

Robert Knox (Cambus) Ltd, *Forth Brewery, Cambus.* Founded at Tullibody 1786 and had moved to Cambus by 1792. Forth Brewery opened 1866. Registered July 1951. Acquired by Blair & Co. (Alloa) Ltd. September 1954 and was closed in 1955. Later used as a whisky distillery.

Maclay & Co.Ltd, *Thistle Brewery.* Founded by 1830 when James Maclay leased the Mill Brewery. The Thistle Brewery was built in 1870 and the Mill Brewery was leased to Robert Henderson. Registered 1897. Still brewing independently 1990 with 25 public houses.

Robert Meiklejohn & Sons, *Bass Crest Brewery.* Founded 1774 by Robert Meiklejohn and moved to the Candleriggs Brewery 1787 and c.1852 to the Grange Brewery, the Candleriggs Brewery being leased to George Younger & Co 1852 and was sold to them in 1871. Registered as Meiklejohn's Brewery Ltd March 1890. Wound up April 1900 but they continued to trade as the Bass Crest Brewery Co. Acquired by Bass, Ratcliff & Gretton Ltd 1918 after

a lengthy dispute over trademarks. Brewery sold to George Younger & Sons Ltd 1919. Brewing ceased 1941.

John Thomson, *Caponcroft Brewery, Jamaica Street* (1902)

George Younger & Son Ltd, *Meadow & Candleriggs Breweries.* Founded by 1745 and the Meadow Brewery was established by 1764 and the Candleriggs Brewery was leased from Meiklejohns 1852. Registered February 1897. Acquired by Northern Breweries of Great Britain 1960 and brewing ceased on 31st December 1963.

Dollar

Harviestoun Brewery, *Dollarfield Farm.* Founded by Ken Booker 1985. Still brewing 1990.

Falkirk

James Aitken & Co.(Falkirk) Ltd, *17 Lint Riggs.* Founded by James Aitken 1740. Registered June 1900. Acquired by United Caledonian Breweries 1960. Brewing ceased in 1966.

Stirling

Peter Burden Ltd, *Stirling Brewery, Irvine Place.* Founded 1795. Offered for sale February 1925 and a new company was registered in the same year. Ceased brewing December 1931.

James Duncan, *31 Broad Street* (1902)

J.& J.Miller, *St.Ninian's Well Brewery, Burghmuir* (1918)

Alderney

Braye Brewery Ltd. Founded by Roger Curtis. In operation 1984-85.

Guernsey

Guernsey Brewery Co.(1920) Ltd, *South Esplanade, St.Peter Port.* Founded by John le Patourel 1856. Registered March 1895 as the Guernsey Brewery Co.Ltd to acquire the business of Schreiber & Skurray with registered offices at Morlands Brewery, Abingdon. Re-registered February 1920 as above in Guernsey. Acquired 1977 by Bucktrout & Co.Ltd, who in turn were acquired by the Ann Street Brewery Co.Ltd. 35 tied houses.

R.W.Randall Ltd, *Vauxlaurens Brewery, St.Julians Avenue, St.Peter Port.* Possibly founded c.1650 and was acquired by R.H.Randall in 1868. Registered February 1929. Still independent 1990 with 17 public houses.

Jersey

Ann Street Brewery Co.Ltd, *57 Ann Street, St.Helier.* Registered 1905. Still brewing independently 1990 with 48 public houses.

Randalls Vautier Ltd, *Clare Street, St.Helier.* Founded 1823. Registered 1936. Still brewing 1990 with 27 tied houses.

Sark

Sark Brewery. Founded 1983 by Jim Shelley but closed in the same year. Plant sold to the Braye Brewery.

Appleton

Alcuin Cowley (1892)

Bollington

Heaver Brothers Ltd, *Bollington Brewery*. 18 public houses offered for auction 20th January 1920. Acquired by Ind Coope Ltd 1931.

Bridge Trafford

George Williamson (1890)

Burtonwood

Burtonwood Brewery Co.(Forshaws) Ltd, *Bold Lane*. Founded 1867 by James & Jane Forshaw. Registered 1910 as the Burtonwood Brewery Co.Ltd and was re-registered as above April 1949. Some of the public houses were sold to Higson's Brewery Ltd 1925 and a further 23 houses went to Joshua Tetley & Sons Ltd 1949. Still brewing independently 1990.

Chelford

Thomas Heald Gledhill. Founded 1880. Brewing ceased 1906.

Chester

Chester Lion Brewery Co.Ltd, *Pepper Street*. Founded 1642. Registered May 1896 to acquire the business of Thomas Montgomery with 40 public houses. Acquired by Bent's Brewery Co.Ltd 1902 and brewing ceased. Brewery demolished 1969 and replaced by a multi-storey car park with the lion from the brewery tower on top.

Chester Northgate Brewery Co.Ltd, *Northgate Street*. Founded 1760 at the Golden Falcon Hotel. New brewery built in the 1850s. Registered March 1889. Acquired by Greenall Whitley & Co.Ltd 1949 with about 140 tied houses. Brewing ceased 1969 and was demolished 1971. Centurion House now occupies the site.

Edward R.Seller, *Foregate Street*. Acquired by the Albion Brewery Co.Ltd of Wigan *c.*1890

Other Breweries
Robert Cooper Drury, *Francis Street* (1890)
John Dutton, *Egerton Street* (1892)
Henry Knight, *Park Street* (1902)
James Parry, *Barr's Brewery, Foregate Street* (1890)

Crewe

Woolf's Ltd, *South Cheshire Brewery, Wistaston Road*. Founded by 1877. Registered 26th March 1897 to acquire the business of Edward Samuel Woolf with 20 tied houses. Acquired by Ind Coope Ltd 1923 with 42 public houses and was closed.

Croft

Jane Ann Owen, *Croft Brewery* (1926)

Ellesmere Port

Samuel Hough, *Ellesmere Port Brewery* (1895)

Oak Brewery, *59 Merseyton Road*. Founded August 1982 by Tony Allen. Still brewing 1990.

Farndon

Joseph Salmon. Acquired by the Chester Lion Brewery Co.Ltd in 1898

Handforth

Handforth Brewery Co. (1908)

Knutsford

Alfred John Claxton, *Knutsford Brewery*. Acquired by Chesters Brewery Co.Ltd 1906.

Macclesfield

Harry Evans & Co, *Star Brewery, Bond Street*. Acquired by Bindley & Co.Ltd of Burton-on-Trent 1890 for £23,000 with 20 tied houses.

William Hamson, junior, *Royal Oak Brewery, 89 Hill Street* (1892)

C.A.Hordern & Co, *Grapes Brewery, Lord Street*. Acquired by the North Cheshire Brewery Co.Ltd 1910.

Lonsdale & Adshead Ltd, *Macclesfield Brewery, 45 Park Green*. Founded 1790. Registered 1899 with 129 tied houses. Acquired by Ind Coope Ltd 1950. Brewery offered for sale 1967 and was bought by Whitbread.

F.W.Maurice & Co, *Queen's Brewery, Albert Place* (1905)

North Cheshire Brewery Co.Ltd, *Charles Street*. Founded 1862. In liquidation 1867 as the Macclesfield Brewery & Wine Co.Ltd. Operating as the Macclesfield Brewery Co.Ltd 1869-73. Registered 1897 as the North Cheshire & Manchester Brewery Co.Ltd. Name changed as above 1898 after legal action by the Manchester Brewery Co.Ltd who objected to the use of that part of the name which coincided with their own. Acquired by Lonsdale & Adshead Ltd 1928 with about 87 tied houses.

W.A.Smith & Sons Ltd, *Crown Brewery, Bond Street*. Acquired by Marston, Thompson & Evershed Ltd 1962 with about 20 public houses.

Stancliffe Brothers Ltd, *Sutton Brewery, Byrons Lane*. Registered 1897 to acquire Stancliffe Brothers of Mirfield and Macclesfield. Acquired by Lonsdale & Adshead Ltd July 1920 with 40 houses.

Malpas

Frederick Batterbee (1898)

Mollington

G.Williamson. Sold by auction 11th May 1912, to Thomas Crump of Chester.

Nantwich

Walley & Dutton, *Cock Inn Brewery* (1892)

Peover

George Bell & Sons, *Tabley Arms Brewery* (1921)

Runcorn

Bass Charrington Ltd, *Whitehouse Industrial Estate*. A large scale brewery opened 1973.

Thomas Jones, *Navigation Brewery, Canal Street*. Home brew house closed 1906. The Navigation is now a Marston, Thompson & Evershed house. Thomas Jones was a close friend of Edward J.Smith, Captain of the Titanic and an executor of his will.

Warrington

Bolton Brothers, *38 Mersey Street*. Acquired by Greenall Whitley & Co.Ltd November 1931.

Cunningham Brothers Ltd, *Owen Street*. Founded 1895 as a wine & spirits merchants, moved to Owen Street 1908 and began brewing in 1909. Known as B.Cunningham Ltd until 6th June 1969. In 1951 63 properties were sold, of these, 34 public houses and 18 off-licences were bought by Joshua Tetley & Son Ltd for £550,000. Merged with Howcroft's Brewery Ltd of Bolton 1969, but due to financial difficulties they were wound up in December of that year.

Greenall Whitley & Co.Ltd, *Wilderspool Brewery, Wilderspool Causeway and Hall Street, St.Helens*. Founded 1762 at St.Helens and the Warrington brewery was established in 1787. Private company registered October 1880 and public company formed 1952. Late in 1990 it was announced that the breweries at Warrington and Nottingham were to close and their 1,510 tied houses would be supplied by Allied-Lyons under a 5 year contract.

John Evans, *33 Church Street* (1920)

Walker Cain Ltd, *Dallam Lane*. Founded 1864 at King Street, Dallam Lane brewery built 1866 and was replaced by a new brewery on the same site in 1967. Registered 1889 as Peter Walker & Sons, Warrington & Burton Ltd. Also at the Midland Brewery Burton-on-Trent 1890-1923 when lager brewing ceased. New company registered September 1921 as Peter Walker (Warrington) and Robert Cain & Sons Ltd. Name changed as above in 1946. Merged with Joshua Tetley & Son Ltd 1960 to form Tetley Walker Ltd, now part of Carlsberg-Tetley.

Widnes

Peter Laughton, *Spring Brewery, Hough Green*. Acquired by Greenall Whitley & Co.Ltd 1898.

Winsford

John Crompton Armitage, *Over Brewery, Over.* Offered for auction 1908 with 2 public houses and was presumably closed.

CLEVELAND

Hartlepool

J.W.Cameron & Co.Ltd, *Lion Brewery, Stockton Street.* Founded 1852 by William Waldon. Leased to John William Cameron 1872 with 16 public houses and he bought the brewery in 1893. Registered as above November 1894 with 50 tied houses. Acquired with 750 houses in 1974 by Ellerman Lines Ltd, which in turn was acquired by Barclay Brothers 1983 and finally sold to the Brent Walker Group in January 1989. Still brewing 1990 with 480 public houses.

Harker & Co.Ltd, *Minerva Place.* Private company registered 1911. Acquired by North-Eastern Breweries Ltd 1925

Nixey, Coleclough & Baxter Ltd, *Brunswick Brewery, 16 Church Street.* Registered July 1890. Acquired by J.W.Cameron & Co.Ltd 1894 and was closed in 1898.

Rickinson & Sons Ltd, *9 Church Street.* Acquired by J.W.Cameron & Co.Ltd 1895.

Middlesborough

Amateur Winemakers, *Goliath Brewery, 37 Princes Road.* Home brew shop where Paul Gray began brewing 1979 to supply off-licences with bottled beer. Ceased brewing 1983.

Norton-on-Tees

J.Heslop, *Norton Grange Brewery.* Founded 1878. Their 27 public houses were bought by J.W.Cameron & Co.Ltd 1909. The brewery was acquired by Vaux & Sons Ltd 1923 and used as a distribution centre.

Stockton-on-Tees

Kirk Brothers & Co, *Castle Brewery, Bridge Street.* Formed part of North-Eastern Breweries Ltd 1896.

E.J.Sait (late Kirtley & Son). Acquired by J.W.Cameron & Co.Ltd 1896.

CLWYD

Acrefair

Thomas Richards (1923)

Bagillt

Cambrian Brewery Co.Ltd. Registered 6th April 1898 to acquire William Pierce & Son, also known as the Cambrian Brewery. Formed as a subsidiary of the Kelsterton Brewery Co.Ltd, with 41 public houses. As the latter went into liquidation on 22nd December 1899, the company never traded and was dissolved on 2nd August 1904.

Bettisfield

Samuel Preston (1923)

Buckley

Cestrian Brewers, *Pinfold Brewery, Pinfold Lane Industrial Estate.* Founded July 1981. Closed 1983.

Caergwrle

Lassell & Sharman Ltd. Founded at Milton Street, Liverpool by 1832 and the Caergwrle brewery was established by 1873. Registered 1894. Acquired by the Burtonwood Brewery (Forshaws) Co.Ltd 1945 with 57 tied houses and was later closed. Premises later used by C.R.Averill Ltd, paint manufacturers.

Cefn

Daniel Bowen, (1920)
Mary Ann Cartwright, (1920)
William Davies, (1921)
Mary Alice Hughes, *Queen's Hotel.* The last home brew house in Clwyd. Acquired by Border Breweries

1944.
John Morris, (1921)
Walter Wright, (1920)

Chirk

James Edwards & Son, (1926)
Henry George Jones, (1920)

Denbigh

Angel & Co, *Denbigh Brewery, 6 Halls Square* (1915)
Margaret Parry, *Graig Brewery, Beacon's Hill* (1935)
Robert Brothers, *High Street Brewery* (1895)
William Williams, *Hawk & Buckle, Vale Street* (1895)
Pryce Edward Storey, *Coppy Brewery* (1934)

Ewloe

John Fox & Co, *Castle Hill Brewery.* Founded 1844. Acquired by the Burtonwood Brewery (Forshaws) Co.Ltd 1949 with 16 public houses and brewing ceased.

Eyton

Plassey Brewery, *The Plassey.* Founded October 1985 in old dairy buildings using some former Border Breweries equipment. Still brewing 1990.

Glyn Ceiriog

Edward Hughes (1910)

Holywell

St.Winefrid's Brewery Co, *Greenfield Street.* Founded by 1844. Under the name of J.Lloyd Price until 1892. 44 tied houses offered for auction on 21st November 1928, 34 being sold for £30,000 and brewing ceased.

Kelsterton

Kelsterton Brewery Co.Ltd. Registered March 28th 1890 to acquire the business of Thomas Bate trading as the Kelsterton Brewery Co. Acquired by the Chester Northgate Brewery Ltd 1899 with 93 public houses. Brewing ceased 1904.

Llangollen

Charles Baker, *Prince of Wales Brewery, Regent Street* (1918)
Robert Baker & Co, *Sun Brewery, 26 Regent Street.* Founded before 1886. Ceased brewing January 1925 due to the death of Robert Baker.
John Jones, *Crown Brewery, Butler's Hill* (1912)
Miriam Jones, *Hall Street* (1910)
John S.Tanqueray & Co, *Llangollen Brewery, Berwyn Road.* Founded by J.S.Tanqueray 1870 who was originally a partner in Combe's Brewery, London until 1869 when he opened a brewery off New Oxford Street before moving to Llangollen. Brewery sold 1919 and was converted into a milk & cheese factory. Public houses acquired by F.W.Soames & Co.Ltd of Wrexham. A later attempt to re-establish the brewery was not realised.

Minera

Minera Brewery, *City Arms, Wern Road.* A home brew house founded February 1984 by Lloyd & Trouncer (Allied Breweries) but ceased brewing 1989.

Mold

Owen Jones, *Glanrafon Brewery, Wrexham Street* (1895)

Old Mold Brewery Co.Ltd, *New Street.* Founded by 1844. Registered 14th January 1897 to acquire the business of David Clark Radcliffe trading as Jones, Lloyd & Co. Acquired by the West Cheshire Brewery Co.Ltd March 1898.

Pontmadog

C.R.Fendick, *Glyn Brewery* (1923)

Rhosymedre

Robert Godfrey Evans (1910)

Ruabon

James Edwards & Son, *Lodge Brewery* (1926)
John Thomas Gabriel, *Newbridge* (1923)
John T.Jones, *Rhos* (1906)
Alfred Edward Pemberton (1930)

Ruthin

Margaret Jones, *Park Place Brewery, Mwrog Street* (1920)
William Owen, *Corporation Arms Brewery, Castle Street* (1895)
Charles Phillips, *Spread Eagle Brewery, Upper Clwyd Street* (1895)
Robert Roberts, *Hand Brewery, Well Street.* Acquired by Ind Coope Ltd 1917.

Wrexham

C.Bate & Son Ltd, *Union Brewery.* Registered May 1905 to acquire breweries at Wrexham & Liverpool with 32 public houses. Acquired by Walker's Warrington Brewery 1909. Receiver appointed and trading ceased on 7th June 1910. Brewery and 27 tied houses offered for sale 23rd February 1927. Dissolved 12th January 1932.

John Beirne, *Albion Brewery, Bridge Street.* Closed 1938 and their 23 tied houses were bought by the Wrexham Lager Beer Co.Ltd.

Border Breweries (Wrexham) Ltd, *Nag's Head Brewery, Mount Street.* Registered June 1931 to acquire: F.W.Soames & Co.Ltd (in liquidation), Nag's Head Brewery: The Island Green Brewery Co.Ltd & Dorsett, Owen & Co, Oswestry. Public company registered 1938. Acquired by Marston, Thompson & Evershed Ltd in November 1984 with 170 public houses and brewing ceased.

Julius Augustus Chadwick, *Burton Brewery, Bridge Street.* Public houses sold to F.W.Soames & Co.Ltd September 1922.

Island Green Brewery Co.Ltd. Founded *c.*1840 by John Jones. Registered January 1925 to acquire the business carried on by F.O.J.Huntley & G.A.S.Mowat as the Island Green Brewery Co. with 23 tied houses. Formed part of Border Breweries in 1931.

William John Sisson, *Cambrian Brewery, Bridge Street.* Brewery closed 1922 and their 48 tied houses were leased to the Island Green Brewery Co.

F.W.Soames & Co.Ltd, *Nag's Head Brewery, Mount Street.* Founded *c.*1750 and was acquired by F.W.Soames 1879. Registered April 1931. Formed part of Border Breweries in 1931.

Wrexham Lager Beer Co.Ltd, *Central Road.* Founded by Ivan Levenstein in 1878 as the Wrexham Brewery Co. and Robert Graesser soon acquired the majority shareholding. Name was changed to the Wrexham Beer Co. in 1881. Registered April 1900. Acquired by Ind Coope Ltd 1949. Still brewing 1990.

Other Breweries

Heasman & Co, *Eagle Brewery, Bridge Street* (1922)
Thomas Manley, *Vicarage Hill Brewery* (1894)
Murless & Co, *Wynnstay Brewery, York Street* (1894)
Margaret Price (exors of), *Mitre Brewery, Brook Street* (1914)
Thompson & Co, *Sun Brewery, Bridge Street* (1910)

CORNWALL

Albaston

Edward Bowhay & Brothers. Founded by 1877. Brewing continued until about 1930. The maltings are still standing.

Bodmin

John Billing, *Bodmin Brewery.* Acquired by the Redruth Brewery Co.Ltd 1900.

Chacewater

Chacewater Brewery Co.Ltd, *Station Road.* Originally known as Moyle & Son. Closed 1920.

Gradwell & Co. Founded 1889. Acquired by Sydney Hatch of Penryn 1901 with 16 tied houses and was closed.

Dinham's Bridge

Miss E.Bate (1920)

Egloshayle

Ambrose Matthews (1926)

Falmouth

W.& E.C.Carne, *Falmouth Brewery Co, Killigrew Street.* Acquired by Devenish & Co.Ltd 1921 and brewing ceased in 1926. Brewery demolished *c.*1935 and was replaced by the Odeon cinema.

Gulval

Pensans Brews, *Little Chyauster Farm.* Founded December 1982 by Tim Sears, brewer at the Blue Anchor, Helston. Supplied a number of free houses. Ceased brewing Summer 1985.

Hayle

Christopher Ellis & Son Ltd, *Steam Brewery, Brewery Road.* Founded 1815. 32 public houses.

Merged with Walter Hicks & Co.Ltd 1934 to form the St.Austell Brewery Co.Ltd and brewing ceased at Hayle in the same year.

Paradise Brewery Co.Ltd, *Paradise Bird Sanctuary, Trelissick Road.* Founded by Mike Reynolds, May 1981 to supply the Bird-in-Hand pub at the bird sanctuary. Still in operation 1990.

Helland

Stallion Ales, *Helland Grange.* Founded by Ken Jones and Maureen Hurst December 1985. Closed 1987.

Helston

Blue Anchor Inn, *50 Coinagehall Street.* Home brew house founded by 1400 as a monastic foundation and became an inn by the 18th Century. Still in operation 1990.

William Edward Oates, *Meneage Street* (1923)
Sleeman & Co, *62 Meneage Street* (1920)

Liskeard

D. Venning & Son Ltd, *East Cornwall Steam Brewery, Baytree Hill.* Founded c.1800 by Edmund Venning. 11 public houses. Brewhouse destroyed by fire 1942 and brewing ceased but business carried on as bottlers and wine & spirit merchants. Acquired by Watney, Combe, Reid & Co.Ltd January 1955 and ceased to trade March 1963.

The Lizard

Caroline Hill (1930)

Mevagissey

Robert Thomas Pearce (1940)

Mount

Bodmin Ales, *Higher Tawna Farm.* Founded December 1982 by John Holden. Closed 1984.

Newquay

William Hancock, *St.Columb Minor* (1910)

Padstow

T.Henwood & Sons, *Mill Road.* Brewing ceased 1914 but the business was still in existence 1990 as an off-licence in the Strand.

Penryn

Arthur George Chapman, *Broad Street* (1920)
Sydney Hatch, *Treluswell Brewery.* The 12 tied houses were acquired equally by the St.Austell Brewery Co.Ltd & the Redruth Brewery Co.Ltd after brewing had ceased in 1943.

Poundstock

North Cornwall Brewery Co.Ltd. Registered April 1907 to carry on the business of Slaughter & Dominy. Wound up 1912.

Probus

Thomas Bailey (1920)

Redruth

Cornish Brewery Co.Ltd. Founded before 1827. Registered February 1887 as the Redruth Brewery Co.Ltd to acquire the businesses of the Redruth Brewery Co. and W.C.Wickett of Penryn. 194 public houses. Acquired by Devenish & Co.Ltd of Weymouth 1934 and name changed to Devenish Redruth Brewery Co.Ltd 1960 and again as above 1985. Still brewing 1990.

St.Austell

St.Austell Brewery Co.Ltd, *Trevarthian Road.* Formed by a merger of Walter Hicks & Co.Ltd and Christopher Ellis & Son Ltd of Hayle 1934. Walter Hicks was founded as wine merchants 1851 and began brewing 1860. New brewery built 1891. Still brewing independently 1990 with 130 public houses.
John Job, *Bodmin Road* (1906)

St.Dominick

Joseph Martin, *Towell Brewery* (1910)

St.Mabyn

Mrs John Baker (1892)

Saltash

Frederick Richard Vaughan, *Saltash Brewery.* Formed part of Plymouth Breweries Ltd 1889.

Tintagel

Min Pin Inn. Home brew house founded 1986 when a farmhouse was converted into a brewery by Marie Hall and daughter Stefanie. Still in operation 1990.

Truro

John Allen, *42 Fairmantle Street* (1920)
William Arthur Davey, *25 New Bridge Street* (1926)
Edith Evans, *93 Pydar Street* (1923)
James Edgar Libby, *7 Richmond Hill* (1923)
Richard Mainwaring, *11 Richmond Hill* (1923)
Mallett's Brewery. Acquired by Devenish & Co.Ltd 1921.
William Martin, *30 Carclew Street* (1920)
Thomas Passmore, *5 Calenick Street* (1923)
William Henry Passmore, *61 Lemon Street* (1923)
William J.Passmore, *1 Bodmin Street* (1930)
Elizabeth Penrose, *26 Pydar Street* (1920)
Martha Ellen Rapson, *Quay Street* (1935)
John Alexander Smith, *83/84 Pydar Street* (1926)
Joseph Tabb, *77 Kenwyn Street* (1923)
William John Thomas, *85 Kenwyn Street* (1935)
Richard Trudgen, *Mitchell Hill* (1923)
Robert Venton, *12 Fairmantle Street* (1923)
Walter J.Wilkins, *57 Pydar Street* (1935)

Wadebridge

James Collins, *Station Road* (1898)
John Irons, *Molesworth Street* (1914)

CUMBRIA

Allithwaite

William Lambert (1906)

Alston

Walton & Little (1926)

Appleby

Alfred Bertwistle & Sons, *Low Brewery, Doomsgate.* Acquired by Marston, Thompson & Evershed Ltd 15th August 1928.
Westmorland Brewery Co.Ltd, *Cross Croft.* Founded October 1979 as the Appleby New Brewery. Name changed as above December 1980. Closed for financial reasons 1984.

Aspatria

Yates Brewery, *Ghyll Farm, Westnewton.* Home brew house founded 1986 by Peter Yates. Still in operation 1990.

Barrow-in-Furness

R.F.Case & Co.Ltd, *Cavendish Brewery, Cavendish Street.* Founded 1860 at King Street, Ulverston and had moved to Barrow by 1865. Registered 1904. Acquired by Hammond's United Breweries Ltd 1959 with 60 tied houses. Brewing ceased 3rd March 1972.
G.S.Heath Ltd, *Devonshire Brewery, Hindpool Road.* Private company registered 1913. Acquired by Hammond's United Breweries Ltd 1959 with 21 public houses and was closed.
James Thompson & Co.Ltd, *237 Dalton Road.* Founded 1871 as wine & spirit merchants. Thompsons never owned a brewery but from 1932 they brewed at Hartley's Brewery, Ulverston, under the supervision of their own brewer, this continued until 1969. Before 1932 they had brewed at Heath's Brewery and also at the Whittle Springs Brewery, Chorley, Lancs. Acquired by Whitbread & Co.Ltd 1966 with 47 public houses.

James Tyson, exors of, *Barrow Brewery, Burlington Street* (1900)

Brampton

Brampton Old Brewery Co.Ltd. Founded 1785. Known as J.Armstrong and the name was changed c.1910. Acquired by Glasson's Penrith Breweries Ltd 1926.

New Brampton Brewery Co. Brewing ceased c.1919 but continued in business as ale & stout merchants until at least 1926.

Burton-in-Kendal

Joseph Titterington. Acquired by William Mitchell of Lancaster c.1923.

Caldbeck

John Emmerson (1898). Brewery still standing.

Carlisle

During the 1914-18 war there were a number of munition factories in the Carlisle area, and to control the drinking habits of the workers, all the breweries and public houses were brought under State control in 1916. The controlling body was the Carlisle & District State Management Scheme.

It was announced on 19th January 1971 that the brewery and the 206 tied houses in the Carlisle/Gretna area would be sold to private enterprise. The main purchasers were: Greenall Whitley & Co.Ltd - 49 properties for £2,428,408; John Smith's Tadcaster Brewery Co.Ltd - 30 properties for £1,082,902 and Scottish & Newcastle Breweries Ltd - 27 premises for £1,267,000. Jennings Brothers Ltd of Cockermouth bought 3 public houses for £32,000 and other purchasers were Whitbread West Pennines Ltd and Bass Charrington Ltd. 34 of the smaller public houses were sold to the sitting tenants. An attempt to recommence brewing as Lakeland Breweries by Peter Lewis & Associates of Alston was not realised and the brewery was sold to T.& R.Theakston Ltd of Masham, North Yorkshire for £90,000 in May 1974.

Carlisle New Brewery Co.Ltd, *Shaddongate.* Originally registered 1879 as the New Brewery (Carlisle) Ltd and was re-registered as above 1899. Brought under state control 1916 and was closed. Later used as maltings and sold to the Border Dairy Co.Ltd.

Carlisle Old Brewery *(Sir Richard Hodgson & Co.Ltd), Bridge Street.* Founded 1756. Used as the State Management brewery until 1973 and was bought by Theakstons 1974.

F.P.Dixon *(Jos.Iredale's trustees), High Brewery, Currock Street.* Brought under state control 1916 and closed.

Graham & Sons, *Queen's Brewery, Caldewgate.* Founded 1860. Brought under state control 1916 and closed. Premises now used by a firm of motor engineers.

David Hall & Sons, *Crown Street* (1895)

Cleator Moor

Cleator Moor Brewery Co.Ltd, *Birks Road.* Registered 1896 to take over Paitson's Brewery Co.Ltd, Cleator Moor, registered 1875 and William Foster Charter, Main Street, Egremont. Acquired by Matthew Brown & Co.Ltd 1947 and brewing ceased 1977.

Cockermouth

Jennings Brothers Ltd, *Castle Brewery, Castlegate.* Founded at Lorton 1828 and moved to Cockermouth 1887. Public company registered in the same year with 41 tied houses. Still independent 1990.

Dalston

W.T.Trimble, *Dalston Old Brewery.* Acquired by the Maryport Brewery Ltd 1891.

Dalton-in-Furness

W.E.Ashburner, *Dalton Brewery Co, Market Street.* Offered for auction 9th October 1901, with 21 public houses and was sold privately for £35,000.

James Holmes & Co, *Beckside* (1895)

Egremont

William Foster Charter, *Main Street.* Merged with Paitson's Brewery Co.Ltd of Cleator Moor 1896 to form the Cleator Moor Brewery Co.Ltd.

Flookburgh

George Fell (1910)

Kendal

Jonas Alexander & Sons Ltd, *Beezon Lane Brewery, Sandes Avenue.* Founded 1822 as E.Hayton & Co. Registered December 1927. Acquired by Dutton's Blackburn Brewery Ltd 1947 with 31 tied houses. Brewing ceased 1954. Premises now an insurance office.

Collin Croft Brewery Co.Ltd, *Beezon Road.* Founded by 1884. Registered 1905 to acquire the business of John Geldred. Acquired by William Younger & Co.Ltd September 1933 and brewing ceased but continued to bottle Younger's beers until 1965. Dissolved July 1965.

Edwin Hetherington, *Gillingate Brewery, 99 Highgate.* Acquired by Hartley's (Ulverston) Ltd 1918 with 3 public houses.

Whitwell, Mark & Co.Ltd, *Highgate.* Founded 1757 by John Whitwell. Private company registered 1883. Acquired by Vaux & Associated Breweries 1947 with 30 tied houses. Brewing ceased 18th September 1968. Now converted into the Brewery Arts Centre.

Other Breweries

J.J.Banks & Son, *Old Brewery, Wildman Street* (1903)

John Graham, *Tower Brewery, Allhallows Lane* (1926)

George Hoggarth, *Highgate Brewery* (1895)

Edward Rishton, *Seven Stars Brewery, Stricklandgate* (1921)

Keswick

Faulder's Brewery Co.Ltd, *Browfoot Brewery.* Registered 1883 to acquire the business of the late Robert Faulder. Acquired by Jennings Brothers Ltd 1926 and brewing ceased 1927. Wound up March 1946.

Old Brewery Co.Ltd, *Brewery Lane.* Registered September 1889 to acquire the business of Henry John Allinson. Brewery for auction 25th June 1896 with 4 public houses. Went into liquidation November 1896 and was dissolved July 1907.

Kirkby Stephen

Henry Paul Mason, *High Brewery* (1894)
James Rowlandson, *Eden Bank Brewery, Mellbecks* (1929)

Kirkoswald

William Hodgson (1892)

Kirksanton

J.W.Brockbank & Sons Ltd, *Bank Springs Brewery.* Acquired by Matthew Brown & Co.Ltd 1954 and was liquidated in the same year.

Longtown

Longtown Brewery Co. (1902)

Maryport

Maryport Brewery Ltd, *Wood Street.* Founded c.1780. Registered November 1890 to acquire the business of Frederic Robinson Sewell with 63 public houses. As a result of their tied houses in Carlisle being brought under state control in 1916, the brewery output was reduced by more than 50%.

So the houses left were sold to the State Management scheme in November 1916 and brewing ceased November 1921.

Milnthorpe

Mary C.Hodgson (1921)
Thomas James Titterington (1921)

Penrith

Glasson's Penrith Breweries Ltd, *Union Court Brewery, Roper Street.* Founded by 1884. Registered February 1898 to acquire the businesses of Robert James Glasson and the Old Brewery Co.Ltd, Stricklandgate, Penrith. Acquired by Dutton's Blackburn Brewery Ltd 1959 with 110 tied houses.

H.Newton & Co, *New Brewery, Middlegate.* Acquired by the Carlisle Old Brewery Co.Ltd 1899 with 34 public houses for £60,000.

Old Brewery Co.Ltd, *Stricklandgate.* Merged with Robert James Glasson 1898 to form Glasson's Penrith Breweries Ltd.

Penrith Middlegate Brewery Ltd, *Middlegate.* Registered November 1900 to acquire the New Brewery, formerly owned by H.Newton & Co. Acquired by Glasson's Penrith Breweries Ltd 1906 with about 40 public houses.

Tirril

J.Siddle, *Tirril Brewery.* Acquired by Glasson's Penrith Breweries Ltd September 1899. Brewery still standing 1990.

Ulverston

Hartleys (Ulverston) Ltd, *Old Brewery, Brewery Street.* Founded 1819. Private company registered October 1918. Acquired by Frederic Robinson Ltd of Stockport 1982 with 54 tied houses.

Whitehaven

Joseph Dalzell's Parton & Harrington Breweries Ltd, *Tower Brewery, Duke Street.* Registered March 1892. The Parton brewery was sold to the Maryport Brewery Ltd 1905 with 74 public houses. Merged with Jennings Brothers of Cockermouth 1906 but was still operated as a separate concern, the profits being divided each year. This arrangement ended in September 1923 after a dispute over the accounts. Harrington Brewery was acquired by Matthew Brown & Co.Ltd 1925 with 75 tied houses and is now a garage.

T.C.Dixon & Co. (1910)

Henry Spencer & Co.Ltd, *Old Brewery, Irish Street.* Founded c.1790. Registered August 1891 to acquire the business of Spencer Broadbent and Henry Taylor carried on as Spencer & Co. Acquired by the Workington Brewery Co.Ltd November 1929 with about 40 tied houses and was closed.

Workington

J.P.Bennett & Sons Ltd, *Griffin Brewery, Ramsay Brow.* Private company registered October 1924. Acquired by the Workington Brewery Co.Ltd 1939.

Workington Brewery Co.Ltd, *High Brewery.* Founded by John Curwen 1792. Registered May 1891 to acquire the business of P.& T.Iredale. Acquired by Mount Charlotte Investments Ltd 1973 with 110 public houses and was sold to Matthew Brown & Co.Ltd June 1975. Renamed the Lakeland Lager Brewery and ceased brewing in 1986.

DERBYSHIRE

Ashbourne

Wilson, Allaway & Co.Ltd, *Burton Brewery, Clifton Road.* Traded as Thomas Cooper until 1881. Registered as above November 1886. Acquired by Bindley & Co.Ltd of Burton-on-Trent April 1897.

Belper

Herbert Bradley, *Rose & Crown, King Street.* Home brew house in operation 1895.

Buxton

Saxon Cross Brewery, *Harpur Hill Industrial Estate.* Founded January 1979 by Clive Winkle. Known locally as Winkle's Brewery. One tied house at Mow Cop, Cheshire. Went into liquidation March 1987.

Castle Gresley

Gresley Brewery Ltd. Operating as Beard Brothers from c.1870 and by 1886 known as Beard, Hill & Co. Registered as above October 1892. Voluntary liquidation 30th October 1894. For sale by private tender August 1895 with 43 tied houses which were acquired by the Albion (Burton-on-Trent) Brewery Ltd. Wound up 21st November 1898.

Chapel-en-le-Frith

John S.Simpson, *Park Brewery.* Acquired by Stancliffe Brothers Ltd of Macclesfield, Cheshire 1910.

Chesterfield

Brampton Brewery Co.Ltd, *Chatsworth Road, Brampton.* Registered June 1897 with 142 public houses. Acquired by Warwicks & Richardsons Ltd 1955.

Chesterfield Brewery Co.Ltd, *Tapton Lane.* Founded 1853. Registered August 1897. Acquired by the Mansfield Brewery Co.Ltd 1934 and brewing ceased.

A.Hollingworth, *Grassmoor* (1920)
Joseph Minkley, *Whitwell* (1902)

Scarsdale Brewery Co.Ltd, *Spa Lane Brewery.* Registered June 1865. Acquired by Whitbread & Co.Ltd February 1958.

Cromford

Hill's Cromford Brewery Co.Ltd. Founded c.1825. Registered July 1866 to acquire the business of Matthew Hill. Acquired by Offiler's Brewery Ltd 1914. Brewery used as a depot until 1926 and converted into a laundry which was demolished c.1968.

Derby

Alton & Co.Ltd, *Wardwick Brewery, 15 Wardwick.* Founded by Thomas Lowe 1788. Registered 1888 and a new company was registered in July 1899 with 91 public houses. Acquired by Stretton's Derby Brewery Ltd January 1903 with 154 tied houses. Brewery not closed until 1922 as it was run as a separate concern.

Derby Brewery Co.Ltd, *Nottingham Road.* Registered May 1893 to acquire the business of H.J.E.Scott & H.B.Craven. Acquired by Stretton's Derby Brewery Ltd 1899 with over 57 tied houses.

Flamingo & Firkin, *Becket Street.* New home brew house opened December 1988.

Home Brewed Ale Co.Ltd, *Old Mill, Agard Street.* Registered 1903.

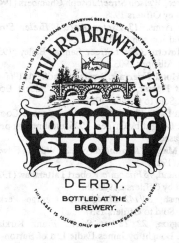

Offiler's Brewery Ltd, *7 Ambrose Street, Normanton Road.* Founded 1876 when George Offiler acquired the Vine Inn brewery, Whitaker Street. Ambrose Street brewery opened 1881. Registered November 1890 and reconstructed company formed February 1892. Acquired by Charrington United Breweries 1965 with 238 public houses and was closed 30th September 1966.

John Stretton, *Kedleston Road Brewery*. Formed from business of Henry Sherwin declared bankrupt December 1905. New building opened 1907. John Stretton ran the firm until 1916 with Thomas Salt & Co.Ltd as the principal shareholders. New syndicate formed 1916 primarily to brew non-alcoholic beer with L.Harvey as the manager and was later known as Harvey & Harvey. Became a malt vinegar brewery and continued as such until the early 1980s.

Stretton's Derby Brewery Ltd, *Manchester Brewery, Ashbourne Road*. Founded before 1868 when acquired by Stretton Brothers. Acquired by Samuel Allsopp & Sons Ltd 1927 with 143 public houses. Brewery closed 1929 and sold to Burrows, Sturgess & Severn, mineral water manufacturers.

Weall Brothers, *Ashbourne Road*. Partnership of B.& A.F.Weall dissolved 3rd December 1897 and was acquired by Alton & Co.Ltd.

Other Breweries

Albert Vaults, *21 Whitecross Street/195 Brook Street*, H.D.Leonard, sold to Strettons 1924.
Barleycorn, *105 Canal Street*, Thomas Carter, sold to Offilers, continued to brew probably until 1960s
Black Swan, *49 Siddals Road*, Thomas Boden (1932). A Pountain's house sold to Ind Coope after 1945.
Castle Tavern, *40 Castle Street*. George Bull (1962). Sold to Offilers 1942 but continued to brew.
Cheshire Cheese, *105 St.Peter's Street*. William Sutton (1935). Sold to Alton & Co.Ltd 1897 but continued to brew.
Cobden Arms, *45 Cobden Street*. Louisa Spriggs (1931). A Pountain's house from 1901.
Copeland Arms, *18 Copeland Street*. Annie Winter (1963)
Crystal Palace, *42 Rosehill Street*. Frederick Shreeve, sold to Offilers 1924 but still brewing under Charringtons September 1966.
Devonshire Arms, *27 Devonshire Street*. John Hirst (1932 +). Sold to Offilers 1931.
Dog & Partridge, *55 Bedford Street*. Harold Brooks (1967)
Duke of Cambridge, *34 Whitecross Street*. Charles Roberts (1952)
Duke of Devonshire, *55 Goodwin Street*. John Hilton (1932 +)
Eagle Tavern, *20 Green Street*. James Revill (1952)
Elm Tree, *25 Boroughs Walk*. May Reynolds, sold to Offilers 1950 after her death.
Elm Tree, *Watson Street*. Joseph Chambers (1945). Bought by Offilers 1928.
Exeter Arms, *13 Exeter Place/1 Exeter Street*. Winifred Jackson (1970)
Fleet Tavern, *3 Fleet Street*. Samuel Bailey (1953). Sold to Allsopps 1903.
Friary Hotel, *Friargate*. Rowland Hadfield (1960-68)
Gallant Hussar, *Ashbourne Road*. Albert Boyce (1932). Sold to Offilers 1925.
Golden Eagle, *27/55 Agard Street*. Joseph Cooper (1926). Bought by Offilers 1925 and brewing probably ceased.
Green Man, *32 Kensington Street*. William Edward Dawes (1965)
Greyhound, *76 Friargate*. Robert Tattershaw (1928). Bought by Offilers c.1923/28.
Hollybush, *84/142 Bridgegate*. George Perkins (1936). Sold to Offilers 1937.
Kensington, *22 Talbot Street*. Frank Kirkland (1928). Bought by James Eadie Ltd of Burton-on-Trent in 1920s.
Lamb, *St.Alkmund's Churchyard*. Margaret Keenan (1941)
Lamb Inn, *Park Street*. Sarah Carter (1940). Sold to Offilers c.1938.
Lion & Tigress, *42 Bradshaw Street*. Henry Thornhill (1925). Sold to Home Brewery Co.Ltd 1904/28.
Lord Raglan, *38 Clover Street*. William Jackson (1940). Sold to Home Brewery Co.Ltd c.1928.
Malt Shovel, *44 Kedleston Street*. John Tivey (1938)
Melbourne Arms, *11/33 Siddals Road*. Gerald Roberts (1961)
Napoleon, *103 Parker Street*. John Brook (1956). Sold to Strettons c.1935.
Newmarket, *53/54 East Street*. Florence Sharp (1928). Sold to Allsopps 1910/19.
Nottingham Castle, *12 Queen Street*. Henry Groome (1958)
Old Dolphin, *7 Queen Street*. John Edward Felix (1928). Sold to Offilers c.1945.
Old Dove, *1 William Street*. George Leech (1928). Sold to Allsopps 1919/23.
Old Eagle & Child, *1 St.Alkmund's Churchyard*. Harold Anthony (1964). Sold to Offilers 1941.
Prince Regent, *57 Regent Street*. Thomas Harness (1949). Sold to Ind Coope (Strettons) c.1945.
Quarn Tavern, *34 Quarn Street*. Charles Henderson (1925). Leased to John Hair & Son from 1925.
Queen Adelaide, *13 Canal Street*. William Guest (1942). Sold to Offilers 1928.
Ram, *84 Bridgegate*. John Willgoose (1940)
Ring O'Bells, *36 Bradshaw Street*. William Renshaw (31st December 1925)
Rising Sun, *67 Osmaston Road*. Charles Roberts (1933)
Seven Stars, *97 King Street*. Philip Henry, sold to Scottish & Newcastle Breweries 1962.
Shakespear, *16 Sadlergate*. Kate Tomlinson (1925)
Sir Henry Wilmot's Arms, *50 Rivett Street*. Ellen Bailey (1932). Sold to Offilers c.1935.
Sitwell Tavern, *21 Sitwell Street*. Henry Edwin Bailey (1926). Sold to Shipstones c.1937.
St.Helens Inn, *25 Duffield Road*. William Francis (1925). Sold to Home Brewery Co.Ltd by 1928.
Wagon & Horses, *149 Ashbourne Road*. Fred Buxton (1956)
Wheatsheaf, *6/8 Liversage Street*. Ernest Palfree (1942). Sold to Offilers 1931.
White Bear, *18 Derwent Row*. William Beckett (1962)
Woodlark, *80 Bridge Street*. Edward Carter (1939). Sold to Offilers 1926.
Woolsack, *164/66 Parliament Street*. Sold to Ind Coope 1941/54 and Stone family (1955)
Ye Old Spa Inne, *204 Abbey Street*. Founded 1892. Albert McLocklin (1947). Sold to Strettons (Allsopps) 1932 and later brewing not known of, although McLocklin was a brewer.

Glossop

Alfred & Job Pickford, *Whitfield Brewery, Simmondley Springs*. Originally registered as the Glossop Brewery Co.Ltd 2nd February 1880 to acquire the Whitfield Brewery and the Roebuck, Whitfield. Wound up voluntarily 26th February 1882. Pickfords ceased brewing 1910.

Ilkeston

Fletcher's Erewash Valley Brewery Ltd, *Chapel Street*. Registered July 1899. Receiver appointed July 1904 and was dissolved 26th February 1909. Apparently no tied houses.
Ilkeston Brewery Co.Ltd, *14 East Street*. Registered 22nd June 1895. Liquidator appointed 21st December 1922. Wound up 16th January 1923. Two public houses: Gladstone Inn, Ilkeston and Nag's Head, Ripley.
Truman & O'Hara, *Northgate Brewery* (1898)

Ingleby

John Thompson Inn. Home brew house founded March 1977. Still in operation 1990.

Little Eaton

Little Eaton Brewery Ltd. Registered March 1906 to acquire the business of Herbert Alfred Searle. Receiver appointed 6th January 1909 and was dissolved 29th August 1911.

Long Eaton

John Marshall, *Trent Brewery* (1906)
Steam Boat, *Trent Lock*. Home brew house founded 1987. Still in operation 1990.

Melbourne

Francis William Dalman, *Derby Road*. Acquired by John Hair & Son.
John Hair & Son, *Church Street*. Founded 1851. Acquired by Offiler's Brewery Ltd 1954 with one tied house. Brewery converted into a house.

Pilsley

Ellen Hollis (1910)

Shardlow

Z. Smith & Co, *Trent Brewery*. Founded 1865. Acquired by Marston, Thompson & Evershed Ltd. 1922 with over 80 public houses and brewing ceased.

Thornsett

Louisa Barbara Jones (1920)

Woodville

Brunt, Bucknall & Co.Ltd, *Hartshorne Brewery*. Founded 1832. Registered October 1890. Acquired by Thomas Salt & Co.Ltd 1919.

DEVON

Ashburton

William Henry Mortimer, *Old Mill Brewery* (1900)
Thompson's Brewery, *London Inn, 11 West Street*. Home brew house founded August 1981. Still in operation 1990 with 2 public houses and also supplies the free trade.

Atherington

John Brownscombe (1910)

Barnstaple

Barnstaple Brewery Co, *Taw Vale Brewery*. Founded by John Kay 1851. Acquired by Arnold, Perrett & Co.Ltd 1895 and was sold to Starkey, Knight & Ford Ltd 1897. Closed 1900.

E.Petter & Son, *Anchor Brewery, Boutport Street*. Brewery and 7 public houses sold to Hancock & Sons (Wiveliscombe) Ltd 1918 for £2,000. The other 3 houses were bought by Starkey, Knight & Ford Ltd.

William Pugsley & Son, *Yeo Vale Brewery, 35 Bear Street* (1930)
Seldon & Son, *Boutport Street* (1898)
Bessie Yeo, *Bear Street* (1923)
Samuel Yeo, *Boutport Street* (1895)

Bideford

James Barrow, *East-of-the-Water Brewery, Torrington Street* (1910)
William Brownston, *Higher Brewery, 29 High Street* (1900)
James Crang, *Old Town Brewery, 4 Bridge Street* (1895)
Samuel Jewell Dark, *The Quay* (1926)
Henry Hopkins, *Honestone Lane* (1926)
James Little, *5 Cooper Street* (1926)

Blackawton

Blackawton Brewery. Founded 1977. Moved to Washbourne 1981.

Black Torrington

Joseph Chapman, *Woodhill Brewery* (1914)

Bovey Tracey

Bate's Brewery, *Unit 4, Western Units, Pottery Road.* Founded by Ron Bate October 1983. Ceased brewing September 1986.

Braunton

William Mitchell (1926)

Brixham

M.P.Hunt, *Lakeman's Brewery, Fore Street.* Originally under the name of Thomas Lakeman. Sold to H.& G.Simonds Ltd November 1937 with 50 tied houses. Brewing ceased 1950 and the brewery was demolished. The bus station now occupies the site.

Chittlehampton

Harry Carder Watts. Acquired by Petter & Son of Barnstaple 1905.

Colyton

Axe Vale Brewery, *Cownhayne Lane.* Founded by Harry Kingsbury July 1983. Closed 1986.

Combe Martin

John Buse (1940)
Samuel Creek (1921)

Crediton

Arthur George Bicknell, *St.Lawrence Green* (1926)
William Burrows, *Exeter Road* (1930)
Creedy Valley Brewery, *Commercial Road.* Founded by Brian Bell and Henry Drew July 1984. Closed 1985.
John Richard Gover, *High Street* (1906)
John Spry, *74 High Street* (1921)

Dartmouth

Bartlett & Co, *Warfleet Brewery.* Acquired by the Heavitree Brewery Ltd 1926. Premises now used by the Dartmouth Pottery.

Dawlish

Richard Brock Ferris, *Dawlish Brewery, High Street.* Founded 1827. Acquired by the Heavitree Brewery Ltd 1926 with about 30 tied houses and a mineral water factory. Brewery was still standing in 1983.
Frederick E.Lendon, *Albert Place* (1910)

Exeter

Aylwin & Snowden, *Well Park Brewery, Alphington Road.* Originally under the name of Ross & Pidsley 1911 and Ross & Son until 1913 when it was acquired by Aylwin & Snowden. Acquired by Devenish & Co.Ltd 1925 with 22 public houses and was used as a depot until 1958 and is now trading units.

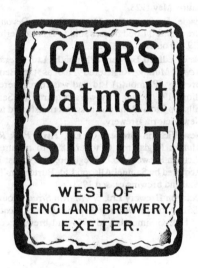

Carr & Quick Ltd, *West of England Brewery, 15 Queen Street.* Founded 1853. Brewery and 7 public houses acquired by Carr & Quick January 1909. Brewing ceased after 1926 but business continued as Ash, Carr & Quick Ltd, beer, wine & spirit merchants. Became a subsidiary of Bass, Ratcliff & Gretton Ltd. Premises now a waste paper depot.
Crowson & Son, *Windsor Brewery, Heavitree.* Acquired by the Heavitree Brewery Ltd 1899 for £50,000.
Heavitree Brewery Ltd, *16 Church Street, Heavitree.* Founded 1790. Registered February 1890 to acquire E.N.Birkett. 135 tied houses. Brewing ceased April 1970 due to increased demand for national beers. Brewhouse demolished 1972 but some buildings remain.
William Mortimore, *St.Thomas' Brewery, Okehampton Street.* Brewery and 7 public houses sold to W.H.Morton 1919 for £10,000.
Norman & Pring Ltd, *City Brewery, 1 Commercial Road.* Founded 1700. Acquired by Whitbread & Co.Ltd April 1962 with 102 tied houses and the business was merged with Starkey, Knight & Ford Ltd 1964. Brewing ceased at the City Brewery in 1956 when production was concentrated at the St.Anne's Well Brewery, but bottling continued until 1968 when the brewery burnt down.

St.Anne's Well Brewery Co.Ltd, *Low North Street.* Founded c.1819. A partial amalgamation with Norman & Pring Ltd took place in 1944, both companies being run separately until completely merged in 1956. 78 public houses. Brewing ceased 1967/68.
Other Breweries
Frederick George Brand, *3 Sidwell Street* (1920)
William John & Susan Cannett (1890)
John Dodd, *54 Cowick Street, St.Thomas* (1926)
Elizabeth Ebbels, *Woodbury Brewery* (1895)
John William Frost, *57 Sidwell Street* (1926)
Edwin Glade, *Black Dog Brewery, 4/5 Lower North Street* (1910)
Harry Lamacraft, *Clifton Road* (1923)
John Charles Lamacraft, *146 Sidwell Street* (1920)
C.H.Stevenson & Son, *George & Dragon Brewery* (1914)
Tapper, Farley & Ladds, *Commercial Road* (1906)
Emma Williams, *53 Bartholomew Street* (1920)

Exmouth

James Salter, *18 High Street* (1920)

Frithelstock

Sydney May (1892)

Harbertonford

W.G.Grills. Brewery advertised for sale 1925 but not sold. The 3 tied houses were sold separately.

Holsworthy

John Bassett (1906)

Honiton

Harold A.Fitch, *High Street* (1923)
Hann & Co.Ltd, *Mill Street.* Registered December 1918 to acquire J.G.Hann & Co. with 10 public houses. Acquired by the Dorsetshire Brewery Co.Ltd, Sherborne in 1927.

Horsebridge

Royal Inn. Home brew house founded by P.Weymouth 1982. Ceased brewing 1984 but pub and brewery sold to Terry Wood August 1985 and brewing recommenced. Still in operation 1990.

Ilfracombe

Charles Walker, *23 Portland Street* (1914)

Kingsbridge

John Kelland, *London Brewery, Church Street.* Offered for auction 22nd July 1904 with 11 tied houses and was bought by the Bedford Brewery (Plymouth) Ltd.
Philip N.Rundle, *Mill Street* (1906)
South Devon Brewery Ltd, *South Devon Steam Brewery, Union Road.* Known as W.H.Prowse & Sons Ltd until 1946. Brewing ceased 1st October 1948, all beer then being supplied by H.& G.Simonds Ltd from the Tamar Brewery, Devonport. Acquired by Simonds 1951 with 25 public houses owned by them and their associate company, C.W.Blundell (Plymouth) Ltd.

BLUNDELL'S SOUTH DEVON PALE ALE

THE SOUTH DEVON BREWERY LIMITED KINGSBRIDGE

Kingskerswell

William H.Mortimer (1927)

Littleham

Edward Philbrick, *Apps Brewery*. Acquired by Starkey, Knight & Ford Ltd 1901 and was closed.

Lundy Island

Marisco Tavern. Home brew house founded 1984. Still in operation 1990.

Milton Damerel

William Vodden, *Woodford Bridge Brewery* (1914)

Newton Abbot

Mill Brewery, *Unit 19c, Bradley Lane*. Founded by Dave Hedge and Paul Bigrig August 1983. Still in operation 1990.

Mills Brothers, *Old Brewery, Wolborough Street*. Offered for sale August 1921 due to the advanced age of the owner and was bought by the St.Anne's Well Brewery Co.Ltd 1924 with 6 public houses. Brewery demolished.

Pinsent & Sons, *Highweek Street*. Acquired by the Heavitree Brewery Ltd 1919 with 44 tied houses. Brewery was still standing 1983 as a garage & club.

Newton St.Cyres

Beer Engine. Home brew house founded by Peter Hawkesley March 1983. Still brewing 1990.

Okehampton

Fred Andrews, *Fore Street* (1902)

Paignton

Torbay Brewery & Cyder Co.Ltd, *44 Victoria Street*. Founded 1884. Registered May 1890 to merge Gottwaltz & Lind, Paignton Brewery and John Mortimer, Fordton Cider Works, Crediton. Acquired by Arnold, Perrett & Co.Ltd June 1893 and was sold to Starkey, Knight & Ford Ltd 1896.

Parracombe

Crocombe & Son. Originally maltsters. Brewery built c.1870. Brewing ceased 1940 due to the death of Mr Crocombe senior. 16 public houses.

Plymouth

G.Crake, *Tamar Brewery, 12 Tamar Street, Devonport*. Founded by 1820. Acquired by H.& G.Simonds Ltd 1919 with about 28 tied houses. Brewing ceased 1975 and some of the equipment is now used by the Blackawton Brewery. Brewery was standing derelict 1983.

Devonport & Tiverton Brewery Co.Ltd, *New Passage Brewery, John Street and Old Brewery, Bampton Street, Tiverton*. Registered December 1876. Old Brewery Tiverton bought by William Hancock & Son (Wiveliscombe) Ltd 1919. Voluntary liquidation May 1923.

Eagle Brewery Co, *Queen Street, Devonport*. Brewery & 11 tied houses sold to B.A.Letherby for £29,850 on 19th July 1921.

New Bedford Brewery (Plymouth) Ltd, *Alexandra Road, Mutley*. Registered 1900 as the Bedford Brewery (Plymouth) Ltd and was re-registered as above 1919 when they were acquired by Samuel Allsopp Ltd and the business was transferred to the New Victoria Brewery.

New Victoria Brewery Co.Ltd, *Hyde Park Road, Mutley*. Registered October 1898 to acquire the Victoria Brewery Co.Ltd registered in August 1893. Acquired by Samuel Allsopp Ltd, Burton-on-Trent 1920 and brewing ceased 1953.

Octagon Brewery Ltd, *5/7 Martin Street*. Founded 1861 by Joseph Godfrey. 48 public houses. Acquired by H.& G.Simonds Ltd 1954 and brewing ceased 1970.

ANCHOR STOUT BREWED & BOTTLED BY THE PLYMOUTH BREWERIES LTD. PLYMOUTH & TORQUAY.

Plymouth Breweries Ltd, *Regent Brewery, Stonehouse*. Registered October 1889 to amalgamate: Samuel Vosper, Regent Brewery; Amanda Henrietta Butcher, Anchor Brewery, Chapel Street, Stonehouse; G. Ryall, Frankfort Street Brewery; Hicks & Co, South Devon Brewery, 2 Willow Street, all in Plymouth and Frederick Richard Vaughan, Saltash Brewery. Acquired by Courage Ltd December 1970 for £6.5 million. Brewing ceased in 1983.

Plympton Brewery, *Valley Road, Plympton*. Founded November 1984 by Allied Breweries to supply their 40 tied houses in the area. Still in operation 1989.

William Rew, *Richmond Brewery, 6 Richmond Street* (1894)

Annie Shillabeer, *Brownlow Street, East Stonehouse* (1895)

Summerskills Brewery, *15 Pomphlett Farm Industrial Estate, Broxton Drive, Plymstock*. Founded 1983 at Ringmore, Kingsbridge and moved to Plymstock 1985. Closed 1986.

Shaldon

James Green, *Fore Street* (1920)

Sidmouth

Vallance's Brewery Ltd, *Temple Street*. Founded 1832 by Richard Searle. Acquired by Woodhead's Brewery Ltd of London 1946 with 35 public houses and was sold to Devenish & Co.Ltd 1957.

Silverton near Exeter

Barrons Brewery, *Land Farm*. Founded November 1984. Still in operation 1989.

South Molton

Charles Frederick Harris, *East Street* (1910)
Mrs C.Vickery, *Barnstaple Street* (1930)

Swimbridge

Swimbridge Brewery, *Old Tannery, Hannaford Lane*. Founded August 1981. Closed July 1983.

Tavistock

Johnstone & Johnstone, *Tavistock Brewery, Brook Street*. Founded by 1877. Registered January 1897 as the Tavistock Brewery Co.Ltd as a subsidiary of Flower & Sons Ltd. Ceased trading April 1899. Offered for auction as Hilton & Sons, July 1913 with 7 tied houses but was withdrawn at £3,050. Brewing ceased 1927 when they were acquired by H.& G.Simonds Ltd.

Teignmouth

Brown & Bishop, *Teign Brewery, 21 Teign Street* (1931)
Fore Street Brewery Co.Ltd, *Fore Street* (1914)
William Henry Gray, *Black Horse Brewery, 32 Commercial Road* (1926)
John Leggett, *Half Moon Brewery, 2 Hollands Road* (1910)
Phoebe Emma Tucker, *Dawlish Inn Brewery, Regent Street* (1898)
Campbell Ward, *Teignmouth Brewery, Mere Lane* (1914)
Joseph Wills, *Devon Arms Brewery, Northumberland Place* (1900)

Tiverton

Devonport & Tiverton Brewery Co.Ltd, *Old Brewery, Bampton Street*. See also:- Plymouth.
Sarah Edbrooke, *97 Barrington Street* (1920)

Thomas Ford & Son, *Fore Street.* Founded 1852. Acquired by Starkey, Knight & Co.Ltd 1895. Brewing ceased 1982.

Torquay

J.B.Gilley, *Prowse's Brewery, 29a Higher Fleet Street* (1900)

Greenslade Brothers, *St.Mary Church Brewery, Fore Street.* Founded before 1880. Acquired by Plymouth Breweries Ltd 1925. Brewing ceased 1927. Still standing at the rear of the Palk Arms.

Swayne & Co.Ltd, *Ellacombe Brewery, Church Road.* Acquired by Plymouth Breweries Ltd 1925. Brewery was still standing 1983.

Torquay Brewing & Trading Co.Ltd, *34 Fleet Street.* Registered 1865 to acquire Matcham & Hussey. Acquired by Plymouth Breweries Ltd 1897.

Ansty

Hall & Woodhouse Ltd. See also:- Blandford St.Mary.

Bere Regis

Johnson & Tozer, *Royal Oak.* Brewery built c.1830. Acquired by Strong & Co.Ltd 1921. Brewhouse demolished 1923.

Blandford Forum

George Henry Jones, *The Crown, West Street.* Home brew house bought by Hall & Woodhouse Ltd 1931 for £14,000.

J.L.Marsh & Sons Ltd, *Town Brewery, Bryanston Street.* Founded 1735. Registered 1912. Acquired by H.& G.Simonds Ltd 1939 with 8 tied houses. Sold to Brutton, Mitchell & Toms Ltd 1950 and used as a depot. Mostly standing 1988. Situated behind the King's Arms public house.

Blandford St.Mary

Totnes

Laura Dobree, *Castle Street* (1898)
William Sawyer, *Castle Brewery, Fore Street.* Acquired by Walter & Phillips 1899.
Walter & Phillips, *Lion Brewery, 52 High Street.* Brewery and 16 public houses offered for auction 31st October 1921.

Uffculme

Furze & Co.Ltd. Registered 1903. Acquired by Starkey, Knight & Ford Ltd 1918 with 26 tied houses and was closed. Brewery still standing 1983.

Washbourne

DORSET

Hall & Woodhouse Ltd, *Blandford Brewery.* Founded 1777 at Ansty and acquired by John Hector, Blandford Brewery in 1883 with 15 public houses. Registered 8th June 1898 to acquire Hall & Woodhouse and Godwin Brothers, Durweston. Ansty brewery closed c.1900. Still independent 1990 with 160 public houses.

Bournemouth

George Catersh, *Westminster Tap, Branksome.* Home brew house in operation 1895.
Dorset & West Hampshire Private Brewers Institute, *c/o 8 Brackendale Road.* A non-commercial brewery run from a private house. Members of the institute paid an annual subscription to keep the brewery in operation and to buy the brewing ingredients. Brewing 1970 but closed shortly afterwards.
New Bell, *Christchurch Road, Pokesdown.* Home brew house acquired by Frampton Brothers of Christchurch c.1908.
Mrs Hilda G.Ogden, *Bournemouth Brewery, 117 Holdenhurst Road.* Founded at the Railway Inn, Boscombe 1868. Registered September 1898 as Crane & Osmond Ltd. Acquired by Strong & Co.Ltd 1923. Demolished 1973.
Elizabeth Walton, *Pokesdown Brewery, 27 Southdown Road, Pokesdown.* Acquired by Frampton Brothers 1902 and brewery closed 1907.

Bourton

White Lion. Home brew house acquired by Frome United Breweries c.1890.

Bridport

William George Knight, *The Bull* (1920)
J.C.& R.H.Palmer Ltd, *Old Brewery, West Bay Road.* Founded 1794. Private company registered 1975. Still independent 1990 with 68 tied houses.
William Scalding, *The Castle, South Street.* Home brew house. Ceased brewing December 1914.

Cerne Abbas

New Inn, *Long Street.* Home brew house. Ceased brewing c.1900. Acquired by Eldridge, Pope & Co.Ltd April 1920.

Blackawton Brewery. Founded 1977 at Blackawton. Moved to Washbourne 1981. Still brewing in 1990.

Washfield

Cotleigh Brewery. See also:- Wiveliscombe, Somerset.

Woodbury

Tom Glanvill (1923)

Yelverton

George Ryall (1894)

James Northover, *Northover Brewery, Ackerman Street.* Bankrupt 1896 and was acquired by Eldridge, Pope & Co.Ltd 1902.

Christchurch

Frampton Brothers Ltd, *Steam Brewery, 11 High Street.* Brewery originally occupied by Aldridge & Co, who became bankrupt 1906. Acquired by Frampton Brothers 1907 who were brewing at Pokesdown. Public houses sold to Eldridge, Pope & Co.Ltd 1920 but they carried on the business supplying the family trade until 1934 when it was sold to Hammerton & Co.Ltd of London. Brewery demolished 1956.
John King, *Christchurch Brewery, High Street.* Acquired by Strong & Co.Ltd 1891.
Old London Brewery, *West Street.* Acquired by Habgood & Son of Wimborne 1891.
William Shentlebury, *Bargate Brewery.* Possibly acquired by Eldridge, Pope & Co.Ltd January 1900.
Stanpit Brewery, *92/106 Stanpit.* Acquired by Charles Absalom of Fordingbridge 1886 and brewing ceased 1909.
C.Thomas, *Duke of Wellington.* Home brew house acquired by Strong & Co.Ltd 1900.
Alfred & Henry Youngman, *Avon Brewery, 56/64 Stanpit, Mudeford.* Acquired by Crowley & Co.Ltd of Alton 1897 with 5 tied houses.

Dorchester

Eldridge, Pope & Co.Ltd, *Dorchester Brewery, Weymouth Avenue.* Founded 1837 when Charles Eldridge leased the Dragon Brewery, Ackland Road/Durngate Street (closed 1883). Dorchester Brewery opened 1880. Registered May 1897 with 74 public houses. Still independent 1990 with 189 tied houses.
Galpin & Masters, *Phoenix Brewery, High East Street.* Acquired by John Groves & Sons Ltd 1910 with 5 public houses.
J.R.Taylor, *Plume of Feathers, Princes Street/Back West Street.* Home brew house acquired by John Groves & Sons Ltd 1903.
Tom Brown's Goldfinch Brewery, *47 High East Street.* Home brew house founded by landlord Alan Finch 1987. Still brewing 1990.

Durweston

Godwin Brothers, *Durweston Brewery.* Founded 1753. Acquired by Hall & Woodhouse Ltd 1898.

East Burton

Seven Stars. Home brew house acquired by John Groves & Sons Ltd 1895.

Fiddleford

Philip Charles Adams, *Travellers Rest (now Fiddleford Inn)* (1903)

Fontmell Magna

A.& T.Sibeth, *Crown Brewery.* Founded 1780. Ceased brewing 14th December 1904 and was sold with 21 public houses for £25,410, the houses being divided between Hall & Woodhouse Ltd, Baxter & Sons and Marston's Dolphin Brewery Ltd. Still standing in 1990, last used as a pottery.

Gillingham

Matthews & Co, *Wyke Brewery.* Founded 1750. Acquired by Hall & Woodhouse Ltd 1963 with 61 tied houses and closed. Partly demolished 1985, the remainder converted to multiple residential use in 1988. This part having been built *c.*1860.

Langton Matravers

Charles Chunchen Edmunds, *Coombe Farm.* Acquired by Panton's Swanage Brewery 1892.

Litton Cheyney

Francis James Gladwyn (1897)

Lyme Regis

Lyme Regis Brewery. Acquired by Carr & Quick of Exeter *c.*1919 with 7 public houses.

Maiden Newton

Robert Rixon. Founded by 1848. Acquired by John Groves 1886 and brewing ceased 1894.

Marnhull

Jennings, Styring, White & Co. Founded by 1821. Acquired by Eldridge, Pope & Co.Ltd 1913 with 36 tied houses. 5 public houses sold to Hall & Woodhouse Ltd 1937. Brewery still standing.
John Parham & Co, *Walton Elm Brewery, Caraway Lane.* Acquired by Jennings, Styring, White & Co.1897 with 2 tied houses.

Melcombe Horsey

Melcombe Horsey Brewery. Founded 1761. Acquired by Hall & Woodhouse Ltd 1900.

Melplash

William Garland, *Mangerton Brewery.* Bankrupt 1896 and was acquired by Palmers of Bridport with 2 public houses.

Milton Abbas

Fookes Brothers, *Milton Brewery.* Founded *c.*1775 and acquired by Robert Fookes 1848. Acquired by John Groves & Son Ltd 1950 with 6 public houses. Converted into a private house 1986.

Poole

Marston's Dolphin Brewery Ltd, *Market Street.* Founded 1750. Registered 1897. Acquired by Strong & Co.Ltd 1923 with 58 tied houses and used as a depot. Demolished 1974.
Poole Brewery, *38 Sandbanks Road.* Founded 1981 by David Rawlins at Sterte Avenue and moved to present address 1987. Still brewing 1990.
Styring & Co, *Poole Brewery, Towngate Street.* Sold to Eldridge, Pope & Co.Ltd 1900 with 34 public houses for £81,200. Brewing ceased 1928.

Portland

Comdon, *Chesil Brewery.* Acquired by John Groves with 3 public houses *c.*1900.

Shaftesbury

F.E.Browning, *King's Arms.* Home brew house sold to Hall & Woodhouse Ltd 1924.
F.Jackson, *Rose & Crown, High Street* (1939)
Ship Inn, *6 Bleke Street.* Home brew house acquired by Matthews of Gillingham 1916.
W.E.Watts, *St.James Brewery, 67 St.James Street.* Home brew house acquired by Matthews & Co. *c.*1950.

Sherborne

Blake & Cooper, *Long Street.* Acquired by Baxter & Sons *c.*1914.
Dorsetshire Brewery Co.(Sherborne) Ltd, *Long Street.* Founded 1796. Registered June 1926 to acquire Baxter & Sons. Acquired by Brutton, Mitchell & Toms Ltd 1951 with 78 public houses and brewing ceased.
Woolmington Brothers, *Cheap Street.* Acquired by Eldridge, Pope & Co.Ltd 1922 with 8 public houses.

Stalbridge

Edwin White. Merged with Jennings, Styring & Co. of Marnhull *c.*1900 to form Jennings, Styring, White & Co.

Sturminster Newton

Harry Richard Chapman, *White Hart, Market Place.* Home brew house acquired by Hall & Woodhouse Ltd *c.*1910 and brewing ceased.

Swanage

Henry John Panton & Co, *Swanage Brewery, Pound Lane.* Acquired by Strong & Co. 1893.

Wareham

Stephen W.Bennett, *South Street.* Acquired by Strong & Co.Ltd 1906 with 11 tied houses.

Weymouth

Devenish Weymouth Brewery Ltd, *Hope Square & Redruth, Cornwall.* Founded 1742 by Fowler family and acquired by William Devenish 1824. Registered 1889 as J.A.Devenish & Co.Ltd and name was changed as above 1965. 330 tied houses. Brewing ceased at Weymouth November 1985 and is now concentrated at Redruth as the Cornish Brewery Co.Ltd. Houses acquired by Boddingtons 1993.
John Groves & Sons Ltd, *Hope Brewery, Hope Square.* Founded 1840. Acquired by Devenish 1960 with 115 public houses.

Reynolds Brothers & Heathorn, *Melcombe Brewery, St.Thomas Street.* Acquired by John Groves & Sons Ltd 1896 with 9 tied houses.

Wimborne

Charles E.Ellis, *Town Brewery, The Square.* Acquired by Hall & Woodhouse Ltd 1937 with 18 public houses and brewing ceased.

George Habgood & Son, *Julian Brewery, West Street.* Acquired by John Groves 1915 with 17 public houses.

Edward Willis, *Walsford Brewery* (1892)

Yetminster

White Hart. Home brew house acquired by Baxter & Son of Sherborne *c*.1910.

DUMFRIES & GALLOWAY

Castle Douglas

John McDonald & Son, *Queen Street Brewery* (1920)

Dumfries

George Black, *Whiter Sands* (1900)

Newton Stewart

South-Western Brewery Co.Ltd, *High Street.* Registered July 1898 to acquire the business of W.T.Solomon. Acquired by Campbell, Hope & King Ltd of Edinburgh 1925 with 6 public houses.

DURHAM

Barnard Castle

McLean & Co, *Bank Brewery.* Founded by early 1870s. Offered for auction 25th January 1907 but was withdrawn at £525.

Bishop Auckland

King's Arms, *Market Place.* Home brew house founded December 1982. Closed 1985.
Nixey, Coleclough & Baxter Ltd, *Crown Brewery.* See also:- Hartlepool, Cleveland.

Bishop Middleham

Forsters' Bishop Middleham Brewery Ltd. Founded 1705 and was acquired by C.F.& M.Forster 1874. Registered March 1897. Brewery burnt down December 1899 and rebuilt 1900. Acquired by Newcastle Breweries Ltd October 1910 and was closed.

Castle Eden

J. Nimmo & Sons Ltd, *Castle Eden Brewery.* Founded by John Nimmo 1826. Registered December 1892. Public company formed 1952. Acquired by Whitbread & Co.Ltd October 1963 with 202 tied houses. Still brewing as Whitbread East Pennines Ltd 1990.

Consett

Derwent Brewery. Founded 1979. Closed 1981.
Richard Murray. Wine, spirit & ale merchant who owned 182 public houses. Formed part of North-Eastern Breweries Ltd of Sunderland 1896.

Darlington

Haughton Road Brewery Co, *South Durham Brewery, Haughton Road.* Registered December 1882 as the South Durham Brewery Co.Ltd which was liquidated before 1898 and was succeeded by the above concern. Acquired by John Smith's Tadcaster Brewery Co.Ltd June 1934 with 41 public houses.
T.M.& E.W.Hinde, *National Brewery, Ridsdale Street, Eastbourne.* Registered December 1880 as the Eastbourne Brewery Co.Ltd which was dissolved August 1889 and was succeeded by the above concern. Acquired by the Tadcaster Tower Brewery Co.Ltd November 1930 with 14 tied houses.
Kelly's Brewery, *38 Balmoral Road, Hurworth.* A new small brewery founded 1979. Closed 1983.
Plews & Sons Ltd, *4 Houndgate & Vale of Mowbray Brewery, Leeming, N.Yorkshire.* Vale of Mowbray brewery founded by Henry Plews 1795. Acquired by J.W.Cameron & Co.Ltd 1925 with about 100 public houses.
J.P.Simpson & Co, *Neasham Road* (1909)

Warwick's Brewery Co.Ltd, *Victoria Brewery, L'Anson Street, Rise Carr.* Registered 1903. Acquired by North-Eastern Breweries Ltd 1925.

Durham

John Colpitt, *133 Framwellgate Bridge.* Established prior 1855. Acquired by John Smith's Tadcaster Brewery Ltd *c*.1890.
Joseph Johnson (Durham) Ltd, *City Brewery, 74 New Elvet.* See also:- Westoe Breweries Ltd, South Shields, Tyne & Wear.
Plews & Sons Ltd, *Old Elvet Brewery, 59 Old Elvert.* (1906)
James Robert Thurlow, *Weirs Brewery, 119 Framwellgate.* Founded *c*.1836. Offered for auction 1st December 1890 but no bids were received. One public house at Church Merrington.

Hunwick

Bertram Bulmer, *Quarry Burn Brewery* (1892)

Satley

John Howe, *Greenfield Brewery* (1895)

Seaham Harbour

Thomas Chilton, *Adolphus Place.* Acquired by J.Nimmo & Son Ltd 1912 with 12 public houses.

West Auckland

West Auckland Brewery Co.Ltd, Founded 1840 as the West Auckland Joint Stock Brewery Co. Went into liquidation 1877 and was bought in January 1878 by a group of brewers and maltsters headed by J.W.Cameron. Acquired by J.W.Cameron & Co.Ltd 1959 with 70/80 public houses. Ceased brewing 1962.

Willington

Francis Nicholson, *Sunnybrow* (1898)

Aberaeron

Ann Evans, *12 Market Street* (1920)
David Evans, *Quay Parade* (1920)

Aberystwyth

Red Kite Brewery, *Glanyrafon*. Founded December by Kieran Healy & Martin Paterson 1982. Closed November 1983. Believed to have re-opened as the Teifi Brewery but brewing has ceased.

David Roberts & Sons Ltd, *Trefechan*. Founded 1848. Merged with T.E.Issard & Co of Newtown 1890 to form the Montgomeryshire Brewery Co.Ltd but this company was liquidated in 1893. Registered as above May 1897. Re-registered 26th April 1935 as Robert's Brewery Ltd, liquidated 24th October 1941 and was registered as above. Acquired by William Hancock & Co.Ltd 1960 with 117 public houses and brewing ceased.

Cardigan

J.Bedford, *1 Pendre* (1940)
Thomas Burgess, *Three Mariners Brewery, High Street* (1930)
Davies Brothers. Acquired by Swansea Old Brewery in 1899
Mrs E.Davies, *Cardigan Brewery, College Row* (1923)
Thomas Davies, *Pritchard's Arms Brewery, North Street* (1920)
Daniel R.Evans, *Red Lion Brewery, Church Street* (1906)
Maggie Evans, *Half Moon Brewery, Green Street* (1920)
Daniel Griffiths, *Saddler's Arms Brewery, High Street* (1910)
Seph James, *Eagle Inn Brewery* (1930)
Jane Johns, *Plasterer's Arms Brewery, Mwldan* (1920)
Thomas Lewis, *Farmer's Arms Brewery, Catherine Row* (1910)
Mrs M.A.Rees, *Angel Hotel Brewery, St.Mary's Street* (1935)
Mary Ann Thomas, *Lamb Brewery, Finch's Square* (1923)
Sarah Williams, *Bridge Street* (1923)

Carmarthen

Carmarthen United Breweries Ltd, *John Street*. Registered 1890 to acquire Norton Brothers (founded by 1847), Springside; David Evan Lewis & Sons, Merlin Brewery and Evans & Son, all of Carmarthen. Acquired by Buckley's Brewery Ltd in 1900 and brewing ceased.
Owen Norton, *Vale of Towy Brewery, St.Peter's Street* (1899-1910)

Clynderwen

Rachel Davies (1914)

Cosheston

John White, *Cosheston Brewery* (1890)

Fishguard

Globe Inn (Black Fox Brewery), *Main Street*. Home brew house founded June 1981. Brewing ceased 1988.

Haverfordwest

Charles Davies, *Fox & Hounds Brewery, Hill Street* (1902)
Mrs James Pugh, *Oak Brewery, St.Thomas's Green* (1921)

Laugharne

Elizabeth Davies, *Wogan Street* (1930)
Mrs L.E.Richards, *Victoria Street* (1930)

Llandilo

Morgan Roderick, *King's Head Brewery, Bridge Street* (1890)
South Wales Brewery Co.Ltd, *Railway Terrace*. Registered 23rd June 1888 to acquire the business formerly carried on by D.Lewis. 4 tied houses. Voluntary liquidation 30th November 1912.

Llandissilio

Phoebe Evans (1902)

Llandovery

H.V.Watkins, *Victoria Brewery, Stone Street* (1910)
Thomas Watkins & Son, *Stone Street*. Some connection with the Anglo-Bavarian Brewery. Ceased brewing 1927 but continued in business as mineral water manufacturers and a brewer's agent.

Llandysul

Black Sheep Brewery (Bragdyr Defaid Du), *Henllan Industrial Estate, Henllan*. Founded April 1980 by Bob Parker & Gareth Lewis. Brewing ceased June 1982.

Llanelli

Buckley's Brewery Ltd, *Gilbert Road*. Brewery founded by Henry Child in 1769 and became known as Buckley Brothers 1877. Registered 10th December 1894 with 120 tied houses. Acquired by the Brodian property group in 1987. With the backing of Harp Lager merged with the Crown Brewery Co.Ltd of Pontyclun to form Crown Buckley PLC. Independence was restored under a mangement buy-out in 1993.
William Bythway & Co, *New Brewery*. Founded 1875 by William Bythway, formerly manager of Buckley's Brewery. Acquired by Buckley's Brewery Ltd June 1896 with 85 public houses.
Felinfoel Brewery Co.Ltd, *Felinfoel*. Founded by David John c.1840 as the King's Head home brew house. New brewery built 1878. Registered October 1906. The first brewery in Britain to introduce canned beer in December 1935. Still brewing independently in 1990 with 74 tied houses.

Llanteg

Pembrokeshire Own Ales, *Benfro Brewery, Llanteglos Holiday Complex*. Founded August 1985 by Peter Johnson but ceased brewing 1990.

Milton

Elizabeth Jones, *Milton Brewery*. Recorded as being owned by a Mr Griffiths in 1895. By 1901 John James and above in 1910.

Narberth

Richard C.Davies, *Water Street* (1920)
James Eynon, *Church Street* (1923)
Ann Jones, *Water Street* (1906)
Ann Phillips, *St.James Street* (1920)
Arthur E.Thomas, *High Street* (1923)

Newcastle Emlyn

William Harries, *White Lion Brewery, Bridge Street* (1906)
Samuel Jones, *Lamb Inn Brewery, Bridge Street* (1902)
Walter Jones, *Drover's Arms Brewery, Adpar* (1910)
Evan Williams, *Carrier's Arms Brewery* (1914)

Pembroke

Robert George & Son, *Cromwell Brewery, Main Street*. Founded 1790. Merged with the Swansea Old Brewery 1896. Closed by 1914.
Pembroke Dock Brewery Co.Ltd, *1 Meyrick Street*. Registered 25th September 1897 to acquire the business of George Hamer Jones Cullwick. Compulsorily wound up 1898 and the brewery was offered for auction on 25th September 1899. Reopened as White & Long until 1906. Dissolved 27th August 1909.
James Williams, *Pembroke Steam Brewery, Main Street* (1923)

Pontardulais

Cambrian Brewery Co.Ltd. Registered 1893 to acquire North & Heitzman. Closed by 1895

Pontyberem

C.W.Evans, *Cwmmawr Brewery* (1900)

St.Clears

Sarah Davies, *Station Road* (1940)
Gwilym Evans, *Santa Clara Brewery*. Became part of Carmarthen United Breweries Ltd 1890.
W.Evans, *Butcher's Arms Brewery* (1940)

St.Dogmael

George Adams, *Treffynon Inn Brewery* (1921)
Mary Evans, *White Hart Brewery* (1915)

ESSEX

Abridge

Hurdle & Wileman, *Anchor Brewery*, and at Hertford. Listed as William Willett 1870 and was acquired by Percy Hargreaves 1880. By 1897 known Hurdle & Wileman and the Abridge Brewery Company from 1900. Acquired by Whitbread & Company Ltd 12th December.1898 with 32 public houses and was used as a depot until November 1922. Brewery still standing 1990.

Belchamp Walter

James Morgan, *Eight Bells* (1910)

Birdbrook

Harriett Blacklock, *The Plough* (1910)

Braintree

Sidney Hodges Amos, *Sun Inn Brewery, Upper Railway Street*. Acquired by the Notting Hill Brewery Co.Ltd 1907 and ceased brewing.
Jacob Bearman, *Rose & Crown, Church Street, Bocking* (1890)
Braintree Brewery Co, *Upper Railway Street*. Known as Ingold & Co. until 1907 when the name was changed as above. Merged with Randall, Gibbons & Co. of Dunmow 1916 to form Randall, Gibbons, Ingold & Co.
Oliver Gosling, *Bocking Brewery, Bradford Street*. Founded before 1813. 13 public houses. Acquired by Greene King & Sons 1904. Brewing continued until 1939. Still in use as a Greene King depot.
Frederick Rankin, *King's Head Brewery, Bradford Street* (1899)
Jabez Rankin, *Orange Tree Brewery, Cattle Market*. Acquired by Greene King & Sons, December 1891 with 8 tied houses.
Silas Richardson, *Sandpit Road* (1898)
Wigan's Black Lion Brewery, *Great Square*. Founded by William Hawkes in 1869 and acquired by Wigans in 1890. Sold to Benskin's Watford Brewery 1898 with 8 public houses. Ceased brewing 1916.

Brentwood

Fielder & Co, *King's Road*. Founded by 1855. Acquired by S.R.Conron & Co. of Hornchurch 1923. Buildings still standing.
J.Hill & Co.Ltd, *Brentwood Brewery, Warley Road*. Founded by 1859. Registered July 1895. Acquired by Ind Coope Ltd September 1900 with about 31 public houses.

Brightlingsea

C. & W.R.Seabrooke, *Marine Brewery, New Street*. Originally Frederick Miller from 1874 and sold to Seabrookes 1899. Acquired by Daniell & Sons of Colchester 1935 with 6 tied houses. Demolished 1954.

Bures Mount

Anne Downes, *Thatcher's Arms*. Home brew house sold to Greene King & Sons 1892.

Burnham on Crouch

Harry Pannell, *Eagle Brewery, High Street* (1930)

Canvey Island

Golden Brewery, *Water's Edge Public House, Western Esplanade*. Home brew house founded August 1981 by Stan Barrett and sold to Peter Burton but closed 1985.

Chelmsford

Baddow Brewery Co.Ltd, *Church Street, Great Baddow*. Founded by Crabb 1798 and new brewery built 1868. Operated as Crabb, Veley & Co. until 1887. Registered October 1895. Acquired by Seabrooke & Sons Ltd 1927 with 53 tied houses and was closed. Buildings still standing.

Chelmsford Brewery (Wells & Perry) Ltd, *26 Duke Street*. Founded 1792 as Bird, Hawkes & Woodcock. Registered June 1890 to acquire Wells & Perry founded 1792. Acquired by Taylor, Walker & Co.Ltd 1934 with 72 public houses. Brewery demolished 1936.
Andrew Durrant, *Tonic Ale Brewery, Conduit Street*. Founded by 1855. Acquired by Ind Coope Ltd 1897.
Gray & Sons (Brewers) Ltd, *Springfield Road & Gate Street, Maldon*. Founded 1828 by Charles Stanton Gray. Maldon brewery acquired c.1896 and ceased brewing 1952. Registered 1958. Name changed to Gray & Sons (Chelmsford) Ltd 1973. Chelmsford brewery closed September 1974 and their 49 public houses are now supplied by Greene King & Sons. Depot established at Galleywood.

Coggeshall

John Beard, *Church Street*. Founded c.1810. Acquired by Charrington Nicholl & Co.Ltd 1905 with 11 tied houses for £16,000. Still standing.
William Bright & Sons Ltd, *Stoneham Street*. Founded by 1837. 30 public houses sold to Ind Coope. Acquired by the New London Brewery Co.Ltd 1921. Partly standing.
E.Gardner & Son, *Bridge Street*. Founded by 1877. Leased to Greene King & Sons January 1941 with 11 public houses and closed in 1943. Brewery still standing 1990.
W.& S.J.King, *Gravel End Brewery, The Gravel*. Founded 1793 as seed growers. Brewing from 1870. Acquired by Daniell & Sons Breweries Ltd 1907.

Colchester

Charrington, Nicholl & Co.Ltd, *East Hill Brewery*. Founded in 1830 as a porter brewery. Registered 1904. Acquired by the Colchester Brewing Co.Ltd 1920. Brewery demolished in 1971.
Colchester Brewing Co.Ltd, *Eagle Brewery, East Hill*. Founded 1828 by Christopher Stopes and Robert Hurnard. Christopher Stopes & Sons were acquired in January 1887 by the Norfolk & Suffolk Brewery Co.Ltd who then changed their title as above in September 1887. Also at Langham until 1887. Acquired by Ind Coope Ltd 1925 and was closed. Some of their 225 public houses were sold to Lacon & Co.Ltd in 1926. Brewery still standing.
Cook Brothers, *Mersea Road*. See also:- Halstead.
Bernard Cuddon, *Old Heath*. Acquired by Daniell & Sons Breweries Ltd 1912.
Daniell & Sons Breweries Ltd, *Castle Brewery, 6 Maidenburgh Street*. Founded 1866. Merged with Daniell & Sons of West Bergholt in January 1887 to form Daniell Brothers & Co. Castle Brewery closed by March 1892. Acquired by Truman, Hanbury and Buxton 1958 with 150 tied houses. Brewery mainly standing.

Dunmow

Randall, Gibbons, Ingold & Co, *Dunmow Brewery, North Street*. Founded 1803. Merged with Webb & Gibbons 1911 to form Randall, Gibbons & Co. Acquired Ingold & Co. of Braintree in 1916 and name changed to above. Finally renamed the Dunmow Brewery Ltd in 1945. Acquired by Charrington United Breweries in 1965 with 50 tied houses and brewing ceased. Brewery demolished in 1975.
Walter Mead (1899)
Webb & Gibbons, *Crown Brewery, Market Place*. Founded 1866. Merged with Randalls in 1911 and brewing ceased after 1918 but continued bottling until 1939. Brewery has been demolished.

Essex

T.D.Ridley & Sons Ltd, *Hartford End*. Founded 1842. Registered 1906. Still brewing independently 1990 with 65 tied houses.
Saward & Sons, *Tindal Street* (1898)
Writtle Brewery Co.Ltd, *Writtle Brewery*. Founded by 1855. Registered April 1888 to acquire Pattisson & Co. Acquired by Russell's Gravesend Brewery Ltd September 1901.

Epping

Epping Brewery Co, *Lindsey Street*. Founded 1840. Partnership of C.W.W.Roberts & J. Pearson dissolved 1907 and was acquired by McMullen & Sons Ltd of Hertford in the same year. Used as stores until at least 1937. Brewery has been demolished.

Finchingfield

Frederick Allen, *Prince of Wales Brewery, Head Street*. Founded by 1842 and had ceased brewing by 1902.

Fordham Heath

Edward Ernest Smith, *Huxtable Lane* (1910). Buildings still standing.

Foxearth

Ward & Son Ltd, Founded 1848 by George Ward, a beer retailer. Brewing began 1878. Registered 1921. Acquired by Taylor, Walker & Co.Ltd 1957 with 31 tied houses. Repurchased by the Ward family from Ind Coope Ltd 1960 but it proved not to be a viable propostion and the brewery was demolished in 1962.

Gestingthorpe

Ruth Paul, *The Pheasant*. Home brew house founded August 1981. Ceased brewing 1984.

Grays

Seabrooke & Sons Ltd, *Thorrock Brewery, Bridge Street*. Founded 1799 by Thomas Seabrooke. Registered 1891. Acquired by Charrington & Co.Ltd 1929 with 120 public houses and brewing ceased. Brewery demolished 1969.

Great Bardfield

Edward Smith. Founded by Thomas Smith by 1855. Acquired by Hawkes & Co. of Bishops Stortford 1898 with 4 public houses.
Elizabeth Smith (1898)

Great Chesterford

E.& H.Pilgrim. Acquired by Dale & Co.Ltd of Cambridge with one tied house for £2,750 August 1913 and was converted into maltings and stores. Still standing 1990.

Great Horkesley

George Collins, *Fordham Horse Shoe Brewery* (1892)

Great Oakley

Robert Swinborne Cole, *Holt Farm Brewery* (1892)

Halstead

Thomas Francis Adams, *Halstead Brewery, Trinity Street*. Founded 1859 by Charles Stanton Gray of the Chelmsford brewery and was acquired by Adams in 1876. Acquired by Isherwood, Foster & Stacey Ltd, then a subsidiary of Fremlins Ltd, June 1939 with 46 public houses. Now mainly demolished.
George Burford, *Mount Hill Brewery, Trinity Terrace* (1886-1892)
Frederick Clark, *Domestic Brewery, High Street* (1890)
G.E.Cook & Sons Ltd, *Tidings Hill Brewery*. Founded 1885 at the Griffin, Parsonage Lane. New brewery built in Mersea Road, Colchester 1913. Registered 1961. No tied houses but own 15 off-licences. Brewery closed October 1974. Still extant 1990.

Harlow

Chaplin & Co.Ltd, *Front Street*. Founded 1832. Acquired by Barclay, Perkins & Co.Ltd January 1926 with 25 tied houses. Buildings now demolished.

Hatfield Peverel

Charles Brown & Sons Ltd. Founded by 1855. Private company registered 1906. Their 6 public houses were sold to T.D.Ridley & Sons Ltd in June 1920 after they had acquired the brewery in April 1918.

Kelvedon

John Fuller & Sons, *Kelvedon Brewery, High Street*. Founded 1837. Acquired by Daniell & Sons Breweries Ltd 1930. Brewery demolished 1971.

Maldon

C.Brown. Founded *c*.1840. Ceased brewing 1929.
Gray & Sons Ltd, *Maldon Brewery, Gate Street*. See also:- Chelmsford.
F.G.Stone, *19 Spital Road*. (1949) A general stores and off-licence with brewery attached.

Manningtree

E.J.Alston & Sons. Founded by 1793.
Brightlingsea Brewery Co.Ltd, *2 Jubilee End, Langford*. Founded by Paul Janssens September 1982. Bankrupt February 1984.

Marden Ash

Ernest James Palmer, *Marden Ash Brewery, Sandon Hill, Ongar*. Brewery built 1849 for William Cooper. Acquired by McMullen & Sons Ltd 1912. Brewery now demolished.

Messing

Charles Thomas Thorn, *Crown Public House & Brewery*. Brewing 1839-1892 when sold to Thorn & Livermore of Tiptree.

Ongar

Francis Starkey, *Cock Public House, High Street*. Founded by 1766. Sold to Grays of Chelmsford & Maldon in March 1897.

Radwinter

Edwin Newell, *Brewery Tavern, 23 Gold Street*. Founded by 1871.

Rayleigh

C.J.Barnard. Established *c*.1780. Acquired by Henry Luker, Southend on Sea in 1884 with 4 public houses.
John Woolston, *Anchor Brewery, High Street*. Acquired by Henry Luker 1884. Closed 1906.

Rayne

Misses Newman, *Cherry Tree Public House* (1892)

Rochford

Henry Luker & Co. Branch of the Southend brewing company 1882-1906. Demolished 1922.

Romford

Ind Coope Ltd, *Star Brewery.* Founded 1709 at the Star Inn by George Cardon. In 1799 Star Inn and brewery purchased by Edward Ind and J.Grosvenor. C.E.Coope joined firm in 1845. Registered November 1886 as Ind Coope & Co.Ltd. In receivership January 1909 and was re-registered 1912 as Ind Coope & Co.(1912) Ltd. Name reverted to Ind Coope & Co.Ltd 1923. Merged with Samuel Allsopp & Sons Ltd 1934 and became Ind Coope & Allsopp Ltd. Name changed as above 1959. Now part of Carlsberg-Tetley.

Rowhedge

S.T.Daniell & Co, *East Donyland Brewery, High Street.* Founded by 1808 as a maltings. Brewing from 1874. Acquired by Daniells c.1887 and brewing ceased but continued malting until 1902. Demolished 1937.

Saffron Walden

W.H.Day & Co, *Castle Brewery, 17 Gold Street.* Acquired by Watney, Combe, Reid & Co.Ltd June 1892 and closed 1903.

Martha Hunt, *Fairycroft Road/East Street* (1921)

Charles George Payne, *Rose & Crown Hotel, Market Place.* Brewing after 1887.

J.W.& J.L.Taylor, *Anchor Brewery, High Street.* Founded 1805. Acquired by Reid & Co.Ltd of London 1897 with 80 tied houses and was sold to Benskin's Watford Brewery Ltd 1916 due to wartime transport difficulties.

Shalford

Thomas George Brunwin, *Sheering Hall Brewery.* Founded by 1855. 1 tied house. Acquired by T.F.Adams & Sons of Halstead c.1898. Brewing ceased 1906. Brewery still standing.

Sible Hedingham

Sarah Clarke, *The White Horse* (1902)

Southend-on-Sea

Henry Luker & Co.Ltd, *Middleton Brewery, 123 High Street.* Founded before 1875. Registered July 1895. Acquired by Mann, Crossman & Paulin Ltd 1929 with 43 public houses for £285,000.

South Woodham Ferrers

Crouch Vale Brewery, *12 Redhills Road.* Founded October 1981 by Rob Walster & Colin Bocking. Still in operation 1990 with one tied house: the Cap & Feathers, Tillingham.

Stanford-le-Hope

Blyth & Squier. Founded 1868. Acquired by Seabrookes in 1914 and brewing ceased. Mainly still standing.

Stansted Mountfichet

Samuel Smith Rogers & Co, *Stansted Brewery.* Acquired by Randall, Gibbons, Ingold & Co.1922.
Thomas Irvine Rowell, *Stansted Brewery, Lower Road.* Founded by 1872. Brewery and public houses sold July 1925. Has been demolished.

Terling

John Smith, *Rayleigh Arms.* Home brew house operating from 1855 until 1921 when sold to Ind Coope Ltd.
Edward Whiffen (1899).

Thaxted

Mordecai Charles Andrews, *Park Street.* Brewing between 1855-1921. Owned 4 public houses.
H.Grout, *Bull Ring* (1899)

Tiptree

C.T.Thorn & Co, *Crown Brewery, Factory Lane.* Founded by 1902. Acquired by Fuller & Sons of Kelvedon 1926. Demolished during the 1970s.

Tollesbury

Stone & Sons, *Brewery Road.* Brewery built before 1897. See also:- Maldon.

Toppesfield

Charles Rider Barker (1882-1906)

Wakes Colne

C.& F.Patten Brothers, *Colne Green* (1861-1914)

Waltham Abbey

Hurdle & Co, *Eagle Brewery, Sun Street.* Acquired by McMullen & Sons Ltd 1898.
G.H.Lee, *Waltham Abbey Brewery, Sun Street.* Ceased brewing 1906.
Edward Parker, *Eagle Brewery, High Bridge Street.* Founded c.1855 by W.R.Clark. Closed c.1887.

West Bergholt

Thomas Daniell & Sons, *West Bergholt Brewery.* Founded c.1815. Registered and merged with Daniell Brothers & Co. of Colchester in 1887. Acquired by Truman, Hanbury and Buxton & Co. 1958. Brewing ceased 1959, brewery mainly demolished 1989.

Wethersfield

Elizabeth V.Raven, *Wethersfield Brewery.* Founded by 1855. Brewery & 15 tied houses sold to Greene King & Sons 25th November 1901 for £17,000.

White Notley

Isabella Chappell, *Cross Keys Public House* (1874-1905)

Witham

Cornelius W.Hodges, *Swan Brewery, Bridge Street.* (1882-1906)

Anstruther

William Key (1906)

Crail

Thomas Key (1914)

Cupar

R.& J.Mitchell, *3 Bonnygate* (1906)

Dunfermline

R.M.Cullen & Son, *Dunfermline Brewery, 129 High Street* (1902)

East Wemyss

John & George Brown. Acquired by William Murray & Co.Ltd of Edinburgh 1926.

Grange

John Blyth (1910)

Kirkcaldy

James Rintoul, *Bridgeton Brewery* (1910)

Leuchars

Alexander K.Scott (1902)

Newton of Falkland

David Bonthrone, *Newton Brewery*. Founded 1600. Brewing ceased 1916 but malting continued until *c.*1960. Acquired by the Distillers Co.Ltd 1947. The brewery was still standing in 1990.

William Meiklejohn, *Glen Newton Brewery* (1906)

St.Andrews

D.S.Ireland Ltd, *Argyle Brewery*. Founded *c.*1833. Registered January 1893. Offered for sale in 1900 and was closed in 1902. Brewery was still standing in 1990.

MID-GLAMORGAN

Aberaman

Abergawr Brewery Co.Ltd. Registered 26th November 1890 to acquire the business of Taliesin James. Acquired by William W.Nell of Cardiff 1898 and was dissolved 21st June 1907.

Aberavon

Henry Jones, *Avonside Brewery, High Street* (1895)

Aberdare

Aberdare & Trecynon Brewery Co.Ltd, *Mill Street*. Founded 1865. Registered 2nd December 1887 to acquire the business of Thomas Rees. Offered for auction June 1911 but only the public houses were sold. Wound up 27th April 1914. Merged with New Black Lion Brewery Co.Ltd and was closed 1921.

Thomas Jones & Son, *George Brewery, George Street*. Brewery and 26 public houses offered for sale on 3rd March 1909. Business carried on by executors until *c.*1950.

New Black Lion Brewery Co.Ltd, *Monk Street*. Registered 19th March 1890 as the Black Lion Brewery Co.Ltd to acquire the business of A.S.Pleace. Voluntary liquidation 26th October 1898 and was wound up 15th July 1899. New company registered as above 17th March 1899 which went into liquidation on 2nd November 1910. A.S.Pleace relinquished the managing directorship on 1st April 1911 and bought the Rock Brewery. Brewery and 22 tied houses offered for sale and were acquired by Samuel Allsopp & Sons Ltd 1912.

Rock Brewery Co.Ltd, *High Street*. Registered 8th March 1897 to acquire the business of Morgan Richard David for £40,500 with 19 public houses. Acquired by A.S.Pleace 1st April 1911. Sold to Samuel Allsopp & Sons Ltd 1913 and merged with the New Black Lion Brewery Co.Ltd to form Aberdare Valley Breweries Ltd. The Rock Brewery was renamed the Town Brewery. Closed 1921.

Bridgend

R.H.Stiles. Acquired by H.& G.Simonds Ltd of Reading 1938 with 27 tied houses.

Brynmenyn

John Brothers Abergarw Brewery Co.Ltd, *Lake Brewery*. Founded 1884. Registered June 1895 to acquire John Brothers. Ceased brewing 1940.

Caerphilly

Caerphilly Brewery Co.Ltd, *Castle Street*. Registered 22nd May 1890 to acquire the brewery lately carried on by Thomas Reynolds. Merged with the Castle Brewery Co. (Caerphilly) Ltd and the name was changed to the Caerphilly & Castle Brewery Co.Ltd on 8th November 1893. Acquired by Crosswell's Cardiff Brewery Ltd February 1898 with 18 public houses.

Castle Brewery Co.(Caerphilly) Ltd, *Castle Brewery, Nantgarw Road*. Registered 4th December 1889. Merged with the Caerphilly Brewery Co.Ltd 1893. Ceased brewing 1900.

Dowlais

Mrs S.A.Huggins, *East Street* (1940)
David Thomas, *Union Street* (1900)

Llantrisant

Taliesin Morgan & Co, *Llantrisant Brewery* (1895)
Griffith Jenkins, *Phoenix Brewery* (1891)

Maesteg

Maesteg Brewery Co.Ltd. Registered 18th December 1897 to acquire the business of John & Valentine Pegg. Acquired by W.J.Rogers Ltd of Bristol 1898 with 42 public houses and was closed.

Merthyr Tydfil

Emily Botteril, *Wheafsheaf Brewery, Glebeland Street*. Recorded as Henrietta Mackintosh in 1897 and as above 1910.

David Thomas Braddick, *Ship Brewery, Bethel Street*. Listed in 1901. Closed 1910. Took over the Cyfartha Brewery, Nantygwenith Street by 1914 and the Ship Brewery was closed.

Cefn Viaduct Brewery Co.Ltd. Founded by Robert Millar *c.*1800. Registered 1912 as the Pont-y-Capel Brewery Co.Ltd which was wound up 1921. The brewery and 60 tied houses were offered for auction 18th February 1925. A new company was registered as above on 13th May 1925 and was wound up 29th November 1930.

Christmas Evans, *Six Bells Brewery, Hoelgerrig*. Acquired by D.F.Pritchard Ltd 1916 and was closed.

Giles & Harrap, *Merthyr Brewery, Brecon Road*. Acquired by William Hancock & Co.Ltd 1936 with 62 public houses.

Richard Lloyd, *Cyfartha Brewery, Nantygwenith Street*. Acquired by D.T.Braddick by 1914 and was closed *c.*1935.

Penydarren Brewery Co.Ltd, *Pennydarren*. Registered 9th November 1892 to acquire the business of Thomas Davies. Wound up 1905 after the brewery had been destroyed by fire in 1904.

David Williams & Co.(Merthyr) Ltd, *Taff Vale Brewery, George Town*. Founded by 1877 by David Williams. New brewery built 1904. Registered November 1922. Acquired by Andrew Buchan's Breweries Ltd of Rhymney in 1936.

Other Breweries

Thomas Cochrane, *Picton Brewery, Picton Street* (1894)

James Gould, *Windsor Arms Brewery* (1920)

John J.Jones, *Ship & Bell Brewery, Plymouth Street* (1914)

WHEN THE 'ROCKET' FIRST
RAN FROM LIVERPOOL
TO MANCHESTER,
THE HOUSE OF

J.OULES

HAD BEEN BREWING ALE
FOR FORTY·THREE YEARS

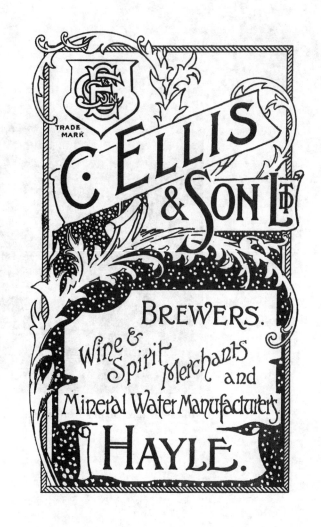

TRADE MARK

C.ELLIS & SON LTD

BREWERS.
Wine & Spirit Merchants and
Mineral Water Manufacturers
HAYLE.

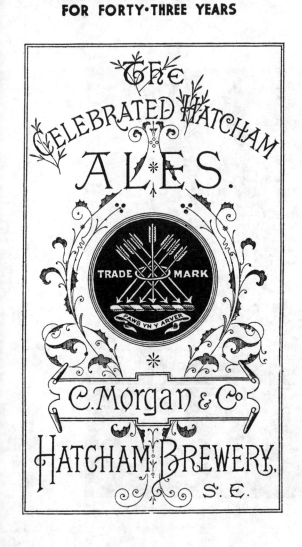

The
CELEBRATED HATCHAM
ALES.

TRADE MARK

CAWB YN Y ARVER

C.Morgan & Co

HATCHAM BREWERY,
S.E.

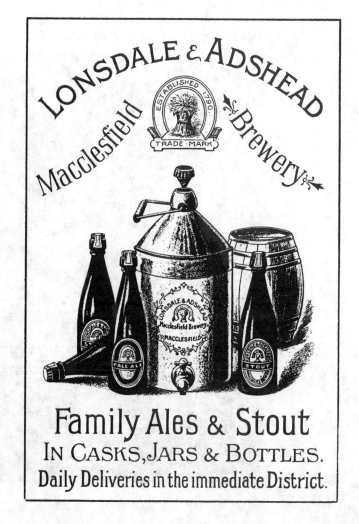

LONSDALE & ADSHEAD
Macclesfield   Brewery

ESTABLISHED 1790.
TRADE MARK

Family Ales & Stout
IN CASKS, JARS & BOTTLES.
Daily Deliveries in the immediate District.

Molesworth & Bean's Ketton Brewery, Demolished in 1926

Star Brewery, Eastbourne in the 1920s

John Meredith, *Cefn Hill Brewery* (1923). Renamed [N]ew Brewery by 1910. (1926)

[O]wen & George, *Iron Bridge Brewery, Albert Street* [1]921)

[D]avid Price, *Tydfil Brewery, Tramroad Side* (1890)

Mountain Ash

[J]ohn Rees (1906)

Newton

[C]rown Brewery Co. (1914)

[T]homas Woolacott, *Rock & Fountain Brewery* [1]940)

Pendre

[M]aria E.W.Lewis (1914)

[C]aradoc Rees, *Hope & Anchor Brewery* (1935)

[J]ames Thomas, *Commercial Hotel Brewery* (1940)

[H]annah Williams (1940)

[S]amuel Williams, *Sailor's Home Brewery* (1926)

Pentre

[W]illiam Hockaday, *Llewellyn's Brewery* (1900)

[D]avid John & Co.Ltd, *Pentre Brewery, Llewellyn [S]treet.* Registered September 1888 to acquire the [P]entre Brewery and John Davies, Mardy Brewery, [G]went. Acquired by Webb's (Aberbeeg) Ltd 1946 [w]ith 26 tied houses and brewing ceased.

Pen-y-Graig

[E]vans, Jenkins & Co, *Great Western Brewery.* [O]riginally recorded as Rachel Rees & Son, followed [b]y T.M.Rees in 1901. Closed by 1910. Revived as [ab]ove but closed by 1918.

Pontlottyn

[B]last Furnace Brewery. Acquired by Andrew [B]uchan & Co. of Rhymney in 1916.

Pontyclun

[C]rown Brewery Co.Ltd, *Llantrisant.* Registered 10th [J]uly 1919 as the South Wales & Monmouthshire [U]nited Clubs Brewery Co.Ltd when D.& T.Jenkins' [b]rewery was bought by the South Wales branch of [th]e Working Men's Club & Institute. New brewery [b]uilt 1954. The title was changed as above in 1977. [M]erged with Buckley's Brewery Ltd to form Crown [B]uckley PLC. Still brewing 1990.

[M]iskin Arms. Home brew house in operation [19]76-79 founded by Cliff Davies.

Pontygwaith

[F]ernvale Brewery Co.Ltd, *Tylorstowwn.* Registered [5t]h April 1918 to acquire the business of D.L.Tre-[h]arne. Acquired by Webb's (Aberbeeg) Ltd 1949 [an]d brewing ceased in 1970.

Pontypridd

Anne Evans, *Station Steam Brewery, Tram Road.* (1906)

David Leyshon, *Graig Brewery, Rickard Street.* Founded 1867. Merged with the New-bridge-Rhondda Brewery Co.Ltd 1903 to form Pontypridd United Breweries Ltd. Brewery closed 1904 and remained unused until 1922 when it was converted into a church.

Newbridge-Rhondda Brewery Co.Ltd, *Glenview Brewery, Court House Street.* Registered 1891. Merged with David Leyshon 1903 to form Pontypridd United Breweries Ltd. Acquired by Rhondda Valley Breweries Co.Ltd in 1918.

Pontypridd Brewery Co.Ltd, *Taft Street.* Founded c.1854 and was operated by William Williams until registered in 1887. Merged with the Rhondda Valley Brewery Co.Ltd, Treherbert, 1896 to form Rhondda Valley Breweries Co.Ltd. Brewing ceased at Ponty-pridd in 1930.

Pontypridd United Breweries Ltd, *Court House Street.* Registered 1903 to acquire the businesses of the late David Leyshon and the Newbridge-Rhondda Brewery Co.Ltd. Acquired by the Rhondda Valley Breweries Co.Ltd, Treherbert in 1918.

Porth

John Leyshon, *Eirw Brewery* (1904)

Rhymney

Rhymney Breweries Ltd. Founded 1839 by William Copeland, Chairman of the Rhymney Iron Co. to supply beer to their employees. Control of the parent company passed to the Powell Duffryn Steam Coal Co.Ltd in 1920 and the brewery became a separate company which was registered as Andrew Buchan's Breweries Ltd on 9th October 1929 to acquire the businesses of Andrew Buchan & Co. and Griffith Brothers Ltd, Blaina. The name was changed as above on 25th May 1959. Acquired by Whitbread & Co.Ltd in January 1966. Brewing ceased in 1978.

Tonypandy

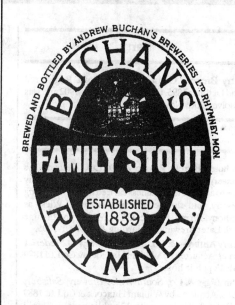

Mrs M.Rees, *Dinas Road* (1906)

Tonypandy Brewery Co.Ltd, *Dunraven Arms Hotel.* Registered 31st January 1885 to establish a brewery at Tonypandy. Voluntary liquidation 28th January 1892 and was re-registered as above 30th May 1892. Acquired by Crosswell's Cardiff Brewery Ltd 1899 and was wound up 10th July 1901.

Treharris

Treharris Brewery Co.Ltd. Private company regis-tered 4th October 1886 to acquire the business of Thomas Lewis Williams. Ceased trading March 1900 and was dissolved on 21st February 1911.

Treherbert

Rhondda Valley Breweries Co.Ltd. Registered 10th April 1873 as the Rhondda Valley Brewery Co.Ltd. Merged with the Pontypridd Brewery Co.Ltd 30th June 1896 to form the above company with 97 public houses. Took over the Ely Brewery Co. of Cardiff 1920 and adopted their name in 1928. Acquired by Rhymney Breweries Ltd in December 1959 with 265 tied houses. Brewing ceased at Treherbert in 1928.

Treorchy

Mary Lewis, *Pencelli Brewery, Cardiff Arms Hotel* (1891)

Upper Boat

Janet Nicholas (1921)

Wick

Jane Harry, *Broughton Court Brewery* (1926)

William Herbert, *Severn Side Brewery.* Merged with the Fleur de Lys Brewery, Gwent, in 1898 to form Anthony, Birrell, Pearce & Co.Ltd.

Barry

Barry Brewery Co.Ltd, *Holton Road.* Registered 22nd October 1895. Ceased trading July 1902 and was dissolved 20th November 1908.

Cardiff

Anthony, Birrell, Pearce & Co.Ltd, *Fleur-de-Lys Brewery, 61 Clare Road.* Registered 4th January 1898 to acquire the business carried on at the existing brewery, and the Severn Side Brewery, Wick, as Anthony, Birrell, Pearce & Co. Wound up 8th June 1899. Later brewing as Harding & Co 1901-1905.

Henry Anthony & Co, *Castle Brewery, 44 Frederick Street.* Acquired by William Hancock & Co.Ltd 1899 with 12 public houses.

John Biggs & Co, *South Wales Brewery, Salisbury Road.* Acquired by William Hancock & Co.Ltd 1889 as Biggs & Williams with 12 public houses. Closed 1892 but revived as Biggs & Co 1899-1900.

S.A.Brain & Co.Ltd, *Old Brewery, St.Mary Street.* Founded 1713 and was acquired by S.A.Brain in December 1882. Registered 12th April 1897 with 74 public houses. New brewery built 1914. Still brewing independently 1990 with 120 tied houses.

Canton Cross Brewery Co.Ltd, *Cowbridge Road, Canton.* Registered 12th October 1897 to acquire the Canton Cross Brewery Co. Acquired by William Hancock & Co.Ltd 1904 and was closed.

Cardiff Brewery Co.Ltd, *John Street, Bute Street.* Registered 21st December 1885 to acquire the Crown Brewery. Ceased trading 1901 and was dissolved 2nd August 1904.

County Brewery Co, *Crawshay Street.* Acquired by William Hancock & Co.Ltd in 1899.

Crosswell's Cardiff Brewery Ltd, *Penarth Road, Ely.* Founded for the sale of Showell's Brewery Ltd beers in South Wales. Registered 22nd July 1897 to amalgamate the Caerphilly & Castle Brewery Co.Ltd and Crosswells Ltd. Acquired by Andrew Buchan's Breweries Ltd of Rhymney in 1936 and brewing ceased 1947.

Dowson Brothers, *Phoenix Brewery, 20 Working Street.* Acquired by William Hancock & Co.Ltd 1887 and was closed in 1896.

Fred Dunkley, *Black Lion Brewery, St.Mary Street.* Merged with S.A.Noel 1903.

Ely Brewery Co.Ltd, *Ely.* Registered November 1887. Acquired by Rhondda Valley Breweries Co.Ltd 1920 who then changed their name to Rhondda Valley & Ely Breweries Ltd and to Ely Brewery Co.Ltd in 1928. Acquired by Rhymney Breweries Ltd 1959 with 256 public houses. Ceased brewing 1978.

John Follard, *Ivor Place Brewery, Windsor Road.* Acquired by Yorath & son of Newport 19887 and closed 1895.

William Hancock & Co.Ltd, *Crawshay Street.* William Hancock, brewer of Wiveliscombe, Somerset bought the Bute Dock Brewery of North & Low in 1884. Registered 7th July 1887. Acquired by Bass Charrington Ltd in 1968 with 505 tied houses. Brewery still in operation in 1990 as Bass Brewing (Cardiff) Ltd.

Heritage Brewery, *St.Mellons.* A Whitbread home brew house founded December 1983 with equipment from the defunct Ely Brewery. Brewing ceased January 1986.

Thomas Jenkins, *Marchioness of Bute Brewery, Frederick Street.* Closed 1922

James Jones, *Friendship Brewery, Homfray Street, Bute Terrace* (1893)

King's Brewery (Cardiff) Ltd, *183 King's Road, Canton.* Registered December 3rd 1897 to acquire the business of Percy Richard Drury. Voluntary liquidation 10th August 1898. Was succeeded by the Walpole Brewery Co.Ltd.

F.S.Lock, *County Brewery, Crawshay Street, Penarth Road.* Founded 1889. Acquired by Willian Hancock & Co.1894.

William W.Nell Ltd, *Eagle Brewery, St.John Square.* Registered 18th January 1890. Acquired by Crosswell's Cardiff Brewery Ltd August 1927.

New Walpole Brewery Co.Ltd, *183 King's Road, Canton.* Successors to the King's Brewery (Cardiff) Ltd registered in 1900 to acquire the Walpole Brewery Co.Ltd. In liquidation 1906. New company registered as above on 24th July 1906. Voluntary liquidation 23rd November 1908.

S.A.Noel & Co.Ltd, *Roath Brewery, Bedford Place, Roath.* Merged with Fred Dunkley 1903. Registered in 1946.

H.E.Pearce & Co.(Cardiff) Ltd, *Cross Keys Brewery, Severn Road, Canton.* Registered February 1890 to acquire the business of H.E.Pearce. In liquidation 1895 and was sold to Starkey, Knight & Ford.

Ship Brewery Co.Ltd, *Millicent Street.* Registered 4th October 1888 as William Phillips & Co.Ltd to acquire the business of Morgan Rees Williams. Name changed as above January 1890. Acquired by Rhondda Valley Breweries Co.Ltd 1899 with 11 public houses.

William Steeds, *Albion Brewery, 259 Bute Street.* Acquired by R.W.Miller & Co.Ltd of Bristol by 1897.

Cowbridge

Hansard Brothers, *Malthouse Yard* (1902)
David Jenkins, *Aberthin* (1902)
Lewis Jenkins, *Vale of Glamorgan Brewery.* Acquired by William Hancock & Co.Ltd 1914.
Janet John, *Aberthin Brewery.* Closed 1906.

Thomas Morgan & Sons Ltd, *Cowbridge Brewery.* Acquired by Bass, Mitchells & Butlers Ltd 1955.

Llanwit Major

Boverton Brewery Co. (1921)
Alfred Evans, *King's Head Brewery* (1906)
Cecilia Watts, *White Lion Brewery* (1906)

Penarth

Bullmastiff Brewery, *Anchor Way.* Founded June 1987 using equipment from the former Monmouth Fine Ales Brewery. Still brewing 1990.

Raisdale Sparging & Brewing Co, *Raisdale Road.* Founded 1985 brewing for the Raisdale Hotel guests only. Ceased brewing 1990.

Porthcawl

Gwilym Morgan John, *Crown Brewery, Newtown.* Recorded as G.Williams 1901 and T.Morgan 1906. Registered as above 1910.

Wenvoe

Wenvoe Brewery Ltd. Registered 16th March 1902. Voluntary liquidation 4th November 1903 and was dissolved 10th May 1910.

WEST GLAMORGAN

Gwaun-cae-Gurwen

John Rees, *Abernant Brewery.* Registered December 1921. Acquired by William Hancock & Co.Ltd 1924 with 14 public houses.

Neath

Evan Evans Bevan Ltd, *Vale of Neath Brewery.* Founded by David Evans 1846. Acquired by Evan Evans 1850. Registered 13th December 1935. Acquired by Whitbread & Co.Ltd 1967 and brewing ceased in May 1972.

Tom Skelton Nash, *Somerset Brewery, Green Street* (1890)

Pontardawe

David Bevan, *Swansea Vale Brewery.* Built in 1837/38 for John Jones. Acquired by Evan Evans in the late 1860s but not closed until 1937.

Port Talbot

Afan Brewery, *Brunel Industrial Estate, Cwmafan.* Founded by John McArdle, Ian Barber & John Grimmer January 1982. Closed 1984.

Swansea

Ackland & Thomas, *West End Brewery, Madoc Street.* Acquired by William Hancock & Co.Ltd 1890 and the brewery was closed in 1969.

Glamorgan Brewery. Acquired by William Hancock & Co.Ltd (1901)

Thomas Jones, *High Street Brewery, Tower Lane.* Acquired by William Hancock & Co.Ltd 1891 with 13 public houses. Closed 1894.

Singleton Brewery Co.Ltd, *Little Gam Street.* Registered 22nd December 1899 to acquire the business of Benjamin Hoddinott & Francis D'Oyley Mears. Ceased trading 1st December 1900. No tied houses. Dissolved 26th December 1902. Acquired by William Hancock & Co.Ltd 1917.

Swansea Old Brewery Ltd, *Singleton Street.* Registered 15th May 1896 as the Swansea Old Brewery & Davies (Cardigan) Bonded Stores Ltd to acquire: the Swansea Old Brewery Co.Ltd; Davies Brothers, Cardigan & R.George & Sons, brewers and maltsters, Pembroke, with over 50 tied houses. Name changed as above April 1921. Acquired by William Hancock & Co.Ltd December 1927 and brewing ceased in 1934.

Swansea United Breweries Ltd, *Orange Street.* Registered 21st March 1890 to acquire: Crowhurst & Windsor, Orange Street Brewery and Thomas Jones & Co, Glamorgan Brewery, Little Madoc Street, both of Swansea, with 58 tied houses. Acquired by Truman, Hanbury, Buxton & Co.Ltd in September 1926 and was closed.

Other Breweries

Arthur Dyer, *Market Street, Morriston* (1910)
David Edwards, *The Cross, Morriston* (1923)
David Evans, *Martin Street, Morriston* (1910)
Robert George, *12 Woodfield Street, Morriston* (1910)
Harrison & Co, *21/22 Woodfield Street, Morriston* (1923)
Leyshon Matthews, *Brynhyfryd* (1901)
Prudence Rees, *Graig, Morriston* (1910)

GLOUCESTERSHIRE

Ampney Crucis

Charles B.Radway. Brewery and the Butcher's Arms public house sold to the Stroud Brewery Co.Ltd. on 4th September 1899 for £1,875 due to the ill-health of the owner. Still extant.

Berkeley

Benjamin Fear, *Canonbury Street* (1895)

Blakeney

Samuel P.Evans & Co, *Forest of Dean Brewery* (1895)

Bourton on the Water

Hadley & Sons (1921)

Brockhampton

George Thomas Combe, *Brockhampton Brewery.* Acquired by Combe in 1840 and sold to Showell's Brewery Ltd June 1921. Brewing ceased 1927 but early home brew kits manufactured and sold there until 1939. Date stone on existing brewery buildings implies malting carried out by the Wood family on the site since 1769.

Cheltenham

Benjamin Combe, *Grafton Brewery, Leckhampton.* Merged with the Nailsworth Brewery Co.Ltd 1899.

J.A.Connelly & Co.Ltd, *Crispen Inn, 18 Ambrose Street.* Registered 29th September 1911 to acquire the Crispen Inn and the Gossditch malthouse, Cheltenham. Wound up voluntarily February 1913.

Clement John Cowell, *Anchor Brewery, Warwick Place.* Brewery and 2 public houses offered for auction 18th July 1891 and possibly acquired by Arnold & Perrett & Co.Ltd who were listed at this address in 1906.

Full Moon Hotel, *High Street.* Offered for auction 1st October 1896 with 3 quarter brewery attached.

Old Swan Brewery, *Old Swan, The Strand.* Whitbread home brew house founded 1983. Closed 1987.

Stibbs & Co, *Albion Steam Brewery, Albion Street.* Acquired by the Cheltenham Original Brewery Co.Ltd 1898.

West Country Breweries Ltd, *256 High Street.* Registered 15th April 1888 as the Cheltenham Original Brewery Co.Ltd to acquire the business of J.T.Agg-Gardner founded in 1760. Name changed to Cheltenham & Hereford Breweries Ltd 1945 when the Hereford & Tredegar Brewery Ltd was acquired and was later renamed again to Cheltenham Brewery Holdings Ltd. Merged with the Stroud Brewery Co.Ltd 1958 to form West Country Breweries Ltd with 1,275 tied houses. Acquired by Whitbread & Co.Ltd 1963 and is now known as Whitbread Flowers Ltd.

Other Breweries

William Apperley, *St.Paul's Road* (1898)
Henry Bird, *Grosvenor Brewery, Albion Street* (1906)
Charles Clutterbuck, *Stonehouse Brewery, Swindon Road* (1906)
James Kitching, *Exmouth Arms Brewery, 60 Upper Bath Road* (1921)
George Meek, *Andover Street* (1890)
Mills & Co, *100 High Street* (1914)
George Tanner, *Tewkesbury Road* (1890)
Raymond Edward Walter, *Somerset Brewery, St.George's Street* (1910)
George Wheeler, *Kemble Brewery, Fairview Street* (1910)
James Henry Wheeler, *Central Brewery, Warwick Place.* Receiver appointed 1896.
Arthur Wiffen, *St.George's Street* (1890)
Wire & Burney, *Charlton Kings Brewery* (1895)

Cinderford

Hawthorn Brewing Co, *Steam Mills Road.* Founded October 1985 by Andrew Baber. Closed 1987.

Cirencester

Cellar Brewery, *Cirencester Workshops, Brewery Court.* Founded 1983 in the former cellars of the Cirencester Brewery Co.Ltd. Name changed to Cirencester Brewing Co. 1986 and was closed in 1987. Most of the buildings still exist, including maltings now converted to multiple residential housing 1990.

Cirencester Brewery Ltd, *Cricklade Road.* Operated by Cripps & Co until 1887 when registered as above. Acquired by H. & G.Simonds of Reading in June 1937 when brewing ceased. Largely demolished.

Edmund John Price, *Nelson Brewery, 48 Gloucester Street.* Founded by John Miller at the Nelson public house prior to 1880. John Norris was recorded there in 1887 and traded as E.J.Price until 1930. Buildings still standing.

Coleford

Henry Jenkins, *Boxbush Road* (1921)

Donnington

L.C.Arkell, *Donnington Brewery.* Founded 1865 in the mill acquired by Thomas Arkell 1827. Still brewing independently 1990 with 17 public houses.

Dursley

T.W.Elvy, *Dursley Brewery Co, Silver Street.* Bankrupt May 1906 and the brewery was sold to Marshall & Elvet Ltd, distillers. Their 21 tied houses were sold to Godsell & Sons Ltd of Stroud 1907.

King & Wordsley, *Steam Brewery, Silver Street.* For auction as Chapman & Co. 25th July 1894 with 13 public houses. Acquired by Godsell & Sons Ltd 1900.

Gloucester

R.H.Bailey & Co, *City Brewery, Quay Street.* Offered for auction 14th November 1894 with 15 public houses. Bought by Tayler & Co. of Northleach 1898.

Carpenter & Co, *Black Dog Brewery, Barton Street.* Sold to the Stroud Brewery Co.Ltd 1909 for £4,800.

College Ales, *Gloucester Brewery, Cooperative Industrial Estate, East India Road.* Founded August 1983. Closed 1984.

H.V.Hatton & Co, *Northgate Brewery, George Street.* Acquired by Ind Coope Ltd 1896.

Hawthorne Brewery Co.Ltd, *Norfolk House Hotel, 75 Bristol Road.* Home brew house founded October 1978. Closed 1983.

James & Henry Hill, *Sun Brewery, Northgate Street.* Acquired by Arnold, Perrett & Co.Ltd 1889.

Other Breweries

John Apperley & Co, *Laburnum Brewery, Ryecroft Street* (1895)

William Bayliss, *India Hotel Brewery, Lower Barton Street* (1895)

Henry Goddard Branch, *Crown Brewery, St.Mary's Street* (1895)

Sidney Cummings, *Vauxhall Brewery, Barton Street* (1892)

William Harris, *Golden Heart Brewery, Moor Street* (1895)

J.Wheeler & Co. Acquired by Tayler & Co. of Northleach 1890.

Elizabeth Withers, *London Road* (1923)

Minchinhampton

George Playne & Sons, *Forwood Brewery.* Acquired by the Stroud Brewery Co.Ltd 1897 with 40 tied houses. Most of the buildings are intact.

Mitcheldean

Wintle's Brewery Ltd, *Forest Steam Brewery.* Brewery built 1871. Offered for auction March 1923 but was withdrawn at £174,500. New company registered September 1923. Acquired by the Cheltenham Original Brewery Co.Ltd March 1930 with about 70 public houses. Brewery still standing 1990.

Moreton in Marsh

Charles Joseph Gillett, *Swan Brewery.* Acquired by Flower & Son Ltd 1914.

Nailsworth

Nailsworth Brewery Co.Ltd. Registered August 1889 to acquire the business of Clissold & Sons founded c.1800. Amalgamated with the Cheltenham Original Brewery Co.Ltd 1908 and was closed. Maltings used as a club.

Northleach

Tayler & Co, *Cotswold Brewery.* Acquired by the Cheltenham Original Brewery Co.Ltd 1919 with 14 tied houses. Buildings still extant in 1990, last used as a motor repair business.

Painswick

William Sadler Hall, *Cranham.* Home brew house acquired by Godsell & Sons Ltd August 1904 for £13,800.

Quedgley

Three Counties Brewery. Founded August 1983 by Paul Soden but was closed in 1984.

Redbrook

Oliver Arthur Burgham. Founded 1825. Acquired by Ind Coope Ltd 1923 with 22 public houses.

Ruardean

Edward Thompson, *Hillside Brewery.* Ceased brewing 1910. Brewery still standing 1990.

Soudley

Royal Forest of Dean Brewery. Founded 1980 but ceased brewing 1982.

South Cerney

Isaac B.Howell (1902)

Stow-on-the-Wold

Augustus Barton Green. Acquired by the Cheltenham Original Brewery Co.Ltd 1914. Brewery offices intact. Yard buildings converted to multiple retail units in 1989.

Stroud

Carpenter Ltd, *Cainscross Brewery.* Registered 1904. Offered for auction April 1926. Offices and yard in use as retail outlets.

Cordwell & Sons, *Hamwell Leaze Brewery, Cainscross.* Bankrupt 1907 but a new company was formed. Supplied the free trade only in the Tewkesbury/Bristol area. Brewing ceased 1940/41 due to the shortage of staff and free trade outlets. Continued to operate as bottlers until closed in 1957.

Godsell & Sons Ltd, *Salmon Springs Brewery.* Founded by 1877. Registered 1905. Acquired by the Stroud Brewery Co.Ltd 1928. Brewery demolished 1936 and a mineral water factory and bottling plant was built on the site. The maltings are still extant 1990.

Holmes, Harper & Neame, *Church Street Brewery, 17 Church Street* (1892)

Alan Neame, *Eagle Brewery.* Acquired by the Nailsworth Brewery Co.Ltd 1897.

Smith & Sons Ltd, *Brinscombe Brewery, Brewery Lane.* Offered for auction September 1915 with 22 public houses. The houses realised £18,075 but the brewery was not sold until 1919 when it was bought by the Stroud Brewery Co.Ltd. Used as a garage in 1988.

Stroud Brewery Co.Ltd, *Rowcroft.* Founded 1760 as Watts, Hallewell & Co. Registered 1888. 643 tied houses. Merged with Cheltenham & Hereford Breweries Ltd 1958 to form West Country Breweries Ltd. Used as a Whitbread depot until 1969 and was demolished in 1970.

Tetbury

N.& W.Cook, *Hampton Street.* Founded 1800. Acquired by the Stroud Brewery Co.Ltd 1913 with 33 public houses.

Warn & Son Ltd, *Barton & Dolphin Breweries, Church Street.* Founded 1766 by William Warn. Acquired by the Stroud Brewery Co.1930.

Thomas Henry Witchell, *Dolphin Brewery, Church Street.* Founded c.1820. Acquired by Warn & Sons Ltd 1903. The brewery is still standing, converted into flats.

Tewkesbury

Bayliss & Merrell, *The Distillery.* Founded 1750. Offered for auction 27th April 1921 with 2 public houses: The Nottingham Arms, Tewkesbury and The Seven Stars, Upton on Severn.

Tewkesbury Brewery Co.Ltd, *Original Brewery, Quay Street.* Registered 1890 to acquire Joseph Jupp, Abbey Brewery and James Wilkes Wilson, Original Brewery. Acquired by Arnold, Perrett & Co.Ltd 1893. However, the inscription "Blizard, Colman & Co" is still visible on the brewery.

Uley

Uley Brewery, *Old Brewery, 31 The Street.* Founded by S.Price in 1833 but brewing ceased during early 1900s. Brewing recommenced 1984 by Charles Wright in the derelict buildings. Date on lintel of 1888 shows owner's name. Still in operation 1990.

Wotton under Edge

Coombe Valley Brewery Co.Ltd. Registered 1905 to acquire the business of A.J.P.& J.H.S.Annesley. Receiver appointed March 1908.

A.H.Guinness (1900)

GRAMPIAN

Aberdeen

Devanha Brewery Co.Ltd, *Wellington Road*. Founded 1803. Originally known as W.Black & Co. Registered April 1910. Acquired by William Younger & Co.Ltd 1930.

Thomson, Marshall & Co.Ltd, *Aulton Brewery, High Street*. Founded before 1800. Originally known as Smith, Irvine & Co and was acquired by Thomson, Marshall & Co. 1863. Registered February 1902. Voluntary liquidation and the brewery was offered for sale on 8th April 1904.

Other Breweries
McAdam & Co, *146 Hardgate* (1914)
Hugh McCauley & Co, *Lochside Brewery, 112 Loch Street* (1902)
James Milne & Son, *69 Virginia Street* (1910)

Alford

Aberdeen Ales Ltd, *Devanha Brewery, Old Station Yard*. Established October 1982 by John Hammond and Dixie Taylor. In receivership 1985 and purchased by Jim Moffat and Alastair Byres. Ceased brewing 1986.

Banff

Aberbeeg

Webbs (Aberbeeg) Ltd. Founded by William Webb 1838. Private company registered 10th December 1900 as J.R.& T.A.Webb Ltd. Acquired Webb Brothers & Co, brewers and the name was changed as above in 1905. Public company registered 1942. Acquired by Northern Breweries of Great Britain Ltd 1960 with 88 public houses. Brewing ceased in 1969.

Abergavenny

William Graham & Co, *83 North Castle Street*. Founded c.1750. Converted into a mineral water bottling plant 1908 and is now a laundry.

Craigellachie

Craigellachie Brewery Co.Ltd. Registered 1895. Voluntary liquidation May 1907.

Cullen

Joshua Roberts

Cuminestown

Alexander Fraser (1906)

Elgin

A.& Y.Young, *Elgin Brewery* (1910)

Ellon

T.Yelton Ogilvie & Co. (1906). Also at Biffic Brewery, Old Deer (1910)

Fraserburgh

William S.Grant, *Shore Street* (1902)
John Hendry, *Castle Brewery, 21 Castle Street* (1927)
John Watt, *Water Mill Brewery* (1910)

Hill of Maud

Bin Hill Brewery. Founded March 1986 by Phil Gilbert but has since ceased brewing.

Huntly

Huntly Brewery Co. (1902)

Inverurie

William Hay & Sons, *Inverurie Brewery, Beverley Road* (1926)
Philip Brothers, *Port Elphinstone* (1914)

GWENT

Claude S.Atkin, *King's Arms, Nevill Street*. Brewing by 1864. King's Arms continued as a home brew house until c.1934. Acquired by Cheltenham & Hereford Breweries.
S.H.Facey & Son Ltd, *Market Street Brewery*. Founded 1864. Market Street Brewery built 1892. Acquired by David Roberts & Sons Ltd 1950 with 12 public houses and brewing ceased in 1960.
King's Arms, *Neville Street*. Home brew house acquired by Cheltenham & Hereford Breweries.
Other Breweries
Edward Bowen, *King David Inn* (1940)
Mrs A.E.Cook, *Baker Street* (1921)
Delafield, *Neville Street*. Acquired by C.S.Atkins c.1914.
William Edwards, *St.John's Square* (1923)
William Jenkins, *Brecon Road Brewery* (1891)

Johnshaven

James Jackson junior (1902)

Keith

James Bruce, *Union Street* (1906)

Laurencekirk

David Cameron Ltd. Registered March 1945. No tied houses. Brewery closed early in 1947 and beer was supplied by McLennan & Urquhart Ltd of Dalkeith.

Old Deer

Biffic Brewery, *Old Deer* (1910). See also:- Ellon.

Old Meldrum

Robert M.Cruikshank (1940)
William Grant (1906)

Peterhead

Heslop & Son, *Peterhead Brewery, 20 Errol Street*. Owned by the Helsop family since 1879. Acquired by Thomas Usher & Son Ltd of Edinburgh 1940.
John Hunter, *Tanfield Brewery*. Bankrupt March 1910.
George L.Stephen, *Brae Brewery* (1902)
James Webster, *Uphill Lane* (1906)

Ruthven

Borve Brewhouse. Originally founded at Borve, Isle of Lewis in 1983. Established July 1989 by James & Gregory Hughes. Still Brewing 1990.

Stonehaven

John Begg & Son, *Bridge of Cowie Brewery* (1914)

Strichen

J.Michie & Sons Ltd, *Newmill* (1914)

Abersychan

Reform Brewery Co.Ltd, *Union Street*. Founded 1832. Brewing revived by Daniel S.Davies in the late 1870s as the Abersychan Brewery. Registered 1933 to acquire the Abersychan Brewery and the public houses of Westlake's Brewery Ltd. Acquired by Andrew Buchan's Breweries Ltd 1938.

Abertillery

Chivers Brothers, *Cwmtillery Brewery*. Recorded as Joseph Chivers until 1895 when name changed to Chivers & Sons. As above from 1910 to 1914.

Blaenavon

Richard James, *Ivor Castle Brewery* (1891)
Westlake's Brewery Ltd. Registered in 1889 to acquire business of Charles Francis Westlake. Moved to Cwmavon in 1900.

Blaina

Griffiths Brothers Ltd, *Blaina Brewery*. Registered 16th September 1890 with 20 public houses. In liquidation from 18th August 1909 to 7th July 1910 when they resumed trading. Merged with Andrew Buchan's Breweries Ltd 1939.

Brynmawr

Walter James, *King Street* (1891)
Catherine Jones, *King Street* (1902)
W.H.Madeley & Sons, (1891)

Caerleon

John Sherwood, *Hanbury Arms, High Street*. Merged with Percy Jones Eastern Valleys Brewery, Pontnewydd in 1910. Acquired by William Handcock of Cardiff in 1914.

Crumlin

D.F.Pritchard Ltd, *Western Valleys Brewery*. Registered 1904. Acquired by Andrew Buchan's Breweries Ltd June 1930.

Cwmavon

Westlake's Brewery Ltd. Founded at Blaenavon in 1884 when Charles Francis Westlake acquired the Cambrian Brewery. Registered 1889. New brewery built at Cwmavon 1900 with a better water supply. Ceased brewing 1928 and the public houses absorbed by the Abersychan Brewery to form the Reform Brewery Co.Ltd 1933.

Ebbw Vale

Ebbw Vale Brewery Ltd. Registered 1919 to acquire the business of William Richard Jones. Bankrupt and was wound up 21st December 1926.
John Briscoe, *Lamb Brewery, Commercial Street* (1891-1901)

Fleur-de-Lis

Gwent Union Clubs Brewery Co.Ltd. Founded by Henry Anthony Birrell. Merged with the Severnside Brewery, Wick, 1898 to form Anthony Birrell, Pearce & Co.Ltd, Fleur-de-Lis Brewery Co. from 1906. Registered 1921 to acquire the business of G.Beames. Voluntary liquidation 1929 and the clubs were then supplied by the South Wales Clubs Brewery.

Llanfoist

Charles Edwards' Brewery Ltd. Founded by Charles Edwards 1865. Registered 1902. Acquired by Andrew Buchan's Breweries Ltd 1945 and brewing ceased. Name changed to Llanfoist Table Waters Ltd in 1949.

Magor

Whitbread PLC, New brewery on stream September 1979. Initally to brew only lager. Still brewing 1990 now also producing ales and stout.

Monmouth

Frances James, *Agincourt Street* (1921)
Gladys Kendell, *Chippenhamgate Street* (1923)
Monmouth Fine Ales, *Queen's Head Hotel, St.James Street*. Home brew house founded July 1983. Closed 1986.
John Redpath, *Dixton Gate* (1921)
Harry W.Rowland, *Monmouth Brewery* (1923). Acquired the business of H.Tipper.
Searle & Co, *Monmouth Brewery, St.Mary Street* (1898)
H.Tipper. Acquired business of Vincent & Co. (1910)
Vincent & Co. Partnership took over from Seale & Co. (1901)

Newport

Clytha Brewery Ltd. *Cannon Street/Dean Street, Caerleon Road*. Registered 1889. Operated by Frederick Cross until 1890s. Ceased trading later in same decade. Brewing restored by James Gorman by 1902. Ceased brewing 1936.
Herbert's Alexandra Brewery Ltd, *Alexandra Brewery, Commercial Road*. Registered 1913 to acquire James Herbert & Son. Offered for auction 14th July 1920 with 4 public houses but was withdrawn.
Edwin Hibbard's Anchor Brewery, *Mountjoy Road*. Acquired by William Hancock & Co.Ltd 1884 and brewing ceased in 1906.
Grove Johnson, *Victoria Brewery, Bridge Street*. Acquired by the Crown Brewery Co.(Pontypool) Ltd in 1900 with 6 public houses and was closed by 1903.
Daniel Lewis, *Star Brewery, West Market Street*. Originally know as the Commercial Brewery but name changed when acquired by Lewis in 1892. Closed 1895.
Lloyd's (Newport) Ltd, *Cambrian Brewery, Cambrian Road*. Registered November 27th 1895 as Lloyd & Yorath Ltd. to acquire William Yorath & Son and J.L.Lloyd & Co.Ltd, wine and spirit merchants, High Street, Newport. Operated by William Henry Gregory until acquired by Yorath & Sons in 1877. Name changed as above in 1946. Acquired by Ansells Brewery Ltd 1951.
Phillips & Sons Ltd, *Dock Road Brewery*. Founded 1874 when Thomas Phillips, previously of the Northampton Brewery, bought the brewery of Thomas Floyde Lewis with 13 tied houses. Registered March 1892. Sold to H.& G.Simonds Ltd 1949 with 125 public houses and brewing ceased in 1968.
Searle & Herring Ltd, *Castle Brewery, The Bridge, Shaftesbury Street*. Registered February 1889. Acquired by Lloyd & Yorath Ltd 1898.

Thatcher's

Thatcher's Brewery Ltd, *Bristol Brewery, 28 Alma Street*. Founded by 1875. Originally registered 1893. Ceased brewing 1931 but reopened 1933 by A.E.Edwards. Registered December 1937 as Thatcher's Bristol Brewery Ltd. Acquired in 1949 by Mitchells & Butlers Ltd with 20 tied houses.

Pontnewydd

Percy Jones, *Eastern Valleys Brewery, Osborne Road*. Merged with John Sherwood of Caerleon 1910 to form Eastern Valleys Brewery Co.Ltd but split up in 1912.
Silverthorne Gwent Ales, *Unit 88, Springvale Industrial Estate*. Founded February 1981 at Little Mill, Pontypool as Gwent Ales Ltd who ceased brewing 1984 and the above brewery was started in 1985 but ceased brewing in the same year.
James Veater, *United Friends Inn, Mill Road* (1901-1923)
Joseph Williams, *Mill Road* (1926)

Pontrhydyrun

Eliza Jenkins, *Terrace Inn* (1910)
John Jenkins, *Terrace Inn* (1914)

Pontypool

Ellen Bayton, *80 High Street* (1920)
Castle Brewery (Pontypool) Ltd, *George Street*. Registered August 1901 to acquire the business of Donald Reid. Acquired by Westlake's Brewery Ltd of Cwmavon in 1912 with 9 public houses and was closed.
Crown Brewery Co. (Pontypool) Ltd, *Osborne Road*. Registered 1901 to acquire the business of Donald Reid. Acquired by Andrew Buchan & Co. 1902.
Gwent Ales Ltd, *Little Mill*. See also:- Silverthorne's Gwent Ales, Pontnewydd.
Harold James, *Crane Street* (1923)
Harold Joshua, *Trosnant Street* (1923)
Granville Probyn, *Crane Street* (1921)

Redbrook

A.Burgham, *Redbrook Brewery*. Acquired with 22 public houses by Ind Coope, Burton, in 1923.

Risca

Cross & Matthews, *Risca Brewery*. Sold to William Hancock & Co.Ltd March 1902 and brewing ceased in 1916.

Tredegar

J.T.Jenkins & Co, *Church Street*. Merged with George Edwards of Hereford 1899 to form the Tredegar & Hereford Brewery Co.Ltd and was closed in 1914.

Usk

George Edmunds, *Bridge Street* (1920)

Amlwch

Anglesey Brewery Co.Ltd, *Quay Street.* Founded c.1780. Originally known as the Amlwch Port Brewery. Operated by T.Paynter Williamson until acquired by Evans & Fanning 1887. Known as the Amlwch Brewery Co. Registered as above in December 1900 with 10 tied houses. Wound up May 1904.

David Jones, *Parys Brewery, Parys Lodge Square.* Operated by John Owen until 1918. Closed 1933 but possibly operated as bottlers until 1946.

Bangor

J.F.Browning, *Tros-y-Carrol Brewery.* Founded 1812. Bought by A.H.Blake, manager to J.Lloyd & Co, Kingsbury Brewery, St.Albans, Herts, in October 1889 from S.Fricker. B.H.Browning late of Brighton was appointed brewer. Acquired by Ind Coope Ltd 1898 and was sold to the Anglesey Brewery Co.Ltd January 1903 for £877.

Beaumaris

John Jones, *Prince of Wales, Church Street* (1895)

Bethesda

John Griffith, *King's Arms, High Street* (1895)

Bontnewydd

J.Williams (1930)

Dolgellau

North Wales Brewery Ltd, *Cambrian Brewery, Arran Road.* Registered August 1906 as the North Wales Brewery Co.Ltd. Receiver appointed 23rd July 1908. New company registered as above in October 1909 and was dissolved 27th March 1914.

Gaerwen

Gwynedd Brewers, *Gaerwen Industrial Estate.* Founded August 1980. Closed 1984.

Llanfachraeth

David Williams (1892). Registered 1882 as the Mona Brewery Co.Ltd.

Llanfairfechan

Sarah Williams, *River View Brewery, Nantyfelin Road* (1895)

Llanfair-PG

Griffith Thomas Roberts, *Garneddwen Brewery* (1895)

Llanwrst

Elias & Co.Ltd, *Wilton Street.* Registered January 1905 to acquire Thomas Elias & Co. Wound up November 1905.

Pwllheli

Thomas Doughton, *Bear Brewery* (1906)
David R.Evans, *Red Lion Brewery* (1930)
John Roberts, *Victoria Brewery, Carnarvon Road* (1893)
David Thomas, *Royal Arms Brewery* (1926)

Aldershot

Army & Navy Co-operative Breweries Ltd. Registered July 1895 to acquire Gerald & Edward Hall, Aldershot and George Belgrave, Folkestone, Kent. The Aldershot brewery and 3 public houses were offered for auction February 1900 but were withdrawn at £7,500. Wound up January 1902.

Crown Brewery Aldershot Ltd, *Elms Road.* Registered 1892 to acquire the Aldershot Brewery Co.Ltd which had been offered for auction in July 1891. The company ceased to exist within a few days of registration. Dissolved September 1896.

Alresford

Hunt & Co, *West Street.* Acquired by Crowley & Co.Ltd 1901. Brewery has been demolished.

William Henry Twine (1910)

Alton

Alton Brewery Co, *Turk Street.* Founded before 1841. Acquired by Courage & Co.Ltd 1903 with 77 tied houses. Courage required the brewery for the production of pale ale, previously brewed for them by Flowers (1872-86) and by Fremlins (1886-1903). Brewing was transferred to Reading in 1970.

Crowley & Co.Ltd, *Turk Street.* Founded by James Baverstock 1763 and was bought by the Crowley family of Croydon 1821. Sold to the Burrell family 1877. Registered 1901. Acquired by Watney, Combe, Reid & Co.Ltd 1947 with 248 public house and brewing ceased in September 1970. See also:- A.C.S.& H.Crowley, Croydon, London.

Andover

Bourne Valley Brewery Ltd, *North Way, Walworth Industrial Estate.* Founded November 1978 by James Lynch & John Featherby. Ceased brewing October 1985. Owned one public house.

H.C.Hammans, *East Street.* Acquired by Strong & Co.Ltd October 1919.

Hampshire Brewing Co.Ltd, *North Way, Walworth Industrial Estate.* Founded 1986 in former Bourne Valley Brewery premises but was closed in the same year.

W.M.Herbert, *Union Street Brewery.* Offered for auction 16th October 1916 after the death of W.M.Herbert, with 8 tied houses and was bought by the Winchester Brewery Co.Ltd.

W.O.Nutley, *Phoenix Brewery, 29/31 Chantry Street.* The brewery tap, the King's Head and the Clatford Arms were offered for auction 7th March 1917.

John Poore & Son, *51 High Street.* Acquired by the Winchester Brewery Co.Ltd 1919.

Bishops Waltham

Edwards' Brewery Ltd, *Abbey Brewery, Abbey Street.* Operated as Heaver & Babbage until 1884. Acquired by Edward Edwards 1895. Registered 1898 to acquire the business, and J.Wiltshire, Droxford Brewery. Acquired by the Winchester Brewery Co.Ltd 1923 with 11 tied houses and brewing ceased. Part still standing & used as a garden centre.

Henry Richard Paice, *Bishops Waltham Brewery* (1895)

Cadnam

New Forest Brewery, *Old Lyndhurst Road.* Founded February 1979 by John Watts. Still in operation 1990.

East Meon

Stephen Parson (1930)

Emsworth

Kinnell & Hartley Ltd, *Crown Brewery, South Street.* Founded 1896 by Arthur Hartley, previously brewer to Kidd & Hotblack of Brighton. Registered 1903. Acquired by Henty & Constable Ltd 1928.

Fareham

Cawte Brothers Ltd, *40/42 West Street* (1906)
Thomas Nicholson, *White Horse Brewery, West Street* (1914)
H.H.& R.J.Saunders, *Wallington Brewery, Drift Road.* Acquired by Hammerton & Co.Ltd 1944. The brewery is still standing.

Fordingbridge

Alfred J.Abbott, *High Street.* Brewery damaged by fire October 1906 but brewing continued until 1922.

Charles Absalom, *High Street* (1914)

Frovle

Raymond Archer Morse (1892)

Gosport

Biden & Co.Ltd, *Sea Horse Brewery, Sea Horse Street.* Founded 1800 and acquired by the Biden family 1846. Registered July 1896. Acquired by Portsmouth United Breweries Ltd 1918.

S.& T.N.Blake & Co.Ltd, *South Cross Street Brewery.* Registered October 1897. Acquired by Brickwood & Co.Ltd 1926 and brewing ceased. Name changed to Blake Properties Ltd 1927 and was liquidated 1941.

Hobbs & Co, *Stoke Brewery, Stoke Road.* Founded by 1885. Their 12 tied houses were sold to Portsmouth United Breweries Ltd 1913.

Alex Hurst & Co, *Haslar Street Brewery.* Acquired by Kinnell & Hartley Ltd 1903.

Hambledon

Hartridge & Sons Ltd, *Alliance Brewery.* Founded before 1882 when acquired by Francis Hartridge. Main buildings destroyed by bombing 1940 and brewing ceased. Business still in operation 1990 as mineral water manufacturers owning 2 public houses. Recommenced brewing on the Isle of Wight in 1991.

Hartley Wintney

Thomas Kenward, *Hartley Row Brewery.* Bought by Thomas Kenward 1876. Acquired by Friary, Holroyd & Healy's Brewery Ltd 1921 with 4 public houses. Some of the buildings are still standing.

Havant

Samuel Clarke, *Homewell Brewery, West Street.* Acquired by Gale & Co.Ltd 1903 with 9 tied houses.

Emma Gloyne, *South Street.* Acquired by Kinnell & Hartley Ltd 1898.

Havant Brewery Co.Ltd, *West Street.* Registered 1897. Acquired by Biden & Co.Ltd. in 1906.

A.C.Nance, *Cygnet Brewery.* Acquired by Bransbury & Co. 1900.

Holybourne

Walter J.Complin, *Holybourne Brewery.* See also:- Southampton.

Horndean

George Gale & Co.Ltd, *The Square.* Founded 1847 when Richard Gale acquired the Ship & Bell home brew house. Registered April 1888 with 80 public houses. Still brewing independently with 96 tied houses.

Hurstbourne Tarrant

Albert Edward Berry (1906)
George Hutchins (1902)

Hythe

Hythe Brewery Co, *Langdown Steam Brewery.* Acquired by Strong & Co.Ltd 1895.

Kingsclere

William Ingram Drake, *Duke Street.* Acquired by John May & Co.Ltd of Basingstoke 1921. The buildings are still standing.

Lymington

G.& W.Olive, *West End Brewery, Queen Street* (1898)

William Stephens, *Solent Brewery.* Acquired by Mew, Langton & Co.Ltd 1887.

Micheldever

C.King & Son (1892)

Odiham

King & Palmer, *Odiham Brewery, High Street.* Acquired by Crowley & Co.Ltd 1895 and was used as stores. Most of the buildings are still standing.

Otterbourne

James Baldwin. Brewing ceased 1910.

Petersfield

Amey's Brewery Ltd, *Borough Brewery, Frenchmen's Road.* Founded by Thomas Amey 1883. Registered 1941. Acquired by Whitbread & Co.Ltd 1951 with 20 public houses and 12 off-licences and brewing ceased. Most of the buildings are still standing.

W.& R.Luker, *College Street Brewery.* Acquired by Strong & Co.Ltd 1929.

Weeks & Co, *Square Brewery.* Acquired by George Gale & Co.Ltd 1907.

Portchester

James Goodman, *Old Oak Brewery, West Street.* Offered for auction 25th July 1907 with 3 tied houses and was sold to Long & Co. of Portsmouth for £8,600.

Portsmouth

Henry Bransbury & Co, *Crown Brewery, Clarendon Street, Landport.* Founded by Henry Bransbury junior 1879. Acquired by Portsmouth United Breweries Ltd 1902 with 40 tied houses. Used as a bottling store.

Brickwoods Ltd, *Portsmouth Brewery, Admiralty Road, Portsea.* In 1851 Fanny Brickwood bought the Cobden Arms Brewery, Arundel Street, Landport, founded in 1823. In 1875 grandsons John & Arthur Brickwood took charge. In 1880 moved to the Hyde Park Brewery, Hyde Park Road, Southsea, founded by Henry Bransbury senior 1851. Then in 1887 to Tessier's Portsmouth Brewery, Penny Street, founded in 1763. Registered as Brickwood & Co.Ltd 1891. In 1899 they bought Jewell's Catherine Brewery, Catherine Row, Portsea, established in 1845, which they rebuilt as the Portsmouth Brewery and moved there 1902. The name was changed as above in 1953. Acquired by Whitbread & Co.Ltd 1971 with 675 public houses. Brewing ceased 1983. Demolished 1990.

Gibb & Son, *Phoenix Brewery, Collingwood Road, Southsea.* Founded 1867 by Rice Brothers as the Dock Mill Brewery. Rebuilt and was renamed the Phoenix Brewery after a fire. Bought by William Gibb in 1882. Acquired by the Lion Brewery (Portsmouth) Ltd 1903 with 31 tied houses and was demolished.

Charles Gillett, *Buckland Brewery, Kingston Road, Buckland.* Founded by Thomas Allen 1847 and acquired by Gillett 1903. Amalgamated with Ernest Whicher's Cosham Brewery 1906 and acquired by J.J.Young & Sons Ltd 1914.

Peter Henry Goodman, *Crescent Brewery, Kingston Crescent, Kingston.* Established by Thomas Russell 1851. Acquired by Goodman 1871. Acquired by Gibb & Son 1890 and brewing ceased.

Dormer Jewell & Son, *Catherine Brewery, Catherine Row, Portsea.* Founded 1845. Acquired by Brickwood & Co.Ltd 1899 and was rebuilt and renamed the Portsmouth Brewery.

Lion Brewery (Portsmouth) Ltd, *Lion Brewery, London Road, North End.* Founded 1870 by William Stephens as the Myrtle Brewery. Became the Lion Brewery 1879 when acquired by G.H.King. Registered 1902 to acquire the business of King & Co. Acquired by Brickwood & Co.Ltd in 1910. Brewery still standing.

Long & Co.(Southsea) Ltd, *Southsea Brewery, Hambrook Street, Southsea.* Founded by William Tollervey 1814 and was acquired by Samuel Long in 1839. Registered March 1924. Acquired by Brickwood & Co.Ltd 1933 when brewing ceased.

Lush & Co.Ltd, *St. George's Brewery, St. George's Square, Portsea.* Founded by Robert Temple 1757 and acquired by the Spicer family 1801. Run by Pike & Co. from 1840 and brewing ceased 1848 after Pike, Spicer & Co. was formed. Brewing recommenced 1859 when George Lush moved from the Hawke Brewery, Hawke Street, founded 1809 by George Clements. Registered July 1895. Brewing ceased 1911 when the company was privately owned by Sir William Dupree, head of Portsmouth United Breweries. Acquired by Portsmouth United Breweries 1924.

George Greetham Palmer, *St. Paul's Brewery, King Street, Southsea.* Founded 1851. Acquired by Long & Co. 1899 when brewing ceased.

A.F.Perkins & Co.Ltd, *Lager Brewery, Hyde Park Road, Southsea.* Originally Henry Bransbury's Hyde Park Brewery and John & Arthur Brickwood 1880-87. Registered 1896. In voluntary liquidation November 1900 and was dissolved 10th July 1908.

George Peters & Co.Ltd, *Kingston Brewery, Kingston Road, Kingston.* Founded 1805 by William Fidlina and bought by auction 1884 by George Peters & Co, wine merchants, Kings Road, Southsea. Registered 1910 when Peters ceased brewing, the brewery being sold to Ernest Whicher.

Albert Phillips, *Castle Brewery, Somers Road, Southsea.* Founded 1863 by William French. Acquired by Florence Phillips 1887. Acquired by W.A.Hobbs of Gosport 1904 with 2 tied houses.

Pike, Spicer & Co.Ltd, *Penny Street.* Founded by William Pike 1719. Amalgamated with David Spicer's St.George's Square Brewery 1847. Registered 1891 with 110 public houses. Acquired by Brickwood & Co.Ltd 1910 and was closed.

Portsmouth & Brighton United Breweries Ltd, *Elm Brewery, King Street, Southsea.* Registered October 1896 as Portsmouth United Breweries Ltd to acquire the Elm Brewery (founded 1851 by John Miles), the Beehive Brewery, Warblington Street (founded by Thomas Weeks 1832) and the Cosham Steam Brewery, Cosham. the latter two had been bought in 1895 by William Dupree from Alexander Stannard and George Henry Dean respectively. The name was changed as above February 1928 after the Rock Brewery (Brighton) Ltd was acquired. Acquired by Brickwood & Co.Ltd 1953 with 271 tied houses. Brewing continued until 1962.

J.Shaft & Co, *Star Brewery, Queen Street, Portsea.* See also:- Ernest Whicher & Co.

Southsea Brewery, *Old Lion Brewery, Pitcroft Lane, North End.* Founded August 1982 in part of original Lion Brewery. Brewing ceased in 1985.

Tessier & Co, *Portsmouth Brewery, Penny Street.* See also:- Brickwoods Ltd.

Ernest Whicher & Co, *Star Brewery, Queen Street, Portsea.* Founded 1891 by James Shaft, passed to Whicher 1897 and closed in that year when Whicher bought the Cosham Steam Brewery from Portsmouth United Breweries Ltd. In 1906 merged with Gillett's Buckland Brewery. In 1910 bought the Kingston Brewery from George Peters and ceased brewing in 1914.

J.J.Young & Sons Ltd, *Victory Brewery, Thomas Street, Landport.* Founded by Daniel Ford 1830 and was acquired by J.J.Young 1860. Registered 1902. Acquired by George Peters & Co.Ltd, wine merchants c.1914 and continued brewing until 1959 when Peters were acquired by Friary Meux Ltd. Was also known as the St.Thomas Brewery.

Privett

Pig & Whistle, *A32 Road.* Home brew house founded August 1982. Closed 1987.

Redbridge

William Stride. Acquired by Strong & Co. March 1890.

Ringwood

Carter & Co, *West Street.* Founded by the Carter family 1725. Acquired by Strong & Co.Ltd 1923 and was closed.

Ringwood Brewery, *138 Christchurch Road.* Founded by Peter Austin 1978 at Minty's Yard, New Street and moved to Christchurch Road 1986. Still brewing 1990 with 2 public houses.

Romsey

Emily M.Cressey, *Hundred Brewery.* Acquired by Strong & Co.Ltd 1894.

Mrs Holloway, *Middle Bridge Street* (1910)

James Smith, *Love Lane* (1923)

Strong & Co.Ltd, *Horsefair Brewery.* Founded c.1778. Brewery and 23 tied houses leased to Thomas Strong 1858, who bought the business in 1883. Registered November 1894. Acquired by Whitbread & Co.Ltd 1969 with 940 public houses. Brewing ceased 1981. Partly intact 1993.

Southampton

Aldridge & Son Ltd, *Bedford Brewery, 24 Bedford Place.* Registered 1925. Acquired by Brickwood & Co.Ltd 1927 and brewing ceased 1930 but bottling continued until 1968.

Ashby's Eling Brewery Co.Ltd, *Rumbridge Street, Totton.* Founded 1824 and acquired by Francis Ashby 1859. Acquired by Strong & Co.Ltd 1920 with 20 public houses. Mainly demolished 1928.

A.Barlow & Co.Ltd, *Victoria Brewery, Commercial Road.* Brewery built 1862 and was under the control of Andrew Barlow 1898. Registered May 1921. Acquired by Brickwood & Co.Ltd 1929 and brewing ceased.

W.H.Complin & Co, *Cobden Bridge Brewery, Bitterne.* Founded 1890 by Walter J.Complin of the Holybourne Brewery. Acquired by Fuller, Smith & Turner 1898 and brewing ceased 1914. The public houses were sold to Courage & Co.Ltd 1920.

William Cooper & Co.Ltd, *East Street Brewery.* Founded c.1786. Acquired by Watney, Combe, Reid & Co.Ltd 1943 and brewing ceased 1950.

Forder & Co.Ltd, *Hampton Court Brewery, 23 French Street & High Street Brewery.* Registered 1909. Acquired by Brickwood & Co.Ltd 1925.

Frog & Frigate, *Dock Brewery, Canute Road.* Founded 1981 by David Welsh. Sold to Tony Sabley. Still in operation 1990.

Gate public house, *Burgess Road.* Whitbread home brew house founded 1983. Ceased brewing 1985.

Hine Brothers, *68 Marland Place.* Founded 1857 when Henry & James F.Hine bought the Netherbury Brewery, Dorset. Acquired the Birmingham Street Brewery, Southampton 1860 and later added the wine & spirit business in Marland Place. Acquired by Strong & Co.Ltd 1898.

Charles King, *Heathfield Brewery, Winchester Road, Shirley* (1906)

Sir Frederick Perkins & Sons Ltd, *Globe Brewery, 40 Orchard Lane.* Registered 1912. Acquired by Brickwood & Co.Ltd 1925.

A.& H.Scovell, *College Street Brewery.* Acquired by Strong & Co.Ltd 1896.

Scrase's Brewery Ltd, *Star Brewery, 29 High Street.* Founded 1829. Registered November 1889 to acquire Henry Scrase. Acquired by Strong & Co.Ltd 1927 and brewing ceased 1947.

Southampton United Brewery Co.Ltd, *52 Waterloo Road, Freemantle.* Registered 1898 as the United Liberal Brewery Co.Ltd. Name changed as above 14th November 1902. Voluntary liquidation 11th August 1905. Some buildings are still standing.

William Stride, exors of, *Redbridge.* Acquired by Strong & Co. 1890.

Henry Welsh, *Wheatsheaf Brewery, Bridge Street.* Founded 1826. Acquired by Scrase's Brewery Ltd 1900, whose premises were adjacent.

Southwick

W.J.Hunt, *Golden Lion Brewery.* Home brew house closed 1956 when the owner became too old to work the brewery. Golden Lion acquired by Courage & Co.Ltd. Brewery & plant still intact.

Stockbridge

Lewis Hart Guinness (1914)

Stratfield Turgis

John Innes, *Wellington Arms.* Home brew house which ceased brewing 1895. Brewing plant removed 1971.

Titchfield

John R.Fielder & Son Ltd, *Titchfield Brewery, Bridge Street.* Founded 1744 and was acquired by the Fielder family 1897. Registered 1947. Acquired by Whitbread & Co.Ltd March 1961 with 12 tied houses. The brewery has been demolished.

Twyford

Young & Co.Ltd, *Twyford Brewery.* Founded 1859. Acquired by Eldridge, Pope & Co.Ltd May 1911 with 7 public houses.

Vernham Dean

George Stroud (1898)

Waterlooville

George Webb (1906)

Weyhill

George Gibbons. Acquired by Strong & Co.Ltd 1894 with 27 public houses.

Whitchurch

Gates & Son (1910)
John Roe, *Whitchurch Brewery* (1914)

Wickham

Wickham Brewery Co.Ltd, *The Square.* Registered 1908. Offered for auction 23rd September 1910 with 3 public houses. Trading ceased when the brewery was sold to Gale & Co.Ltd 25th June 1912. The buildings were redeveloped recently.

Winchester

B.B.Colson & Co.Ltd, *Cheeshill Brewery, Cheeshill Street and Winnall Brewery.* Registered 1900. Voluntary liquidation 28th April 1920. Premises used for many years as a laundry.

Lion Brewery (Winchester) Ltd, *Lion Brewery, 28 Eastgate Street.* Founded by 1880. Registered as Wootten & Co.Ltd December 1896. Name changed to the Lion Brewery Ltd 1900 and as above 1906. Acquired by Strong & Co.Ltd 1931 and brewing ceased.

Lawn Brewery, *Mash Tun Public House, Eastgate Street.* Home brew house founded 1982 by David Welsh. Ceased brewing 1984. Formerly the Halcyon public house.

Frederick Welsh Ltd, *Hyde Abbey Brewery, 31 Hyde Street.* Originally under the name of Hugh Wyeth & Co, who were acquired by Eldridge, Pope & Co.Ltd with 5 public house 1886. Registered as above May 1895 with 21 tied houses. Wound up 10th July 1899 and was re-registered as Welsh & Co.Ltd. Acquired by Cooper & Co.Ltd of Southampton 1929.

Winchester Brewery Co.Ltd, *Winchester Brewery, Hyde Street.* Founded by 1812. Under the control of H.& G.Simonds of Reading from 1850. Registered November 1893. Acquired by Marston, Thompson & Evershed Ltd 1923 with 108 public houses. Brewing ceased 1927 but bottling continued until 1969. Used as a regional depot.

Wootten & Co.Ltd. See also:- Lion Brewery (Winchester) Ltd.

HEREFORD & WORCESTER

Bodenham

Tate Brewery, *Houghten Court Farm.* Founded May 1985 by David Dawson formerly of the Nag's Head, Canon Pyon. Ceased brewing 1988 and was offered for sale.

Broadway

Charles Richardson Drury (1895)

Bromsgrove

Frank Bridgman, *4 Worcester Street* (1940)
Fortescue & Son, *169 Worcester Street.* Acquired by Lewis Fortescue from J.W.Fitch on 30th April 1906 for £7,500, with 9 public houses. Offered for sale April 1922 and was bought by Flower & Sons Ltd in 1926.
J.Martin (1890)
Elizabeth Potter, *Rock Hill, Worcester Road* (1921)
Elizabeth Stiles, *9 High Street* (1921)

Canon Pyon

Nag's Head. Home brew house founded 1984 by landlord, David Tallboys with David Dawson as brewer. Ceased brewing 1985 when the latter moved to Bodenham.

Wye Valley Brewery, *Nag's Head.* Founded May 1985 when the business of the Abbey Brewery, Torworth, Notts was moved to here. Moved to the Lamb Hotel, Owens Street, Hereford in 1986 and was still in operation 1990.

Cow Honeybourne

Reuben Gray (1910)

Cradley

W.Oliver & Sons of Cradley Ltd, *Talbot Brewery, Colley Gate.* Registered December 1915. Acquired by Darby's Brewery Ltd of West Bromwich 1937.

Other Breweries
Hezekiah Dunn, *High Street* (1935)
Llewellyn Robinson, *High Street* (1920)
Ellen Roper, *Colley Gate* (1923)
George H. Stafford, *74 Colley Gate* (1940)
Samuel Taylor, *Two Gate* (1920)
William Thomas, *Two Gate* (1920)
Benjamin Tromans, *Furlong Lane* (1926)
Gilbert Willetts, *Blue Ball Lane* (1940)

Cutnall Green

Thomas Clinton (1926)
Frank Trow (1930)

Almeley

Henry Baird (1895)

Badsey

Walter Richard Warmington (1923)

Belbroughton

Ada Bridgman (1921)
David Harry Riste (1940)

Bewdley

Emma Alcock, *Cleobury Road* (1923)
Frederick T.Bishop, *74 High Street* (1940)
Mrs James Bradbury, *Wribbenhall* (1940)
Leonard A.Brown, *Dog Lane* (1926)
Joseph Gardner, *Wyre Hill* (1940)
Charles H.Green, *Cleobury Road* (1923)
Arthur H.Hall, *30 High Street* (1940)
Invicta Sparkling Hop Ale Co, *Butt Town Meadow*
Frederick Martin, *60 High Street* (1914)
William H.Mucklow, *17 Severn Side* (1910)
George H.Perkins, *Wribbenhall* (1923)
Priscilla Southan, *7 Welshgate* (1930)

Droitwich

Arthur Baggott, *Acre Lane* (1920)
William Baylis, *St.Peter's Street, Witton* (1920)
Thomas W. Bourne, *Hill End* (1923)
Rose Fox, *Friar Street* (1921)
Arthur Harrison, *Ombersley Street* (1920)
James S. Johnson, *High Street* (1921)
Florence F. Small, *Ombersley Street* (1921)

Dunley

Alice Haynes (1920)

Eckington

John Stone (1902)

Evesham

H.Boyd & Co, *Model Brewery, 2 Vine Street*. Originally registered October 1896 as H.& B.Boyd Ltd, a subsidiary of the Albion (Burton-on-Trent) Brewery Ltd, which went into voluntary liquidation on 25th October 1901. Acquired by Hunt, Edmunds & Co.Ltd 1919 with 6 tied houses and was closed in 1921.

William Cooke & Sons, *43 Port Street*. Closed 1914 but was still standing as a garage in 1983.

H.W.Rowlands, exors of, *Rowland's Brewery, 69 Bewdley Street*. Founded by Charles Williams 1832 at Bridge Street. Moved to Bewdley Street 1850 and was acquired by Henry Rowlands 1877. Acquired by Flower & Sons Ltd 1930 but continued as ale and wine & spirits merchants until 1939.

Sladden & Collier Ltd, *3 Brick Kiln Street*. Known as Allard & Son until 1878 when it was acquired by Sladden & Co. Registered March 1890. Acquired by the Cheltenham Original Brewery Co.Ltd 1927 and was closed.

Other Breweries
Charles Byrd, *Bridge Street* (1921)
Henry Byrd, *26 Port Street* (1920)
Frederick Charles Evans, *6 Port Street* (1921)
William Thomas Grove, *17 Vine Street* (1921)
Mary Ann Major, *Bridge Street* (1920)
Louis E.Newbury, *26 Vine Street* (1921)
Thomas Osborne, *36 Port Street* (1920)
Herbert Pettitt, *Merstowe Green* (1921)
William Salmon, *High Street* (1921)

Talbot Hotel. Brewing utensils for sale 11th August 1919.
Thomas Taylor, *Bridge Street* (1920)

Fladbury

Fladbury Brewery. Acquired by Hunt, Edmunds & Co.Ltd 1919 with 2 public houses.

Hanbury

Jane Cope (1920)
John Henry Martin, *Valley Brewery* (1902)

Hartlebury

Mrs E. Davis (1923)
Mrs Julia Meades (1940)

Hereford

Hereford & Tredegar Brewery Ltd, *Imperial Brewery, Bewell Street*. Operated by Charles Watkins and was succeeded by Jenkins & Edwards in 1898. Registered August 1899 as the Tredegar & Hereford Brewery Co.Ltd to acquire Jenkins & Edwards and J.T.Jenkins & Co, Church Street, Tredegar. Name changed as above 1902 and brewing was transferred to the Sunlight Brewery which was renamed the Imperial Brewery. Tredegar Brewery closed 1914. Under the control of Allsopps 1900-1902. Acquired by the Cheltenham Original Brewery Co.Ltd 1945 who then changed their name to Cheltenham & Hereford Breweries Ltd. Many of the public houses were sold to Rhymney Breweries Ltd. Brewing ceased at Hereford 1963.

Herefordshire Ales, *86 Broomy Hill*. Founded April 1985 by Dr Chris Tennant & his brother Paul. Closed in the same year.

Frederick James Hockaday, *Angler Brewery, 24/25 Union Street*. Acquired by Charles Watkins & Sons 1898.

R.W.Miller & Co, *City Brewery, Maylord Street*. Acquired by Arnold, Perrett & Co.Ltd 1889 but not closed until 1939.

Charles Watkins & Sons, *Sunlight Brewery, Bewell Street*. Founded 1834. Acquired by the Tredegar & Hereford Brewery Co.Ltd 1899 who then transferred their brewing to here. Brewing ceased 1963.

Other Breweries

William Henry Bryan, *Cambrian Brewery, 14 White Cross Street* (1914)
John Davies, *Ship Brewery*. Acquired by Charles Watkins & Sons March 1890.
Thomas Hill, *47 Commercial Street* (1926)
Hull & Co, *Sun Brewery, 7 Peter Street* (1921)
Lamb Brewery. Acquired by Ind Coope Ltd 1897.

Hopwood

Southan's Hopwood Brewery Co.Ltd, *Redditch Road, Westmead*. Founded 1830. Registered December 1896. Ceased brewing 1956.

Kidderminster

Ellen Gale, *100 Wood Street*. Premises previously occupied by Frederick Tandy. Acquired by Julia Hanson & Sons Ltd 1923.

Kidderminster Brewery Co.Ltd, *Blackwell Street*. Registered 1896 as the Worcestershire Brewing & Malting Co.Ltd to amalgamate: Bucknall's Brewery, Kidderminster founded 1807 and the Delph Brewery, Brierley Hill established 1876, with a total of 126 public houses. Name changed as above July 1905. Acquired by Wolverhampton & Dudley Breweries Ltd 1913 and brewing ceased in 1914. The Delph Brewery is now used by Daniel Batham & Son Ltd.

F.J.Mumford & B.Combe Ltd, *Royal George Brewery, 65 Coventry Street*. Merged with Allen & Son of Worcester 1900.

Radcliffe & Co.Ltd, *Cross Brewery, 96 Worcester Cross*. Registered 1931. Acquired by W.Butler & Co.Ltd of Wolverhampton in 1946.

Frederick Tandy, *100 Wood Street*. Acquired by Julia Hanson & Sons Ltd 1923.

Other Breweries
Jesse Adams, *61 Cobden Street* (1926)
Frederick James Atkinson, *13 Coventry Street* (1926)
Percy J.E.Bent, *19 Stourbridge Street* (1926)
Beatrice May Bird, *46 Worcester Street* (1940)
Joseph Breakwell, *19 Park Butts* (1921)
Margery C.Buttery, *60 Worcester Street* (1940)
George Clarke, *31 Park Lane* (1926)
Frank W.Cope, *103 Bromsgrove Street* (1926)
Agnes E.Edwards, *10 Worcester Street* (1940)
Charles Frost, *11 Park Butts* (1926)
Henry Gale, *42 Queen Street* (1920)
Fanny Glower, *Churchfields* (1920)
Harry Hardiman, *88/90 Bewdley Street* (1920)
William Hollerton, *South Street* (1920)
Harold Hooper, *1 Broad Street* (1940)
Hopkins, Garlick & Co.Ltd, *Mill Street Brewery, 11/12 Mill Street* (1921)
Annie M.Hughes, *3 Worcester Street* (1921)
Thomas Herbert Hunter, *New Road* (1926)
Lionel Gifford Jefford, *72 Lorne Street* (1940)
John Jennings, *1 Stourbridge Street* (1940)
Jabez Jones, *47 Mill Street* (1926)
Arthur Jordan, *Malt Shovel, Chapel Street* (1940)
George Marshall, *4 Comberton Hill* (1926)
Francis Martin, *23 Stourbridge Street* (1940)
Dorothy May Massey, *84 Dudley Street* (1940)
Stanley E.Massey, *Hoo Road* (1940)
Harry Middleton, *91 George Street* (1926)
Charles R.Mitchell, *8 Mill Street* (1926)
Richard H.Newman, *25 Wood Street* (1926)
William Charles Parker, *41 Mill Lane* (1923)
Harry Leonard Peacock, *Blackwell Street* (1920)
E.J.Reynolds, *St.John's Street* (1921)
Harry Richards, *22 Park Lane* (1940)
William J.Rogers, *74 Blackwell Street* (1926)
Francis Smith, *84 Worcester Street* (1940)
Walter Tanser, *24 Horsefair* (1920)
Albert E.Taylor, *84 Blackwell Street* (1930)
George Taylor, *82 Dudley Street* (1920)
James G.Teague, *76 Lea Road* (1926)

Thomas Titley, *76 Broad Street* (1926)
J. William Troth, *1 Wood Street* (1921)
Blanche E.Waite, *81 Offmore Road* (1940)
Ada Walker, *7 Fairfield* (1930)
Elizabeth Wall, *12 George Street* (1920)
Thomas Ward, *113 Coventry Street* (1923)
Edith A.Weavers, *Hoo Road* (1940)
Alice F.Williams, *Stourbridge Street* (1921)
Dora Jane Yates, *Worcester Street* (1923)
George A.Yates, *86 George Street* (1940)

Kington

Mary Carr, *24 Church Street* (1924)
James George, *19 High Street* (1920)
Reuben Hall, *12 High Street* (1923)
Henry Gwynne Hughes, *31 Church Street* (1920)
Edward Jones, *32 Church Street* (1920)
Evan J.Jones, *23 Bridge Street* (1920)
Frederick Jones, *Railway Inn Brewery, Victoria Road* (1940)
Penrhos Brewery, *Penrhos Court, Lyonshall.* Founded 1977 by Martin Griffiths. Ceased brewing December 1983.
William A.Tarrant, *33 Duke Street* (1923)
William Whislade, *Bridge Street* (1920)

Ledbury

Elizabeth Gurney, *White Hart Brewery* (1920)
Ernest Hambler Hopkins, *Royal Oak Brewery* (1902)
Thomas Harry Howard, *Plough Brewery, Homend Street* (1902)
Frank James, *Bye Street* (1923)
Lane Brothers & Bastow, *Vine Brewery, New Street.* Acquired by the Cheltenham Original Brewery Co.Ltd 1919.

Leigh Sinton

Bailey's Brewing Company, *Cowcroft.* Founded 1983 by Tim Bailey. Ceased brewing October 1985.
Malvern Chase Brewery Ltd, *The Coach House, Sherridge.* Founded 1981 by Michael Fass. Bought by Peter Norbury 1983. Ceased brewing 1984.

Leominster

John J.Biddle, *61 Etnam Street* (1926)
Joe Grimmer, *24 School Lane* (1920)
Paxton & Co, *Leominster Brewery, 38 South Street.* Originally owned by Alexander McNish formerly a partner in Paine & Co.Ltd of St.Neots until 1896. Acquired by the Hereford & Tredegar Brewery Ltd 1926.

Malvern

Jones & Davis, *Link Brewery.* Offered for sale 11th November 1925 and was sold to Lewis Clarkes of Worcester with 2 tied houses.
Royal Well Brewery Co.Ltd, *Royal Well Brewery, West Malvern.* Registered 1897 as Homfray's Brewery Ltd to acquire the business of the late Joseph Henry Edward Tyler. Voluntary liquidation February 1901. New company registered as above May 1903 to acquire the Royal Well Brewery and Allen Brothers. Brewery and 26 public houses offered for auction 21st July 1930, 19 of the houses being sold for £29,165. Went into voluntary liquidation 26th March 1931.
Other Breweries

Allen Brothers, *Brompton.* Formed part of the Royal Well Brewery Co.Ltd 1902.
Samuel Bullus, *Morton Road, Malvern Link* (1921)
John Herbert Jones, *Worcester Road* (1921)
Thomas Morris, *Lower Howsell, Malvern Link* (1921)

Nether End

Henry Herring (1935)
George Johnson (1926)

Newnham Bridge

Bartlett's Brewery, *The Tavern.* Founded September 1981 by Bob Bartlett. Ceased brewing 1986.

Pershore

W.H.Knight, *White Horse Brewery, Church Street.* Acquired by Hunt, Edmunds & Co.Ltd 1919 with 4 tied houses and was closed.

Redditch

Brown & Co, *Shakespeare Brewery, Evesham Street.* Acquired by Ind Coope Ltd 1915.

Ross-on-Wye

Alton Court Brewery Co.Ltd, *Station Street.* Founded 1846. Registered 1865. Acquired by the Stroud Brewery Co.Ltd 1956 and was closed. Liquidated May 1961.
Charles F.Sutcliffe, *Barrel Brewery, Brookend Street* (1930)

Sedgeberrow

Henry Ginnell (1902)

Stoke Prior

Eleanor Crumpton (1921)

Stourport

Ellen Butler, *Areley Kings* (1940)
Walter Ernest Dalley, *Mill Road* (1923)
Ida V.Doughty, *39 High Street* (1940)
Sydney Marshall Glover, *Lion Hill* (1930)
Harold V.Hardwick, *1 Lombard Road* (1940)
Frederick Notts, *Areley Common* (1921)
George R.Robinson, *Worcester Road* (1940)
Sidney Wilcox, *17 Lion Hill* (1921)
Charles Wild, *39 Mitton Street* (1923)

Tenbury Wells

John Sydney Davies, *King's Head. Cross Street* (1926)
Henry Charles Hucker, *Tame Street* (1940)
Samuel Mattock, *Market Street* (1920)
Arthur Powis (1920)

Upton-on-Severn

Edwards & Co, *High Street* (1920)
Hannah Harrison, *Waterside* (1921)
Edward James Oakley, *New Street* (1921)

Jolly Roger Brewery, *Old Anchor Inn, High Street.* Home brew house founded by Paul & Martin Soden June 1983. Sold to Chris Callaghan 1985. Closed 1987.

Upton Snodsbury

Arthur Bullock, *Royal Brewery.* Acquired by Rushton's Brewery Ltd of Birmingham 1906.

Welland

Elizabeth Vevian (1910)

Wilden

Hiram Jay (1926)

Worcester

Allen Brothers, *The Breweries, Angel Street.* See also:- Malvern.
Robert Allen & Co.Ltd, *Barbourne Brewery, New Bank Street.* Registered 1900 as Robert Allen, Mumford & Co.Ltd to acquire Robert Allen & Son, Barbourne Brewery; F.J.Mumford & B.Combe Ltd., Royal George Brewery, Kidderminster. Name changed as above November 1903. Acquired by Wolverhampton & Dudley Breweries Ltd December 1928. Premises still used as a depot.
Lewis Clarkes Ltd, *Angel Place.* Founded 1846. Registered May 1929. Acquired by Marston, Thompson & Evershed Ltd 1937 and brewing ceased.
Harper's Hitchman's Ltd, *Lowesmoor Brewery.* Private company registered July 1917 as a subsidiary of Hitchmnan & Co.Ltd of Chipping Norton. Acquired by Hunt, Edmunds & Co.Ltd 1924 with 13 public houses. Brewing ceased 1929.
William Prosser, *Bull's Head, 32 High Street.* Acquired by Robert Allen & Co.Ltd 1907.

Spreckley Brothers Ltd, *Worcester Brewery, Barbourne Road.* Spreckley Brothers acquired Stallard's Britannia Brewery with 7 tied houses in 1884 and the title was changed to the Worcester Brewery. Registered June 1897 to acquire Spreckley Brothers & George Joseland & Sons with 57 public houses. Acquired by Cheltenham & Hereford Breweries Ltd 1958 with 68 tied houses. Brewing ceased 1960 and was liquidated in the same year.
Other Breweries

William Abbott, *41 Hylton Road* (1921)
Leah Barrington Andrews, *4/8 Barbourne Road* (1920)
Alfred Ayres, *Little Angel Street* (1935)
Sarah Badgery, *Tallow Hill* (1921)
Alfred T.Barker, *26 James Street* (1940)
George H.Barnes, *Vine Street* (1926)
Elizabeth Bearcroft, *Fish Street* (1921)
Arthur Beasant, *The Tything* (1921)
Sarah Bird, *Little Angel Street* (1930)
William Martin Bird, *Mill Street, Diglis* (1930)
Leah Blake, *8 Little Park Street* (1940)
Ada Marguerite Blunt, *Shrub Hill* (1921)
Fanny Bough, *Providence Street* (1926)
William Bowcott, *London Road* (1940)
Edward Brown, *Cumberland Street* (1923)
Percy Edgar Collier, *Severn Street* (1940)
Jane Copson, *Vine Street, Ombersley Road* (1920)
Norman M.Cragg, *Droitwich Road* (1940)
John Denning, *Moorfields* (1923)
Nellie Dredge, *Northfield Street* (1940)
Alfred H.Foakes, *Severn Street* (1920)
Arthur Edward Hale, *53 Lowesmoor* (1930)

Frederick George Hale, *Merryvale* (1940)
Arthur J.Hales, *2 Lowesmoor* (1935)
Jesse Harper, *Newport Street* (1920)
Frederick Harris, *London Road* (1923)
George Harrison, *40 Tything* (1940)
Lester Henney, *Waterloo Street* (1923)
Arthur Speller Horton, *Five Ways Brewery, Angel Place* (1926)
Cecil George Instan, *Lowesmoor* (1940)
Frederick Daniel Jones, *Loves Grove* (1923)
Walter H.Jones, *George Street* (1920)
Edward Knight, *Quay Street* (1930)
Florence Edith Lee, *Silver Street* (1926)
Henry Lock, *North Hallow* (1940)
Laura Moore, *Moors* (1940)
Sydney Alfred Naish, *26 Southfield Street* (1940)
Sam Osborne (1926)
Maria Perkins, *Bransford Road* (1921) and *109 Sidbury* (1926)
Joseph William Pittock, *Powick Lane* (1940)
Harriett Poutney, *School Road, St.John's* (1926)
Edward Price, *Little Angel Street* (1923)
Edward Henry Price, *Droitwich Road* (1926)

Harry Price, *10 Cromwell Street* (1926)
Harry Ranford, *Cannon Street* (1940)
Annie Rencher, *Newport Street* (1930)
Henry Joseph Richards, *25 Pheasant Street* (1940)
John H.Richards, *Bransford Road* (1940)
Frederick J.Roberts, *1 Sidbury* (1920)
William Roberts, *Saracen's Head, Tything* (1930)
Arthur C.Scott, *Bromyard Road* (1940)
Bessie Sefton, *Newport Street* (1940)
Annie Shaw, *Foundry Street* (1921)
Bert Shepherd, *36 & 84 Tybridge Street* (1940)
Joseph Shipton, *Fish Street* (1921)
William Silk, *London Road* (1920)
Catherine Simmonds, *Lowesmoor* (1921)
John Smith, *Sansome Place* (1935)
Sidney Albert Smith, *51 The Tything* (1923)
William Smith, *Malvern Road, St.John's* (1930)
Richard Thompson, *32 James Street* (1921)
Matthew John Tolley, *18 Pitmarston Road, St.John's* (1940)
William Tolley, *Shrub Hill* (1920)
Lucy Jane Treadwell, *48 New Street* (1923)

HERTFORDSHIRE

Ashwell

E.K.& H.Fordham Ltd. Founded about 1832. Registered March 1897 with 124 public houses. Acquired by J.W.Green Ltd 1952 and became a bottling stores which was closed 1965. Flats and houses built on the site 1969.

J.R.Page & Co, *Westbury Brewery.* Founded 1843 by Benjamin Christy and John Sale at Westbury Farm and acquired by J.R.Page, a Baldock maltster, in 1879. Acquired by Wells & Winch Ltd 1921 with 26 tied houses. The Baldock maltings sold to Paine & Co.Ltd of St.Neots in the same year.

Baldock

Baldock Brewery Ltd, *Pale Ale Brewery, Norton Street.* Founded 1823 when William Oliver leased the brewery to John Steed. Bought by William Pickering 1889 with about 60 public houses which were largely disposed of in 1895. Registered February 1898. Acquired by Wells & Winch Ltd 1904 with 22 tied houses and brewing ceased but used as a depot until 1912.

Simpson's Brewery Ltd, *High Street.* Founded in the 1730s when it was owned by John Thurgood. Leased by the Pryor family 1775 before buying it outright 1799, and owned it until 1853 when it was bought by Joseph & Thomas George Simpson, nephews of John Phillips of the Royston Brewery. Private company registered March 1935. To avoid death duties sold to Greene King & Sons Ltd 1954 for £525,000 and was closed 1965. Sold to Baldock U.D.C. 1966 and demolished 1968 to make way for a housing estate.

Barkway

John Johnson Balding, *High Street.* Brewing c.1862-1908. Their 2 public houses were acquired by J.& J.E.Phillips Ltd of Royston.

Barley

Fox & Hounds, *High Street.* Home brew house founded July 1982. Still in operation 1990.

Berkhamsted

Foster's Swan Brewery, *High Street.* Founded 1797 at the Swan Inn dating at least from 1607. Acquired by T.J.Nash of Chesham 1897 with 9 public houses. Brewing may have continued until about 1901.

Locke & Smith Ltd, *Water Lane.* Founded 1868 when they acquired the business of Alfred Healey. Registered January 1897 with 42 public houses. Receiver appointed 30th June 1911, and after a legal dispute the brewery was offered for sale for a second time in June 1913 and was bought by Benskin's Watford Brewery Ltd for £37,600.

Bishop's Stortford

Bailey Brothers, *Fox Brewery, Dunmow Road.* Founded by 1886. Acquired by Benskin's Watford Brewery Ltd 1915 with one off-licence.

Hawkes & Co, *Water Lane.* Brewery built 1780. Acquired by James Wigan, formerly of the Mortlake Brewery, in 1876 but continued under the same name. Acquired by Benskin's Watford Brewery Ltd 1898 with 157 public houses. The brewery seems to have remained in operation until 1921 and was continued as a depot until 1987. Buildings demolished 1992.

Borehamwood

Elstree Star Brewery Ltd, *Star Brewery.* Founded by Alfred Parkins by 1889. By 1891 it was called the Borehamwood Brewery, but by the time Parkins died in 1909, it was known as the Star Brewery. Registered as above 26th May 1909. Receiver appointed 5th October 1911 and the company was dissolved 6th July 1920. Premises became offices for Shorts Lifts Ltd.

Bourne End

Berkhamsted Brewery, *Bourne End Lane.* Sample brewery founded in the premises of Inn Brewing 1983. Still in operation 1990.

Frithsden

Alford Arms. Whitbread's first home brew house founded August 1981. Still brewing in 1990.

Furneux Pelham

Rayment & Co.Ltd, *Pelham Brewery.* William Rayment brewed and farmed at Furneux Pelham from the 1820s. New brewery built 1860. Acquired privately by King & Lake, partners in Greene King December 1888 and was run separately until officially merged with Greene King in 1931. Private company registered 1912. 36 public houses. Brewery closed 9th October 1987.

Harpenden

Benjamin Bennett, *Harpenden Brewery, High Street.* Founded by James Curtis c.1837. Owned by the Healey family of Watford from 1853 and was leased to Benjamin Bennett of Dunstable from about 1872 to 1893 when it was acquired by Glover & Sons.

Glover & Sons Ltd, *Peacock Brewery, High Street.* Founded by the House family about 1838. Acquired by James Mardell soon after 1871. Sold to Richard Glover of the Wenlock Brewery, Islington, London 1897. Registered 1898 with 40 public houses. Merged with Pryor, Reid & Co.Ltd of Hatfield 1902 to form Hatfield & Harpenden Breweries Ltd. Sold separately to J.W.Green Ltd of Luton 1919 with 19 of their public houses and was closed. Brewery demolished 1936.

Hatfield

Charles Bradshaw, *Newtown Brewery, Hatfield Newtown.* Founded c.1850. Acquired by Pryor, Reid & Co. August 1888 with 3 tied houses.

Pryor, Reid & Co.Ltd. Developed from the Chequers Inn, owned by the Searancke family from about 1635. Eventually acquired by Pryors of the Baldock High Street brewery, who about 1882 went into partnership with the son of the founder of Reid's brewery, London. Merged with Glover & Sons Ltd of Harpenden 1902 but run separately until sold to Benskin's Watford Brewery 1920 for £190,000 with 105 tied houses.

Hemel Hempstead

John Mayo Biggs, *Star Brewery, 23/25 Bury Road, Boxmoor*. James Elliott brewing from at least 1859. Sold to Biggs 1915 but closed in the following year.

Henry Wyman, *Anchor Brewery, Bury Road, Boxmoor*. Founded 1854. Wyman & Hall from 1878 and Henry Wyman from 1884. Acquired by T.J.Nash of Chesham 1891 with at least 8 tied houses.

Hertford

William Baker & Sons, *Hope Brewery, 26 Old Cross*. Originally a maltings acquired by William Baker c.1831 and converted into a brewery. Acquired by McMullens December 1920 with 20 public houses and used as a mineral water factory and offices from 1927. Most of the buildings have gone but part is still used as offices.

Percy Hargreaves & Co, *Crown Brewery, Railway Place*. A branch of the Abridge Brewery, Essex acquired by Hargreaves 1886. By 1895 had become stores and was offered for sale with 9 tied houses December 1895. Benskins bought the brewery and the Saracen's Head for £1,800 but do not seem to have brewed here. The other houses went to various brewers.

McMullen & Sons Ltd, *Hertford Brewery, Hartham Lane*. Founded 1827 at Railway Street by Peter McMullen. Moved to Mill Bridge 1832 and Hartham Lane brewery built 1891. Registered March 1897 with 90 public houses. Still brewing independently 1990 with 160 tied houses.

W.H.& G.Nicholls, *4 West Street*. Brewing began by 1850. 5 public houses. Also specialised in supplying large country houses in the area. Brewing ceased November 1965 when the brewery was bought by the County Council and was demolished 1967 for a road scheme.

E.J.Wickham, *Mill Bridge Brewery, 7 Mill Bridge*. Founded 1829 when Edward Wickham bought Ireland's brewery. E.J.Wickham was the brother of William Wickham of the Ware Brewery. Acquired by Wells & Winch Ltd April 1938 with 7 tied houses. Brewery destroyed by a flying bomb 1944.

Benjamin Young & Co, *Fore Street*. Founded 1754. Acquired by Pryor, Reid & Co. October 1893 with 48 public houses and brewing ceased.

Hitchin

William Chapman, *The Peacock, 20 Queen Street*. A home brew house in operation 1859-1902. On 3rd June 1903 the Peacock Brewery and pub were sold, with the brewery realising £1,000. Acquired by the Herts & Essex Public House Trust in October 1906.

W.S.Lucas Ltd, *Sun Street*. Established 1709. Registered 1898. Acquired by J.W.Green Ltd 1921 with 52 tied houses. Closed 1923 and brewery demolished 1963.

George Rochford, *Sun Hotel*. A home brew house in operation 1902.

Hoddesdon

Christie & Co.Ltd, *High Street*. Founded by the Plomer family c.1700. Acquired by Christie & Cathrow 1803 with 7 public houses. Registered 1903. Acquired by the Cannon Brewery Co.Ltd of London 1927 with 159 tied houses. The brewery contents were sold by auction 30th May 1928. Part was demolished except for the offices which became flats and shops.

Ickleford

John Foster, *Mayfield Villa, Arlesey Road*. Originally a beer retailer but was brewing by 1871 until at least 1895 at the brew house behind Mayfield Villa.

Kimpton

George Chalkley, *Lion Brewery*. Founded by Joseph Kingsley c.1835 and was under various names until 1862 when the brewery was put up for sale and Pryor, Reid bought the public houses, but the brewery was not sold and stood empty for 2 years. Owned by Hornsey & Co. by 1899. Registered as the Hertfordshire Brewery Co.Ltd 27th June 1900 to acquire Hornsey & Co. Offered for auction January 1901 with 2 public houses: The Greyhound, Kimpton and the Plough Inn, Egginton and was bought by Brass & Abbott. George Chalkley was the owner by 1906 and was closed c.1911 and converted into a laundry. Has recently been used as an arts centre.

King's Langley

John Edward Groome. Founded 1767. The owner retired 1897 and the brewery was sold by auction with 32 public houses to Benskin's Watford Brewery Ltd for £64,000 in October 1897.

Swannell's Brewery, *Numbers Farm, Station Road*. Founded November 1982 by Alan Swannell. Ceased brewing 1983.

Lilley

Mickles Brewery, *Dog Kennel Farm, Hitchin Road*. See also:- Walkern.

Little Gadesden

Bridgewater Arms. Home brew house founded October 1981 at the pub which ran its own brewery in the 19th Century. Still in operation 1990.

Little Hadham

Drake & Lawson, *Nag's Head*. A home brew house acquired by Rayment & Co.Ltd 1912.

Puckeridge

Puckeridge Brewery Ltd. Registered September 1892 to acquire the business carried on by Charles & Edwin Chapman as Chapman & Co. The lease of the brewery and its attached off-licence was sold at the Dimsdale Arms, Hertford on 1st October 1898 although a court order had wound up the company on 19th February 1894. Dissolved 27th August 1907.

Redbourn

Benjamin Bennett. Founded as the Bull Inn home brew house. Thomas & John Edwards had at least nine tied houses in 1878. Benjamin Bennett of the Dunstable Brewery acquired the lease of the brewery and the public houses in March 1879. Offered for auction March 1900, but no buyer was found for the brewery and the pubs went to various local brewers, such as the Bull to McMullens.

Rickmansworth

Salter & Co.Ltd, *Rickmansworth Brewery, High Street*. Founded by 1741. Registered December 1889 to acquire Salter & Co. Acquired by the Cannon Brewery Co.Ltd of London 1924 with 76 tied houses and was closed. Brewery used for various purposes until demolished 1972 and an office block built on the site.

Thomas Wild & Sons, *Mill End Brewery*. Founded c.1870. Acquired by Sedgwick & Co. of Watford 1900 with two public houses. Continued as mineral water manufacturers and beer dealers and was later used as a laundry.

Royston

J.& J.E.Phillips Ltd, *Baldock Street*. Founded by the Phillips family some time after 1725. Registered November 1897 and took over the businesses of J.& J.E.Phillips and P.A.Meyer of Orwell, Cambs. Acquired by J.W.Green Ltd 1949 with 150 tied houses. The brewery was later used by a wholesale confectionery manufacturer.

St.Albans

Adey & White Ltd, *St.Albans Brewery, Chequer Street*. Founded by the Kinder family by 1737. Acquired by Adey & White 1868. They also brewed at St.Peter's Brewery 1878-1902. Private company registered 1921. Acquired by J.W.Green Ltd May 1936 with 56 public houses and was closed in July of that year. Most of the buildings were demolished.

T.W.Kent & Son, *Holywell Brewery, Holywell Hill.* Founded 1826. Acquired by Adey & White 1918 with 8 tied houses and was closed.

Kingsbury (St.Albans) Brewery Co.Ltd, *Verulam Road.* Possibly founded by 1722. Registered December 1894 to acquire the business of William Bingham Cox, who had bought it in 1889, with 52 public houses, and also to acquire from T.O.Pugh, the Peckham Road Brewery, Camberwell, London with 13 tied houses and the Camberwell Distillery, Addington Square. T.O.Pugh was made managing director. Acquired by Benskin's Watford Brewery Ltd November 1897 with 34 public houses.

Sandon

W.R.Baker, *Hyde Hall Farm.* A commercial farm brewery founded by 1846. Acquired by Fordhams of Ashwell 1898 and was closed in 1899.

Sawbridgeworth

George Rochester, *William IV public house.* Brewing at the pub from about 1852 to 1865, from 1866 the William IV was a Christie's tied house and was acquired by McMullens 1872. However, Rochester carried on as a brewer in Knight Street, followed by his son Henry until at least 1906, presumably supplying off-sales only. Brewery still standing as the Masonic Hall.

Tring

Frederick William Brown, *Tring Brewery, 24 High Street.* Founded by John Brown 1826. Sold to Locke & Smith Ltd of Berkhamsted 1898 and the brewery became a slaughterhouse.

William Jesse Rodwell, *Akeman Street.* Started by John Batchelor in Hastoe about 1852 and moved to Akeman Street c.1872. Batchelor & Rodwell from about 1894-1898. Ceased brewing 1923 and most of the public houses were sold, the last five going to Meux's Brewery Co.Ltd in 1935. In existence as mineral water manufacturers 1985.

Walkern

Mickles Brewery, *Victoria Brewery Maltings, High Street.* Founded at Lilley 1982 and moved to Walkern 1983 into Samuel Wright's former brewery. Ceased brewing October 1984.

S.Wright & Co, *Victoria Brewery.* Founded by 1866. Brewing ceased 1924 and their 12 public houses were sold to Simpson's Brewery Ltd of Baldock. Cider production continued until 1955.

Ware

Silas Barker, *25 New Road.* Brewing commenced c.1878. Acquired by Christie & Lucas, the wine & spirit side of Christie & Co.Ltd of Hoddesdon, in 1929. Brewing continued for a few months. Silas Barker carried on as a beer retailer until about 1933. In 1936 the Ware Brewery Co. operated here for a year. It was owned by Herbert Lynn and was registered as the Ware Brewery Co.Ltd on 25th November 1946. They had transferred to the Star Brewery in 1937 where they continued until 1951. Bought by Wells & Winch 1952. Still extant behind the Old Two Brewers public house.

John Jeffrey, *Bridge Foot.* Brewing 1890-1902.

William Wickham, *Star Brewery, Watton Road.* Founded by Caleb Hitch in 1862. Leased to Isaac Everitt in 1872 and bought by McMullens in November 1874. Leased to William Wickham, elder brother of Edward Wickham of Hertford, in 1878. Brewery still standing and being used as a builders merchants. Date on foundation stone confirms 1862.

Watford

Benskin's Watford Brewery Ltd, *Cannon Brewery, 194 High Street.* Founded by 1722 by John Pope at New Street. Moved by his great-grandson, John Dyson to 194 High Street about 1820. Bought by Joseph Benskin 1867 with 42 public houses for £34,000. Registered July 1894. Acquired by Ind Coope Ltd 1957 and brewing ceased 1972. 636 tied

houses. The brewery buildings were demolished 1978 but the offices were converted into the Watford Museum.

E.J.& C.Healy Ltd, *King Street.* Founded 1851. Registered February 1893. Acquired by Benskins 1898 with 15 tied houses. The brewery is now Pickford's Repository.

M.A.Sedgwick & Co, *High Street.* Probably founded by the Smith family about the middle of the 18th Century. Bought by William Fellowes Sedgwick 1862. Acquired by their neighbours, Benskins on 23rd November 1923 with 97 public houses and was converted into maltings 1927. Demolished 1965-66.

Well's Watford Brewery Ltd, *Lion Brewery, St.Albans Road.* Brewery built June 1890 by Ralph Thorpe. Registered 25th April 1925 to acquire Wells & Co. with 20 tied houses. Acquired by Benskins 1951.

Welwyn

Alfred Edward Macalister Hadwen, *Welwyn Brewery, School Lane.* Founded by 1833. Under the control of Mews' of the Newport Brewery, Isle of Wight 1892-95. Sold to McMullens with the Fox public house in March 1897 for £245. Brewery still in use as a store.

Wheathampstead

Chambers & Co, *Hope Brewery.* Brewery built 1781. Acquired by Chambers c.1902 with 7 tied houses. Offered for sale November 1904.

HIGHLAND

Inverness

Alice Brewery, *Harbour Road.* Founded by Oliver Griffin & Roger Duncan 1983. Possibly closed 1988.

Guild & Co, *Thornbush Brewery, Kessock Road.* Sold by auction 3rd December 1913 for £1,000. Brewery dating from c.1840 later used as a seed store.

Highland Brewery Co.Ltd, *Haugh Brewery, Haugh Road.* Registered January 1914 to acquire the Highland Brewery, formerly Richard Buchanan &

Co. Closed 1920.

Nairn

Ainslie & Co. *Nairn Brewery* (1902)

Barmston

William Hought (1892)

Barrow-upon-Humber

Schofield & Dannatt (1895)

Barton-upon-Humber

Hunt & Son, *Anchor Brewery, Pasture Road* (1910)

Beverley

Martin Henry Cross (1892)

J.R.Spencer, *Steam Brewery, Ladygate*. Acquired by Simpson & Co. of Market Weighton 1895.

R.Stephenson & Son, *Golden Ball Brewery, Walkergate*. Acquired by the Hull Brewery Co.Ltd 1920 with 13 tied houses.

Bridlington

Haggitt & Co, *Old Original Brewery, 71 High Street*. Brewery plant offered for sale 20th March 1890 by order of John Smith's Tadcaster Brewery.

Mary Catherine Simpson (exors of), *Promenade* (1892)

Brigg

A.M.& E.Sergeant & Co.Ltd, *Bridge Street*. Founded 1832. Registered 1928. Acquired by Hewitt Brothers Ltd of Grimsby 1954 and brewing ceased 1968.

Sutton & Bean Ltd, *Britannia Brewery, Queen Street*. Acquired by the Hull Brewery Co.Ltd 1925 with 17 public houses.

Cottingham

Henry & William Thurlow, *Hallgate* (1892)

Crowle

James Fox & Sons Ltd, *Isle of Axholme Brewery, Brewery Avenue*. Founded 1856. Private company registered July 1917. Bought by the Barnsley Brewery Co.Ltd 1949 with 40 tied houses.

New Trent Brewery Co.Ltd, *New Trent Brewery, Spen Lane*. Registered 1911 to acquire the business of John Dymond. Closed for financial reasons 1915 and their 36 public houses were supplied by the Barnsley Brewery Co.Ltd who gained control in 1918.

Goole

Icon Heppenstall & Son, *24 North Street*. Originally known as Frederick Pemberton and was sold to Samuel Allsopp & Son Ltd 1897 and resold to Heppenstall 1901. Closed 1939.

Old Mill Brewery, *Mill Street, Snaith*. Founded June 1983 by Bryan Wilson. Still brewing 1990 with 3 tied houses.

Great Driffield

Thomas Holtby, *Eastgate North*. Acquired by John Smith's Tadcaster Brewery Co.Ltd 1895.

John William Turner, *Market Place*. Acquired by John Smith's Tadcaster Brewery Co.Ltd 1897.

Grimsby

John Jack Darnill, *Grainthorpe*. (1895)

Robert Gale, *Humber Brewery*. Acquired by Hewitt Brothers Ltd 1891.

C.A.Guy & Co, *1 Flottergate*. Acquired by Moors & Robsons Breweries Ltd 1919.

Hewitt Brothers Ltd, *Tower Brewery, Pasture Street*. Founded before 1808. Registered March 1888 and public company formed 1934. Acquired by by United Breweries Ltd 1961 with 320 public houses. Brewery closed 19th April 1968.

Lewis & Barker, *Wellow Brewery, Wellowgate*. Founded 1802. Acquired by the Nottingham Brewery Ltd 1900 with 19 tied houses. Closed 1944.

Willy's, *17 Highcliffe Road, Cleethorpes*. New brewery opened May 1989.

Hedon

Mary Elizabeth Cautley, *Eagle Brewery* (1892)

Hessle

Thomas Dewhirst (1898)
Edward T.Saunders (1914)

Hull

Brodrick & Peters, *59 Wincolmlee*. Partnership dissolved 5th November 1895. Brewing ceased 1928.

Martin Henry Cross, *Osborne Brewery, 86 Osborne Street*. Acquired by the Hull Brewery Co.Ltd 1890.

William Glossop & Bulay Ltd, *Globe Brewery, Northumberland Avenue*. Registered 1898 as William Glossop Ltd. Acquired by the Hull Brewery Co.Ltd 1920.

Hull Brewery Company, *English Street, Hessle Road*. New brewery opened late 1989. Still brewing 1990.

Hull Brewery Co.Ltd. See also:- North Country Breweries Ltd.

Minerva Brewery, *Nelson Street*. A Joshua Tetley home brew house founded 1985. Still brewing 1990.

Moors' & Robsons' Breweries Ltd, *Crown Brewery, Francis Street*. Registered March 1888 as Hull United Breweries Ltd to acquire Henry & Charles Moor, Crown Brewery and Edward Robson, Waterwork Street, at a purchase price of £310,000. Name changed June 1888. Acquired by Hewitt Brothers Ltd 1960 with 138 tied houses and was closed.

North Country Breweries Ltd, *Anchor Brewery, Silvester Street*. Founded 1765 as John Ward's Brewery, Dagger Lane. Moved to Anchor Brewery 1868. Registered January 1888 as the Hull Brewery Co.Ltd to acquire Gleadow, Dibb & Co.Ltd. Acquired by Northern Dairies Ltd 1971 with 212 tied houses and name changed as above. Bought by the Mansfield Brewery Co.Ltd May 1985 and brewing ceased.

Smith's Brewery Co.Ltd, *Green Lane*. Acquired by Worthington & Co.Ltd 1901 with 40/50 tied houses.

H.& J.G.Smithson Ltd, *Tower Brewery, Waverley Street*. Acquired by the Hull Brewery Co.Ltd 1896.

Other Breweries

Goodson Brothers Ltd, *Victoria Brewery, Bowlalley Lane* (1892)

W.Low & Co

William Wilson, *56 Somerset Street* (1910)

Keyingham

James Jackson (1910)

Kilham

Francis Boynton (1902)
Richard Knaggs (1895)

Kirton-in-Lindsay

Edward E.Duckering, *High Street* (1910)

Leven

Jane Turnbull (1914)

Market Weighton

Simpson & Co. Founded before 1888. Acquired by John Smith's Tadcaster Brewery Co.Ltd 1899 with 51 public houses.

Pocklington

Robert Cattle & Co, *Old Brewery, Chapmangate*. Brewery and 10 tied houses bought by the Tadcaster Tower Brewery Co.Ltd 27th October 1921. In 1924 the Yorkshire Clubs Brewery was founded here and occupied the premises until moving to York in 1933.

George Scaife, *New Pavement* (1895)

Young & Co, *Waterloo Brewery, Chapmangate* (1910)

Scunthorpe

William Brunt, *53 Manley Street*. Acquired by Sutton & Bean Ltd of Brigg 1900.

West Cowick

Hartley's Brewery Co.Ltd, *Crown Brewery*. Founded 1850 by J.& T.Hartley. Acquired by the Hull Brewery Co.Ltd 1957 with 27 public houses and was closed.

Winteringham

Henry Grassby, *Tinkle Brewery* (1898)

ISLE OF MAN

Castletown

Castletown Brewery Ltd, *Victoria Road.* Registered 1920 as the Castletown Brewery (1920) Ltd and was controlled by the Cain family. Acquired by Hope & Anchor Breweries Ltd, Sheffield in 1946. Re-registered as above January 1948 to acquire the Castletown Brewery and Clinch & Co.Ltd. Merged with Okell & Sons Ltd 1986 to form Isle of Man Breweries Ltd. 34 public houses.

Douglas

Bushy's Brew Pub, *Victoria Street.* Founded 1986. Still brewing 1990 with 1 tied house.

Clinch & Co.Ltd, *Lake Brewery.* Founded 1779. Registered August 1897. Acquired by J.W.Clinch 1868. Acquired by the Castletown Brewery Ltd in 1948.

Thomas Kewley Ltd, *Ridgeway Street.* Acquired by Ind Coope Ltd 1902.

Okell & Sons Ltd, *Falcon Brewery.* Founded by William Okell 1850. Acquired by Heron & Brearley, wine & spirit merchants 1972. Merged with the Castletown Brewery Ltd 1986 to form Isle of Man Breweries Ltd. 71 tied houses.

ISLE OF WIGHT

Brading

William Clare Wright. Home brew house acquired by Mew, Langton & Co.Ltd in 1923.

Chale

Sprake Brothers, *Star Brewery.* Founded by Robert Sprake 1833. Acquired by Brickwoods Ltd 1928 with 6 tied houses. Ceased brewing April 1934.

Freshwater Bay

John Emberley & Sons, *Church Place* (1902)

Newport

Charles James Dashwood, *Carisbrooke Brewery, Castle Street.* Acquired by Mew, Langton & Co.Ltd 1910.

W.B.Mew, Langton & Co.Ltd, *Royal Brewery, Crocker Street.* Founded by 1814. Registered December 1888. Acquired by Strong & Co.Ltd 1965 and brewing ceased in 1969.

Frank Saunders, *Coppin's Brewery, Coppin's Bridge.* Bankrupt 1912.

Ryde

James Garland Duffett, *181 High Street.* Acquired by Brickwoods Ltd 1921.

Henry Charles & Walter Sweetman, *George Street Brewery.* Acquired by Mew, Langton & Co.Ltd 1920.

Shanklin

Shanklin Brewery Co.Ltd, *Rectory Road.* Bought by Frank Saunders of Coppin's Brewery, Newport 1902 and was acquired by Herbert Hoare in 1913 and was known as H.Hoare & Son until registered as above in 1945. Brewing ceased in 1953.

Ventnor

Burt & Co, *High Street.* Founded 1840. Acquired by Albert Phillips in 1906 and continued trading under the name of Burts until 1992 when brewing ceased. Acquired by Hartridges. Brewing transferred to the Island Brewery, Newport.

West Cowes

William Waterman, *St.Mary's Brewery, St.Mary's Street.* Acquired by Brickwoods Ltd 1919.

Yarbridge

Isle of Wight Brewery Co.Ltd. Founded c.1860. Registered April 1896 to acquire the Yarbridge Brewery Co. Offered for sale 11th January 1900.

KENT

Ash

Gardner & Co.Ltd, *Ash Brewery.* Founded 1837 when John Bushell converted the parish workhouse into a brewery. Acquired by William Gardner 1840 with 49 tied houses. Traded as Gardner & Godden from 1855. Registered 1898. Amalgamated with Tomson & Wotton Ltd of Ramsgate 1951 to form Combined Breweries (Holdings) Ltd, which was acquired by Whitbread & Co.Ltd June 1968. Brewing ceased at Ash in 1954, although ginger beer production continued until 1962. Brewhouse demolished but some buildings remain.

Ashford

Ashford Brewing Co.Ltd, *Units 125/26, Ellingham Way.* Founded by Roger Spence January 1983. Ceased trading in October and acquired by David Butler and Christopher Stamp in February 1984. Purchased by Sapphire Ltd October 1985 and merged with the Royal Tunbridge Wells Brewery to form Kentish Ales and brewing ceased 1985.

Ashford Breweries Ltd, *Lion Brewery, Dover Place.* The Lion Brewery was established 1850 and traded as Green & Laud. Sold by Sharman & Cooper to a Mr.Newport 1866. Thomas Chapman & Sons, whose brewery at Lenham had been established by a Mr Mercer in 1785, purchased the Lion Brewery in 1868 and the Lenham brewery was closed. New brewery erected after a fire in November 1869. Above style registered September 1898 to acquire Chapmans and W.M.Richardson's Original Brewery. Acquired by Style & Winch Ltd in 1912 and premises used as stores until 1921 when converted for the production of cider by Ashford Valley Cider Co.Ltd. Brewery demolished 1971.

Packhorse Brewery, *Folkestone Road.* Established 1990 by Roger Quinn & Chris Butler to brew lager only for Flatfoot Sam's pub and Gale's nightclub in a converted flour mill dating from 1901.

Walter M.Richardson, *Original Brewery, Brewer Street.* Established prior to 1847 by Thomas Lewis Elliot. Acquired by W.M.Richardson after Elliot's bankruptcy in 1888. Acquired by T.Chapman & Sons 1895.

Aylesford

Metropolitan & Home Counties Clubs Brewery, *Anchor Brewery, Aylesford.* Founded by Henry Baker at the Anchor Inn c.1840. Known as Thomas

-43-

Danes & Son until 1920 when registered as the Medway Federation of Clubs Brewery Ltd. Name changed as above 1944. The Northants & Leicestershire Clubs Brewery supplied the beer from 1946 until Fremlins took over the club trade. Bankrupt 1956. The buildings have been mainly demolished.

Broadstairs

Charles Frederick Wacher, *The Brewery, Crowhill* (1872-1895)

Canterbury

Ash & Co, *Dane John Brewery, St.John's Lane*. Founded 1772. Amalgamated with the East Kent Brewery Co.Ltd of Sandwich 1920 to form Ash's East Kent Brewery Co.Ltd. Acquired by Jude, Hanbury & Co.Ltd 1923 who then closed their brewery at Wateringbury. Acquired by Whitbread & Co.Ltd 1929. Brewing ceased 1933.

Beer & Co, *Original Brewery, Broad Street*. Founded c.1770 at St.Augustine's Brewery. Original Brewery built 1848. Bankrupt 1891. Acquired by B.C.Bushell & Co.Ltd of Westerham 1894. Brewing ceased 1899.

George Beer & Co.Ltd, *Star Brewery, Broad Street*. Established prior to 1851. Registered December 1919. Took over Rigden & Co.of Faversham in January 1922 to form George Beer & Rigden Ltd and brewing was concentrated at Faversham.

Canterbury Brewery Co, *Northgate Brewery, St.George's Street*. Established prior to 1869. Registered as Johnson & Co.Ltd May 1881 brewing mainly for export. The name was changed as above in 1898 when acquired by Wilson & Towgood. Acquired by Fremlins Ltd 1923 with one tied house and two off-licences.

Canterbury Brewery, *28 St.Radigunds*. Founded February 1979 by Simon & Anthony Taylor in the sample room of Flint's former brewery. Ceased brewing 1983 and they then licensed other breweries to produce their draught beers.

Flint & Co.Ltd, *St.Dunstan's Brewery, St.Dunstan's Street*. Founded 1797. Registered before 1892 as Flint & Sons Ltd and was re-registered as above September 1903. Acquired by Alfred Leney & Co.Ltd of Dover 1923 with 350 tied houses. Brewing ceased 1929 and much of the brewery is still standing.

Henry Holden, *Eagle Brewery, 25 Longport Street*. Holden acquired C.Small's Eagle Brewery between 1866 & 1870. Sidney Holden was a mineral water manufacturer only by 1893.

Chatham

Charles Arkcoll & Co, *Lion Brewery*. Bought by the Arkcoll family c.1870. Upon the death of Charles Arkcoll in 1912,the business was sold at auction to A.J.Brown, trading as Owen J.Carter, wine & spirit merchants for £75,000. He resold the licensed houses to Style & Winch Ltd.

Edward Winch & Sons Ltd, *Chatham Brewery, High Street*. Operated by the Best family from at least 1666. Leased to Edward Winch 1851 and acquired by Edward Winch & Sons 1894. Registered January 1895. Merged with Style & Co. of Maidstone 1899 to form Style & Winch Ltd. Brewing at Chatham ceased and the brewery has been demolished.

Cranbrook

Sharpe & Winch, *Baker's Cross*. Established prior to 1846 by William Barling Sharpe and above title assumed 1892. Acquired by Frederick Leney & Sons Ltd of Wateringbury 1928 who were then a subsidiary of Whitbread & Co.Ltd.

Dartford

Dartford Brewery Co.Ltd, *Lowfield Street*. Registered July 1897 to acquire Miller & Aldworth Ltd which had been registered in November 1890. 67 public houses. Acquired jointly by Style & Winch Ltd and its subsidiary the Royal Brewery, Brentford Ltd 1924 and was later under the sole control of Style & Winch. Brewery demolished.

C.N.Kidd & Sons Ltd, *Steam Brewery, Hythe Street*. Operated by William Miskin as the Oak Brewery before 1870. Name changed after 1890. Registered February 1920. Acquired by Courage & Co.Ltd 1937 and brewing ceased. Brewery demolished 1939. A Co-op store stands on the site.

Wilmington Brewery Co.Ltd, *14 Hythe Street*. Established 1860 by Thomas Chapman and later run by Caswall & Berrall as the Eagle Brewery. Acquired by Russell's Gravesend Brewery Ltd 1899. Was used as a laundry until demolished to make way for a housing estate in 1984.

Deal

W.Hills & Sons, *High Street & Great Mongeham*. Established c.1850. William Hill had acquired John Noakes Coleman's brewery at Great Mongeham around 1860. Acquired by Thompson & Son Ltd of Walmer 1901 with 63 tied houses and both breweries were closed.

Dover

John James Allen, *Diamond Brewery, Folkestone Road, Maxton*. Brewery operated by George Chamer 1862 but Herbert Edward Wright by 1874. Above title assumed c.1880 and acquired by Edwin Dawes, late of the Standard Brewery, Long Sutton, in 1892. Acquired by Thomas Phillips of West Malling in 1897 and resold to Alfred Leney & Co.Ltd in 1912. Brewing ceased 1916.

Alfred Leney & Co.Ltd, *Phoenix Brewery, Dolphin Lane*. Founded 1740 and acquired by Alfred Leney 1860. Registered December 1896. Acquired by Fremlins Ltd 1926 and brewing ceased 1927. Business continued as Leney's Table Waters Ltd registered 1927, until 1950. Brewery demolished 1965.

Eastry

Owen Clark, *Eastry Brewery*. Established c.1840 by John Bowes and run by various members of his family until at least 1898. Acquired by Leonard Alston Fawsett, late of Findlay's Brewery, Leeds, from Owen Clark in 1902. Thomas Neville Cheatle by 1912 and Top & Co, by 1922. Ceased brewing c.1924.

Edenbridge

Larkin's Brewery, *Chiddingstone*. Founded 1986 when the Dockerty family acquired the Kentish Ales brewery at Rusthall, Tunbridge Wells. The plant was moved to Larkin's Farm and the above title assumed. Still brewing.

Faversham

W.E.& J.Rigden Ltd, *Court Street*. Founded in the early 1700s by Edward Rigden. Registered 1902. Merged with George Beer & Co.Ltd 1922 to form George Beer & Rigden Ltd which was acquired by Fremlins Ltd in 1948 and brewing ceased 1954. Production recommenced in 1961, coming under the control of Whitbread after Fremlins acquired in 1968. Brewery closed 1990.

Shepherd, Neame Ltd, *17 Court Street*. Founded 1698 by Richard Marsh and was acquired by Samuel Shepherd 1741. Registered as Shepherd, Neame & Co.Ltd November 1914 and name changed as above 1919. Still brewing independently 1990 with 250 tied houses.

Folkestone

Army & Navy Co-operative Breweries Co.Ltd, *Gun Brewery, Cheriton Road & Friary Brewery, Aldershot*. Registered July 1895 to acquire the breweries at Folkestone and Aldershot. Sold to Alfred Leney & Co.Ltd 1898 and brewing ceased. Used as a bottling plant until 1922.

Martin Ales

Martin Ales, *Marston Hall*. Founded 1983 by Merrick Johnson. Still brewing 1990.

Woodhams & Levi, *Bulwark Hill Brewery*. Founded 1823 by J.A.Rolls. Bankrupt May 1890. Acquired by the East Kent Brewery Co. in 1895.

Gravesend

Hilton Brewery, *Pier Hotel, West Street.* Home brew house founded 1981 by Ian Hilton. Closed 1985 when brewing was concentrated at Strood.

Russell's Gravesend Brewery Ltd, *West Street.* Operated as Plane & Heathorn until acquired by the Russell family in 1858 with 22 public houses. Registered January 1893. Acquired by Truman, Hanbury & Buxton & Co.Ltd 1930 with 223 tied houses. Brewery plant for sale 18th June 1935. Buildings remain as private dwellings.

Walker & Son Ltd, *Wellington Brewery, Wellington Street.* Founded at least by 1850 and acquired from John Keddell junior by Alexander Walker 1854. Registered June 1896. Acquired by Charrington & Co.Ltd 1904 with 29 public houses. Brewing ceased 1928 when the premises were damaged by fire. Brewery office remains on opposite side of the road.

George Wood & Son Ltd, *8 East Street.* Possibly founded in the late 1770s and was acquired from Charles Beckett by George Wood c.1857. Acquired by Russell's Gravesend Brewery Ltd 1911 and was closed.

Hadlow

Kenward & Court Ltd, *The Close Brewery.* Established prior to 1840 when run by Mrs Mercy Barton and acquired c.1850 by Harrison & Taylor. Known as Kenward & Barnett from 1858 and Kenward & Court from 1871. Registered July 1888. Acquired by Hammerton & Co.Ltd. of London 1945 and was sold to Charrington & Co.Ltd 1952 after brewing had ceased in 1949. The brewery has been redeveloped.

Henry Simmons, *Style Place Brewery.* Acquired by Style & Winch Ltd 1905 and was closed. Buildings now private houses.

Hawkhurst

Charlotte Wicken, *Moor Brewery.* Established c.1840 by John Wicken and in the hands of members of the family until its acquisition by Mackeson & Co.Ltd in March 1919 when brewing ceased. Had only brewed for private trade, owning no public houses. Brewery demolished.

Herne Bay

Burton Brewery Co, *Burton Brewery, William Street.* Established at Herne Street, 1 1/2 miles from Herne Bay, prior to 1832 by George Harris. Moved to William Street by 1874 and owned by Richard Sydney King in 1882. Known as G.E.Furber, Burton Brewery between 1891 & 1895, Flinn & Co. between 1895 & 1905 when above title assumed. Brewing had ceased by 1910 when premises used as stores by the Canterbury Brewery Company and later by Fremlins in the 1930s.

Hythe

Mackeson & Co.Ltd. Founded 1669 by James Pashley and acquired by Mackeson family 1801. Registered In September 1900. Acquired by H.& G.Simonds Ltd of Reading 1920 and was sold to Jude, Hanbury & Co.Ltd 1929, which came under the control of Whitbread. Brewing ceased 3rd May 1968. Brewery demolished for housing.

Lamberhurst

Lamberhurst Brewery Co.Ltd. Registered March 1924 to acquire the business of H.P.Dungay. Closed 1935.

Smith & Co.(Lamberhurst) Ltd. Trading as Smith & Simpson from before 1839. Registered 1899. 68 tied houses. Offered for auction 9th September 1921 and 54 of the houses were sold for £134,610. The brewery was not sold but was acquired by the Dartford Brewery Co.Ltd 1922.

Littlebourne

Humphrey E.De Trafford, *Sun Brewery.* Occupied by Hewitt & Clark in 1877, Herbert D.Phelps 1882-1894, and R.& H.Havens 1894-1898. Registered as De Trafford & Co. 1903 with 6 licensed houses. Sold by auction to Mackeson & Co.Ltd 1907.

Rolfe Field, *Two Brewers.* Home brew house which had been in the Field family since at least 1832. Acquired by Bushell, Watkins & Smith Ltd c.1898 and brewing ceased. Name of pub changed to the Basketmakers Arms, finally closing in 1973.

Lydd

Edward Finn & Sons Ltd, *Pale Ale Brewery.* Established 1862 when Edwin Finn bought Catherine Green's Sun Brewery which had been trading since c.1830. Acquired Alfred White's brewery in the High Street and brewing transferred there, the old brewery being used for the production of ginger beer. New brewery built 1885. Registered November 1896. Acquired by Style & Winch Ltd 1921 with 42 tied houses and was closed. Brewery bought by Mr Kenward of Kenward & Court Ltd to brew a near beer for export to the USA, but without much success and was closed when prohibition was repealed. The brewery has been demolished.

Maidstone

Joseph Barker, *Shernold Brewery, Loose.* Established by Joseph & Mark Barker prior to 1844. Partnership dissolved 1871. Also at 10 High Street, Maidstone from c.1890. Brewing ceased 1898 and High Street premises used as stores by New Northfleet Brewery Co. and its successors 1899-1902.

Fremlins Ltd, *Pale Ale Brewery, Earl Street.* Founded c.1790. Acquired by Ralph Fremlin from the executors of John Heathorn in 1861. Acquired by Whitbread & Co.Ltd 1967 with 714 public houses. Brewery closed October 1972. Brewery mostly demolished but in use as a depot.

Goacher's Bockingford Brewery, *5 Hayle Mill Cottages, Bockingford.* Founded May 1983 by Philip & Deborah Goacher. Still brewing 1990.

Isherwood, Foster & Stacey Ltd, *Lower Brewery, Lower Stone Street.* Possibly founded before 1650. Registered August 1891. Acquired by Fremlins Ltd 1929 with 151 public houses and was closed. Brewery demolished.

William Henry Martin, *Havock Lane* (1890)

E.Mason & Co.Ltd, *Waterside Brewery.* Acquired by Shepherd, Neame Ltd 1956 with about 80 tied houses and was closed. Brewery demolished.

Style & Winch Ltd, *Medway Brewery, St.Peter's Street.* Medway Brewery built by William Baldwin 1806. Registered March 1899 to acquire A.F.Style & Co, and E.Winch & Sons Ltd, Chatham Brewery with a total of 256 public houses. Chatham Brewery closed 1899. Acquired by Barclay, Perkins & Co.Ltd March 1929 with 600 tied houses. Ceased brewing 1971 and demolished.

Margate

Cobb & Co.(Brewers) Ltd, *Margate Brewery, 27 King Street.* Founded 1673. Private company registered July 1947. Acquired by Whitbread & Co.Ltd January 1968 with 40 public houses. Brewery closed October 1968 and was demolished July 1971.

Paramor & Son, *Phoenix Brewery.* Acquired by Tomson & Wotton 1891.

Reeve & Co.(Margate) Ltd, *24 Hawley Street.* Registered September 1903. Brewing ceased 1907 but continued in business as ale & porter merchants until 1939.

Webb & Co, *Fort Brewery, Fort Road.* Registered as the Fort Brewery Co. Margate Ltd on 26th November 1873 to acquire the Fort & Phoenix Breweries and the Saracen's Head Brewery, Margate & Cambridge Arms, Walmer, but never proceeded beyond registration of the company. Acquired by Russell's Gravesend Brewery Ltd 1897. Brewery is still standing behind the Fort Tap public house.

Northfleet

New Northfleet Brewery Co, *Dover Road.* Registered July 1889 as Pope & Co.Ltd. Name changed to Northfleet Brewery Co.Ltd April 1894 and this company was liquidated in March 1899. Succeeded by the partnership of Barkway & Hitchcock under the above title. Acquired by the Dartford Brewery Co.Ltd 1908. Buildings are extant.

Ramsgate

Edgar Austen, *Regent Brewery, 32 Belmont Street.* Established in Broad Street c.1775. Brewery leased to Gardner & Co.Ltd of Ash 1921 and brewing was concentrated at Ash. Bought by Gardners 1927 with 2 public houses for about £15,000. Brewery demolished 1937.

Cannon Brewery Co, *Cannon Brewery, Cannon Road/High Street.* Successors to R.S.Cramp & Sons. Acquired by Tomson & Wotton 1878 with 12 licensed houses but brewing continued until 1920.

James Fleet, *Broad Street.* Premises previously occupied by James Austen. Acquired by Russell's Gravesend Brewery Ltd 1899 with 9 tied houses. Brewing ceased 1919.

Tomson & Wotton Ltd, *Queen Street.* Founded 1634 and acquired by Thomas Tomson 1680. Private company registered 1892. Merged with Gardner & Co.Ltd 1951 to form Combined Breweries (Holdings) Ltd, controlling 102 tied houses. Acquired by Whitbread & Co.Ltd June 1968 and was closed October 1968.

E.G.Wastall & Co, *Thanet Brewery, Queen Street.* Established 1862. Acquired by W.Williams May 1889 from Ingold & Lewis. Williams & Co in receivership 1890. Brewed only for private trade owning no licensed houses and ceased brewing after 1906.

Rochester

Woodhams & Co.Ltd, *Steam Brewery, Victoria Street.* Founded 1750 and known as the Troy Town Brewery. Registered November 1895. Acquired by Style & Winch Ltd. April 1918 and was closed. Brewery still standing.

Sandwich

Baxter & Co, *Export Brewery.* Acquired by the East Kent Brewery Co.Ltd 1895 after the fincial collapse of the Baxters.

East Kent Brewery Co.Ltd, *Sandwich Street.* Founded c.1823 by John Hoile. Merged with Ash & Co. of Canterbury 1920 to form Ash's East Kent Brewery Co.Ltd. Acquired by Jude, Hanbury & Co.Ltd 1923. Brewery sold June 1923, and is still standing in use as a corn & feed merchants.

Sevenoaks

John Samuel Bligh, *Holmesdale Brewery, 117 High Street.* Founded 1868. Acquired by Watney, Combe, Reid & Co.Ltd 1911 with 27 tied houses.

Golding & Co, *Bat & Ball Brewery, Crampton Road.* Established 1900 to brew for the private trade. Premises renamed the Oak Brewery after the acquisition of the goodwill and private trade of Fox & Sons of Farnborough 1910. Acquired by Hoare & Co.Ltd from the Standard Brewery Co-Operative Society 1912 and brewery closed. Premises used as a furniture repository until its demolition in the early 1970s.

Sevenoaks Brewery, *Crown Point Inn, Seal Chart.* Home brew house founded June 1981 by Gordon Emery. Closed 1986.

Alfred Smith & Co, *Sevenoaks Brewery, High Street.* Founded c.1848. Acquired by Bushell, Watkins & Co. 1899 with 25 public houses to form Bushell, Watkins & Smith Ltd. Brewery closed and subsequently demolished.

Sittingbourne

Edward Hartridge, *Milton Brewery.* Established c.1850 and acquired by Frederick Leney & Sons Ltd. 1895.

H.& O.Vallance, *Napier Brewery, High Street.* Founded before 1828 by William Vallance. Traded as Paynes Steam Brewery c.1860-1880. Acquired Style & Winch Ltd 1905 and was closed.

Southborough

Matthew Mark Phipps, *Modest Corner.* Robert John Phipps 1870-1882. Ceased brewing after 1895.

Staple

Frank Vincent Tritton, *Staple Brewery.* Acquired by Gardner & Co.Ltd 1912. Used for some years for the production of ginger beer. Premises now the Black Pig public house.

Stone

Walter Ray, *Stone Steam Brewery* (1898)

Stourmouth

Francis Alexander White, *Stourmouth Brewery.* The brewery had been in existence since before 1845 when it was run by the partnership of Impett & Gardner who soon sold out to H.& W.Gibbs. The Lemarque Brothers came into possession of the firm in 1868 and White assumed control in November 1875. There was a connection by marriage between White and the Flints of Canterbury. Brewery & 11 public houses offered for sale 9th July 1904 and bought by Flint & Sons Ltd of Canterbury.

Strood

Budden & Biggs Brewery Ltd, *Steam Brewery, 11 High Street.* Founded by 1823 by Samuel Tayler and later run by Thomas William Clark. Registered July 1897 as Budden & Biggs Ltd to amalgamate the wine & spirit business of James Budden of Chatham with Biggs Brothers Steam Brewery. 66 public houses. Name changed as above 1924. Acquired by Ind Coope Ltd 1931. Brewery demolished c.1975 for Safeway supermarket.

Henry Ludwell Dampier, *Frindsbury Brewery, 23/25 Frindsbury Road.* Established c.1830 by William Wood and acquired by Dampier 1875. Amalgamated with Woodhams & Co.Ltd of Rochester October 1906. Brewery still standing.

Hilton Brewery, *South Eastern Hotel, 51 Static Road.* Home brew pub founded 1983 by Ian Hilto of the Gravesend Brewery. Still in operation 1990.

Tenterden

Tenterden Brewery Co.Ltd, *Vine Brewery.* Founde 1745 and was bought by Obadiah Edwards 1872 wh had previously brewed at Tunbridge Wells. Regis tered as above 1922. Acquired by Jude, Hanbury & Co.Ltd February 1922 with 10 tied houses and wa closed.

Tonbridge

Benjamin Baker, *Royal Victoria Brewery, Quarr Hill.* Established before 1842. Royal Victori Brewery built 1874. Acquired by E.& H.Kelsey 1908

James Taylor Baker, *Quarry Hill Brewery.* Lease to Frederick Leney 1892. Possibly same brewery a above.

W.& G.Bartram Ltd, *Bridge Brewery, High Stree* Registered January 1894 to acquire the business o R.H.& G.W.Bartram. Acquired by the Dartfor Brewery Co.Ltd 1902 with 51 public houses and wa demolished.

Tunbridge Wells

E.& H.Kelsey Ltd, *Culverden Brewery, St.John Road.* Founded c.1738 as Thomas Jarrett's brew house. Acquired by the Kelsey family 1851. Regis tered July 1920 to amalgamate E.& H.Kelsey an Thomas Phillips & Co.Ltd of West Malling Acquired by J.W.Green Ltd of Luton 1948 with tied houses. Brewing ceased 1956. Brewery demol ished 1967.

Kentish Ales, *Grange Brewery, Grange Road, Rus thall.* Successors to the Royal Tunbridge Well Brewery in 1984. Acquired by Sapphire Ltd Octobe 1985. Closed 1986.

Royal Tunbridge Wells Brewing Co.Ltd, *Grang Brewery, Grange Road, Rusthall.* Founde November 1982 by Charles Stirling, Roger McBride Shaun Goodman & Ian Dorman. Ceased brewing 1983 and was re-opened 1984 trading as Kentis Ales.

T.& W. Edwardes, *Grosvenor Brewery, Good Station Road.* Established prior to 1874. Acquire by W.E.Young 1899. 2 tied houses. Ceased brewing 1902.

Walmer

Thompson & Son Ltd. Founded 1820 by Edmund Thompson. Registered February 1894 to acquire Thompson & Son. Acquired by Charrington & Co.Ltd 1950 and brewing ceased c.1960. Used as a depot and maltings until 1974 when brewery demolished.

Wateringbury

Jude, Hanbury & Co.Ltd, *Kent Brewery.* Founded 1840. Registered October 1919. Moved to Canterbury 1924 after acquiring Ash & Co. and the Kent Brewery was sold. Acquired by Whitbread & Co.Ltd 1925 with about 200 public houses. Brewery sold to the Yalding Soap Co. and was later demolished.

Frederick Leney & Sons Ltd, *Phoenix Brewery.* Founded by Augustus Leney 1843. Registered 1895 with 156 tied houses. Acquired by Whitbread & Co.Ltd 1927 and was sold to Fremlins Ltd in 1960. Closed 1981. Brewery demolished and is now a housing estate.

Westerham

Bushell, Watkins & Smith Ltd, *Black Eagle Brewery.* Brewery founded by Nathaniel Davis c.1840. Registered July 1894 as B.C.Bushell & Co.Ltd with 63 public houses. Took over Watkins & Son, Swan Brewery, Hosey Hill, Westerham 1897 and name was changed to B.C.Bushell, Watkins & Co.Ltd and finally as above when Alfred Smith & Co, of Sevenoaks were acquired. Acquired by Taylor, Walker & Co.Ltd of London 1948 with 102 tied houses. Ceased brewing 1965 and premises used as an Ind Coope depot until demolished November 1989.

West Malling

Thomas Phillips & Co.Ltd, *Abbey Brewery.* Registered March 1898 to acquire the Abbey Brewery; the Diamond Brewery, Dover and the Park Brewery, Camberwell, London with 70 public houses. Acquired by E.& H.Kelsey of Tunbridge Wells 1920. Premises used by the Abbey Brewery Co.Ltd, registered November 1934, until about 1939. Brewery still standing.

Wrotham

Walter Morgan, *Nepicar Brewery.* Founded by Jonathon Biggs at the Spring Tavern c.1840. He later moved to Strood leaving the Nepicar Brewery under the control of his two sons. Upon their father's death they too moved to Strood & brewery sold to C.G.& J.M.Reed. Morgan assumed control c.1880. Brewery purchased 1906 for its retail license by Golding & Co. of Sevenoaks. Brewing ceased c.1912 and brewery demolished.

Yalding

H.T.Wickham & Co. Brewery and 11 public houses sold to Frederick Leney & Sons Ltd 1921 for £20,000.

LANCASHIRE

Accrington

Bentley's Milnshaw Brewery Co.Ltd, *Milnshaw Lane.* Founded before 1895. Private company registered July 1911. Acquired by John Smith's Tadaster Brewery Co.Ltd 1926.

New Brewery, *Manor Street* (1900)

Adlington

Edward Eccles, *Market Street* (1902)

John Mercer Ltd, *Plough Brewery, Market Street.* Registered December 1907. Acquired by Dutton's Blackburn Brewery Ltd March 1929. Brewing ceased 1936.

Henry Seddon, *Chorley Road* (1902)

Bacup

Rochdale & Rossendale Brewery Ltd, *Stacksteads.* Originally registered as the Brandwood Brewery Ltd April 1894 but never traded. Brewery sold to a firm of chemical manufacturers. Dissolved 28th July 1899.

Bamber Bridge

Albert W.Greenhalgh, *McKenzie Street* (1940)

James Reddy (1926)

Barnacre

Mrs F.Smith (1921)

Barrowford

John Kenyon Ltd, *Rossendale Brewery, Wheatley Lane Road.* Founded 1869. Registered 1896 to acquire the Rossendale & Clough Springs Breweries. Acquired by Massey's Burnley Brewery Ltd December 1928 with 78 tied houses.

Lancashire Clubs Federation Brewery Ltd, *Clough Springs Brewery.* Registered March 1920. Originally brewed at 179 Spa Road, Bolton before moving to Kenyon's former brewery. Ceased trading 1960 and the trade was acquired by the Yorkshire Clubs Brewery. Gibbs, Mew & Co.Ltd of Salisbury, Wilts bought the brewery in 1962 to produce keg beer for Northern clubs. Brewing ceased after two years for economic reasons.

John Strickland, *Carr Mill Brewery* (1902)

Blackburn

Blackburn Brewery Co.Ltd, *Lark Hill Street.* Registered June 1876 as Joseph Eatough & Co.Ltd. Name changed to the Higher Eanam Brewery Co.Ltd September 1879 and was wound up March 1881. Registered as above June 1882. Acquired by Dutton's Blackburn Brewery Ltd 1928 with over 100 public houses.

Thomas Bourn, *Crown Brewery, Canterbury Street* (1892)

Matthew Brown & Co.Ltd, *Lion Brewery, Coniston Road.* Founded at Pole Street, Preston 1830. Brewing transferred to Blackburn 1927 when Nuttall & Co. (Blackburn) Ltd were acquired. Acquired by Scottish & Newcastle Breweries October 1987 with 550 tied houses.

Cunningham's & T.W.Thwaites Ltd, *Snig Brewery, Malt Street.* Registered April 1897 to acquire J.Cunningham & Co, brewers and T.W.Thwaites, wine & spirit merchants. In 1913 they leased all their licensed properties to Matthew Brown & Co.Ltd for 999 years, but retained the brewery and a number of unlicensed houses which were later sold.

Dutton's Blackburn Brewery Ltd, *Salford Brewery, Bow Street.* Founded by 1799. Registered November 1897 with 92 public houses. Acquired by Whitbread & Co.Ltd 1964 with 784 tied houses and was operated as Whitbread West Pennines Ltd until closed in 1978.

Fountain Free Brewery Co.Ltd, *Mother Redcap, Accrington Road, Rishton.* Founded 1849. Registered December 1898. Acquired by Thwaites & Co.Ltd May 1927 with 6 public houses.

Richard Holden Ltd, *Nova Scotia Brewery,* 81 Bolton Road. Registered March 1898. Acquired by Matthew Brown & Co.Ltd 1920.

Little Harwood Brewery Co.Ltd, *Lettice Ann Street, Little Harwood.* Registered 1875 to acquire Beardsworth & Whalley. Acquired by Nuttall & Co. 1892 and brewing ceased.

Nuttall & Co.(Blackburn) Ltd, *Lion Brewery, Coniston Road.* Registered June 1897 as Nuttall & Co.Ltd, name changed as above 1906. Acquired by Matthew Brown & Co.Ltd 1927 with 172 tied houses.

Henry Shaw & Co.Ltd, *Salford New Brewery.* Founded 1834. Registered April 1897 to acquire the business of John Rutherford known as Henry Shaw & Co. Acquired by Thwaites & Co.Ltd August 1923 with 87 public houses and brewing ceased in 1925.

-47-

William Smith, *Brookhouse Well New Brewery, 9 Townhall Street.* Acquired by Thomas Whewell 1896.

Daniel Thwaites & Co.Ltd, *Star Brewery.* Acquired by Daniel Thwaites 1807. Registered March 1897. New brewhouse built 1966. Still independent 1990 with 411 tied houses.

Thomas Whewell Ltd, *Victoria Brewery, Mary Ann Street & Albert Brewery, Cort Street.* Private company registered 1922. Acquired by Nuttall & Co.(-Blackburn) Ltd 1925 and was closed.

Blackpool

Catterall & Swarbrick's Brewery Ltd, *Queen's Brewery, Talbot Road.* Founded at Poulton-le-Fylde 1871. Registered July 1894. Blackpool brewery built 1927. Acquired by Northern Breweries 1961 with 104 public houses.

Marton Brewery Co.Ltd, *Green Lane, off Preston Road, Marton.* Registered July 1905 to acquire the business of Moses Kay. Brewing ceased 7th December 1910. Brewery and adjoining Boar's Head Inn were acquired by the Burtonwood Brewery Co.Ltd February 1913 and were sold again on 17th August 1921 for £8,500.

Brierfield

Thomas Horsfall, *Brierfield Brewery.* Acquired by the Blackburn Brewery Co.Ltd 1925 and was closed.

Burnley

Thomas Bradshaw, *Manchester Road* (1890)

G.D.L.Fernandez, *Old Brewery.* Fernandez was of Spanish descent, the son of the owner of the Old Bridge Brewery, Wakefield, West Yorkshire. He married the daughter of John Hargreaves, owner of the Old Brewery, which passed into his control. Acquired by J.Grimshaw Ltd 1918 with 23 public houses and was closed.

J.Grimshaw Ltd, *Keirby Brewery, 15/20 Church Street.* Founded c.1840. Acquired by Massey's Burnley Brewery Ltd 1928 with 120 tied houses.

Lancashire Clubs Brewery Ltd, *Bank Parade.* Registered 1901 as the Burnley Clubs Brewery Ltd. Name changed as above 1949. Bankrupt and was acquired by the Yorkshire Clubs Brewery Ltd 1950 and the brewery was demolished.

Massey's Burnley Brewery Ltd, *Bridge End Brewery, Westgate.* Founded 1750. Registered March 1889 to acquire the business of Lord Massey with 118 public houses. Acquired by Charrington United Breweries Ltd 1966 with 227 tied houses. Brewing ceased 1974.

Moorhouse's Brewery, *Moorhouse Street, Accrington Road.* The Moorhouse family have been involved in brewing since 1865, producing hop bitters concentrate for drinks. Started brewing real ale in 1977. Bought by the Hutchinson Leisure Group 1981 and was resold to Apollo Leisure 1984. Acquired by Bill Parkinson 1985 and is still brewing 1990 with two tied houses.

J.Pletts & Sons Ltd, *Borough Brewery, 11 Stanley Street.* Founded c.1866 as bottlers and Wine & spirits merchants. Brewing began about 1886. Liquidator appointed 12th September 1923 and the brewery was offered for sale.

Burscough Bridge

J.Thoroughgood & Son. Merged with Thoroughgood's Breweries Ltd of Liverpool 1896. The brewery built 1893. was offered for sale in July 1922.

Chorley

Gardner, Thompson & Cardwell Ltd, *Crown Brewery* (1898)

Alice Hilton, *113 Market Street* (1920)

John Lancaster & Co, *10 Water Street* (1890)

Thomas Sharples, *46/48 Parker Street.* Bought by Wilkins Ltd of Longton July 1904 with one tied house, the Prince Consort, Parker Street, for £2,475.

Speak & Marsden (1890)

G.H.Wilding, *Market Street* (1905)

Clitheroe

E.& J.Crabtree Ltd, *Victoria Brewery, Shawbridge Street.* Registered May 1892. Acquired by the Blackburn Brewery Co.Ltd 1920 with 45 public houses.

Tempest Seedall, *Swan & Royal Brewery* (1910)

John Tillotson & Son, *Waterloo Brewery.* Acquired by E.& J.Crabtree Ltd February 1904.

Colne

William Blackburn, *Albert Brewery, Buck Street* (1911)

John Fort, *Bent Lane Brewery* (1907)

Darwen

Spring Vale Brewery Ltd, *Spring Vale Brewery, Grimshaw Street.* Brewery bought by Samuel Allsopp & Sons Ltd 1898 for £325,000, with about 70 tied houses and was registered as above August 1899. Allsopps sold the brewery to Nuttall & Co.Ltd for £200,000 June 1901.

James Tootall (1910)

Edenfield

Edenfield Brewery Co.Ltd, *Spring Bank Brewery.* Registered September 1898 as Grant's Tower Brewery Co.Ltd to acquire the business of T.Mercer. Wound up 1909 and a private company was registered as above in the same year. Acquired by John Kenyon Ltd of Barrowford in 1919.

Fleetwood

Fylde Home Brewery Co.Ltd, *Dock Street.* Registered 28th February 1907. Supplied the household trade only. Brewery destroyed by fire 4th July 1903 and was wound up voluntarily 29th September 1903.

United Clubs Brewery (Fleetwood) Ltd, *6 Kemp Street.* Private company registered 1920. Voluntary winding up 1922.

Fulwood

Sumner's Brewery Ltd, *Watling Street Road.* Registered February 1896 to acquire the business of William Sumner, brewer, army contractor, farmer and canteen proprietor. 6 public houses. Went into voluntary liquidation 4th October 1915.

Gauxholme

John Bulcock, *Rock Spring Brewery.* Acquired by J.Grimshaw Ltd of Burnley 1914.

Gisburn

Ribblesdale Arms. Home brew house founded by Richard Vernon October 1977. Ceased brewing 1979 and the public house was sold.

Haslingden

W.H.Baxter & Co.Ltd. Acquired by John Baxter Ltd of Waterfoot 1922 with 40 tied houses.

Hoghton

John Thomas Robinson (1923)

Lancaster

Mitchells of Lancaster (Brewers) Ltd, *Central Brewery, 11 Moor Lane.* Founded 1871 when William Mitchell leased the Black Horse Inn with brewery attached. Central Brewery built 1880. Registered as above 1965. Brewing transferred to the Old Brewery after Yates & Jackson's closure in 1984. Still brewing independently 1990 with 50 public houses.

Yates & Jackson Ltd, *Old Brewery, Brewery Lane, Brock Street.* Founded 1669 and was acquired by William Jackson and John Proctor in 1811. Registered 1923. Acquired by Daniel Thwaites & Co.Ltd 1984 and brewing ceased. The Old Brewery was sold to Mitchells.

Other Breweries

William Bell, *50/52 Penny Street* (1902)

Frederick Cornforth, *8 Brock Street*. Acquired by Yates & Jackson Ltd 1923.

John Martin, *Bull's Head Brewery, Common Garden Street* (1940)

James Newsham, *Friar Street Brewery* (1898)

James Patterson, *Marton Street* (1890)

Leyland

Leyland Brewery, *7 Towngate Street*. Founded October 1983 by Ian Bignell. Ceased brewing 1985.

Longton

James Pye & Son. Acquired by Walmesley & Co. of Preston 1905.

W.& R.Wilkins Ltd, *Marsh Lane*. Private company registered February 1937. Acquired by Groves & Whitnall Ltd of Salford 1952.

Lytham St.Annes

William Arthur Ogden, *Ship Brewery, Ship & Royal Hotel, Clifton Street*. Offered for auction 27th October 1920.

Morecambe

Robert Garnett (1920)

Nelson

William Astley, exors of, *Nelson Brewery, Sagar Street*. Acquired by Massey's Burnley Brewery Ltd 1924 with 75 tied houses and was closed.

Arthur W.Catlow, *Home Brewery, Pendle Street* (1926)

John Strickland, *Pendle Street*. Offered for sale December 1904.

Victoria Brewery Ltd, *Victoria Brewery, Railway Street*. Registered February 1903 to acquire the business of Joseph Wooliscroft and William Thomas trading as William Thomas & Co. Went into voluntary liquidation 25th April 1905.

Ormskirk

Ellis, Warde & Co.Ltd, *Snig's Foot Brewery, Church Street*. Founded by 1871 as Thomas Nixon. Registered October 1897 as Ellis, Warde, Webster & Co.Ltd. Brewing transferred to the Bath Springs Brewery 1902. Name changed as above September 1919. Acquired by Walker Cain Ltd 1929 with 102 public houses. Brewing ceased September 1955.

Forshaw's Brewery Co.Ltd, *Bath Springs Brewery, Derby Street*. Founded 1871. Registered May 1898. Acquired by Ellis, Warde, Webster & Co.Ltd June 1901, who then moved their brewing to here in 1902.

Richard Knowles & Sons, *Church Street Brewery*. Moved to the Snig's Foot Brewery when Ellis, Warde, Webster transferred to the Bath Springs Brewery. Acquired by the Burtonwood Brewery (Forshaws) Ltd 1947 with 8 tied houses.

Thomas Sumner Parker, *Aughton Brewery, Townend*. Founded 1871. Acquired by Ellis, Warde, Webster & Co.Ltd 1906 with 11 public houses.

Benjamin Stockley, *Burscough Street* (1910)

Richard Taylor (Ormskirk) Ltd, *Wheatsheaf Brewery, 20 Burscough Street*. Home brew house founded 1884. Private company registered 1916. Acquired by Ellis, Warde & Co.Ltd 1919.

Daniel Webster, *Hillmount Brewery, Southport Road*. Founded 1871. Acquired by Ellis, Warde & Co. October 1897.

Preston

H.C.Breakell & Co.Ltd, *Victoria Brewery, 12 Church Street*. Founded 1839. Registered October 1929. Acquired by Catterall & Swarbrick Ltd 1947.

W.M.Cross, *24 Lord Street*. Acquired by Chester's Brewery Co.Ltd 1944. Brewing ceased 3rd April 1950 and the brewery has been demolished.

Hall, Hale & Co.Ltd, *71 Tithebarn Street*. Founded by Henry Cardwell at Cannon Street 1866 and moved to Tithebarn Street 1877. Acquired by Alfred Bertwistle & Sons 1895 and by William Hall & Co. 1900. Registered 1906. Acquired by Matthew Brown & Co.Ltd 1920 with 28 tied houses and was closed. Brewery demolished 1964.

Hull's Brewery Ltd, *Glover Street*. Registered May 1895 to acquire James Hull & Sons. Acquired by Boddington's Breweries Ltd 1900 with 60 public houses.

New Preston & Fylde Brewery Co.Ltd, *Syke Street, Avenham Lane*. Registered May 1899. Acquired by Hall, Hale & Co.Ltd 1906.

Preston Breweries Ltd, *Chester Road*. Registered February 1936. Acquired by Thwaites & Co.Ltd 1955 with 17 public houses.

Preston Labour Clubs Brewery Ltd, *Brierley Street*. Founded 1928 and supplied about 8 clubs. Closed 2nd January 1962.

Ribble Brewery Co.Ltd, *75 St.George's Road*. Registered October 1936 to acquire the business of Richard Maguire trading as the Moor Park Brewery Co. In liquidation 1939 and the brewery and 12 tied houses were sold to Matthew Brown & Co.Ltd 1943.

William Sharples Ltd, *Croft Street*. Founded c.1884. Registered 1918. Acquired by Matthew Brown & Co.Ltd 1919 with 28 public houses.

Walmesley & Pye Ltd, *Church Street & Victoria Street, Ormskirk*. Founded 1883. Registered December 1904. Acquired by Hall, Hale & Co.Ltd 1906.

Other Breweries

Arthur Ainsworth, *24 Victoria Street* (1935)

Henry Allsopp, *93 North Road* (1935)

Robert Anyon, *212 Ribbleton Lane* (1921)

Samuel Ashton, *41 Salter Street* (1920)

Joseph Aspinall, *27 Fylde Road* (1940)

William Atkinson, *11 Deepdale Street* (1921)

Samuel Baines, *44 Meadow Street* (1940)

Thomas Bamber, *32 Brook Street* (1920) & *32 Tithebarn Street* (1921)

Arthur Barnes, *114 Church Street* (1930)

Harry Barnes, *90/91 Moor Lane* (1940)

John Barnes, *24 Lancaster Road* (1940)

Richard Barnes, *28 Deepdale Mill Street* (1921)

John T.Baron, *62 Newhall Lane* (1940)

John Bateson & Co.Ltd, *12 Grimshaw Street* (1940)

Cattle Market Hotel (1938)

James Christopher, *3 Fylde Road* (1923)

Thomas Christopher, *332 North Road* (1935)

Fred Danson, *6 Great George Street* (1935)

Walter Dawber, *79 London Road* (1940)

Robert Dewhurst, *24 North Hawkins Street* (1921)

John Dixon, *135 Ribbleton Lane* (1921)

Nancy Dixon, *111 Bowl Lane* (1921)

Wilfred Dixon, *8 Egan Street* (1935)

William Dobson, *185 Fylde Road* (1935)

Mary E.Edmundson, *St.John's Place* (1940)

Stanley Eteson, *1 Ribbleton Lane* (1935)

Stanley Nicholas Fazackerly, *2 Great Avenham Street* (1940)

Frank Fecitt, *29 Adelphi Street* (1935)

Robert Finch, *1 Pedder Street* (1923)

Mary E.Garland, *66 Avenham Lane* (1940)

Thomas Gorman, *180 Lancaster Road* (1935)

William Gorse, *16 Hammond Street* (1921)

Mrs James Gorton, *61 Berry Street* (1926)

Frederick Grayson, *82 Byron Street* (1935)

Frederick Grayston, *14 & 25 Brackenbury Street* (1940)

Annie Gregson, *97 Marsh Lane* (1926)

Edward Hacking, *112 Friargate* (1940)

Samuel Hackling, *42/44 Fletcher Road* (1940)

George D.Hale, *Avenham Lane* (1906)

John Hall, *197 Lancaster Road* (1930)

Proctor R. Hall, *84 Adelphi Street* (1940)

Joseph Halsall, *70 Wellfield Road* (1920)

James Halstead, *Salmon Street* (1935)

Charles Hargreaves, *30 Larkhill Street* (1940)

George Harrison, *370 North Road* (1935)

Thomas H.Helm, *33 Cannon Street* (1921)

John Hesketh, *155 Marsh Lane* (1921)

William Hesketh, *15 Ratcliffe Street* (1926)

Frank Hodgkinson, *93 Marsh Lane* (1940)

Joseph Hodgkinson, *1 Dunderdale Street* (1935)

William Holden, *30 Meadow Street* (1940)

John Holland, *85 Plunginton Road* (1940)

Elizabeth Hornby, *30 Tithebarn Street* (1920)

Henry Hothersall, *Lancaster Road* (1920)

Agnes Houghton, *43 Bow Lane* (1921)

Mary E.Howarth, *16 Hudson Street* (1940)

William H.Howarth, *Globe Commercial Hotel, Corporation Street* (1935)

Arthur Hughes, *11 Manchester Road* (1940)

Richard Kay, *50 Water Lane* (1935)

Robert Lackey, *115 Lancaster Road* (1921)

William Lakeland, *403 Brook Street* (1940)

Arthur Lambert, *129 Manchester Road* (1940)

William Lawson, *36 Plunginton Road* (1940)

Jane Leah, *319 Cemetery Road* (1923)

John L.Lilley, *186 Aqueduct Street* (1930)
James Livesey, *262 Fylde Road* (1923)
William H.Livesey, *70 Fylde Road* (1940)
Fred McCartney, *14 Jutland Street* (1940)
Thomas McGuinness, *St.Paul's Road* (1940)
Hugh McKerney, *81 Peel Hall Street* (1921)
John Maddock, *86 Ribbleton Lane* (1921)
Ben Markland, *107 Kent Street* (1930)
Thomas Martin, *Wharf Street* (1940)
Nicholas Mercer, *16 Dunderdale Street* (1930)
Thomas Moore, *58 Fishergate Hill* (1920)
Martin Moran, *100 Walker Street* (1921)
Agnes Moss, *1 Maudland Bank* (1940)
Thomas Nichol, *63 Ribbleton Lane* (1921)
John Nightingale, *53 Plunginton Road* (1921)
Thomas Noblett, *Heatley Street* (1935)
Edward Ormerod, *180 Marsh Lane* (1940)
Joseph Partington, *236 Brook Street* (1940)
Edward A. Pimbley, *New Cock Yard, Fishergate* (1940)
Annie Preston, *44 Friargate* (1935)
James Preston, *10 Saul Street* (1921)
Joseph C.Price, *157 Ribbleton Lane* (1935) & *10 Brierfield Road* (1940)
Herbert Ernest Quayle, *27 Manchester Road* (1935)
James L.Reynolds, *27 North Road* (1921)
Albert E.Rhodes, *16 Gorst Street* (1930) & *17 Maudland Bank* (1940)
Thomas Richardson, *24 Avenham Lane* (1940)
James Ridge, *125 Fylde Road* (1935)
Modona Riley, *Corporation Street* (1940)
Tom Roberts, *144 North Road* (1935)
Peter James Rourke, *26 Richmond Street* (1935)
George David Russell, *112 Park Road* (1940)
Alfred Sandiford, *295 Lancaster Road* (1920)
Thomas Norman Saul, *St.Ann's Street* (1923)
Arthur Saxton, *27 Queen Street* (1935)
Walter Scott, *85 Water Lane* (1935)
Evelyn Sherlicker, *297 Marsh Lane* (1940)
John Simmill, *14 Brook Street* (1935)
John Thomas Simpson, *36 Newhall Lane* (1935)
Sarah Jane Simpson, *24 North Road* (1921)
Alfred J.Smith, *240 Fylde Road* (1935)
Herbert Smith, *150 Ribbleton Lane* (1935)
John Smith, *70 Victoria Street* (1920)
Harold A.Spencer, *139 Adelphi Street* (1940)

Joseph Standing, *208 Aqueduct Street* (1923)
Herbert Steer, *76 North Road* (1940)
Richard Stevens, *194 Marsh Lane* (1940)
William Swarbrick, *53 Marsh Lane* (1921)
Alfred Taylor, *23 Newhall Lane* (1935)
John Taylor, *270 North Road* (1940)
Margaret A.Taylor, *114 North Road* (1940)
Richard Taylor, *72 Atkinson Street* (1949)
Joseph Walsh, *30 Maudland Bank* (1940)
Thomas Walton, *95 Adelphi Street* (1940)
Herbert Wareing, *73 Ribbleton Lane* (1935)
Joseph Waring, *262 Lancaster Road* (1920)
Leonard Wearden, *200 North Road* (1923)
Mary Jane Wearden, *68 Fletcher Road* (1921)
John J.Webster, *20 London Road* (1940)
John Wharton, *Herman Hotel Brewery, 70/72 Aqueduct Street* (1956)
John William Wharton, *289 Ribbleton Lane* (1920)
Annie White, *46 Park Road* (1940)
Joseph Ernest Wilding, *6 Mason Street* (1940)
Arthur Wilkinson, *7 William Street* (1935)
Maria Wilkinson, *7 Edgar Street* (1940)
Mary Wilkinson, *13 Harrison Hill* (1935)
Stafford Wilkinson, *20 Elliott Street* (1935)
Fred Wilson, *145 Victoria Street* (1935)
Harry Wilson, *Garstang Road* (1940)
Joseph Wilson, *New Cock Inn Brewery, 123a Fishergate* (1930) and *126 Ribbleton Lane* (1940)
George Winnard, *230 North Road* (1940) and *26 Fish Street* (1935)
Robert Woan, *57 Bow Lane* (1921)
Thomas Wood, *205 Brook Street* (1921)
Elizabeth Woodcock, *49 Moor Lane* (1940)
H.Woodhouse, (1951)
James Woodhouse, *Nile Street* (1930) & *2 St.Austin's Road* (1921) & *77 Church Street* (1926)
Frederick Yates, *30 Avenham Street* (1940)

Ramsbottom

Two Shires Brewery, *Rose Bank Mill, Bolton Road North, Stubbins.* Founded March 1981 by Bob Ward, David Murray, Peter Walker & Graham Newman. Closed 1983.

Rufford

New Fermor Arms, *Station Road.* Home brew house founded by Alan Mawdesley 1976. Sold to Tetley Walker 1981 and was resold back to Alan Mawdesley 1985 and is still in operation 1990.

John Radcliffe, *Hesketh Arms Brewery* (1926)

Samlesbury

Whitbread West Pennines, *Cuerdale Lane.* A new large scale brewery opened April 1972.

Waterfoot

John Baxter Ltd, *Glen Top Brewery.* Founded before 1850. Registered December 1895. Acquired by Beverley Brothers Ltd of Wakefield, Yorkshire 1952 with 127 public houses.

Whittle Springs

Whittle Springs Brewery Ltd, *Crown Brewery.* Registered October 1891 as Gardner, Thompson & Cardwell Ltd and the name was changed as above on 6th April 1897. Acquired by Nuttall & Co.Ltd 1928 with 54 tied houses, who were then a subsidiary of Matthew Brown & Co.Ltd.

Whitworth

Hardman Jackson (1920)

Wrightington

John Foster Wright (1920)

LEICESTERSHIRE

Anstey

Daniel Pettifor & Sons, *Steam Brewery.* Acquired by J.Marston, Thompson & Co.Ltd 1900 with 20 public houses.

Beeby

North Leicestershire Brewery Co.Ltd. Registered February 1894 to acquire the business of T.Nuttall. Acquired by the Midland Brewery Co.Ltd of Loughborough 1898.

Belton

William Toone (1902)

Burrough-on-the-Hill

Parish Brewery, *Stag & Hounds Inn, Main Street.* Home brew house founded 1986 by landlord Barrie Parish. Still in operation 1990.

Cavendish Bridge

George Trussell Eaton, *Cavendish Bridge Brewery.* Acquired by Offiler's Brewery Ltd 1896 and was closed in January 1923.

Cropston

Emma Burchnall (1892)

Donisthorpe

G.& W.F.Cooper, *Acresford Brewery.* Acquired by Sidney Evershed Ltd 1900.

Geeston

Claude Walker. Situated at the Geeston Tap public house. Closed 1914 when Mr Walker went to war.

Harby

Vale Brewery Co. Acquired by W.S.Davy of Newark-on-Trent February 1899.

Hathern

Albert Cooper (1935)

Hinckley

William & Thomas Beardsmore. Acquired by John Marston & Son Ltd 1895.

Huncote

Thomas Harvey (1910)

Kegworth

Hugh Wilson (1900)
Sydney Wells & Sons (1925)

Ketton

W.Bean & Co, *Rutland Brewery.* Trading as Molesworth & Bean in 1894 before becoming T.C.Molesworth & Son in 1895. Above named adopted in 1902.

Ketton & King's Cliffe Brewery Co.Ltd, *Ketton Brewery.* Trading as Thomas W.Whincup in 1887 then Sealy & Wilde by 1895. Registered as Ketton Brewery Co. in 1898 before merging with King's Cliffe Brewery, Northants in 1900. Acquired by Smith & Co. in 1910.

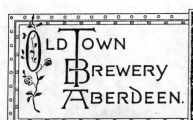 

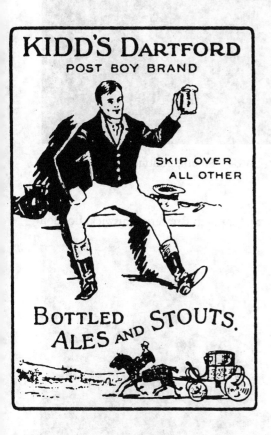

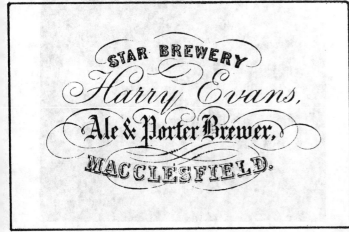

Threlfalls Chesters Ltd, Salford

A & T Sibeth, Fontmell Magna, Dorset

Ludlow & Craven Arms Brewery, c.1930

Sich's Lamb Brewery, Chiswick, London

Langham

Ruddles Brewery Ltd. Founded by Richard Baker 1858. Under the name of H.H.Parry 1895. After the death of Parry in 1910, the brewery and 22 public houses were offered for sale in April 1911 and were bought by George Ruddle, the brewery manager, for £19,500. Registered as G.Ruddle & Co.Ltd December 1945. Their 38 tied houses were sold in 1978, the majority to Everards, to allow the company to concentrate on supplying beer to supermarkets. Acquired by Grand Metropolitan July 1986 and the name was changed as above 1987. Still brewing 1990.

Leicester

Richard Charles Allen Ltd, *26 Newark Street.* Acquired by the Leicester Brewing & Malting Co.Ltd 1900 and closed.

All Saints' Brewery Co.(Leicester) Ltd, *21 Silver Street.* Owned by Cock & Moon from the 1860s. Registered September 1896 to acquire Langmore & Bankart, All Saints' Brewery and Watts & Son, wine and spirit merchants, Leicester. Brewing ceased 1925 and was acquired by Ind Coope & Co.Ltd March 1929 with 81 public houses.

Beaumanor Brewery. Founded by Stephen Hoskins and Simon Oldfield.

Everard's Brewery Ltd, *Castle Acres, Narborough.* Founded 1849 when Thomas Hull and William Everard leased the Southgate Brewery, Southgate Street, Leicester, from Wilmot & Co. In 1893 acquired the Bridge Brewery, Burton-on-Trent from Henry Boddington & Co.Ltd. As this proved to be too small for the firm's output, they leased the Trent Brewery from the Trent Brewery Co.Ltd (in liquidation) in February 1898 and the Bridge Brewery was closed June 1898. Registered 1925 as W.Everard & Co.Ltd. Southgate Brewery. Closed 1931 and all brewing was concentrated at Burton-on-Trent. Public company registered as above October 1936. Trent Brewery renamed the Tiger Brewery c.1970 and was closed 1983. In 1985 it was sold for conversion into a brewery museum and the Castle Acres brewery was established. Still brewing independently 1990 with 137 tied houses.

T.Hoskins Ltd, *Beaumanor Brewery, Beaumanor Road.* Founded 1877 by Jabez Penn and acquired by Thomas Hoskins 1906. Registered June 1947. Acquired by Barrie and Robert Hoar July 1983 and by Hoskins Brewery PLC November 1985. Still in operation 1990 with 10 public houses.

Hoskins & Oldfield Brewery Ltd, *North Mills, Frog Island.* Founded 1984 by Philip Hoskins, former brewer at Hoskins. Still in operation 1990.

Leicester Brewery, *6 Half Croft, High Street, Syston.* Founded May 1983 to brew keg beer for clubs. Closed 1985.

Leicester Brewing & Malting Co.Ltd, *Eagle Brewery, Upper Charnwood Street.* Operated by Frederick Bates 1877. Registered June 1890 to acquire Bates, Son & Bishell and the malting business of Needham & Crick, Leicester. Acquired by Ansells Brewery Ltd 1952 with about 140 public houses and was closed.

Midlands Clubs Brewery Ltd, *822 Syston Street.* Founded 1919. Known as the Northants & Leicestershire Co-operative Clubs Brewery until 1957. Closed 24th January 1969.

Welch Brothers, *St.Martin's Brewery, 10/12 Loseby Lane.* Acquired by the Leicester Brewing & Malting Co.Ltd 1920 and was closed.

Other Breweries

John Victor Barker, *Melton Road, Syston* (1930)
Percy William Barradale, *Syston Brewery* (1898)
John Henry Booth, *Syston* (1920)
George Brown, *Hinckley Road Brewery* (1891)
John Burgess, *The Green, Bath Street* (1920)
George Collins, *28 Thornton Lane* (1890)
Thomas Baxter Collison, *73 Sanvey Gate* (1920)
Cornelius Gurden, *86 High Cross Street* (1892)
John J.Hull, *16 Archdeacon Lane* (1920)
John L.Hurst. Thurmaston (1923)
Charles Luck, *44 Oxford Street* (1920)
S.D.McIver, *Syston* (1921)
William Marshall, *51 Welford Street* (1921)
George Richards, *158 Belgrave Gate* (1920)
Tom Richardson, *116 Churchgate* (1921)
Ernest Ealing Riley, *Chapel Street, Syston* (1920)
John Sharpe, *2 Lower Churchgate* (1923)
Fred Townsend, *14 Gravel Street* (1923)
Tom Willson, *14 Carley Street* (1920)

Long Clawson

Coleman Brothers Ltd, *Belvoir Hunt Brewery.* Wound up 1900.

Loughborough

Midland Brewery Co.Ltd, *Derby Road.* Registered September 1865. Acquired by Stretton's Derby Brewery Ltd 1902 but brewing continued until 1932. 22 tied houses.

Herbert North, *Britannia Inn, 29 Pinfold Gate.* Home brew house. Brewing ceased shortly after the death of Mr North.

Frederick Alan Stenson, *Steam Brewery, King Edward Road.* Originally ale & porter merchants who began brewing c.1930. Closed 1958.

Other Breweries

Charles Dakin, *14 Pinfold Gate* (1921)
Edward A.Hitherly, *Nottingham Road* (1921)
Herbert Holmes, *47 Ward's End* (1921)
Robert Watson Oldershaw, *Wellington Brewery, The Rushes* (1922)
Henry Tyler, *6 The Rushes* (1920)
Leonard Walley, *46 Woodgate* (1930)
Thomas Webster, *53 Ward's End* (1926)

Lutterworth

Arthur Bannister, *High Street* (1895)

Thomas P.Buck, *George Street.* Originally established by Arthur Bannister at the Windmill, Walton, but moved to Lutterworth by 1895. Above title assumed 1900. Brewing ceased c.1926 but firm continued as bottlers and brewer's agents until 1982. Four pubs sold 1945. Brewery demolished 1985 for Co-op superstore.

Market Bosworth

William Henry Trivett (1921)

Market Harborough

Eady & Dulley Ltd, *St.Mary's Road.* Registered June 1895 to acquire the business of Joseph Chamberlain and James Dulley carried on as Eady & Dulley. Acquired by the Northampton Brewery Co.Ltd 1929 and brewing ceased 1938.

Measham

John Gilles Shields (1892)

Melton Mowbray

Adcock, Pacey & Co, *Egerton Brewery.* Acquired by Ind Coope Ltd December 1919.

Langton & Sons, *Thorpe End Brewery, Thorpe Road.* Offered for auction 3rd March 1901 and again on 23rd October 1906 with 14 public houses. Closed 1910.

Mountsorrel

Leake Brothers Ltd, *Castle Brewery, Main Street.* Registered May 1899 to acquire the business of Charles Rowley Leake and William Leake trading as Leake Brothers. Voluntary liquidation 18th July 1907. Apparently no tied houses.

Oakham

Morris' Rutland Brewery Ltd, *Rutland Brewery, New Street.* Founded 1842. Acquired by Warwicks & Richardsons Ltd 1905 with 19 public houses.

Rearsby

Edward Benskin (1921)

Sileby

William Barber, *Brook Street* (1923)
Henry Parkinson (1921)
Sharpe's Sileby Brewery Ltd, *Sileby Brewery, High Street.* Registered March 1912. Acquired by Stretton's Derby Brewery Ltd September 1920 with 15 tied houses and 20 off-licences. Brewing ceased 1922.
James Henry Sneesby, *High Street* (1923)

Stoney Stanton

George Middleton (1920)

Whissendine

Green & Hacker, *Whissendine Brewery.* Partnership dissolved February 1892/93. Converted into a dwelling house.

Whitwick

Thomas S.Grimey (1902)

Wymeswold

John Henry Hubbard, *Far Street* (1921)

LINCOLNSHIRE

Alford

Christopher Robinson, *East End* (1898)

Soulby, Sons & Winch Ltd, *West Street*. Registered December 1896 to acquire E.H.Soulby & Sons, Alford (founded in the 1840s) and T.M.Winch & Co, Louth Brewery, with a total of 83 public houses. Louth Brewery closed 1902. Acquired by J.W.Green Ltd 1951 with 144 tied houses and brewing ceased 1952.
Frederick Ward, *Red Lion Brewery, South End*. Acquired by Soulby, Sons & Winch Ltd 1900.

Billingborough

William Barrand (1898)

Bolingbroke

Maltby & Co. (1902)

Boston

E.G.N.Harper, *Eagle Brewery, Wide Bargate*. Originally under the name of T.W.Thorpe and was bought by Harper in August 1907 with 7 public houses. Merged with the Hundleby Brewery Ltd 1911 and brewing ceased.
W.Horry & Sons Ltd, *Rout Green Brewery, Horncastle Road*. Registered April 1913. Acquired by Soames & Co.Ltd 1924.
Other Breweries
Montague William Coward & Co, *Phoenix Brewery, Grove Street* (1922)
Horace Everitt, *New Bolingbroke Brewery* (1898)
William Henry Hubbert, *67 High Street* (1902)
Peacock Brewery, *Market Place* (1914)
John Swinn & Sons, *104 High Street* (1912)
John Thorpe, *Spilsby Road* (1895)

Bourne

Bourne Brewery Co.Ltd, *Manning Road*. Registered August 1891 as Joseph Wyles & Co.(Bourne Brewery) Ltd. Voluntary liquidation 27th September 1897. New company registered as above May 1898 and this was dissolved in March 1910. Later under the name of Charles Campbell McLeod and was amalgamated with Soames & Co.Ltd 1916. Brewery converted into stores and was later demolished.
Thomas B.G.Thomas, *Manning Road* (1910)

Branston

Alfred Healey (1898)

Burgh-le-Marsh

T.E.Walls, *Kiln House Brewery* (1920)
Mathias Wharram & Co, *Steam Brewery* (1923)

Caistor

John William Christian, exors of, *Fountain Street* (1920)
James Rose & Co, *Nettleton Brewery*. Acquired by the Nottingham Brewery Ltd 1900.

Coningsby

Spencer Harrison Whitan (1910)

Corby Glen

Fighting Cocks, *Market Place*. Home brew house founded 1975. Ceased brewing 1983.

Dunholme

William Moffatt (1892)

Firsby

Cartwright & Fordham (1910)

Fiskerton

William Goulding (1895)

Folkingham

E.J.Gummitt & Son (1910)

Gainsborough

William Pickering, *Half Moon Inn* (1898)

Gosberton

Godfrey Smith (1928)

Grantham

Mary Ann Chambers, *1 Chambers Street, Little Gonerby* (1892)
Sarah Gibson, *1/2 Grantley Street* (1921)
Mowbray & Co.Ltd, *Grantham Brewery, London Road*. Founded in the early 19th Century. Registered May 1888 to acquire Mowbray & Co and Burbridge & Hutchinson, wine and spirit merchants. Acquired by J.W.Green Ltd March 1952 with 200 tied houses and the name was changed to Flowers Breweries (East Midlands) Ltd in 1959. Brewing ceased in 1964.
Redhead & Co, *Spittlegate Brewery, London Road*. Acquired by Mowbray & Co.Ltd 1891.

Hainton

Henry Edwin Flintoff (1923)

Halton Holegate

Anthony Shaw (1914)

Hoffleet Stow

William Sharpe & Son, *Hoffleet Stow Brewery* (1939)

Holbeach

J.Annison, *Penny Hill Brewery* (1910)
John Hardy Carter, *High Street*. Public houses bought by Soames & Co.Ltd of Spalding 1904.
Ridlington & Son, *Old Foundry Brewery, Barrington Gate* (1898)

Horncastle

Walter Gaunt, *Horncastle Old Brewery, 29 Prospect Street*. Offered for auction 27th July 1905. Brewing ceased c.1914.
Horncastle & Kirkstead Brewery Co.Ltd, *Phoenix Brewery, South Street*. Operated by Robert Clifton Armstrong until 1887 as the Phoenix Brewery Co. Merged with Atkinson Harrup of Kirkstead 1914. The merged business was registered as above in 1916. Ceased brewing 1931.
Other Breweries
W.Bell, *12 Stonewall Row* (1903)
Bellamy Brothers Ltd, *Foundry Street* (1931)
Joseph Bower, *16 North Street* (1907)
Alfred Healey & Sons, *The Wharf* (1895)
Walter Levett, *Old Brewery* (1900)
William Frederick Snartt & Son, *1 Bull Ring* (1895)
George Woods, *Mill Lane* (1902)

Hundleby

Hundleby Brewery Ltd. Registered November 1900 to acquire the business of Frederick Thomas Maltby with 30 public houses. Voluntary liquidation 4th January 1921 and the houses were sold as separate lots.

Ingoldmells

Walkin Reed (1895)

Kirkby-on-Bain

James William Green (1898)

Kirkstead

Atkinson Harrup. Merged with the Phoenix Brewery Co. of Horncastle 1914 to form the Horncastle & Kirkstead Brewery Co.Ltd registered in 1916.

Kirton Fen

Thomas Sharpe, exors of, *Witham Brewery* (1912)
Henry Wileman (1890)

Langrick

Joseph Bucknall (1910)

Lincoln

William Henry Brook, *Crown Brewery, Waterside North.* Acquired by Arthur & Bertram Hall of Ely 1892 and brewing ceased in 1923.
Dawber & Co, *Carholme Road.* Founded 1826. Acquired by Mowbray & Co.Ltd November 1905 with 52 tied houses.
John Dawber, *Monson Street* (1895)
Charles Wilson Ludgate, *270 High Street* (1920)
Norton & Turton Ltd, *5 Drury Lane.* Founded 1861 by William Ellis at the Leopard Inn, Steep Hill and the Drury Lane brewery was founded in 1872 and was acquired by Norton & Turton 1898. Acquired by Hewitt Brothers Ltd of Grimsby *c.*1922.

Long Sutton

Edward Dawes, *Standard Brewery, London Road/Roman Bank.* Founded by 1872. Sold to Burton & Lincoln Breweries Ltd *c.*1890.

Louth

Richard Dawson, *5 Corn Market & 1/5 New Street* (1902)
Thomas Dobbs, *Ramsgate* (1890)
Baltmer & Co, *Ramsgate* (1898)
T.M.Winch & Co, *Louth Brewery, Queen Street and Maiden Row.* Merged with E.H.Soulby & Sons of Alford 1896 to form Soulby, Sons & Winch Ltd.

Market Deeping

Hereward Brewery, *10 Peacock Square, Blenheim Way.* Founded May 1983. Ceased brewing November 1984.

Valentine Stapleton, *Church Street.* Brewery and 7 public houses sold for £900 on 24th July 1907.

Market Rasen

Robert Fletcher, *Market Place* (1920)
Market Rasen Brewery Co.Ltd, *17 Oxford Street.* Registered 11th February 1901. Originally registered 4th April 1879 as Favill & Co.Ltd to acquire the business of Robert Favill and the name was changed as above on 28th April 1881. Acquired by Hole & Co.Ltd 1926, with 33 tied houses, for £57,000.

Martin

George & Henry Cawdron (1914)

Moulton Chapel

George Henry Bradford (1926)

Nettleham

William Nicholson (1914)

Nettleton

Charles Henry Colton, *Pelham Brewery.* Founded by 1887. Acquired by the Market Rasen Brewery Co.Ltd *c.*1914.

North Somercotes

Susannah J.Youhill (1902)

Old Leake

George Henry Horton, *Old Leake Brewery* (1898)

Partney

Harry Goodwin, *Partney Lane.* Acquired by Walter Gaunt of Horncastle October 1898 with one fully licensed house and three beerhouses for £3,550.

Pinchbeck

Aoltie Bainbridge Orbell (1914)

Revesby

Robert Cole (1914)

Silk Willoughby

Benjamin Money (1920)

Skellingthorpe

Ann Emmons (1895)

Sleaford

Bellamy & Ashton, *Phoenix Brewery, Southgate.* Acquired by Soulby, Sons & Winch Ltd 1900 with 12 public houses.
Thomas Bird, *63 Westgate* (1923)
John Taylor Marston, *Albion Brewery, Southgate* (1892)
Richard Roberts, *Boston Road* (1895)

South Kyme

Samuel T.Coulson (1921)

Spalding

Kate Ground, *Railway Tavern, 21 Winsouver Road.* Home brew house acquired by Samuel Smith's Old Brewery, Tadcaster 1940/45.
Soames & Co.Ltd, *Cowbit Road.* Operated by Joseph Henry Burg until 1887 when it was acquired by Soames & Co. Registered 1909. Acquired by Steward & Patteson Ltd in 1949. Brewery now mainly demolished.
Thomas Upton, *1 Cowbit Road* (1892)

Stamford

Bartholomew William Aldwinckle, *1 Water Street, St.Martin's* (1921)
G. & H. R. Hunt, *Water Street, St.Martin's.* Acquired by Mowbray & Co.Ltd, in March 1927 with 61 tied houses and was closed.
Lowe, Son & Cobbold Ltd, *St.Michael's Brewery, 6/7 Broad Street.* Founded 1819. Operated as Lowe & Son until 1895 when it was registered as above. Acquired by James Hole & Co.Ltd 1935 with 26 public houses and brewing ceased. Brewery is now a petrol station.
Christopher Martin, *30 Foundry Street* (1921)

Melbourns Brewery Ltd, *All Saints Brewery, 21 All Saints Street.* Founded 1825 and was acquired by Melbourn Brothers in 1869. Brewing ceased 1974 and their 32 tied houses were supplied by Samuel Smith Ltd until sold to J.W.Cameron & Co.Ltd 1987. Part of the brewery is now a museum.
Phillips Stamford Brewery Ltd, *St.Martin's Brewery, Water Street.* Operated by the Phillips family from 1825. Registered September 1937. Acquired by the Northampton Brewery Co.Ltd 1952 with 70 public houses and brewing ceased. Part of the brewery is now used by an agricultural machinery firm and part as a girl's school.

Surfleet

Alfred Ernest Smith (1940)

Swineshead

John Bramley, *Wheatsheaf Brewery* (1895)

Tattershall

John Short (1902)

Waddington

Elizabeth Howden (1898)

Wainfleet All Saints

George Bateman & Son Ltd, *Salem Bridge Brewery*. Founded in 1824 by William Crow. Leased by George Bateman from Edwin Crow 1874 and bought by him in 1875. Registered 1928. Still brewing independently 1990.
Edwin Eyres (1895)
W.H.Gunson, *High Street.* Brewing ceased 1934 but the business was continued as wine & spirit merchants until the premises were bombed in 1940.

Wragby

Charles Phillipson (1910)

Wrangle

John Robert Collins (1902)

GREATER LONDON

Barking

Barking Brewery, *Riverside Works, Hertford Road.* Founded August 1985 by David Jones. Closed 1986.
Glenny's Brewery Ltd, *18 Linton Road.* Registered November 1917 to acquire the business of Thomas Wallis Glenny. Acquired by Taylor, Walker & Co.Ltd January 1930 with 15 public houses. Buildings demolished.

Barnet

Old Barnet Brewery Co.Ltd, *Wood Street.* Founded 1694. Registered January 1906. Liquidator appointed 11th March 1909 and was dissolved 21st June 1912.
Harris Browne Ltd, *Hadley Brewery, Hadley High Street.* Founded 1700. Acquired by J.Harris Browne 1887. Registered December 1930. Acquired by Fremlins Ltd 1938 with 4 public houses and 2 off-licences and was closed. Brewery demolished 1979.
Arthur O.Crooke, *Hendon Brewery, The Hyde, Hendon NW9.* Acquired by Michell & Aldous Ltd 1895.
John Dix, *Farmhouse Brewery, Hendon.* In receivership January 1891.
Windsor Castle, *The Walks, Church Lane, East Finchley N2.* Home brew house founded by landlord David Eaves, September 1981. Ceased brewing 1983.

Bexley

Jolly Fenman, *64 Blackfen Road, Sidcup.* Founded by Clifton Inns August 1986. Still brewing 1990.
Reffell's Bexley Brewery Ltd, *Bourne Road, Bexley.* Founded 1874 by H.Reffell. Registered December 1898 to acquire Reffell Brothers and the London properties of Showell's Brewery Co.Ltd. Acquired by Courage & Co.Ltd 1956 with 19 tied houses and brewing ceased. Brewery still standing 1990.

Brent

Arthur Guinness, Son & Co.Ltd, *Park Royal Brewery, NW10 & St.James's Gate Brewery, Dublin.* Founded in 1759 at Dublin. Registered October 1886. Park Royal Brewery opened 1936 to supply the southern half of England.
Michell & Aldous Ltd, *Kilburn Brewery, 289/91 Kilburn High Road NW6.* Registered August 1894. Acquired by Truman, Hanbury, Buxton & Co.Ltd 1920.
Watson Brothers Ltd, *Wembley Brewery, Harrow Road, Sudbury.* Registered February 1894. Went into liquidation and was wound up May 1914. One tied house: The Jolly Gardeners, Harrow Road.

Bromley

George William Burrows, *Cray's Brewery, St.Mary Cray.* Established prior to 1870 by John Carnell Snelling and above style adopted between 1902 and 1905. Acquired by Reffell's Bexley Brewery Ltd October 1910.
Fox & Sons, *Oak Brewery, Sevenoaks Road.* Founded 1836. Offered for auction June 1909 and 28 of the public houses were sold to Hoare & Co.Ltd for £54,695. See also:- Golding & Co, Bat & Ball Brewery, Sevenoaks.
Jones & Co, *Steam Brewery, Brewery Road, Bromley Common.* Established c.1840 by William & Thomas Davis and trading as the Bromley Steam Brewery Company by 1870. Acquired by Jones & Spreckley before 1882. Acquired by Whitbread & Co.Ltd 31st October 1901.
Powell & Co, *Palace Brewery, Madeline Road, Anerley SW20.* Registered April 1912 as the West of England Brewery Co.Ltd to carry on the business of P.G.Simpson. This company was dissolved on 25th May 1919. Brewery bombed 1941 and was closed.
West Kent Breweries Ltd, *Upper Elmers Road, Beckenham.* Established prior to 1847 when owned by James Learner. Run by William Snelling and auctioned upon his retirement in 1869. Traded as E.Stillwell 1874, Arthur Peacock & Co 1878 and Pontifex & Hall 1882. Registered as above May 1888 to acquire the Norwood Brewery, the West Kent Brewery, the Crown Brewery, Lewisham and the Pioneer Brewery, Chelsea. Partnership dissolved October 1892 and the West Kent Brewery passed to McMullen & Son. Brewing was transferred to Bailey's Berkshire Brewery, Camberwell 1900. Premises sold to the Notting Hill Brewery Co.Ltd by 1908.

Camden

Camden Brewery Co.Ltd, *Hawley Crescent, Camden NW1.* Founded 1859 by Richard Garrett, Abram Garrett, Thomas Whittaker and George A.Grimwood of Leiston, Suffolk. Registered July 1889 to acquire Whittaker, Grimwood & Co. with 84 public houses. Receiver appointed 1912 and a new company of the same name was registered in January 1913. Acquired by Courage & Co Ltd 1923 with 78 tied houses. Brewing ceased in 1925.
Hampstead Brewery Co.Ltd, *9a Hampstead High Street NW3.* Registered August 1906 to acquire Mure & Co. Acquired by Reffell's Bexley Brewery Ltd 1931. The remains of the brewery are still standing at the rear of Thresher's wine & spirit merchants.
Reid's Brewery Co.Ltd, *Griffin Brewery, Liquorpond Street (now Clerkenwell Road) EC1.* Founded 1757 when Richard Meux and Mungo Murray acquired Jackson's Brewery, Mercer Street. Griffin Brewery built 1763. Andrew Reid became a partner in 1793. Registered 1888. Merged with Watney & Co.Ltd and Combe & Co.Ltd July 1898 to form Watney, Combe, Reid & Co.Ltd. Brewing ceased 1899.
Yorkshire Grey, *2 Theobalds Road WC1.* Home brew house founded 1984. Still brewing 1990.

City of London

City of London Brewery Co.Ltd, *Hour Glass Brewery, 89 Upper Thames Street EC4.* Founded before 1431. Recorded under John & William Reynolds 1587 and was run by the Reynolds family until 1730 when it was acquired by Calvert & Co. Registered as above February 1860, re-registered as the New City of London Brewery Co.Ltd September 1891. Reverted to the original title March 1895. In 1919 took over Nalder & Collyers Brewery Co.Ltd Croydon and Stansfeld & Co.Ltd, Swan Brewery Fulham. Brewing was transferred to the Swan Brewery in 1922 and the Hour Glass Brewery was converted into a warehouse. Brewing ceased at Fulham in 1936 when many public houses were sold to Hoare & Co.Ltd. The majority of the Nalder & Collyer public houses were sold to Ind Coope Ltd in 1956. The Hour Glass Brewery was destroyed by bombing in the Second World War. The final connection with brewing ended in 1968 with the sale of 20 public houses to Allied Breweries, but the company is still in existence as an investment trust.

Croydon

A.C.S.& H.Crowley, *137/139 High Street.* Brewed at Waddon since 1600 and acquired the Croydon brewery in 1808. Acquired by Hoare & Co.Ltd 1919 and brewing ceased in 1929. See also:- Alton, Hants.

John Dyke, *Church Street* (1890)

Lion Inn, *Pawsons Road.* Home brew house founded 1981 by Ulick Burke. Ceased brewing 1986 after a boiler explosion.

Nalder & Collyers Brewery Co.Ltd, *Croydon Brewery, 123 High Street.* Founded by Wylim Chapman Baker prior to 1586. Leased by Nalder & Collyer 1848 from the trustees of Anthony Harman and they bought the freehold 1890/91. Registered May 1888 with 255 public houses. Acquired by the City of London Brewery Co.Ltd 1919 with 170 tied houses. Brewing ceased 1936.

Page & Overton's Brewery Ltd, *Shirley Brewery, Overton's Yard, Surrey Street.* Ludlam & Grant operated the Shirley Brewery, Shirley, Street, Croydon until 1889 when it was acquired by Nathaniel Page. Henry Overton founded the Royal Oak Brewery, Surrey Street 1854. Registered August 1892 to merge Page's Shirley Brewery and Overton's Royal Oak Brewery. The Shirley Brewery was closed in 1903 and the Royal Oak Brewery was then renamed the Shirley Brewery. Acquired by Hoare & Co.Ltd 1929 but brewing continued until 1954. Brewery demolished 1972.

G.Yeldram, *Tower Brewery, Station Road, West Croydon.* Founded 1872. Acquired by Thorne Brothers Ltd 1905.

Ealing

Nolder & Co, *Anchor Brewery, 54 Bollo Bridge Road, S.Acton W3* (1906)

Stratton's Brewery Ltd, *The Vale, Acton W3.* Private company registered February 1909 to acquire the business of Cyril Paul Stratton and Harold West carried on as Stratton's Brewery Co. Ceased trading November 1910 and was dissolved 29th August 1913.

Enfield

Gripper Brothers, *Stag Brewery.* See also:- Haringey.

John Freeborn Webb, *Ponders End.* Receiving order made July 1893.

Greenwich

Charles Beasley Ltd, *North Kent Brewery, Lakedale Road, Plumstead SE18.* Founded by L.Davis 1845 as the Park Brewery and name had been changed to the North Kent Brewery by 1878. Registered April 1943. Acquired by Courage, Barclay & Simonds 1963 and brewing ceased. The brewery has been demolished.

Eltham Brewery Co, *Eltham Brewery, High Street.* Established prior to 1850 at the Beehive Brewery when run by Leare & Turner. J.Leare by 1859, Berners & Kemp 1870 and Berners & Co. by 1874. Traded variously as Grier & Shepherd 1878, J.C.F.Grier 1882 and Kenward Brothers 1900. Old timber brewery replaced by new brewery on the tower principle by Arthur Kinder prior to 1900. It is not known when brewing ceased but the premises were in use as a paint and varnish works until mostly destroyed by enemy action during the Second World War.

John Lovibond & Sons Ltd, *Greenwich Brewery, 177 Greenwich High Street SE10 & St.Anne's Brewery, Salisbury, Wilts.* Founded 1826 by John Lovibond at the Nag's Head Brewery, Esther Place, Bridge Street, Greenwich and moved to Greenwich High Street 1865. Salisbury brewery opened before 1884. Registered July 1896. Ceased to brew 1962 and the public houses were sold, mainly to Courage, Barclay & Simonds. An attempt to reopen the brewery by the Alan Greenwood Beer Agency (Brewing) Ltd in 1978 was not realised. The Greenwich buildings are extant.

McDonnell's, *428 Woolwich Road, Charlton SE7.* Home brew house. Founded in the former Antigallican public house December 1985. Still brewing 1990.

Queen Victoria, *118 Wellington Street, Woolwich SE18.* Founded by John McDonnell October 1983 but later closed and production concentrated at Charlton.

Hackney

Falcon & Firkin, *274 Victoria Park Road E9.* Home brew house opened January 1986. Still brewing 1990.

Hoxton Brewery Ltd, *Bell's Brewery, Hoxton Street N1.* Registered October 1896 to acquire H.B.Bell & Co, with 13 tied houses and George Wyatt, wine & spirit merchants, East Harding Street EC4 with 18 public houses. Acquired by John Lovibond & Sons Ltd 1900.

Michell, Goodman, Young & Co.Ltd, *Belfast Road, Stoke Newington N16.* Brewery acquired by Matthew Michell 1880. Registered December 1894. Acquired by Mann, Crossman & Paulin Ltd 1919.

Pitfield Brewery, *The Beer Shop, Pitfield Street N1.* Founded by Brian Brett August 1981 at the Two Brewers off-licence. Sold to Rob Jones 1982 and renamed the Beer Shop. Moved to Hoxton Square 1986. Merged with Premier Midland ales 1990 and brewing transferred to Stourbridge.

Hammersmith & Fulham

Joseph Friend Bell, *Peterborough Road, Parsons Green SW6.* Acquired by Charrington & Co.Ltd 1890.

Grigg Brothers, *Albion Brewery, 11/13 Uxbridge Road, Shepherd's Bush W12.* Brewery and 12 public houses offered for auction 3rd November 1924.

Henry Lovibond & Son (1900) Ltd, *Cannon Brewery, 80/84 Lillie Road SW6.* Registered 1900 to acquire the business of the same name registered February 1897. Acquired by John Lovibond & Sons Ltd 1901. Founded 1831. Premises used as an aircraft factory during the First World War.

Stansfeld & Co.Ltd, *Swan Brewery, Walham Green SW6.* Founded 1765. Registered January 1889. Acquired by the City of London Brewery Co.Ltd 1914.

Haringey

Caffyn & Son Ltd, *Hornsey Brewery, Clarendon Road N8.* Samuel F.Rhodes recorded here 1884 but Richard Caffyn by 1877. Registered January 1899. Wound up September 1921. Premises later used by V.F.Rhodes & Co.Ltd, bottlers, until about 1971 and were destroyed by fire c.1974.

Gripper Brothers, *Bell Brewery, High Road, Tottenham N15 & Stag Brewery, Enfield.* Founded 1760. Acquired by Whitbread & Co.Ltd 1896 who used it as a regional depot until the mid 1980s.

Imperial Lager Brewery Ltd, *Portland Road, Tottenham N15.* Registered 5th May 1886 as the Tottenham Lager Beer & Ice Factory Ltd to acquire the business of Leopold Seckendorff. Voluntary liquidation 6th March 1895 and a new company was registered as above in February 1895. Brewing ceased 1903 and the name was changed to Imperial Cold Stores Ltd.

Lewis G.Williams & Co, *Hornsey Rise Brewery, Hornsey Rise.* E.& O.Nash recorded here 1871. Then William Trimmer in 1877 and Robert Hurman, 1884. Above style adopted before 1887. In receivership February 1891. Acquired April of same year by Cressey & Co who continued trading. It is not known when brewing ceased.

Wooldridge & Co.Ltd, *Bruce Grove Brewery, 551a High Road, Tottenham N15.* Founded 1834. Registered August 1903 to acquire Wooldridge, Hill & Co. with 8 public houses. Acquired by Hoare & Co.Ltd 1910. In 1923 the premises were occupied by Linnell's Tottenham Brewery Co.Ltd and Davenport's Ltd of Birmingham were listed here in 1939.

Harrow

Thomas Clutterbuck & Co, *Stanmore.* Founded c.1749 and was definitely brewing by 1763. Ceased brewing 1916, all beer being purchased from Bass until 1923 when they were acquired by the Cannon Brewery Ltd with 84 tied houses.

Havering

S.R.Conron & Co, exors of, *Old Hornchurch Brewery, Church Hill, Hornchurch.* Founded 1789. S.R.Conron was trading as Sweetman & Co, Francis Court Brewery, Dublin in 1889. The Hornchurch brewery was bought by his father in 1892. Acquired by Harman's Uxbridge Brewery Ltd 1924 and was sold to Mann, Crossman & Paulin Ltd in 1925. Brewing ceased 1929.

Hornchurch Brewery Co.Ltd, *White Hart Lane.* Registered as the Hornchurch Brewery Ltd August 1883 with 37 public houses. Dissolved September 1884. Registered as above July 1890 to acquire the business of Henry and Benjamin Homes, Hornchurch, and Charles Dagnall, Horley, Surrey. Voluntary liquidation 19th December 1890.

Ind Coope Ltd, *Romford, Essex.* See also:- Burton-on-Trent, Staffs.

Hillingdon

Harman's Uxbridge Brewery Ltd, *Old Brewery, 180 High Street, Uxbridge.* Founded c.1730. Registered September 1924 to acquire S.R.Conron, Hornchurch & Alice F.Webb, Uxbridge carried on as Harman & Co. Acquired by Courage, Barclay & Simonds Ltd 1962 with 83 tied house and 5 off-licences. Brewing ceased March 1964.

Mercer & Sons, *Colne Brewery, 82 High Street, Uxbridge.* Acquired by M.A.Sedgwick & Co. of Watford 1896.

Joseph Shepherd, *Hayes Brewery, Hayes* (1894)

James Thatcher & Co.Ltd, *Britannia Brewery, West Drayton.* Registered 1903. Acquired by the Isleworth Brewery Ltd 1910 with 30 public houses.

Union Brewery (B.& W.Beer Co.), *Silverdale Road, Pump Lane Industrial Estate, Hayes.* Founded October 1982. Closed February 1983.

R.Wills & Son, *High Street, Uxbridge* (1898)

Hounslow

Belgrave Brewery Co.Ltd, *Wellington Road North.* Registered December 1879. Voluntary liquidation 10th February 1883 and was wound up March 1886.

Deane & Lewis, *Belgrave Brewery, Wellington Road North.* Successors to the New Hounslow Brewery Co.Ltd. New brewery built 1901. Bankrupt February 1907 and the brewery and 6 public houses were offered for sale in the following month.

Dobell & Courtauld, *Boston Brewery, Boston Road, Brentford.* Acquired by Fuller, Smith & Turner 1897.

Fuller, Smith & Turner Ltd, *Griffin Brewery, Chiswick Lane South W4.* Founded 1699 by Thomas Mawson. Acquired by John Fuller 1842. Henry Smith and John Turner became partners in November 1846. Registered August 1929. Still independent 1990.

William Gomm & Son, *Beehive Brewery, Catherine Wheel Yard, 93 High Street, Brentford.* Acquired by Fuller, Smith & Turner 1908 with 34 tied houses.

Isleworth Brewery Ltd, *St.John's Road, Isleworth.* Founded by 1726 when owned by John Atfield. Acquired by William Farnell 1800. Registered 1886 to acquire Farnell & Watson. Voluntary liquidation November 1923 and was acquired by Watney, Combe, Reid & Co.Ltd 1924. Brewing ceased 1946 and is now used as a bottling store.

New Hounslow Brewery Co.Ltd, *Wellington Road North, Hounslow.* Registered May 1896 to acquire the Hounslow Brewery Co.Ltd which had been registered in August 1891 and was wound up April 1895. Possibly successors to the Belgrave Brewery Co.Ltd.

Royal Brewery (Brentford) Ltd, *Royal Brewery, 23 High Street, Brentford.* Operated as Gibbon & Croxford until 1880 when it was acquired by Montague Ballard. Registered August 1890 as the Royal Brewery Co.Ltd with 102 tied houses. Name changed as above 1900. Acquired by Style & Winch Ltd 1922. Brewing ceased June 1923.

Sich & Co.Ltd, *Lamb Brewery, Church Street, Chiswick.* Founded by 1819. Registered November 1888. Acquired by the Isleworth Brewery Ltd 1920. Brewery plant sold 17th October 1922. Buildings still extant.

Islington

Barnsbury Brewery Ltd, *109 Roman Way, Barnsbury N7.* Registered 9th December 1897 as the Union Brewery (Barnsbury) Ltd to acquire the business of the late Frederick William Blogg with 2 public houses. Name changed to William Blogg & Co.Ltd 15th January 1898 and was dissolved 23rd July 1901. Re-registered as Blogg's Brewery Ltd 6th June 1899 with 6 tied houses. Receiver appointed 13th February

1914 and was wound up 27th November 1914. Finally registered as above 11th July 1912 and was wound up voluntarily 24th December 1913.

Cannon Brewery Co.Ltd, *160 St.John Street, Clerkenwell EC1.* Founded about 1720 by Rivers Dickson. Registered January 1895 with 110 public houses. Acquired by Taylor, Walker & Co.Ltd 1930 but brewing continued until 1955 and was converted into a distillery and bonded warehouse in 1959. Carlsberg-Tetley headquarters were located here. Now closed.

Flounder & Firkin, *52/54 Holloway Road N7.* Home brew house founded March 1985 in the former Highbury Brewery Tap and is now known as Bruce's Highbury Brewery.

A.Gordon & Co, *425 Caledonian Road N1.* Brewery offered for auction on 21st September 1915.

Highbury Brewery Ltd, *52/54 Holloway Road N7.* Founded c.1740 by a Mr Willoughby. Registered March 1896 to acquire the business of Frederick Henry and Arthur Selmes Taylor. Acquired by Taylor, Walker & Co.Ltd 1912 with about 40 public houses and was closed.

King of Beasts, *65 Graham Street N1.* Home brew house founded May 1981. Still brewing 1990.

E.A.Morgan, *192/194 Balls Pond Road N1.* Offered for sale in 1917.

Pheasant & Firkin, *166 Goswell Road EC1.* A Bruce's home brew house founded 1981. Still brewing 1990.

Herbert Santer & Sons, *Albion Brewery, 69/71 Caledonian Road N1.* Acquired by Hoare & Co.Ltd 1918.

Wenlock Brewery Co.Ltd, *Wenlock Road, City Road, Shoreditch N1.* Operated by Richard Alfred Glover until 1887. Registered 1893 to acquire Glover, Bell & Co. Acquired by Bass, Ratcliff & Gretton Ltd 1961 and brewing ceased 1962.

Whitbread & Co.Ltd, *Chiswell Street EC1.* Founded 1742. Registered July 1889. New brewery built at Luton in 1969 and brewing ceased at Chiswell Street 1976. The Luton brewery was closed in 1985. Now operates breweries at Samlesbury, Lancs; Magor, Gwent; Castle Eden, Durham and Cheltenham Glos. Headquarters of the Whitbread group.

Woodhead's Brewery Ltd, *Canonbury Brewery, 112 St.Paul's Road E1.* Registered in 1915 as Edmund Woodhead & Sons Ltd. Re-registered April 1936 as Woodhead's Canonbury Brewery Ltd. Name changed as above September 1946. Brewing was transferred to the South London Brewery, Southwark in 1949. Acquired by Charrington United Breweries Ltd 1965 and brewing ceased.

Kensington & Chelsea

Campbell-Johnstone & Co.Ltd, *Phoenix Brewery, Latimer Road W10.* Registered March 1896. Acquired by Charrington & Co.Ltd 1909 with 100 public houses.

Chelsea Brewery Co.Ltd, *533 King's Road, Chelsea SW3.* Registered February 1897 to acquire Bowden & Co. Merged with the Welch Ale Brewery Ltd March 1900.

Ferret & Firkin, *114 Lots Road, Chelsea SW10.* A Bruce's home brew house founded June 1983. Still brewing 1990.

Frog & Firkin, *41 Tavistock Crescent W1.* A Bruce's home brew house founded February 1981. Still brewing 1990.

Matthews & Canning, *Anchor Brewery, Britten Street, Chelsea SW3.* Amalgamated with Whitbread & Co.Ltd 1899 and closed in 1907.

Notting Hill Brewery Co.Ltd, *243 Portland Road W11.* Established prior to 1876 when run by Charles Clarke. In receivership October 1891. Registered as above 1905. Brewing ceased 1920 and 80 of the tied houses were sold to Whitbread & Co.Ltd, a number of these being resold to Charrington & Co.Ltd.

William Wells & Co.Ltd, *Britannia Brewery, Allen Street, Kensington W8.* Registered June 1903. Acquired by Young & Co's Brewery Ltd March 1924.

Kingston-upon-Thames

Walter & John Flint East, *Oil Mill Lane.* Acquired by Charrington & Co.1891.

Flamingo & Firkin, *88 London Road.* Bruce's latest home brew house opened in a former Watneys house noted as having Isleworth Brewery tiles on the exterior. Still brewing 1990.

Fricker's Eagle Brewery, exors of, *High Street.* Acquired by Hodgson's Kingston Brewery Co.Ltd 1903 with 28 tied houses.

Hodgson's Kingston Brewery Co.Ltd, *Brook Street.* Founded *c.*1610. Acquired by William Hodgson 1854 with 90 tied houses. Registered October 1886 to acquire Hodgson Brothers. Acquired by Courage & Co.Ltd 1943 and brewing ceased 1965. Brewery demolished October 1971.

Nightingale Brothers, *Steam Brewery, Wood Street* (1891)

Lambeth

Allen & Co, *Brixton Brewery, 18 Atlantic Road SW9* (1902)

A.C. Beaton & Co, *Norwood Brewery, Chapel Road SE27.* Offered for auction October 1919 with 5 public houses and was bought by Hoare & Co.Ltd.

Brixton Brewery, *The Warrior, 242 Coldharbour Lane, Stockwell SW9.* Founded 1984. Still brewing 1990.

The Greyhound, *151 Greyhound Lane, Streatham SW16.* Home brew house founded July 1984. Still brewing 1990.

Lion Brewery Co.Ltd, *Lion Brewery, Belvedere Road, Lambeth SE1.* Originally known as Goding's Brewery. Registered April 1865. Acquired by Hoare & Co.Ltd 1923 and was closed. In 1929 the London County Council offered the brewery to the Southern Railway as the site for a new terminus on the condition that they gave up Charing Cross Station, but this scheme was shelved in 1931. Brewery demolished 1949 to clear the site for the building of the Royal Festival Hall.

New London Brewery Co.Ltd, *Durham Street, Vauxhall SE11.* Registered March 1897 to acquire the concern of the same name in liquidation. Voluntary liquidation 13th January 1925 and their 76 public houses were bought by the Wenlock Brewery Co.Ltd.

Stockwell Brewery Co.Ltd, *16 Stockwell Green SW9.* Founded 1730. Registered as Charles Hammerton & Co.Ltd 1902. Registered as above on 25th February 1937. Acquired by Watney, Combe, Reid & Co.Ltd May 1951 with 7 tied houses and 207 off-licences. Brewing ceased before 1964 and the brewery has been demolished.

Waltham Brothers Ltd, *Half Guinea Ale Brewery, Stockwell Road/Combermere Road SW9.* Originally known as Rhodes' Brewery. Acquired by Edward Waltham in 1851. Acquired by the Lion Brewery Co.Ltd 1908 with 4 public houses. Brewery still standing 1990.

Lewisham

Forest Hill Brewery Co.Ltd, *61 Perry Vale SE23.* Registered November 1885 to acquire Morgan Brothers. Acquired by Whitbread & Co.Ltd 1924. Premises bought by United Dairies 1927 and was converted into a bottling plant.

Fox & Firkin, *316 Lewisham High Street SE13.* A Bruce's home brew house founded May 1980. Still brewing 1990.

New Cross Brewery Co.Ltd, *26 Pomeroy Street SE14.* Originally registered April 1888 as the Hatcham Brewery Co.Ltd to acquire Charles Morgan & Co. Dissolved October 1892 and was succeeded by the South Metropolitan Brewing & Bottling Co.Ltd registered January 1890, which was wound up 17th January 1891. Registered as Burney's New Cross Brewery Ltd in December 1898 to acquire

the business of George Burney. Closed 1905 and was finally registered as above in September 1905. Voluntary winding up on 17th April 1925 and the public houses were acquired by Hoare & Co.Ltd.

H.& V.Nicholl Ltd, *Anchor Brewery, 170 Lewisham Road SE13.* Registered November 1887. Acquired by Whitbread & Co.Ltd 1891. Converted into a bottling and distribution centre.

Thomas Norfolk & Sons Ltd, *Deptford Brewery, 2 Deptford Bridge SE8.* Registered October 1894. Acquired by the Dartford Brewery Co.Ltd in 1904 with 55 tied houses.

Southwark Park Brewery Ltd, *Brewery Tap, 19 Trundleys Road SE8.* Registered September 1900 as London United Breweries Ltd to acquire the business carried on by J.F.Smith, H.Sampson and J.Silvester at the Southwark Park Brewery. New company registered as above July 1906 after the original one was wound up in 1905. Voluntary liquidation 26th January 1914.

Wilmington Brewery Co, *Crown Brewery, 99 Loampit Vale SE13.* Founded 1837. Acquired by Thorne Brothers from West Kent Breweries Ltd 1895.

Merton

Thunder & Little Ltd, *London Road, Mitcham.* Registered September 1895 to acquire the business of Francis Thunder and Edward Armstrong Little with 13 tied houses. Merged with Edward Boniface of Cheam 1898 to form the Mitcham & Cheam Brewery Co.Ltd. Acquired by Hoare & Co.Ltd 1914 and brewing ceased.

Newham

Holt & Co, *Marine Brewery, 52 Broad Street, Ratcliff Road, East Ham.* Founded 1837. Acquired by the Cannon Brewery Co.Ltd October 1912 with 27 public houses.

Richard W.Reeve, *West Ham Brewery, 242 Romford Road, Forest Gate E7.* Brewery plant for sale 9th April 1900. Used as a piano factory until *c.*1929.

Savill Brothers Ltd, *Maryland Road, Stratford E15.* Founded 1856. Registered December 1893. Acquired by Charrington & Co.Ltd 1925 and was closed.

Richmond

Jacob Claridge, *Ham Common* (1892)

Cole & Burrows, *Twickenham Brewery, 13 London Road.* Founded by 1635. Acquired by Brandon's (Putney) Brewery Ltd in 1892 and brewing ceased in 1906.

Phillips, More & Co.Ltd, *Mortlake Brewery, 14 Mortlake High Street SW14.* Founded in the 15th Century. Acquired by Charles James Phillips in the 1840s, Registered June 1888 as More & Co.Ltd. Acquired by Watney & Co.Ltd 1889 and the name was changed as above. Renamed the Stag Brewery 1959 after the closure of Watney's Stag Brewery, Westminster. Still brewing 1990. Now under Courage's control.

Roskilly & Sons, *Wheatsheaf Brewery, 65/66 Colne Road, Twickenham.* Possibly acquired by London United Breweries Ltd who were listed here in 1902.

D.Watney & Son Ltd, *Lansdown Brewery, Petersham Road, Richmond.* Registered April 1895. Acquired by Brandon's (Putney) Brewery Ltd 1915 and was closed. Premises now part of the Royal British Legion poppy factory.

Southwark

T.Bailey & Co, *Berkshire Brewery, 15 Wyndham Road, Camberwell SE5.* Acquired by West Kent Breweries Co.Ltd 1900 who then concentrated their brewing here.

Barclay, Perkins & Co.Ltd, *Park Street, Southwark SE1.* Founded 1616 by James Monger and became Barclay, Perkins in 1781. Registered June 1896. Merged with Courage & Co.Ltd 1955 to form Courage & Barclay Ltd. Brewing ceased in the early 1980s and the brewery site demolished.

E.J.Brooks, *Peckham Brewery, 133 Peckham Hill Street, SE15.* Acquired by Charrington & Co.Ltd 1916.

Courage & Co.Ltd, *Anchor Brewery, Horselydown, Bermondsey SE1.* Acquired by John Courage in 1787. Registered April 1888. Merged with Barclay, Perkins & Co.Ltd 1955 to form Courage & Barclay Ltd. Acquired by the Imperial Tobacco Group Ltd August 1972. Anchor Brewery closed 1981 and brewing was transferred to Worton Grange, Reading. Name changed to Courage Ltd October 1970. The Imperial Group was acquired by the Hanson Trust in 1986 who sold Courage as a separate concern to Elders IXL. Courage have now taken over all of the Grand Metropolitan breweries. All Courage public houses and 3/4 of Grand Met's houses are now run by a jointly owned company, Inntrepreneur Estates.

Goose & Firkin, *47/48 Borough Road SE1.* The first of the Bruce's breweries, founded July 1979. Formerly the Duke of York public house.

Market Brewery, *Market Porter Public House, 9 Stoney Street, Borough Market SE1.* Founded December 1981 by John Beach. Closed 1984 reopened May 1985.

New Phoenix Brewery Ltd, *North Surrey Brewery, 37 Peckham Road, Camberwell SE5.* Registered June 1896 to acquire the North Surrey Brewery and the Phoenix Brewery, Dorset Road, Lambeth. Wound up March 1905. A new company of the same name was registered in July 1907, Worthington & Co.Ltd holding the majority of the shares. Wound up voluntarily December 1927 and some of their public houses were sold to the Wenlock Brewery Co.Ltd.

Noakes & Co.Ltd, *Black Eagle Brewery, 27 White's Grounds, Bermondsey SE1.* Reputedly founded in 1697. Acquired by Day, Payne & Co. 1848 with 19 public houses and became Day, Noakes & Sons 1852. Registered March 1897. Brewing ceased at the Black Eagle Brewery 1921 and was transferred to Windsor. Acquired by Courage & Co.Ltd 1930 with 120 tied houses and brewing ceased.

Park Brewery Co, *54a Southampton Street, Camberwell SE5.* Acquired by Thomas Phillips & Co.Ltd of West Malling, Kent 1898 and was later under the control of Courage & Co.Ltd.

Phoenix & Firkin, *Windsor Walk, Denmark Hill SE5.* Founded 1984 in Denmark Hill railway station. Still brewing 1990.

Richard Ray & Son, *Camberwell Brewery, 52 Camberwell Green SE5.* Founded 1860. Acquired by the Winchester Brewery Co.Ltd 1895 and was sold to Samuel Allsopp & Sons Ltd with 53 public houses in 1907. Brewing ceased in 1919.

Simon's Tower Bridge Brewery Ltd, *218 Tower Bridge Road, Bermondsey SE1.* Founded by Simon Hosking February 1980. Ceased brewing 1981.

South London Brewery Ltd, *134 Southwark Bridge Road SE1.* Founded 1760. Registered April 1937 as Jenner's Brewery Ltd. Name changed as above 1939. Acquired by Woodhead's Brewery Ltd 1944 and brewing ceased in 1964.

Tooley Street Brewery, *52/54 Tooley Street SE1.* Founded by Mike Harwood 1984 to supply the Dickens Inn, St.Katharine's Dock. Closed 1986.

Tower Brewery, *218 Tower Bridge Road, Bermondsey SE1.* Founded July 1981 in the former Simon's Tower Bridge Brewery. Renamed the Bridge Brewery 1981 and brewing ceased in the same year.

Welch Ale Brewery Ltd, *561 Old Kent Road SE1.* Registered 1898 to acquire the business of Liddell & Co. Amalgamated with the Chelsea Brewery Co.Ltd and the Lion Brewery, Princes Risborough, Bucks in March 1900. The Old Kent Road brewery was offered for sale, brewing being concentrated at Chelsea. Acquired by Watney, Combe, Reid & Co.Ltd 1920.

Sutton

Edward Boniface, *High Street, Cheam.* Merged with Thunder & Little Ltd of Mitcham 1898 to form the Mitcham & Cheam Brewery Co.Ltd. Acquired by Hoare & Co.Ltd 1914 and brewing ceased.

Boorne & Co.Ltd, *London Road, Wallington.* Founded c.1810. Acquired by Thomas Boorne 1855. Registered July 1927. Acquired by Ind Coope Ltd 1931.

Tower Hamlets

Best & Co, *5 Heneage Street, Whitechapel E1* (1902)

Chandler's Wiltshire Brewery Ltd, *505 Hackney Road, Bethnal Green E2.* Registered May 1900 to acquire the business carried on by George Charles Porter and William Henry Dieseldorff as Chandler & Co and was a branch of Usher's Wiltshire Brewery Co.Ltd. Brewery and 35 tied houses offered for sale on 13th December 1910 and a half interest was acquired by Charrington & Co.Ltd 1911. 14 public houses in Hastings were bought by Watney, Combe, Reid & Co.Ltd.

Charrington & Co.Ltd, *Anchor Brewery, Mile End Road E1.* Founded 1738 at Bethnal Green and moved to the Anchor Brewery 1757. Founded the Abbey Brewery, Burton-on-Trent 1872. Registered July 1897. The Abbey Brewery was sold in 1926 with 86 tied houses. Merged with Bass, Mitchells & Butlers Ltd 1967 to form Bass Charrington Ltd. Anchor Brewery closed January 1975.

Commercial Brewery Co.Ltd, *500 Commercial Road, Stepney E1.* Registered February 1887. Acquired by Hammerton & Co.Ltd 1928 and was closed.

Cygnet Brewery Co.Ltd, *251 Bow Road E3.* Registered December 1906 to acquire Wonder & Co.Ltd. Receiver appointed 13th December 1908 and was dissolved 24th March 1914. No tied houses.

Falcon Brewery Ltd, *Old Ford Brewery, Paines Road, Bow E3.* Registered May 1899 to acquire the Old Ford Brewery Co.Ltd. Voluntary liquidation July 1903.

John Furze & Co, *St.George's Brewery, Whitechapel E1.* Acquired by Taylor, Walker & Co.Ltd 1901 and was closed.

Godson, Freeman & Wilmot Ltd, *Black Horse Brewery, Chisenhale Road, Old Ford E3.* Founded at Atherden Road, Clapton, September 1977 and moved to Bow in June 1978 and to the above address April 1979. Ceased brewing 1982 and beer was supplied by the Tisbury Brewery with whom they had intended to merge, but this was not realised. Brewing recommenced and they merged with Chudley Ales 1984 to form Godson, Chudley & Co. Brewing ceased 1987.

Harvey Greenfield & Co, *Eagle Brewery, 51 Wellclose Square, Stepney E1.* Brewery offered for sale on 5th March 1914.

Hoare & Co.Ltd, *Red Lion Brewery, Lower East Smithfield E1.* Founded 1700. Red Lion brewhouse built 1792. George Matthew Hoare became a partner in 1802. Registered August 1894 with 110 public houses. Acquired by Charrington & Co.Ltd 1933 and ceased brewing on 23rd June 1934.

Ironbridge Tavern, *447 East India Dock Road, Limehouse E14.* A Brewpubs home brew house founded 1980. Ceased brewing 1982.

London & Burton Brewery Co.Ltd, *12 Medland Street, Stepney E14.* Originally registered 21st February 1862 to acquire the Old Queen's Head Brewery and Meakin's Brewery, Burton-on-Trent. This company was wound up 20th June 1865. Registered as above 1892. Acquired by Watney, Combe, Reid & Co.Ltd 1929 and ceased to brew.

Mann, Crossman & Paulin Ltd, *Albion Brewery, Whitechapel Road E1.* Albion Brewery built 1808. Became Blake & Mann 1818 and James Mann was in control in 1826. Crossman and Paulin became partners in 1846. Also at the Albion Brewery, Burton-on-Trent 1875-96. Registered October 1901. Merged with Watney,Combe, Reid & Co.Ltd 1958 to form Watney Mann Ltd. Albion Brewery closed 1979.

Smith, Garrett & Co.Ltd, *Bow Brewery, 246 Bow Road, Bow E3.* Registered July 1882. Acquired by Taylor, Walker & Co.Ltd in July 1927 and was closed.

Taylor, Walker & Co.Ltd, *Barley Mow Brewery, Church Row, Limehouse E14.* Founded 1730 as Salmon & Hare at Stepney. Acquired by John Taylor 1796 and Isaac Walker became a partner in 1816. Moved to Fore Street Limehouse by 1823 and the Barley Mow Brewery was built in 1889. Registered March 1907. Acquired by Ind Coope Ltd 1959 and brewing ceased in 1960.

Edward Tilney & Co, *Alma Brewery, Spelman Street, Whitechapel E1.* Acquired by Charrington & Co.Ltd 1927. The Alma public house marks the site.

Truman, Hanbury, Buxton & Co.Ltd, *Black Eagle Brewery, 91 Brick Lane, Stepney E1.* Black Eagle Brewery built by Thomas Bucknall in about 1666 and it was acquired by Joseph Truman in 1679. Acquired Phillip's Brewery, Burton-on-Trent 1873 and brewed there until 1971. Registered January 1889. Acquired by Grand Metropolitan Hotels Ltd 1971 and was merged with Watney Mann Ltd 1974. Name changed to Truman Ltd 1971. Brewing ceased 1988.

Albert Ward, *Tower Brewery, Ashenden Road, Homerton E3.* Acquired by Edmund Woodhead & Sons 1910.

West's Brewery Co.Ltd, *Three Crown Brewery, 313/315 Hackney Road, Bethnal Green E2.* Registered 1895. Acquired by Hoare & Co.Ltd November 1929 with over 60 public houses and was closed.

Waltham Forest

Collier Brothers, *Essex Brewery, St.James' Street, Walthamstow E17.* Acquired by Tollemache's Ipswich Brewery Ltd August 1920. Brewing ceased in 1972 and the buildings were demolished.

Wandsworth

Battersea Brewery Co, *Prince of Wales, 339 Battersea Park Road SW11.* Founded July 1983. Still brewing 1990.

Battersea Park Brewery Co, *181 New Road.* Established prior to 1882 when run by William Featherstonehaugh. Above style assumed between 1899 & 1906. Ceased brewing before 1919.

Best's Brewery Co.Ltd, *Larkhall Lane, Clapham SW4.* Registered 1910. Possibly successors to the Larkhall Brewery Ltd registered in December 1890. Acquired by Mann, Crossman & Paulin Ltd 1924 with 6 tied houses.

Brandon's Putney Brewery Ltd, *66 Putney High Street SW15.* Founded c.1800. Registered July 1896 to acquire A.J.Brandon Ltd and Jason Gurney's Star Brewery, Walton-on-Thames. Acquired by Mann, Crossman & Paulin Ltd 1920 with 76 public houses. Closed 1949.

Chambers Brothers & Co, *638/640 Wandsworth Road SW8.* Recorded as Richard Edward Rawes & Co before 1860 until after 1880. Traded as Charles Lyon Meek, South Western Brewery by 1887 and South Western Brewery Co. by 1895. James Warne by 1900 and above style by 1902. Brewing ceased before 1919.

Holsten Brewery Ltd, *Union Brewery, Point Pleasant, Wandsworth SW18.* Joseph Langton was brewing in Wandsworth High Street in 1850 but by 1860 Langton & Sons were at the Union Brewery. A new 26 quarter steam brewery was built 1866. Traded as the Union Brewery Co. under Walter Gordon 1890, Perrett Brothers 1898 and Arthur C.Nance to 1900. Registered as above December 1902 as a subsidiary of the Holsten Brauerei of Hamburg until c.1904. Voluntary liquidation 4th June 1920.

Plowman, Barrett & Co.Ltd, *Vauxhall Brewery, 87 Wandsworth Road SW8.* Founded 1883. Registered 1886 as Barrett's Brewing & Bottling Co.Ltd. New company registered as above February 1907 when they amalgamated with Plowman & Co.Ltd. Acquired by the Wenlock Brewery Co.Ltd 1951 and ceased to brew.

Shuckford & Speedy, *Clifton Brewery, 67 Clifton Street, Wandsworth SW18.* Acquired by Taylor, Walker & Co.Ltd 1927.

Thorne Brothers Ltd, *41 Nine Elms Lane, Vauxhall SW8.* Founded by 1833 and was acquired by John Mills Thorne in 1841 with 16 public houses. Registered January 1898. Acquired by Meux's Brewery Co.Ltd 1914 who transferred their brewing to here in 1921. Brewery closed 1964.

Tooting Brewery Ltd, *Tooting High Street SW17.* Registered 1901 to carry on the business of the late Charles Attlee. Acquired by Style & Winch Ltd November 1907 with 14 tied houses.

Thomas Woodward & Son, *Plough Brewery, 516 Wandsworth Road SW18.* Founded 1801 and acquired by Thomas Woodward 1868 and the Plough Brewery was opened on 3rd February 1869. Bought by H.& G.Simonds Ltd in 1925. Brewery still standing 1990 being leased for business purposes.

Young & Co's Brewery Ltd, *Ram Brewery, High Street, Wandsworth SW18.* Under the control of the Draper family from 1675. Registered in November 1890. Still brewing independently in 1990 with 145 public houses.

Westminster

C.J.Bill, *Sovereign Brewery, Queens Road, Bayswater W2.* Acquired by Usher's Wiltshire Brewery Ltd 1890 with 46 tied houses. Premises acquired by Carter, Wood & Co. in the same year. Brewing ceased in 1921.

J.Carter, Wood & Co, *Artillery Brewery, Victoria Street SW1.* Founded by Joseph Wood c.1823. Acquired by Watney & Co.Ltd 1889 and brewing ceased.

Chudley Ales, *1a Saltram Crescent, Maida Vale W9.* Founded by Tim Chudley in July 1981. Merged with Godson, Freeman & Wilmot 1984 to form Godson, Chudley & Co. Ceased brewing 1985.

Combe & Co.Ltd, *Woodyard Brewery, Castle Street (later Shelton Street), Long Acre WC2.* Founded c.1722. Acquired by Combe June 1787. Registered 1888. Merged with Watney & Co.Ltd July 1898. Woodyard Brewery closed in 1905.

Huggins & Co.Ltd, *Lion Brewery, Broad Street (now Broadwick Street), Golden Square W1.* Founded by 1836. Registered May 1894 to acquire John Huggins & Co. Went into voluntary liquidation 26th March 1898 and a new company of the same name was registered on the same day. Mainly export trade. Acquired by Watney, Combe, Reid & Co.Ltd 1929 and was closed.

Meux's Brewery Co.Ltd, *Horseshoe Brewery, Tottenham Court Road WC1.* Founded prior to 1764. After a dispute amongst the partners of Reid, Meux & Co, Griffin Brewery, Sir Henry Meux left the concern in 1807 and acquired the Horseshoe Brewery. Registered August 1888. Brewing was transferred to Thorne Brothers former Nine Elms Brewery in 1921 and this renamed the Horseshoe Brewery. The former Horseshoe Brewery was demolished in 1921 and the Dominion Cinema now occupies the site. Merged with Friary, Holroyd & Healy's Breweries Ltd 1956 to form Friary Meux Ltd. Brewing ceased at Nine Elms 1964.

New Westminster Brewery Co.Ltd, *Westminster Brewery, Earl Street, Horseferry Road SW1.* Operated as Thorne & Son until 1857. Registered 1872 as the Westminster Brewery Co.Ltd which went into liquidation and was and was registered as above in 1873. Acquired by the Lion Brewery Co.Ltd 1914 and brewing ceased. I.C.I. House now occupies the site.
Orange Brewery, *37 Pimlico Road SW1.* Home brew house founded February 1983 and still brewing 1990.
Watney, Combe, Reid & Co.Ltd, *Stag Brewery, Pimlico SW1.* Founded by William Greene 1641. Came under the control of James Watney 1858. Registered 1885 as Watney & Co.Ltd. Registered as above June 1898 to amalgamate Watney & Co.Ltd;

Combe & Co.Ltd and Reid's Brewery Co.Ltd. Merged with Mann, Crossman & Paulin Ltd 1958 to form Watney Mann Ltd. The Stag Brewery was closed on 23rd April 1959 and brewing was concentrated at Mann's Albion Brewery and Mortlake. Acquired by Grand Metropolitan Hotels Ltd 1972 and was merged with Truman, Hanbury, Buxton & Co.Ltd in 1974.
Woodbridge & Co, *Yorkshire Stingo Brewery, 18? Marylebone Road W1.* Operated by Richard Stains from about 1828 and became Woodbridge & Co 1877. Acquired by Watney, Combe, Reid & Co.Ltd 1907 and brewing ceased. Premises bought by the Church Army 1909.

LOTHIAN

Dalkeith

A Naturally Conditioned and Matured Beer.
McLENNAN & URQUHART, LTD., BREWERS, DALKEITH, EDINBURGH.

McLennan & Urquhart Ltd, *Dalkeith Brewery, Back Street.* Founded by 1867. Registered 1909. Acquired by John Aitchison & Co.Ltd December 1955 with 6 tied houses. Brewing ceased 1958 but bottling continued until 1961.

Dunbar

Belhaven Brewery Co.Ltd. Founded 1719. Acquired by Ellis Dudgeon in 1815. Registered as Dudgeon & Co.Ltd 1944. Acquired by Clydesdale Commonwealth Hotels Ltd 1972 with 7 tied houses and the name was changed as above. Public houses increased to 25 but these had all been sold by 1984, others have since been acquired. Acquired by Control Securities Ltd in December 1988 with 41 tied houses. Still brewing 1990.

Edinburgh

John Aitchison & Co.Ltd, *Canongate Brewery, 21 Holyrood Road.* Founded at Peebles 1730 by William Kerr and was acquired by William Aitchison in 1810. Moved to Edinburgh 1830. Registered April 1895. Acquired by Northern Breweries of Great Britain 1959 with 68 public houses. Brewing ceased in 1961 and was merged with John Jeffrey & Co.Ltd to form Aitchison Jeffrey Ltd.

Thomas & James Bernard Ltd, *Edinburgh Brewery, Slateford Road.* Founded 1840 by Daniel Bernard at the Old Edinburgh Brewery, North Back, Canongate. Slateford Road brewery built 1888. Registered March 1895. Acquired by Scottish Brewers Ltd April 1960 and was closed.

Archibald Campbell, Hope & King Ltd, *Argyle Brewery, Chambers Street.* Founded 1710. Registered November 1896 to acquire: the Argyle Brewery and Hope & King, wine & spirit merchants, Glasgow. Acquired by Whitbread & Co.Ltd 1967 and brewing ceased in 1970.

Drybrough & Co.Ltd, *Craigmillar Brewery, Duddingston Road.* Founded by 1750 and brewed at various sites before moving to Craigmillar in 1892. Registered December 1895. Acquired by Watney Mann Ltd 1966. Sold to Allied-Lyons January 1987 with 187 tied houses and brewing ceased in the same month.

Edinburgh United Breweries Ltd, *Bell's Brewery, 46 Pleasance.* Registered December 1889 to acquire: the Edinburgh & Leith Brewing Co, Old Playhouse Close, Canongate; Robert Disher & Co.; Ritchie & Sons, Bell's Brewery; Robert McMillan & Co, Summerhall Brewery and David Nicholson, Palace Brewery, 8 Abbey Mount, for £320,000. Closed down in 1935 by Customs & Excise due to brewing irregularities and was acquired by John Jeffrey & Co.Ltd.

Gordon & Blair (1923) Ltd, *Craigwell Brewery, 65 Calton Road.* Registered May 1898 as Gordon & Blair Ltd to acquire: James Gordon & Co, 167 Vincent Street, Glasgow; Charles Blair & Co, Craigwell Brewery and the Home Brewery, Parkhead, Glasgow. Registered as above 1923. Ceased brewing September 1953. Acquired by George Mackay & Co.Ltd in November 1954. The brewery has been converted into flats.

John Jeffrey & Co.Ltd, *Heriot Brewery, Roseburn Terrace.* Founded 1837. Private company registered July 1934 and a public company was formed in 1958. Acquired by Northern Breweries of Great Britain 1960.

Lorimer & Clark Ltd, *Caledonian Brewery, Slateford Road.* Founded by George Lorimer 1865. Registered January 1920. Acquired by Vaux & Associated Breweries Ltd 1946. Their 214 tied houses were sold to Allied Breweries in 1980. Vaux ceased brewing here in 1987 and it is now operated as the Caledonian Brewery Co.Ltd.

William McEwan & Co.Ltd, *Fountain Brewery, 19? Fountainbridge.* Founded 1856. Registered July 1889. Merged with William Younger & Co.Ltd 1931 to form Scottish Brewers Ltd. Still brewing 1990.

George Mackay & Co.Ltd, *St.Leonard's Brewery St.Leonard's Street.* Registered January 1908 to acquire the business founded in 1867. Acquired by Seager-Evans Ltd 1962 and was resold to Watney Mann Ltd in 1963 and brewing ceased.

Maclachlans Ltd, *Castle Brewery, Duddingston Road.* Originally wine & spirit merchants. Castle Brewery, Maryhill, Glasgow built 1889 and the Castle Brewery, Edinburgh opened in 1901. Registered 1907 and public company formed in 1947. Acquired by J.& R.Tennent Ltd 1960 and brewing ceased in 1966.

Alexander Melvin & Co, *Boroughloch Brewery Buccleuch Street.* Founded by 1805. and was acquired by Alexander Melvin c.1850. Ceased brewing January 1907 and the goodwill was acquired by William McEwan & Co.Ltd.

J.& J.Morison Ltd, *Commercial Brewery, 16? Canongate.* Founded 1868. Registered November 1946. Acquired by Scottish Brewers Ltd 1960 and brewing ceased.

James Muir & Son Ltd, *Calton Hill Brewery, 2? Calton Road.* Founded before 1815 by James Muir. Registered 1883. Wound up in February 1916.

William Murray & Co.Ltd, *Craigmillar Brewery Duddingston.* Founded by William Murray a Ednam 1880. Moved to Edinburgh 1886. Registered December 1897. Acquired by Northern Breweries of Great Britain Ltd 1960 and was closed in May 1963.

T.Y.Paterson & Co.Ltd, *Pentland Brewery, Craigmillar and Petershill Brewery, Springburn, Glasgow.* Registered 1889 to acquire Oswald Paterson & Co of Glasgow. Acquired by James Aitken & Co. (Falkirk) Ltd in 1936 and was closed.

Pattissons Ltd, *New Brewery, Duddingston.* Registered 1896. Voluntary liquidation January 1899 and was bought by Robert Deuchar Ltd for £30,000.

William & John Raeburn, *Merchant Street Brewery.* Acquired by Robert Younger Ltd in 1913.

Rose Street Brewery, *55 Rose Street.* Founded August 1983 in the former White Cockade public house by the Alloa Brewery Co.Ltd.

Simson & McPherson Ltd, *St.Mary's Brewery, Canongate and Abbey Brewery, Melrose.* Founded by James Simson at Melrose 1839. St.Mary's Brewery opened 1864. Registered February 1896 to acquire James Simson & Sons and John Ewen McPherson & Co, Sandyford Brewery, Newcastle-upon-Tyne, with 26 tied houses. Acquired by Robert Deuchar Ltd. 1900 and brewing ceased at Edinburgh in 1901 and at Melrose in 1906.

John Somerville & Co.Ltd, *North British Brewery, Duddingston.* Registered May 1897 to acquire John Somerville & Co, wine & spirit merchants, Leith and Blyth & Cameron, North British Brewery. Acquired by William Murray & Co.Ltd 1922.

Steel, Coulson & Co.Ltd, *Croft-an-Righ Brewery, Abbeyhill and the Greenhead Brewery, Glasgow.* Founded 1865. Croft-an-Righ Brewery acquired 1874. Registered May 1888. Greenhead Brewery sold to James Calder & Co. (Brewers) Ltd in 1946. Acquired by Vaux & Associated Breweries Ltd 1959 with 16 public houses. Ceased brewing 1960.

Thomas Usher & Son Ltd, *Park Brewery, 106 St.Leonard's Street.* Founded at the Cowgate Brewery by 1817. Acquired by James Usher & Cunningham 1831. Moved to the Park Brewery 1860. Registered March 1895. Acquired by Vaux & Associated Breweries Ltd 1959 with 170 public houses. Name changed to Ushers Brewery Ltd 1972. Park Brewery sold to Allied Breweries 1980 and ceased brewing 1981.

Robert Younger Ltd, *St.Ann's Brewery, 60 Abbeyhill.* Founded 1854. Registered November 1896. Acquired by Scottish Brewers Ltd 1st March 1961 and brewing ceased.

William Younger & Co.Ltd, *Abbey & Holyrood Breweries.* Founded by William Younger at Leith 1749. Moved to Edinburgh 1778. Registered August 1887 and public company formed in 1889. Merged with William McEwan & Co.Ltd 1931 to form Scottish Brewers Ltd. Merged with Newcastle Breweries Ltd 1960 to form Scottish & Newcastle Breweries Ltd. New brewery built 1974 and Holyrood Brewery closed May 1986.

Other Breweries

Thomas Carmichael & Co, *Balmoral Brewery, 41 Calton Road* (1910)

Cooper & Macleod, *Castle Brewery, 79 Grassmarket* (1910)

John Fulton & Co, *60 Pleasance* (1910)

Taylor, Macleod & Co, *Drumbryan Brewery, Leven Street* (1902)

Haddington

Mark Binnie & Co, *Nungate.* Founded 1882. Trade and goodwill acquired by William Younger & Co.Ltd 1937. The brewery is still standing.

Haddington Brewery Co.Ltd, *Sidegate Brewery, Sidegate Street.* Went into voluntary liquidation 1899 and the brewery was sold. A new company of the same name was registered in 1900 but brewing ceased in 1902.

Leith

Argyle Brewery, *11/13 Arthur Street.* The assets of the Leith Brewery were bought by a consortium in 1985 but the business was closed in March 1986.

Leith Brewery, *11/13 Arthur Street.* Founded February 1982 by Iain Meikle, Ken Garden, Stuart Hyslop, Tony Dean & David Canning. Ceased brewing in January 1985.

Musselburgh

John Young & Co.Ltd, *Ladywell Brewery, North High Street, Fisherrow.* Founded by John Young c.1830. Registered 1891. Acquired by Whitbread & Co.Ltd November 1968 with 11 tied houses and brewing ceased on 31st January 1969.

Prestonpans

John Fowler & Co.Ltd, *High Street.* Founded c.1720 in a former whisky distillery. Registered 1865. Acquired by Northern Breweries of Great Britain Ltd. April 1960 with 36 public houses. Brewing ceased in March 1962.

GREATER MANCHESTER

Altrincham

Richardson & Goodall, *18 Market Place.* Acquired by Chesters Brewery Co.Ltd 1890.

John Siddeley, *Peel Causeway* (1906)

Ashton-Under-Lyne

Gartside's (Brookside) Brewery Ltd, *Pottinger Street.* Founded 1830. Registered March 1892 as Gartsides Ltd and was re-registered as above February 1898. Acquired by Bent's Brewery Co.Ltd 1939 with 180 tied houses.

Schofield's Portland Brewery (Ashton-under-Lyne) Ltd, *Bentinck Street.* Registered 1915. Acquired by Frederic Robinson Ltd February 1926 with 42 public houses.

Shaw & Bentley, *Bardsley Brewery, Oldham Road.* Founded 1832 by Robert Bentley of the Old Brewery, Rotherham, Yorkshire. Acquired by Rothwell's Brewery November 1902 with 40 tied houses.

Stamford Brewery Co.(Ashton-under-Lyne) Ltd, *Stamford Brewery, Portland.* Registered March 1895 as the Portland Brewery Co.Ltd. Street. As there was already a Portland Brewery Co. in existence in the town, the name was changed as above on 22nd April 1895. Merged with the Whitefield Brewery and the Lee Home Brewing Co.Ltd in 1899 to form Whitefield Breweries Ltd.

Atherton

William A.Riley, *Howe Bridge* (1910)

Bolton

John Atkinson & Co.Ltd, *Commission Street Brewery.* Formed part of Boardman's United Breweries Ltd 1896.

J.Halliwell & Son, *Alexandra Brewery, Mount Street.* Founded 1850. Ceased trading 1912 and public houses acquired by Magee, Marshall & Co.Ltd.

Home Brewery Co, *5 Bradshawgate* (1926) Wilson's Brewery of Newton Heath listed here 1928.

Howcroft's Brewery Ltd, *Model Brewery, Spa Road.* Originally at the Rothwell Street Tavern Brewery, 32 Rothwell Street and moved to Spa Lane 1937. Merged with B.Cunningham Ltd of Warrington 1969 and ceased trading shortly afterwards.

James Jackson & Sons Ltd, *Model Brewery, Spa Road.* Acquired the Model Brewery from the Spa Wells Brewery Co. on 26th March 1904. Private company registered April 1913. Acquired by George Shaw & Co.Ltd of Leigh 1927.

Leach's Brewery Ltd, *Albert Brewery, 181/183 Derby Street, Hammond Street.* Registered 1905. Brewing ceased after 1937.

Magee, Marshall & Co.Ltd, *Crown Brewery, Cricket Street.* Founded by David Magee 1853. Crown Brewery built about 1866. Acquired David Marshall & Co, Grapes Brewery, Brown Street and Horse Shoe Brewery, Water Street 1885. Registered March 1888. Acquired by Greenall Whitley & Co.Ltd 1959. Brewing ceased 30th September 1970.

W.T.Settle, *Rose & Crown Brewery, 55 Cross Street.* Acquired by Dutton's Blackburn Brewery Ltd 1951.

Joseph Sharman & Sons Ltd, *Mere Hall Brewery, 143 Mere Hall Street.* Founded by Joseph Sharman at the Crompton Brewery, Mill Street in 1868. Mere

Hall Brewery built 1874. Registered December 1896. Acquired by George Shaw & Co.Ltd 1927 with over 20 tied houses and was closed.

Samuel Smith, *Dog & Snipe Brewery, 181 Folds Road.* Acquired by Dutton's Blackburn Brewery Ltd 1935.

Spa Wells Brewery Co.Ltd, *Park View Brewery, Spa Road.* Registered 2nd June 1900. Ceased trading 14th April 1904 after the brewery was sold to James Jackson & Sons Ltd.

William Tong & Sons Ltd, *Diamond Brewery, Deane Road.* Founded by William Tong c.1820 at the Diamond Brewery, Pikes Lane. Moved to Bridge Street 1894/5 and to Deane Road 1902. Registered

in June 1897 with 66 public houses. Acquired by Walker Cain 1923 with 21 tied houses. Brewing ceased in 1940.

Uncle Tom's Cabin Brewery Ltd, *270/72 Lever Street.* Registered January 1926 to acquire the business carried on by Sarah Green and Emily A.Leach as exors of Henry Hilton. Acquired by J.Hamer of Bromley Cross 1932.

Walker's Bolton Brewery Co.Ltd, *Park View Brewery, Spa Road.* Predecessors to the Spa Wells Brewery Co.Ltd. Registered September 1889 to acquire George Walker & Co.with 10 public houses. Voluntary liquidation 30th August 1899 and was dissolved 25th April 1901.

Wingfield Silverwell Brewery Co.Ltd, *15 Nelson Square.* Registered October 1896 to acquire T.R.& F.Wingfield. Acquired by the Manchester Brewery Co.Ltd 1899.

R.Wood & Sons Ltd, *Prince Arthur Brewery, St.John Street.* Registered July 1915. Closed 1916.

Other Breweries
Albert Booth, *212 Derby Street* (1923)
Daniel Booth, *198/200 Kay Street* (1926)
Charles Brownlow, *383 Halliwell Road* (1926)
Derby Street Brewery Co, *102 Derby Street* (1892)
Thomas Hodson, *564/566 Manchester Road* (1926). *81 Market Street* (1921)
Andrew Lowe, *12 Haigh Street* (1923)
Ellen Porteous, *86 Deansgate* (1921)
Ernest Robey, *Dove Bank* (1926)
Herbert Rostron, *Union Arms Brewery, 76 Folds Road* (1910)
Herbert Scholes, *251 Derby Street* (1921)
James Taylor, *7 Fletcher Street* (1920)
Martha Tonge, *76 Hulme Street* (1920)
Peter Whitehead, *Jolly Carter, 168 Church Street, Little Lever* (1935)
George Yates, *School Hill* (1923)

Bradshaw

Henry Kershaw (1930)

Bromley Cross

J.Hamer (Brewers) Ltd, *Volunteer Brewery, 158 Darwen Road.* Registered October 1950. Acquired by Dutton's Blackburn Brewery Ltd 1951 with 42 tied houses.

Bury

Buckley Wells Brewery Co.Ltd. Registered 27th October 1890. Ceased trading 2nd February 1893 and was dissolved 27th April 1894.

Bury Brewery Co.Ltd, *George Street.* Acquired by Thwaites & Co.Ltd 1949 with about 80 tied houses.

Chadwick's Walmersley Brewery Ltd, *Walmersley Road.* Founded c.1840 by Robert Chadwick. Registered 1891 with 43 public houses. Acquired by the Manchester Brewery Ltd 1927, who were then a subsidiary of Walker & Homfray Ltd. Premises now used by an oil company.

Crown Brewery Co.Ltd, *Rochdale Road.* Registered January 1861 as the Bury Co-operative Brewing & Distilling Co.Ltd. Name changed February 1866. Acquired by Dutton's Blackburn Brewery Ltd 1959 with 127 public houses and brewing ceased.

Alfred Crowther & Co.Ltd, *Star Brewery, Brook Street.* Registered December 1894. Acquired by Wilson's Brewery Ltd 1925.

Davenport Brothers Ltd, *Central Brewery, Clerke Street* (1910)

Ferdinando Kay, 257 Hollins Lane (1895)

Richard Rushton, *Nelson Brewery, Bolton Street.* Acquired by the Crown Brewery Co.Ltd 1895.

Robert Unsworth, *Commercial Brewery, Elton* (1906)

Castleton

Castleton Brewery Co.Ltd, *Spring Brewery.* Registered May 1892 to acquire the business of Thomas Fletcher with 2 tied houses. Acquired by the Phoenix Brewery Co.Ltd 1899.

Dearnley

Parsons & Co, *Dearnley Brewery* (1898)

Delph

James Gartside (1923)

Dukinfield

Henry Shaw, exors of, *Tame Valley Brewery, Park Road.* Founded before 1895. Acquired by John Smith's Tadcaster Brewery Co.Ltd 1941.

Farnworth

John Crompton, *12 Mossfield Road* (1940)
Martha Isherwood, *78 Egerton Street* (1892)
James Longworth, *34 King Street* (1926)
Elizabeth Rostron, *61 Higher Market Street* (1898)
John Saynor & Sons, *Mosegate Brewery, Hall Lane* (1898)
Emily Watson, *53/55 King Street* (1935)

Heywood

Brierley's Woolpack Brewery Ltd, *Woolpack Brewery, Birch Street.* Registered June 1895. Acquired by the Phoenix Brewery Co.Ltd 1898 and brewing ceased.

Thomas Ashworth Greenhalgh, *Yew Tree Inn Brewery, Pool Lane* (1930)

T.& E.Kershaw, *Victoria Brewery, Green Lane* (1921)

Phoenix Brewery Co.Ltd, *Green Lane.* Registered 1874. Acquired by the Cornbrook Brewery Co.Ltd 1939 with about 100 tied houses.

James Rowbotham & Sons, *Sun Brewery, 121 Railway Street* (1921)

Hindley

William Unsworth, *Balmoral Brewery, 51 Atherton Road.* Acquired by Matthew Brown & Co.Ltd 1924.

Horwich

William Smith, *Original Bay Horse Brewery* (1938)

Hyde

Charles Creese & Co.Ltd, *Cheapside.* Founded 1901. Acquired by Walker & Homfrays Ltd 1929 with over 60 public houses and was closed.

Newton Home Brewing & Bottling Co, *180 Muslin Street.* Registered June 1906 to acquire the business of H.Fletcher. Wound up 1909.

Shamrock Working Men's Brewery Co.Ltd, *Henry Street.* Registered October 1929 and was closed in 1930.

Ince

John Ashton, *Lower Ince Brewery, 136 Warrington Road* (1910)

Isaac Lawrence & Son, *Higher Ince Brewery, Belle Green Lane.* Offered for auction 30th January 1914 with 2 public houses but no bids received and was wound up. Brewery plant for sale in February 1917. Isaac Lawrence was also listed at the Crown Brewery, Leigh.

William Morton & Sons Ltd, *Ince Brewery, Pickup Street.* Acquired by B.Cunningham Ltd of Warrington December 1931.

Leigh

Bond Street Brewery Co.Ltd, *Bond Street.* Registered August 1890 to acquire exors of James Shovelton. Acquired by the Bedford Brewing & Malting Co.Ltd 1897.

Richard Fairhurst & Co, *Derby Brewery* (1898)

Isaac Lawrence & Son, *Crown Brewery, Leigh Road.* Acquired by the Bedford Brewing & Malting Co.Ltd in 1888. See also:- Ince.

George Shaw & Co.Ltd, *Leigh Brewery, 31 Brewery Lane.* Founded 1801. Registered October 1866 as the Bedford Brewing & Malting Co.Ltd to acquire the business of R.Guest. Name changed 20th January 1902. Acquired by Walker Cain Ltd 1931 with 169 public houses. Brewery plant for sale in March 1933.

Littleborough

Littleborough Brewery Ltd, *Church Street.* Acquired by Hammond's United Breweries Ltd 1947. No tied houses.

Little Hulton

William Wright, *Little Hulton Brewery* (1920)

Manchester, Ancoats

Joseph Boardman, exors of, *Canning Street.* Founded by Ellis Boardman 1840. Acquired by Joshua Tetley & Sons Ltd 1950 with 7 public houses. The brewery has been demolished.

John Taylor & Co.Ltd, *Pollard Street.* Registered August 1895. Acquired by Walker & Homfrays Ltd in September 1929 with 48 tied houses.

Manchester, Ardwick

George Bentley, *Viaduct Brewery, 266 Viaduct Street.* Acquired by Threlfall's Brewery Co.Ltd 1913.

Chesters Brewery Co.Ltd, *Ardwick Brewery, Princess Street.* Founded before 1830 at the Victoria Brewery, Hyde Street and became Collins & Chesters 1842. Ardwick Brewery opened 1852. Registered April 1888. Merged with Threlfall's Brewery Co.Ltd 1961 to form Threlfall Chesters Ltd. Brewery demolished 1966.

John Foster, *Swan Brewery, Grey Street.* Originally brewed at Dawson's Croft Brewery, Salford c.1866-1886 and moved to the Swan Brewery c.1887. Bought by Chesters 1890 and was let to Simpson & Crummack.

Edward Issott, exors of, *184 Stockport Road.* Founded before 1882 at Heaton Chapel. Acquired by Wilson's Brewery Ltd 1903.

Kay's Atlas Brewery Ltd, *Atlas Brewery, 225 Stockport Road.* Registered December 1896 to acquire: James Kay, Atlas Brewery and Beaumont & Heathcote, Standard Brewery, Jenkinson Street, Chorlton, with a total of 125 tied houses. Brewing was concentrated at the Atlas Brewery and the Standard Brewery was sold. Acquired by Frederick Robinson Ltd 1929 with 86 public houses and brewing ceased in 1936.

Manchester Brewery Co.Ltd, *Britannia Brewery, Broadie Street.* Registered January 1888 to acquire the business of James Henry Deakin. In financial difficulties 1904 due to the purchase of unrenumerative properties and Broadbents Ltd, was sold in 1905. Acquired by Walkers & Homfrays Ltd 1912. 46 of their public houses were sold to the Palatine Bottling Co.Ltd 1935.

Neil Ryrie, *Swan Brewery, Grey Street.* Neil Ryrie was originally a brewer at Wagstaffe's Lion Brewery and acquired the Swan Brewery from the Empress Brewery Co.Ltd. Brewing ceased c.1925 and the brewery was sold in 1926 and was later run as the Swan Brewery Ltd and was converted into a vinegar brewery by 1939.

Simpson & Crummack, *Swan Brewery, Grey Street.* Founded c.1877 at the Neptune Brewery, Garratt Street, Oldham Road and moved to the Swan Brewery c.1893 as predecessors to Neil Ryrie. Acquired by the Empress Brewery Co.Ltd 1898.

Richard Whittaker, *Victoria Brewery, Midland Street.* Merged with William Kay 1900 to form Kay & Whittaker Ltd. Acquired by Wilson's Brewery Ltd 1903.

Yates's Castle Brewery Ltd, *Castle Brewery, Fairfield Street & Castle Brewery, 18/19 Market Place, Birkenhead.* Founded in the 1830s. Registered 1887 as William Yates & Co.Ltd. Registered as above October 1896 as above with 175 public houses. Birkenhead brewery closed 1934. Acquired by John Smith's Tadcaster Brewery 1961 and brewing ceased.

Manchester, Belle Vue

Barber & Co, *Longsight Brewery, Stockport Road.* Formed part of Whitefield Breweries Ltd, March 1899.

J.Jennison & Co, *Belle Vue House, Hyde Road.* Formed part of the Belle Vue Zoo & Amusement Park founded 1836 and brewed mainly for the visitors, although it is believed that there was at least one tied house. There was a connection with Lees Moss Side Brewery as Angelo Jennison was the managing director in 1910. Brewing ceased c.1925 when the Jennison family sold their interest in the concern.

Manchester, Cheetham

Elliott's Brewery Co.Ltd, *Tyson Street, Cheetham Hill Road.* Registered 1902. Receiver appointed 12th August 1904 and was dissolved 8th January 1915.

Joseph Holt Ltd, *Derby Brewery, Empire Street.* Founded 1849 at Oak Street and moved to the Ducie Bridge Brewery, York Street (now Cheetham Hill Road) 1855. Derby Brewery built in 1860. Registered June 1922 and public company formed 1951. Still brewing independently 1990.

Manchester, Chorlton

Beaumont & Heathcote, *Standard Brewery, Jenkinson Street.* Merged with James Kay, Atlas Brewery, Ardwick 1896 to form Kay's Atlas Brewery Ltd.

Broadbents Ltd, *Steam Brewery, 136 York Street.* Registered August 1891. Acquired by the Manchester Brewery Co.Ltd 1899 with 28 tied houses.

West Coast Brewing Co, *King's Arms.* Founded 1990.

Manchester, City Centre

William Ainscow, *Irwell Street Brewery, Gartside Street* (1890)

Boddington's Breweries Ltd, *Strangeways Brewery, New Bridge Street.* Founded 1778 as Caister & Fry and was acquired by Henry Boddington in 1853. Acquired by Whitbread & Co.Ltd 1989 with 280 tied houses.

Lass of Gowrie, *36 Charles Street.* A Whitbread home brew house founded 1983. Still brewing 1990.

Old Bank House, *5 Old Bank Street, St.Ann's Square.* Home brew house founded December 1983 and ceased brewing late 1985.

Manchester, Failsworth

William Henry Mather, *Lamb Brewery, Elm Street, Oldham Road.* Acquired by Taylor's Eagle Brewery Ltd 1889.

Manchester, Gorton

John Buckley & Sons, *Gorton Brewery, Wellington Street.* Acquired by Threlfall's Brewery Co.Ltd 1898.

Manchester, Greenheys

Taylor's Eagle Brewery Ltd, *Eagle Brewery, Burlington Street.* Founded by Joseph Taylor 1849. Registered February 1888. Brewery sold 1924 but the company continued to own 60 public houses. Acquired by Marston, Thompson & Evershed Ltd in 1958.

Manchester, Harpurhey

B. & J.McKenna Ltd, *Harpurhey Brewery, Rochdale Road.* Registered April 1895. Acquired by Walker & Homfrays Ltd 1903.

Manchester, Hulme

Boardman's United Breweries Ltd, *Russell Street.* Registered June 1896 to amalgamate: Boardman's Breweries Ltd, Bolton and Manchester; E.A.Rothwell, Russell Street; J.O.& J.Wood, Denholme, Bradford; John Greenwood, wine & spirit merchants, Halifax and Greenwood Brothers, Crown Brewery, Crown Street, Bradford. The Lancashire properties were sold to the Cornbrook Brewery Co.Ltd 1899 and those in Yorkshire were acquired by Bentley's Yorkshire Breweries Ltd in January 1921. Went into voluntary liquidation in May 1946.

Cardwell & Co.Ltd, *Naval Brewery, Junction Street.* Founded c.1850 by Hargreave Brothers and used by them until 1876 when acquired by Renshaw & Cardwell. The Chester Road Brewery Co.Ltd was registered April 1889 to acquire Joseph Cox, 219 Chester Road. In July 1889 the name was changed to Cox's Brewery Ltd and in May 1894 the business of Henry Cardwell was acquired and the name was changed again as above. Brewing was then concentrated at the Naval Brewery. In July 1899 Wilson's Brewery Ltd acquired Cardwell & Co.Ltd then in liquidation. The premises were later used by Swales & Co.Ltd.

G.F.Carrington & Sons, *Chester Road.* Acquired by the Manchester Brewery Co.Ltd 1899.

James Cronshaw, *Alexandra Brewery, Erskine Street.* Acquired by Groves & Whitnall Ltd September 1899 and brewing continued until 1932.

William Dockray, *Chorlton Road.* Acquired by Groves & Whitnall Ltd 1900.

Handley's Brewery Ltd, *Clarence Brewery, Clarence Street.* Registered August 1904. Acquired by Threlfall's Brewery Co.Ltd in 1912.

Hardy's Crown Brewery Ltd, *87 Renshaw Street.* Registered May 1889. Acquired by United Breweries Ltd 1962 and the brewery was demolished in 1965.

Kay & Whittaker Ltd, *Britannia Brewery, Bradbury Street.* Registered March 1900 to amalgamate William Kay and Richard Whittaker Victoria Brewery, Ardwick. Acquired by Wilson's Brewery Ltd 1903.

Charles Robinson, *Carlton Brewery, Chorlton Road.* Occupied Dockray's former brewery. All the public houses were sold in 1913 but brewing continued until c.1939.

J.G.Swales & Co.Ltd, *Naval Brewery, Junction Street.* Originally brewing at the Victoria Brewery, Ravald Street, Salford until 1899 when the Naval Brewery was acquired from Wilson's Brewery Ltd. Acquired by Boddington's Breweries Ltd November 1970 with 38 public houses and brewing ceased.

J.Wagstaffe & Co, *Lion Brewery.* Acquired by Watson, Woodhead & Co. of Salford December 1898 to form Watson, Woodhead & Wagstaffe Ltd.

Manchester, Moss Side

William Brookes, *Albert Brewery, Bradshaw Street.* Founded 1860 at the Eclipse Brewery, off Deansgate and moved to the Albert Brewery before 1877. Acquired by John Lees Ltd 1894.

Greatorex Brothers, *Queen's Brewery, Moss Lane West.* Founded 1860. Acquired by the Empress Brewery Co.Ltd 1898 with 48 public houses and the brewery was sold to Hyde's Brewery in July 1899.

Hyde's Anvil Brewery Ltd, *46 Moss Lane West.* Founded by Alfred Hyde about 1863 at the Crown Brewery, Audenshaw. They moved to the Victoria Brewery, Lower Moss Lane 1870 followed by the Mayfield Street Brewery, Ardwick in 1882 and the Monmouth Street Brewery, Rusholme 1887 before moving to the present brewery in July 1899 formerly occupied by Greatorex Brothers. Registered December 1912 as Hyde's Queen's Brewery Ltd and the name was change as above in 1944. Still independent 1990.

Moss Side Brewery Co.Ltd, *Moss Side Brewery, Bradshaw Street.* Originally at the Wellington Brewery, Openshaw and acquired the Albert Brewery, Moss Side from the trustees of William Brookes in 1894. Registered as John Henry Lees Ltd November 1897. Receiver appointed 23rd January 1913 and was dissolved on 14th December 1917 New company registered as above January 1920 to acquire the business of J.H.Davies carried on as the Moss Side Brewery Co. Voluntary liquidation 15th March 1930 and was succeeded by the Red Tower Lager Brewery Ltd.

Royal Moss Side Brewery Co.Ltd, *Royal Brewery, Bradshaw Street.* Registered July 1933 as the Red Tower Lager Brewery Ltd to acquire the business of lager brewers carried on by the Palatine Bottling Co.Ltd. Acquired by Scottish Brewers Ltd 1956 and the name was changed as above in 1963. Brewery still in operation 1990 producing Harp Lager.

Manchester, Newton Heath

Failsworth Brewery, *Thornton House, Eager Street, Oldham Road.* Founded August 1982 in an old timber yard next to Wilson's Brewery. Brewing ceased 1985.

W.T.Rothwell Ltd, *Heath Brewery, Oldham Road.* Operated by William Thomas Rothwell from early 1870s. Registered August 1917 with 80 tied houses. Acquired by Marston, Thompson & Evershed Ltd February 1961 and brewing ceased in 1968.

Wilson's Brewery Ltd, *Newton Heath Brewery, Monsall Road.* Founded 1834 by John Collinson and George Simpson and was acquired by Henry Charles Wilson and Thomas Philpot in March 1865. Registered September 1894 as Henry Charles Wilson & Co.Ltd and the name was changed as above later in the same year. After the 1949 merger with Walker & Homfrays Ltd was known as Wilson & Walker Breweries Ltd until reverting to the original title in 1952. Amalgamated with Watney Mann Ltd August 1960. Brewing ceased 1987.

Manchester, Old Trafford

Cornbrook Brewery Co.Ltd, *Ellesmere Street, Chester Road.* Founded by 1797. Registered 1885 to acquire Lawrence O'Neill & Co. Reconstructed company registered November 1896. Acquired by Charrington United Breweries 1961 and brewing ceased in 1973.

Empress Brewery Co.Ltd, *383 Chester Road.* Operated by Charles Dawes 1880. Registered December 1894 as the Old Trafford Brewery Co.Ltd to acquire W.H.Fulford & Co, originally at the Monarch Brewery, St.George Street, Salford until 1884. Registered as above May 1896. 236 public houses. Acquired by Walker Cain Ltd 1929 and brewing ceased.

Manchester, Openshaw

John Battersby & Co, *Wellington Brewery, 234 Wellington Street.* Acquired by Chesters Brewery Co.Ltd on 29th October 1888 and was leased to John Henry Lees until 1895 when brewing ceased. Brewery demolished 1920.

Manchester, Rusholme

Bee Brewery Co.Ltd, *Monmouth Street.* Registered March 1898 at Tyson Street, Crumpsall. Moved to Rusholme February 1902. Receiver appointed 28th December 1910 after a period of financial difficulties. Dissolved 24th March 1914. Apparently no tied houses.

Manchester, West Gorton

Openshaw Brewery Ltd, *Victoria Brewery, Aberavon Street.* Registered as the Openshaw Bridge Brewery Co.Ltd June 1883 to found a brewery at Tamworth Street, Openshaw. Name changed as above on 19th February 1891 when they moved to West Gorton. Acquired by Hope & Anchor Breweries Ltd 1957 with 125 public houses. Brewery demolished 1968.

Stopford's Brewery Co.Ltd, *Imperial Brewery, Birch Street.* Alfred Stopford moved from Ancoats to the Imperial Brewery c.1863. Registered 1889. Bought by Walker & Homfrays Ltd 1927 and the public houses were transferred to their subsidiary, the Palatine Bottling Co.Ltd who occupied the brewery until 1949.

Middleton

William Bastow, *89 Higher Wood Street* (1926)
Alfred Cheetham, *Back High Street* (1898)
J.W.Lees & Co. (Brewers) Ltd, *Greengate Brewery, Lees Street.* Founded by John Lees 1828. Registered 1936 to acquire J.W.Lees & Co. Reconstructed company registered November 1955. Still brewing 1990.

Frank Matthews, *Lodge Street* (1906)
Benjamin Walker, *Irk Street* (1892)
Arthur Henry Whittaker, *16/18 Cross Street* (1921)

Mossley

C.B.Andrew & Co, *Waggon Road* (1914)
John Edward Garside, *Campden Street* (1914)

New Springs

Atherton & Johnson, *Crown Brewery, 106 Wigan Road* (1940)

Oldham

Hollinwood Brewery & Bottling Co.Ltd, *Victoria Brewery, Hollins Road.* Registered November 1898 to acquire the business of Edmunson Scholes. Dissolved 9th December 1902.

Jowett, Waterhouse & Co.Ltd, *Crown Brewery, Cheapside.* Registered March 1874 to acquire John C.Waterhouse, Crown Brewery and Jowett Brothers, wine & spirit merchants, Clegg Street. Acquired by Wilson's Brewery Ltd 1896 with 43 public houses. Brewing probably continued until the early 1900s.

Lee Home Brewing Co.Ltd, *Lee Street.* Registered January 1897. Merged with the Stamford Brewery Co.(Ashton-under-Lyne) Ltd and the Whitefield Brewery Co.Ltd 1899 to form Whitefield Breweries Ltd. Brewing ceased 1902.

Oldham Brewery Co.Ltd, *Albion Brewery, Coldhurst Street.* Founded by William Boothby 1868. Registered July 1873. Acquired by Boddington's Breweries Ltd 1982 with 87 tied houses and closed.

Walter Potts Ltd, *Lamb Brewery, Market Place.* Registered August 1894. Acquired by Threlfall's Brewery Co.Ltd 1898

Taylor & Lees, *Serjeant-at-Arms Brewery, George Street.* Acquired by Threlfall's Brewery Co.Ltd 1899 with 30 public houses. Brewing ceased 1960.

Waterloo Brewery Co.Ltd, *Waterloo Street.* Registered 12th March 1888 with 4 tied houses. Wound up voluntarily 13th March 1890.

Welcome Brewery Co.Ltd, *Henshaw Street.* Private company registered 1919 to acquire the business of C.F.Hyde & C.W.Battersley carried on as the Welcome Brewery Co. Two public houses. Brewing ceased November 1959 after being acquired by Hope & Anchor Breweries Ltd.

Other Breweries
J.Aldred, *Featherstall Brewery* (1900)
John Boardman, *81 Nugget Street, Glodwick* (1920)
George F.Briggs, *Jackson Pit, King Street* (1921)
William Dawson, *185 Shaw Road* (1920)
Giles Hickson (1890)
John W.Matley, exors of, *754 Middleton Road* (1926)
Levi Matley, *391 Ashton Road* (1926)
Frank Mills, *38 Union Street* (1923)
Edward Neild, *237 West Street* (1920)
Samuel Shaw, *189 Lees Street* (1926)
Herbert Sinkinson, *113 Huddersfield Road* (1914)
Joseph Walker, *100 Shaw Road* (1920)

Pendlebury

Worsley Brewery Co.Ltd, *Old Brewery, Bolton Road.* Operated by Mary Anne Hogg from at least 1877. Registered 1898. Acquired by Walker Cain Ltd 1925. Brewing ceased 1929 and their 50 public houses were transferred to the Empress Brewery Co.Ltd.

Radcliffe

Christopher Duxbury, *King Street/Stand Lane.* Acquired by the Spring Lane Brewery Co.Ltd *c.*1890.

Richard Seed & Co.Ltd, *Spring Lane Brewery.* Founded 1827. Operated by James Cunliffe until registered as the Spring Lane Brewery Co.Ltd April 1882. Registered as above March 1896. Acquired by Dutton's Blackburn Brewery Ltd 1938 and brewing ceased.

Ramsbottom

Two Shires Brewery, *Rose Bank Mill, Bolton Road North, Stubbins.* Founded March 1981. Only brewed occasionally and was closed in 1983.

Rochdale

Rochdale & District Clubs Brewery Co.Ltd, *Halifax Road, Hursted.* Acquired by the Littleborough Brewery Ltd 1942.

Rochdale & Manor Brewery Ltd, *86 Molesworth Street.* Originally registered as the Rochdale & Oldham Brewery Co.Ltd April 1887. New company registered as above March 1895 to acquire this concern and the Manor Brewery, Salford. Acquired by Samuel Smith Ltd 1948 and brewing ceased April 1974.

Other Breweries
Thomas Brown, *349 Halifax Road* (1920)
James Butterworth, *Ye Olde Pack Horse Brewery, Yorkshire Road* (1930)
Frank Crabtree, *3 Norreys Street* (1930)
Benjamin Crossley, *13 Elliott Street* (1935)
John Bentley Davies, *148 Spotland Road* (1923)
Anthony Dick, *Newgate* (1920)
Eliza A.Dyson, *Well-i'-th'-Lane* (1926)
John Fallon, *Toad Lane* (1920)
John Garside, *Redcross Street* (1923)
John William Haslam, *242 Halifax Road* (1926)
Edmund Hey, *39 Spotland Road* (1920)
Mary A.Kenyon, *13 Toad Lane* (1940)
George Kershaw, *35/36 Dyehouse Lane* (1926)
Fred Pearson, *16 Milk Street* (1923)
Simon Priestley, *370 Oldham Road* (1920)
Thomas Rhodes, *11 Halifax Road* (1920)
James A.Richardson, *72 Cheetham Street* (1935)
Frederick Sibay, *101 Manchester Road* (1923)
James Tattersall, *Bamford* (1897)
James Tomlinson, *Dyer's Arms Brewery, 143 Oldham Road* (1927)
John Tweedale, *211 Bury Road* (1920)
Percival Tweedale, *320 Halifax Road, Smallbridge* (1920)
Richard Wallwork, *82 Platting Lane* (1921)
John Whitehead, *45 Spotland Road* (1923)
Henry Woolfenden, *1 Falinge Road* (1921)
Christopher Wormwell, *Wilbutts Lane* (1921)

Royton

Fletcher, Travis & Co.Ltd, *Edge Lane Brewery.* Bought by the Oldham Brewery Co.Ltd 1895 and the brewery was sold to the above concern registered in October 1897. Receiver appointed on 3rd November 1915 and was wound up on 1st May 1916. Premises later occupied by the Edge Lane Brewery & Bottling Co. until *c.*1939.
George Gazey, *Fir Lane* (1921)

Salford

Armitage & Co, *Adelphi Brewery, Adelphi Street.* Founded by 1850 and brewing had ceased by 1904.
George Robert Clayton, *Sandywell Brewery, Sandywell Street.* Acquired by Boddington's Breweries Ltd with 17 tied houses 1888.
William Crabtree, *279 West Park Street* (1910)
Groves & Whitnall Ltd, *Regent Road Brewery.* Founded 1835. Acquired by Groves & Whitnall October 1868. Registered February 1899 with 591 public houses. Acquired by Greenall Whitley & Co.Ltd 1961 and brewing ceased in March 1972.
Mottram's Brewery Ltd, *St.Stephen's Brewery, Brewery Street.* Acquired by the Cornbrook Brewery Ltd 1897.
Benjamin Robinson & Co.Ltd, *Church Street, Pendleton* (1930)
Salford Brewery Co.Ltd, *Town Hall Brewery, Ford Street.* Registered April 1888 as the Town Hall Brewery Salford Ltd which was dissolved 5th July 1889. New company registered as above March 1889 to acquire the business of William Midgley. Liquidated 1895. Disused brewery and the adjacent Town Hall Tavern were bought by Chesters from Samuel Ogden June 1896. Brewery sold to Henry Sutcliffe on 30th November 1899 but in 1966 Threlfall Chesters repurchased part of the old brewery buildings, which were later demolished during the rebuilding of the Town Hall Tavern.
Walker & Homfrays Ltd, *Woodside Brewery, Wilmslow Street.* Originally brewed at the Sun Brewery, Ford Lane 1884 and moved to Wilmslow Street 1890/91. Registered February 1896. Merged with Wilson's Brewery Ltd 1949 to form Wilson & Walker Breweries Ltd. The brewery has been demolished.
Watson, Woodhead & Wagstaffe Ltd, *Irwell Street.* Registered December 1895 as Watson & Woodhead Ltd to acquire the Irwell and Bolton Street breweries. Name changed as above 25th April 1898 when John Wagstaffe & Co. were acquired. Merged with Walker & Homfrays Ltd 1912 and was wound up on 10th February 1923.

Shaw

William Stott, *42 Milnrow Road* (1923)

Stalybridge

John Heginbotham Ltd, *Borough Brewery, Borough Street.* Founded 1851. Registered April 1908. Voluntary liquidation 23rd November 1914 and was acquired by Frederic Robinson Ltd 1915.

Standish

J.B.Almond Ltd, *Standish Brewery, 1 School Lane.* Private company registered 1961. Acquired by the Burtonwood Brewery (Forshaws) Ltd August 1968 with 16 tied houses and was closed.

Edward Ball & Co.Ltd, *20 Standish Lower Road.* Registered May 1895 to acquire the Woodhouses Inn, Wigan and to carry on the business of brewers. Closed 1910.

Stockport

George Ball, *Old King Brewery, 60 Great Portwood Street.* Acquired by Hardy's Crown Brewery Ltd 1912.

Bell & Co.Ltd, *Hempshaw Brook Brewery, Hempshaw Lane.* Founded by Avery Fletcher 1835 and was acquired by Smith & Bell in 1850. Acquired by Frederic Robinson Ltd April 1949 with 100 public houses

James Chetham, *Ash Brewery, Manchester Road, Heaton Norris.* A home brew house bought by Daniel Clifton in July 1899 and brewing ceased.

Richard Clarke & Co.Ltd, *Reddish Brewery, Sandy Lane.* Founded 1865 and the Reddish Brewery was built in 1874. Registered 1899. Acquired by Boddington's Breweries Ltd 1963 with 65 public houses and was closed.

Daniel Clifton & Co.Ltd, *Royal Oak Brewery, Clifton Street.* Daniel Clifton owned the Royal Oak Inn where he began brewing by 1850. Due to expanded trade a new brewery was built adjacent to the inn in 1880. At the time of his death in 1900 some 70 public houses were owned. In February 1923 they were acquired by the Manchester Brewery Co.Ltd, then a subsidiary of Walker & Homfrays Ltd. About 1940 the brewery was leased to the Cornbrook Brewery Co.Ltd and was further leased to Whitbread in April 1943 before they bought it in March 1946. Brewery closed 1957.

James Foster, *Nelson Inn, Wellington Road.* Brewing 1830-1895 when they were acquired by Wilson's Brewery.

James Leigh, *Rock House Brewery, Thomas Street, Heaton Norris.* Home brew house brewing 1892-1934.

Sydney Pearson, *Eagle Brewery, 31 Lower Hillgate.* Brewery sold to Frederic Robinson September 1905 after owner's over-speculation in spinning mills. 4 tied houses. Bankrupt January 1912.

Pollard & Co.Ltd, *Reddish Vale Industrial Estate.* Founded November 1975 by David Pollard. Brewing ceased April 1982.

Frederick Robinson Ltd, *Unicorn Brewery, Lower Hillgate.* Founded September 1838 when William Robinson bought the Unicorn Inn from Samuel Hole. Brewing began by 1868. Registered 7th October 1920. Still independent 1990.

Charles Saynor & Sons Ltd, *61 Travis Brow, Heaton Norris.* Registered April 1898. Voluntary liquidation 28th October 1921.

Showell's Stockport Brewery Ltd, *Brookfield Brewery, Hempshaw Lane.* Founded 1890 when Walter Showell & Sons Ltd of Oldbury acquired Sarah Marsland's Brookfield Brewery established 1866. Formed into a separate company as above in 1896. Acquired by Walker & Homfrays Ltd 1910.

Joseph Worrall, *Windsor Castle Brewery, 41 Castle Street, Edgley.* Founded by 1823 at the Windsor Castle public house and was acquired by Joseph Worrall 1871. Acquired by Wilson's Brewery 1899.

Swinton

William H.Edmondson, *Sutherland Street* (1902)
Swinton Brewery Co.Ltd, *Partington Lane.* Registered July 1889. Acquired by the Worsley Brewery Co.Ltd 1897.

Tottington

John Nuttall, *Robin Hood Brewery, Market Street* (1930)
Warburton Brothers, *Walshaw Lane & Pennington Street* (1914)

Wardle

Walter Ashworth, *Littlefield Brewery* (1914)
John & Joseph Butterworth, *Lowerfield Brewery,* (1910)

Whitefield

Whitefield Breweries Ltd, *Higher Lane, Besses o' th' Barn.* Registered March 1899 as above to amalgamate: the Whitefield Brewery Co.Ltd; the Longsight Brewery, Manchester carried by the exors of Daniel Irvine Flattely as Barber & Co; the Stamford Brewery Co. (Ashton-under-Lyne) Ltd and the Lee

Home Brewery Co.Ltd. Name changed as above March 1901. Compulsory winding up order made March 1905.

Whitefield Brewery Co.Ltd, *Higher Lane, Besses o' th' Barn.* Founded 1845. Registered November 1896 to acquire the interest of Arnold Daly Briscoe. Merged with the Stamford Brewery Co.(Ashton-under-Lyne) Ltd and the Lee Home Brewing Co.Ltd of Oldham 1899 to form Whitefield Breweries Ltd.

Wigan

Airey's Brewery Ltd, *Victoria Brewery, Westwood Road, Poolstock.* Founded by Thomas Airey 1869 and brewed at various sites before the Victoria Brewery was acquired by 1898. Registered November 1906. Acquired by Walker Cain Ltd in 1926 with about 40 tied houses which were transferred to the Oldfield Brewery Ltd in 1933.

Albion Brewery Co.Ltd, *Hardybutts & Seller Street, Chester.* Registered July 1872. Acquired by Threlfall's Brewery Co.Ltd 1919 with 11 public houses in the Chester area and 21 in Wigan. The Wigan properties were sold to Walker Cain Ltd in the 1930s.

Edward Ball, *Crooke Brewery* (1930)

James Fairhurst Ltd, *Warrington Lane.* Private company registered September 1915. 57 of their tied houses were offered for sale 8th April 1920, 11 being sold for £66,700, 6 of these to Walker Cain Ltd, the remainder were withdrawn. Wound up 25th January 1921.

Thomas W.Farrimond, *134a Ormskirk Road, Newtown.* Founded by 1883. Acquired by J.G.Swales & Co.Ltd 1946 and brewing ceased 1961.

Henry Heaton & Sons, *Smithy Bank Brewery, 335a Warrington Road, Goose Green, Pemberton* (1923)

Moorfields Ltd, *Atlas Brewery, Lathom's Yard, 20a Millgate.* Registered September 1914. No tied houses, club trade only. Brewery demolished 1970 due to town centre redevelopment and the club trade connections were acquired by Wilson's Brewery Ltd.

Oldfield Brewery Ltd, *Poolstock Brewery, Westwood Road.* Registered August 1876 as the Oldfield Brewery Co.Ltd to acquire the business of Charles Oldfield. Re-registered as above March 1895. Acquired by Walker Cain Ltd 1926 with 90 public houses. Brewing ceased 1936.

Henry Robinson & Co, *Wigan Brewery, King Street.* Founded in the 1780s. Offered for auction 24th September 1894 with 88 tied houses and was bought by Magee, Marshall & Co.Ltd for £175,000.

John Sumner & Co.Ltd, *Haigh Brewery.* Founded before 1851. Private company registered 1918. 9 public houses. Acquired by Greenall Whitley & Co.Ltd October 1931.

Woodhouses

Sarah Taylor (1920)

MERSEYSIDE

Birkenhead

Aldous & Bedford Ltd, *Victoria Road, Seacombe.* Registered April 1896. Wound up voluntarily 17th December 1897.

Birkenhead Brewery Co.Ltd, *73 Oxton Road.* Registered August 1865 as the Birkenhead Amalgamated Brewery Co.Ltd to merge Aspinall's Brewery, Cleveland Street and Cook's Brewery, Oxton Road. Name changed as above March 1872. 120 tied houses. Merged with Threlfall Chesters Brewery Co.Ltd

1962 and closed.

John W.D.King, *Grosvenor Road, Victoria Road, Seacombe.* Acquired by the Chester Lion Brewery Co.Ltd 1898.

West Cheshire Brewery Co.Ltd, *Queen's Brewery, 365 Farm Road, Tranmere.* Operated as Elvin & Ross until 1887 when it became Gatehouse & Son. Registered as Gatehouse & Son Ltd 1st November 1894 and was reregistered as above November 1896 with 50 public houses. Acquired by Threlfall's Brewery Co.Ltd 1927 with 67 public houses and brewing ceased.

Yate's Castle Brewery Ltd, *Castle Brewery, 18/19 Market Place.* See also:- Ardwick, Manchester.

Other Breweries

William Brown, *40 Derby Street* (1891)
Joseph Bruner, *79 Oxton Road* (1891)
William Thorne & Co.Ltd, *Exmouth Street* (1902)

Bootle

Joseph Hanlon, *6 Norfolk Street* (1892)

Eccleston

Copple Brothers, *Portico Lane*. Founded by 1906 when they had at least 6 public houses. These were bought by Greenall Whitley c.1927 but it is believed that they continued to supply the domestic trade until at least 1939.

Formby

T.& W.R.Dickinson, *Old Brewery, Liverpool, Freshfield*. Acquired by Joshua Tetley & Sons Ltd September 1949 with 3 public houses.

John Greig, *Bay Horse Brewery* (1910)

Thomas Rimmer, *Reciprocity Brewery*. Acquired by Charles Thoroughgood, late Managing Director of Thoroughgood's Breweries Ltd, 1906.

Great Crosby

Charles Cawson, *33 Victoria Road* (1891)

Thomas Molyneux, *Tower Brewery, Liverpool Road* (1895)

Halewood

Edward Moss, *Halewood Brewery*. Founded by 1853. Acquired by Greenall Whitley & Co.Ltd 1890.

Haydock

Benjamin Lowe, *Kenyon's Lane* (1892)

Huyton

Richard Barker & Co, *Huyton Brewery, Derby Road*. Acquired by Walker Cain Ltd October 1926 with about 30 tied houses.

Liverpool, City Centre

Beck Brewing Co.Ltd, *Crown Brewery, 90/94 Prescot Street*. Founded c.1849 as Bartlett's Brewery. Registered as above in December 1895 to produce non-intoxicating beer. Liquidator appointed 16th September 1898 and was wound up March 1900.

Bent's Brewery Co.Ltd, *New Brewery, 30 Johnson Street & Stone, Staffordshire*. Founded before 1877. Registered July 1889 to acquire R.Bent & Co and Montgomery's Brewery, Stone. Acquired by Bass Charrington 1967 with 514 public houses. Brewing ceased March 1975.

Bradshaw & Beesley, *34 Vauxhall Road*. Brewing at the Windsor Brewery, Upper Parliament Street 1875-79. Closed 1900.

J.Bramley & Sons Ltd, *Wellington Brewery, 94 Upper Hill Street*. Registered April 1896. Acquired by the Castletown Brewery Ltd before 1935 and was transferred to Hope & Anchor Breweries 1948. Now only a wine & spirit business.

British Lager Brewery Co.Ltd, *24 Devon Street*. Registered 4th March 1899. Wound up 27th November 1902. No tied houses.

Cook Brothers, *Soho Brewery, 99 Soho Street*. Acquired by Robinson's Brewery Ltd 1897 and was still being used by Ind Coope in 1930.

Green & Clarkson, *111 Soho Street & Midland Brewery, Burton on Trent*. Acquired by Peter Walker & Co.Ltd 1889/90.

Harding & Parrington Ltd, *Brunswick Brewery, 57 St.James's Street*. Possibly founded 1848. In 1873 acquired control of John Joule & Sons of Stone, Staffs. Registered 1st January 1898. Acquired by Cain & Sons Ltd 1920.

Joplin's Brewery Ltd, *1/5 Norman Street*. Founded 1871. Registered 11th October 1900 to acquire exors of Henry Joplin and the United Distilleries Co. Acquired by Cain & Sons Ltd 1906 with 16 tied houses. Brewing ceased 1907.

James Mellor & Sons Ltd, *14/24 Hunter Street*. Founded 1823. Registered 1914. Acquired by Higson's Brewery Ltd 1946 and is now only a wine & spirits merchants.

Robinson's Brewery Ltd, *Myrtle Brewery, Holly Street & Union Street, Burton on Trent*. Founded by Thomas Robinson at Burton 1842. Registered March 1896 to acquire Thomas Robinson & Co. and Sykes, Porter & Co, Myrtle Brewery with 109 tied houses. Acquired by Ind Coope & Co.(1912) Ltd 1920 with 135 public houses. Burton brewery closed 1920 and Liverpool brewery 1930.

Segar, Halsall & Co, *Bevington Bush Brewery, 32 Bevington Bush*. Founded c.1834. Closed 1900.

Smart & Co, *Castle Brewery, 8 Chaucer Street*. Founded 1853. Acquired by James Mellor & Sons Ltd or Cain & Sons Ltd c.1926.

Smith, Mumford & Co, *64/66 Highfield Street*. Acquired by Higson's Brewery Ltd 1915.

Tarbuck's Brewery, *1 Rose Hill*. Registered December 1889. Acquired by Peter Walker & Sons Ltd 1913 with 17 tied houses.

Threlfall's Brewery Co.Ltd, *21 Trueman Street & Cook Street, Salford*. Founded 1812. Salford brewery acquired 1861. Registered March 1888 to amalgamate J.M.Threlfall & W.A.Matheson, 3/7 Juvenal Street. From 1961 known as Threlfall Chesters Ltd. Acquired by Whitbread & Co.Ltd 1967 with 800 licensed houses. Cook Street brewery closed 1971 and Trueman Street October 1982.

United Breweries Co.(Liverpool) Ltd, *Windsor Brewery, Feather Street - Upper Parliament Street and Midland Brewery, Soho Street*. Registered March 1887 as the City of Liverpool & District Brewery Co.Ltd to acquire the business carried on as G.G.Houghton and Hammond & Mills. Name changed as above 30th August 1888. Acquired by Duncan Gilmour & Co.Ltd 1892 who operated the brewery until at least 1915.

George S.Willings & Sons, *20/22 Rose Place*. Possibly acquired by Walkers or Cains' c.1892.

Other Breweries

C.Bate & Son, *11/13 Fairhurst Street*. See also:- Wrexham, Clwyd.

William & John Duck, *33 Gildart Street* (1896)

Gardner & Pedder, *Richmond Brewery, 144 Richmond Row* (1890)

Glover & Son, *69/79 Fontenoy Street* (1906)

Lamb & Watt Breweries, *46/48 St.Anne Street* (1910)

John Lane, *Oriel Brewery, 33 Vauxhall Road* (1890)

Lindley's Kensington Brewery, *286/288 Kensington*

Thomas Murphy, *16 Fraser Street* (1892)

James Scotson, *58 Upper Beau Street* (1895)

John Henry Smith, *290 Kensington* (1896)

John Ulyett, *6 Marlborough Street* (1891)

Liverpool, Edge Hill

William Baker, *20 Dove Street* (1890)

William Jones, *4/8 Edge Vale* (1895)

Liverpool, Everton

William J.Birchall, *11 Greenside* (1891)

Robert Blezard, *Liver Brewery, 419 Scotland Road*. Founded c.1840. Acquired by Walker Cain 1921 with 48 public houses.

Thomas Bowman, *26 Jasmin Street* (1895)

Houlding's Brewery Co.Ltd, *32/34 Tynemouth Street*. Founded by John Houlding 1871. Registered January 1914. Acquired by Ind Coope 1938 with 21 tied houses.

Liverpool, Gateacre

Thomas Gregory, exors of, *Gateacre Brewery, 42 Gateacre Brow*. Founded c.1862 at Mersey Road, Aigburth. Closed 1920.

Liverpool, Kirkdale

Thomas Heyes, *Phoenix Brewery, 42 Foley Street*. Acquired by Robert Cain & Sons Ltd 1907 with 40 public houses.

Tower Brewery Co.Ltd, *6/10 Wrexham Street*. Originally registered 14th January 1891 as Orrell's Brewery Syndicate Ltd to acquire the Crown Brewery, Wrexham Street and was wound up voluntarily 5th October 1893. Registered as above February 1898 to acquire Webster & Atkins. Wound up 18th September 1901.

Liverpool, Knotty Ash

Joseph Jones & Co.(Knotty Ash) Ltd, *Knotty Ash Brewery, East Prescot Road*. Founded 1869. Registered September 1924. Acquired by Higson's Brewery Ltd 1927 with over 70 licensed houses. Brewing ceased 1928. The brewery is still standing.

Liverpool, Toxteth

Robert Cain & Sons Ltd, *Mersey Brewery, Stanhope Street*. Founded 1848 when Robert Cain acquired a small brewery in Limekiln Lane. Mersey Brewery acquired c.1850. Private company registered December 1896 with 200 tied houses. Merged with Walkers of Warrington September 1921 to form Walker Cain Ltd and brewing was concentrated at Warrington in 1923 and the Mersey Brewery was sold to Higsons.

Higson's Brewery Ltd, *Mersey Brewery, Stanhope Street*. Founded by William Harvey at Dale Street 1780 and moved to Cheapside 1854. Acquired by Daniel Higson 1875. Moved to Upper Parliament Street 1912 before acquiring Cain's former brewery in 1923. Registered 1888 as Daniel Higson Ltd and was re-registered as above January 1937. Acquired by Boddington's Breweries Ltd June 1985 with 160 tied houses and brewing ceased in 1990.

Liverpool, Tuebrook

Oxford Brewery Co.Ltd, *64 Sutton Street*. Registered February 1899. Voluntary liquidation 4th September 1899.

Liverpool, Wavertree

Burton, Bell & Co.Ltd, *Rose Brewery, 240 Picton Road*. Registered June 1900. Acquired by Robert Cain & Sons Ltd 1907.

Thomas Wright, exors of, *Crown Brewery, 14 Church Road* (1898)

Liverpool, West Derby

John McGregor, *5 Deysbrook Lane* (1891)

Liverpool, Woolton

Dilford's Brewery, *Allerton Road*. Founded October 1985. Closed 1986.

Rainford

James Birch & Co, *Rainford Brewery* (1900)
William Richardson. Acquired by Greenall Whitley with 24 public houses 1893.

Rainhill

George T. Caldwell, *Norlands Lane* (1921). A farm brewery with at least one tied house, the Ship, Warrington Road, later rebuilt as a Higsons house.

St.Helens

Henry Finlay Ltd, *Phoenix Brewery, 78 Peckers Hill, Sutton*. Registered 1911. Voluntary liquidation 4th August 1915.
Greenall Whitley & Co.Ltd, *Hall Street*. See also:- Warrington, Cheshire.
James Stockley & Son, *New Street* (1906)

Southport

Birkdale Brewery Co, *Crown Brewery, 115 Upper Aughton Road*. Closed c.1935 and was probably better known in recent years as the home of race horse Red Rum.

Southport Brewery Co.Ltd, *Scarisbrick New Road*. Registered March 1875. Acquired by Ellis, Warde & Webster & Co Ltd.

Wallasey

E.Spragg & Co.Ltd, *Wallasey Vale Brewery, Leasow Road*. Registered May 1896. Acquired by Higson's Brewery Ltd June 1919 with 5 tied houses. Resold to Walker Cain 1923.

Waterloo

Thoroughgood's Breweries Ltd, *Lion Brewery, Queen Street*. Brewery built 1877/78 by William Okell of the Falcon Brewery, Douglas, Isle of Man to introduce his popular light ale to the mainland. Registered June 1896 as T.W.Thoroughgood Ltd. Name changed as above 15th February 1898. Acquired by Threlfall's Brewery Co.Ltd 1925.

NORFOLK

Blakeney

Augustus Hill (1875-1904)

Diss

Taylor, Sons & Dowson, *Upper Brewery, Shelf-hanger Road*. Founded by 1850. The brewery, maltings and 67 public houses offered for sale in 1896 at £120,000 and were bought by Tollemache's Ipswich Brewery Ltd in 1897 and was resold to Lacon & Co.Ltd shortly afterwards.

Ditchingham

Crowfoot's Brewery Ltd. Founded 1847 at Broome and moved to Ditchingham c.1875 when they acquired William Cuddon's Brewery. Private company registered February 1935. Bankrupt 1953 and was closed. Demolished 1973.

Downham Market

Derek Briggs, *Downham Brewery, Castle Hotel, Paradise Road*. Home brew house founded December 1982. Brewing ceased 1985 and draught beer supplied by Greene King Ltd.
Frank Mills, *Priory Road*. Bankrupt 1912.
Phillips & Co, *St.Edmund's Brewery, Paradise Lane*. Founded before 1869 as Ward & Newell. Acquired by Charles Reginald Phillips in 1894 for £1,400. They acquired the Elm Road Brewery, Wisbech, Cambs in 1908 and brewed there until the brewery was destroyed by fire in 1911 and they returned to brewing at Downham Market. Brewing ceased after 1946.

Drayton

Woodforde's Norfolk Ales. See also:- Erpingham & Woodbastwick.

East Dereham

Bidwell & Co, *South Green*. Founded c.1795 by a branch of the Thetford brewing family. Wound up in 1890 and was offered for auction on 1st August 1890 with 30 tied houses and realised £31,122. The Thetford brewery acquired 27 of the houses. Brewery demolished shortly afterwards.
Charles Pearse, *Crown Brewery, Norwich Street*. In the late 1880s merged with Day's Eaton Brewery, Norwich and traded as Cooper-Brown & Day. Charles Pearse was the owner by 1904. Sold to Steward & Patteson Ltd in 1922 for £26,500. Brewing had ceased by 1925 when the premises were sold.

Eaton

Arthur J.Day. See also:- East Dereham

Emneth

Henry T.Herbert (1904)

Erpingham

Woodforde's Norfolk Ales, *Spread Eagle Brewery*. Founded at Drayton near Norwich in April 1981 and moved here in 1983. Transferred to Woodbastwick 1989.

Fakenham

Thomas Charlton, *Hall Staith*. Founded c.1852 by John Brereton and acquired by Charlton 1872. Brewery and six public houses sold to Greene King & Sons Ltd 1891 for £7,100.

Feltwell

Henry Fairchild (1890)

Great Yarmouth

George Charles Kew, *High Street, Gorleston*. Founded 1872. Receiver appointed March 1893.

E.Lacon & Co.Ltd, *Church Plain*. Founded 1640 and acquired by Lacons 1760. Registered April 1894 with 204 tied houses. Public company formed 1952. Acquired by Whitbread & Co. Ltd December 1965 with 354 public houses. Brewery closed 28th February 1968 and has been demolished.

Grimston

Bourke & Elwes. Acquired by Morgan's Brewery Co.Ltd 1902.

Hempton

John Lane, *King's Head*. Bought by Elijah Eyres & Co. 1896.

Holt

Henry Turner, *Anchor Brewery, High Street*.

King's Lynn

W.& T.Bagge, *King Street*. Founded before 1767, possibly in 1688. Acquired by Steward & Patteson Ltd 1929 with 75 public houses and was closed.
Frederick J.Carpenter Ltd, *Chevalier Brewery, Church Lane*. Founded 1840. Known as Laws & Co. until 1904. Registered 1913. Closed 1921.
Edward Everard & Sons, *Baker Lane*. Brewing before 1850. Acquired by Steward & Patteson Ltd 1929.
Elijah Eyres Brewery Ltd, *Lady Bridge Brewery, Bridge Street*. Founded c.1820. Registered June 1896. Acquired by Morgan's Brewery Ltd 1900 with 133 tied houses. Brewing continued 1951. Now demolished.
Anne Elizabeth Knights, *Queen Street Brewery*. Founded by 1854. Acquired by the Colchester Brewing Co.Ltd 1910.
Edgar Philip Pipe, *The Crown, Church Street*. Founded in South Street in the early 1850s and had moved to Church Street by 1904. Closed c.1912.
John Jex Rolfe, *London Road Brewery*. Founded by 1872. Brewery & 16 public houses sold to Hogge & Seppings Ltd 5th June 1906 for £11,000.

Letheringsett

W.H.Cozens-Hardy & Sons, *Letheringsett Brewery*. Founded before 1780 and was trading as above by 1888. Sold to Morgan's Brewery Co.Ltd with 17 tied houses in 1896. Used as a soft drinks factory. Some buildings are still standing.

Middleton

John Bardell, *Old Tower* (1900)

Mundesley

William S.Juniper (1895)

Narborough

Ship Inn. Brewing ceased when it was leased to Bullard & Sons Ltd on 12th September 1896.

North Walsham

W.& F.Press, *Crown Brewery, New Road* (1910)

Norwich

Alfred Robert Arnold, *St.Margaret's Brewery, St.Margaret's Plain*. Acquired by Lacon & Co. Ltd 1902 with 32 tied houses.

Bullard & Sons Ltd, *Anchor Brewery, St.Mile's Bridge*. Founded 1837. Registered March 1895. Acquired by Watney Mann Ltd 1964 with 530 public houses and brewing ceased in 1968. The remaining buildings are now a residential development.

Morgan's Brewery Co.Ltd, *Old Brewery, King Street*. Founded 1720. Registered March 1887. Controlled 600 tied houses by 1904. Acquired jointly by Bullard & Sons Ltd and Steward & Patteson Ltd 1961. Brewing ceased April 1985.

Norwich City Brewery Co.Ltd, *St.Swithin's Terrace*. Registered 30th November 1897. Never traded and was dissolved 24th September 1899.

Reindeer Freehouse & Brewery, *10 Dereham Road*. Founded May 1987. Still brewing 1990.

Steward & Patteson Ltd, *Pockthorpe Brewery*. Founded 1793. Registered July 1895. Acquired by Bullard & Sons Ltd 1961 with 632 tied houses. Brewing ceased January 1970.

Tap Brewery, *27 Duke Street*. Founded 1981 as the Star Brewery which ceased brewing in 1982. Re-opened as above in December 1982 but was closed in 1984 and the public house was acquired by Greene King & Sons Ltd.

Youngs, Crawshay Ltd, *Crown Brewery, King Street*. Founded by 1807. Registered November 1897. 250 public houses. Acquired by Bullard & Sons Ltd 1956 and was closed in 1958. Now demolished.

Other Breweries

A.W.Bloom, *Minn's Court, Magdalen Street* (1890)

Coleman & Co.Ltd, *Rosary Road*. Founded c.1890. Brewing had ceased by 1900.

Henry Bathurst Long, *Poplar Garden, Aylsham Road* (1892)

Lord, Smith & Carman, *St.George's Brewery, St.Mary's Alley* (1904)

Charles Pearse, *Eaton Brewery, Church Lane*, see also:- East Dereham.

Reepham

Reepham Brewery, *1 Colliers Way*. Founded 1983. Still brewing 1990.

Ringstead

William Clarke, *Compasses Inn* (1910)

South Creake

James Pinchen & Son. Founded c.1750 and was acquired by Pinchen c.1896. Brewing ceased in 1914. Later used as a razor blade factory and has been recently converted into a house.

Setchey

Hogge & Seppings Ltd, *Setch Bridge Brewery*. Founded by 1767. Registered 1911. Acquired by Bullard & Sons Ltd in 1928. The brewery is still standing.

Swaffham

Morse & Woods, *White Hart Lane*. Acquired by Thomas Morse 1809. Sold to Steward & Patteson Ltd 1895 with 51 tied houses.

Thetford

Bidwell & Co, *Old Market Street*. Founded c.1710 and was operated by the Bidwell family until c.1902 when it was sold to Eustace Quilter, with 104 public houses, for £104,250 but still traded as Bidwell & Co until acquired by Bullard & Sons Ltd in 1924 and was closed. Most of the brewery is still standing.

Thomas Lusher, *2 St.Nicholas Street* (1896)

Trunch

Trunch Brewery Ltd, *North Norfolk Brewery, Brewery Road*. Founded 1803. Private company registered February 1939. Acquired by Morgan's Brewery Co. Ltd 1952 with 9 public houses. Now demolished.

Walpole St.Peter

Alma Woods & Co, *Walpole Brewery*. A branch of Wisbech, Cambs. Closed in 1914.

Watton

Thomas Crawshay Frost, *High Street*. Founded c.1812 and was bought by Frost c.1869. Sold to Cann & Co. of Wymondham 1891 for £15,000. Brewery is still standing.

Weybourne

William J.J.Bolding. Bought by Steward & Patteson Ltd 1897 for £17,000.

Woodbastwick

Woodforde's Norfolk Ales, *Broadland Brewery*. Transferred from Erpingham 1989. Still brewing 1990.

Wymondham

William Cann & Co, *Market Place*. Acquired by Morgan's Brewery Ltd in November 1894 for £129,000 and was closed.

Aynho

Frederick W.Scott, *Cartwright Arms* (1910)

Brackley

William Blencowe & Co.Ltd. See also:- Cannock, Staffs.

Hopcraft & Norris Ltd. Founded 1842 by Alfred Hopcraft. Registered July 1895. 119 tied houses. Merged with the Chesham Brewery Ltd July 1946 to form Chesham & Brackley Breweries Ltd.

Corby

Isaac Gibson (1880 - 1895)

Cosgrove

Francis D.Bull. Founded by Daniel Warren 1847. Acquired by Phipps & Co.Ltd *c*.1898.

Cranford St.John

Battle Brothers. Founded by William Battle 1869. Brewing ceased *c*.1930 with 7 licensed houses. Demolished after 1945.

Daventry

Litchborough Brewery, *21 Alvis Way, Royal Oak Industrial Estate*. Founded 1974 at Litchborough and moved to here April 1980. Bought by Liddingtons of Rugby 1983 and the brewery was moved to there.

Wood Brothers, *West Place, New Street*. Founded 1885. 4 licensed houses. Brewing ceased 1922.

Kettering

John Elworthy Ltd, *Crown Brewery, 5 Gold Street*. Founded by William Rose 1830 and was bought by William Elworthy in 1875. Registered 1912. Acquired by Marston, Thompson & Evershed Ltd October 1931 with 30/40 public houses. Brewing ceased 1940. Brewery mainly demolished.

King's Cliffe

Ketton & King's Cliffe Brewery Co.Ltd, *West Street & Ketton, Leics*. Registered March 1898 and was dissolved 26th October 1900. By 1903 was in the hands of G.K.Fapillon and was known as the Malt & Hop Brewery. Owned by Macleod C.Campbell from before 1910 until 1916.

King's Sutton

Colegrove & Son (1906)

Litchborough

Litchborough Brewery. See also:- Daventry.

Long Buckby

Walker & Soames, *Anchor Brewery, Buckby Wharf*. Founded *c*.1869 as Montgomery, Harris & Co and became Walker & Soames by 1898. Acquired by Hopcraft & Norris March 1910 with 48 tied houses and brewing ceased. Brewery later demolished.

Milton Malsor

W.J.East & Co.Ltd, *Hope Brewery*. Founded by J.Cockerill 1806 as a home brew house and was bought by East 1866. New brewery built 1888. Registered December 1896 with 8 tied houses. Acquired by the Northampton Brewery Co.Ltd 1904. Brewery still standing 1990. Brewery buildings used commercially.

Northampton

Abington Brewery Co.Ltd, *Abington Park Brewery, 334 Wellingborough Road*. Brewery built *c*.1900 by Dorman, Pope & Co. Registered October 1902 and was wound up in 1913 and was succeeded by the above concern. Brewing ceased January 1958 and beer was bought from Bass. Acquired by Charles Wells Ltd 1963 with 23 public houses and was demolished shortly afterwards.

Abington Park Brewery, *Wellingborough Road*. Home brew house founded October 1984. Still brewing 1990.

Allen & Burnett, *Lion Brewery, Cotton End*. Founded 1839 by Thomas Haggar and was acquired by Coales, Allen & Cooper 1866 and became Allen & Burnett December 1890. Brewery now demolished.

Carlsberg Brewery Ltd, *140 Bridge Street*. Opened 1970.

Major, Lucas & Co, *Victoria Brewery, 29 Kettering Road*. Founded *c*.1870. Acquired by Walker & Soames 1899 and closed 1910. Brewery demolished 1989.

T.Manning & Co. Ltd, *Castle Brewery, Black Lion Hill*. Founded 1878. Registered February 1889. Acquired by Phipps & Co.Ltd 1933 with 43 public houses.

Northampton Brewery Co.Ltd, *Phoenix Brewery, 116 Bridge Street*. Brewery built 1856 for Thomas Phillips, later owner of the Dock Brewery, Newport, Gwent. Registered February 1887. Merged with Phipps & Co.Ltd 1957. 420 tied houses. Brewery closed 1973 and demolished. Carlsberg Brewery built on the site.

Phipps Brewery Ltd, *Gold Street*. Founded 1801 at Towcester by Pickering Phipps. Brewing began at Northampton in 1817. New brewery built at Towcester 1874 and remained in use until until *c*.1905. Registered September 1881. After the merger with the Northampton Brewery Co.Ltd became Phipps Northampton Brewery Co.Ltd. Acquired by Watney Mann Ltd 1960 and the name was changed as above in 1964. Brewery closed 1974.

Ratliff & Jeffrey Ltd, *Albion Brewery, Commercial Street*. Founded 1864 by Thomas Ratliff. Registered November 1897 with 135 tied houses. Acquired by Phipps 1899. Brewery still standing.

Edward Tresham, *2 Grafton Street* (1874 - 1890)

Old

Tomblin Brothers, *Wold Brewery*. Founded by 1854. Offered for sale 1906 with 3 public houses after brewing had ceased. Brewery still standing.

Oundle

Charles Frederick McKee, *Anchor Brewery, South Road*. Founded by 1864. 5 tied houses. Brewing ceased *c*.1903. Buildings still standing.

Smith & Co.(Oundle) Ltd, *North Street*. Founded 1775. Private company registered December 1935. Acquired by Warwicks & Richardsons Ltd 1955. Some of the buildings were still standing 1989 being used by a builder.

Sudborough

Frederick Tebbutt. 8 public houses sold October 1889. Brewery offered for auction 15th July 1890.

Syresham

King's Brewery. Founded c.1854 and was owned by the Linnell family until c.1900 when it became King's Royal Crown Brewery Co. until the name was changed as above c.1924. Brewing ceased after 1940 and the brewery was demolished and houses built on the site. No tied houses domestic trade only.

Thornby

John Emerton. Home brew house (1894)

Wellingborough

Campbell, Praed & Co.Ltd, *Sheep Street.* Founded by 1823 and was acquired by Praeds' 1878. Registered

November 1896. Acquired by Phipps & Co Ltd 1954 and brewing ceased 1955. The brewery has been demolished.

Dulley & Sons Ltd, *Swan Brewery, Sheep Street.* Founded by 1823. Acquired by Campbell, Praed & Co. Ltd 1920 with 50/60 public houses. Brewery now demolished.

NORTHUMBERLAND

Allendale

James Walton & Co, *Allendale Brewery* (1895)

Alnwick

Alnwick Brewery Co.Ltd, *Dispensary Street.* Registered September 1890 to acquire Mason Brothers. Brewing ceased 1963 and was bought by Dryborough & Co, a Watney Mann subsidiary. 20 tied houses. Sold to Allied-Lyons 1987.

George Stott Smart, *Clayport Street.* Brewing ceased 1900 and the brewery was bought by the Northern Clubs Federation Brewery Ltd, February 1919.

Belford

George Wright & Co, Acquired by Johnson & Darling Ltd 1896.

Berwick on Tweed

Berwick Breweries Ltd, *Tweed Brewery, 12 Silver Street.* Registered July 1899 as the Border Brewery Ltd. Name changed 1924 when they merged with Johnson & Darling Ltd. 78 public houses. Acquired by Associated Breweries Ltd 1937 and brewing ceased.

Johnson & Darling Ltd, *Tweed Brewery, 12 Silver Street.* Registered November 1892. Merged with the Border Brewery Ltd 1924 to form Berwick Breweries Ltd.

Blyth

Blyth & Tyne Brewery Co.Ltd, *Blagdon Street.* Founded before 1884. Registered February 1890. Acquired by Associated Breweries Ltd 1938 with 10 tied houses.

Felton

Joseph Wardle & Co. (1892)

Harbottle

John Pitlock (1891)

Morpeth

John A.Anderson, *Hope & Anchor Brewery* (1921)
Albert Mears Loades, *Well Way* (1898)

Ovingham

William Bedlington, exors of (1926)

Ovington

Robertson, Lumley & Co.Ltd, *Ovington Brewery.* Registered 1915. Closed 1940.

Rothbury

Rothbury Brewery. Acquired by James Aitken & Co. (Falkirk) Ltd 1911.

Warkworth

James William Lamb (1923)

Wooler

Robert Mitchell (1894)

NOTTINGHAMSHIRE

Arnold

Samuel Anthony, *Front Street* (1923)
Tom Harry Hobbins, *Church Street* (1935)
Mary A.Worton, *High Street* (1926)

Beeston

Beeston Brewery Co.Ltd, *Rylands Road.* Registered October 1896 as the New Beeston Brewery Co.Ltd. Name changed November 1897. Acquired by Shipstone & Sons Ltd July 1922 and was converted into maltings.

Tom Stone, *High Street* (1940)

Bulwell

Myrtle & Harwood (1892)

Chilwell

George Brentnall (1920)
John Woodhouse (1923)

Cinder Hill

David Bramley (1926)
George Bramley (1923)

Clarborough

Bilby Chambers (1920)

Daybrook

Home Brewery Co.Ltd, *Mansfield Road.* Registered August 1890 to acquire the business formerly owned by John Robinson. Acquired by Scottish & Newcastle Breweries July 1986 with 447 public houses.

East Leake

Morton Handley (1930)

Everton

The Farmer's Brewery Co.Ltd. Brewing as Tune & Johnson until 1877. Registered May 1894 to acquire the business of Mark Parkinson. Wound up and was sold to Whitworth, Son & Nephew Ltd March 1907.

Granby

George Skinner (1920)

Kimberley

Hansons Ltd. Founded by Stephen Hanson 1847. Registered November 1897 to acquire R.G.Hanson with 84 tied houses.

Hardy's Kimberley Brewery Ltd. Founded 1832 by Samuel Robinson and was acquired by William & Thomas Hardy in 1857. Registered May 1897 with 97 public houses. Merged with Hansons Ltd in October 1930 and all brewing was concentrated here from 1932. Name changed to Hardy & Hansons Ltd 1972. Still independent 1990.

Lowdham

Albert Radford (1914)

Linby

Jacob Jennison (1902)

Mansfield

Mansfield Brewery Co.Ltd, *Littleworth*. Founded 1855. Registered February 1925. Still independent 1990.

Newark on Trent

Walter Shirley Davy, *Devon Brewery*. Merged with Warwicks & Richardsons Ltd October 1919.

Goodwin Brothers Ltd, *Balderton Gate & 83 Barnbygate*. Registered February 1891. Acquired by W.S.Davy 1897

George Hill, *67 Millgate* (1921)

James Hole & Co.Ltd, *Castle Brewery, Albert Street*. Founded 1870. Registered March 1890. Acquired by Courage, Barclay & Simonds Ltd 1967 with 250 tied houses. Brewing ceased in 1986. Buildings still standing 1990.

Henry Jessop, *Rutland Brewery, Barnbygate*. Acquired by Goodwin Brothers 1891.

McGeorge & Heppenstalls Ltd, *Albion Brewery, Kirkgate*. Operated by Christopher Heppenstall until 1884. Registered 1887 as Heppenstalls Ltd and the name was changed as above 1892. Acquired by Warwicks & Richardsons Ltd 1892 and brewing ceased 1895.

Maple Leaf, *Winthorpe Road*. An Allied Breweries home brew house founded May 1982. Closed 1986.

Newark & Sheffield Breweries Co.Ltd, *Cromwell Brewery, Barnbygate & Scotland Street, Sheffield*. Registered 31st August 1881 to acquire the Newark Brewery Co. and H.W.Robinson & Co. of Sheffield. Acquired by Warwicks & Richardsons Ltd 1895.

Priory Brewery, *George Street*. Originally occupied by Westcrown Ltd brewing 1977-80 and was succeeded by the above in operation 1980-83.

Warwicks & Richardsons Ltd, *Northgate*. Founded by Samuel Sketchley at the Tower Wharf Brewery 1766 and was acquired by Richard Warwick in 1856. Northgate Brewery built 1871. Registered 1888 to acquire Richard Warwick & Sons and Richardson, Earp & Slater, Trent Brewery. Acquired by John Smith's Tadcaster Brewery Co.Ltd 1962 and brewing ceased in 1966. Brewery and malthouse still extant 1990.

Nottingham

Carrington Brewery Co, *Jenner Street, Carrington*. Acquired by Shipstone & Sons Ltd 1896 and was closed.

Dickins, Hickton & Co.Ltd, *Oakfields Road*. In liquidation January 1921.

Dolphin Brewery Co, *6 & 10 North Church Street*. Brewery and 6 public houses offered for auction 15th May 1907.

Fellows, Morton & Clayton, *Canal Street*. A Whitbread home brew house founded 1981 and was named after a former canal transport company whose offices they occupied. Still brewing 1990.

George Green, exors of, *2 Howard Street*. Acquired by the Home Brewery Co.Ltd 1921.

George Hooley Ltd, *Wheatsheaf Brewery, Ilkeston Road, Pears Hill Road*. Private company registered January 1911. 13 tied houses. Acquired by Shipstone & Sons Ltd January 1926.

W.H.Hutchinson & Sons Ltd, *Prince of Wales Brewery, Alpine Street, New Basford*. Founded c.1869. Registered June 1894. Acquired by the Home Brewery Co.Ltd 1914.

T.Losco Bradley Ltd, *Midland Brewery, Northgate, New Basford*. Brewery built 1870 by Abraham Poynton & Co. and was acquired by Bradley in 1887. Registered 1928. Acquired by Shipstone & Sons Ltd 1954.

Newcastle Arms Brewery, *Nottingham Ltd, Sherwood Street*. Home brew house. Private company registered March 1931.

Nottingham Brewery Ltd, *52/56 Mansfield Road*. Founded by Edward Field 1847. Registered February 1887. Acquired by Tennant Brothers Ltd of Sheffield 1944 and brewing ceased in 1952.

James Shipstone & Sons Ltd, *Star Brewery, New Basford*. Founded by James Shipstone 1852. Registered February 1891. Acquired by Greenall Whitley & Co.Ltd 1978 with 280 tied houses.

Other Breweries

Thomas Allan Abram, *50 Upper Parliament Street* (1923)

Edward Addicott, *10 St.Michael Street* (1920)

William Archer, *45 Poplar Street* (1923)

William Archer, senior, *Machin Street* (1930)

William Atherton, junior, *19 Rawson Street, New Basford* (1921)

Frank Bailey, *74 Percy Street, Old Basford* (1920)

William Ernest Beardsley, *15 Platt Street* (1920)

John Bell, *41 Newark Street, Sneinton* (1923)

Ada Blackburn, *16 Pelican Street* (1935)

James Bolton, *77 Walker Street* (1920)

John Bonser, *Bobber's Mill, New Basford* (1923)

Joseph Booth, *23 St.James's Street* (1921)

Thomas L.Bramley, *37 Northgate, New Basford* (1923)

Edgar L.Brooke, *19 Coalpit Lane* (1923)

John Brooker, *Lower Parliament Street* (1940)

William A.Brooks, *136 Ilkeston Road, New Basford* (1923)

Walter L.Brown, *257 Mansfield Road* (1921)

Richard Brownley, *Colwick Street* (1920)

William T.Bryan, *Clarence Street* (1923)

George H.Burnham, *16 Alfreton Road* (1923)

Henry Cave, *27/29 Keswick Street* (1923)

Charlie Clarke, *Malin Hill, Plumpte Square* (1940)

Joseph Cooper, *58 Woolpack Lane* (1935)

Harry Croft, *103 Sneinton Road* (1920)

Richard Arthur Daft, *75 Northumberland Street* (1920)

Elizabeth A.Dales, *86 Shakespeare Street* (1935)

Samuel Henry Daws, *41 Robin Hood Street* (1923)

Ann Eden, *53 Beech Avenue, New Basford* (1923)

Percy Eden, *123 Nottingham Road, Basford* (1923)

George Farr, *1 Alfreton Road* (1920)

Frederick Fee, *16 Hunger Hill Road* (1923)

Benjamin Fletcher, *1 Sneinton Road* (1920)

Walter Fletcher, *Weekday Cross* (1920)

Maria Foster, *387 St.Ann's Well Road* (1920)

Ann Freeston, *1 Carlton Road* (1920)

John H.H.Frettingham, *23/34 Coalpit Lane* (1923)

Edward Fretwell, *105 Carlton Road* (1920)

Peter Gavin, *143 Kirkwhite Street* (1935) & *43 Mount Street* (1926)

Ernest W.Giersberg, *Castle Terrace, Castle Road* (1923)

William H.Goode, *1 Clarence Street* (1926)

Fred John Green, *21 Alfreton Road* (1923)

William Hames, *163 Mansfield Road* (1921)

James Henson, *290 St.Ann's Well Road* (1921)

Thomas Harry Hobbins, *1 Watergate* (1920)

Sarah Hoe, *33 Willoughby Street, New Lenton* (1921)

Annie Holehouse, *24 Houndsgate* (1921)

Albert Holland, *286 Alfred Street, Central* (1935)

Tom Hollingworth, *1 Handel Street* (1926)

Frederick I.Hollis, *25/27 Sneinton Road* (1935)
Albert Arthur Hooley, *209 Alfred Street, Central* (1935)
John Hooley, *680 Woodborough Road* (1920)
John Howard, *9 Highhurst Street, Radford* (1920)
William Henry Howard, *50a Castle Gate* (1921)
John Howcroft, *26 Woolpack Lane* (1921)
Jennie Hubbard, *34 Parker Street, Radford* (1921)
E.F.Jolley, *5 Oliver Street* (1926)
William J.Jones, *9 Coalpit Lane* (1921)
Elizabeth Kirk, *Bottle Lane* (1923)
Walter Kirkman, *93 Manvers Street* (1930)
Edward A.Lanes, *4 Cromford Street* (1935)
James Lewis, *67 Derby Road* (1935)
Sarah Lovett, *223 St.Ann's Well Road* (1923)
Herbert Lowe, *47 Duke Street, Basford* (1923)
William Ludlow, *20 Peas Hill Road* (1923)
Marshall Mackintosh, *15 Sneinton Hollows* (1930)
William Major, *21 Burton Street* (1921)
Randolph Kemp Millington, *28 Beaumont Street* (1910)
William Morley, *14 Lewis Street* (1920) & *2 Moorgate Street* (1921)
Edward Moulding, *92 Abbotsford Street* (1914)
Wiliam Murfin, *21 Carlton Road* (1920)
Frances Murphy, *90 Red Lion Street* (1926)
John Newstead, *14 Mansfield Road* (1921)
John Pawley, *10 Mitchell Street* (1921)
William Pike, *Eastville Street* (1921)
Henry Rawson, *23 Pierrepoint Street* (1923)
Mabel H.Redgate, *21/23 Lincoln Street, Old Basford* (1935)
George William Render, *2 Greyfriargate* (1923)
Samuel Richardson, *27 Colwick Street* (1935)
Henry Rider, *45 Canal Street* (1923)
G.H.Robinson, *8 Bath Street* (1926)
George Robinson, *11 Robin Hood Street* (1930)
Samuel G.Salisbury, *Raleigh Street* (1923)
Arthur Shaw, *50 Carlton Road* (1923)
Emma Sheldon, *47 Heathcote Street* (1920)
Annie Smith, *11 Haywood Street* (1920)
Frederick William Smith, *32 Mount Street* (1921)

Sidney Smith, *9 Park Road, New Lenton* (1930) & *95 Union Road* (1926)
George H.Snook, *335 Mansfield Road, Carrington* (1920)
Harold Spencer, *9/15 Denman Street, New Radford* (1926)
Marcus E.Starkey, *180 Dame Agnes Street* (1920)
John Henry Taylor, *36 Denison Street, Radford* (1923)
Mary Edith Tomlin, *313 Ilkeston Road* (1926)
Samuel Turner, *26 Hornbuckle Street* (1926)
Fred Wagg, *37 Carter Gate* (1920)
Wilfred Waggs, *5/7 Meynell Street* (1923)
Frank Ward, *21 Colwick Street* (1930)
George Henry Ward, *Brewhouse Yard, Castle Road* (1910)
Alice Wardle, *70 Woodborough Road* (1921)
Albert Webster, *Watergate* (1920)
Robert Edward West, *25 Platt Street* (1926)
John Whitehead, *49 Cartergate* (1921)
James Whittaker, *548 Woodborough Road* (1920)
Josiah Widdowson, *Queen's Road* (1940) & *2 St.Nicholas Street* (1920)
Cyril Wilkinson, *57 Brown's Croft, Basford* (1930)
Thomas B.Wilkinson, *Mansfield Road, Sherwood* (1920)
Walter Wilson, *64 Mansfield Street* (1910)
George Woodcock, *292 Carlton Road* (1926)
Arthur George Woods, *60 Bloomsgrove Street* (1921)
Lucy Wright, *130 Mansfield Road* (1921)
William Wyvill, *68 North Sherwood Road* (1930)

Radcliffe on Trent

John Fryer (1930)

Ranby

John Thomas Wells (1920)

Red Hill

Charles Skevington (1923)

Rempstone

William Hibbert (1910)

Retford

Abbey Brewery, *Torworth*. Founded at Stainton, S.Yorkshire 1981 and moved to Torworth 1982. Now brewing at Hereford as the Wye Valley Brewery.

Southwell

Ealand's Brewery. Acquired by J.Marston, Thompson & Son Ltd 1904 with 10 public houses.

Sutton in Ashfield

Crown Brewery Co, *Alfreton Road* (1906)

Worksop

Worksop & Retford Brewery Co.Ltd, *Prior Well Brewery*. Operated as Garside & Alderson until 1877. Registered September 1881 to acquire the Prior Well Brewery Co. and Smith & Nephew, Cresswell Holme Brewery, Worksop. Acquired by Tennant Brothers Ltd in 1959 with 192 public houses.

OXFORDSHIRE

Abingdon

Belcher & Habgood Ltd, *Tower Brewery, Ock Street*. Founded 1815 and operated by Thomas and John M.Townsend until 1892 when it was acquired by Belcher & Habgood. Registered 1898. Acquired by Morland & Co.Ltd 1928 and was closed in 1943.

Morland & Co.Ltd, *United Breweries, Ock Street*. Founded 1726 at West Ilsley by Benjamin Morland. Eagle Brewery acquired 1861 and Abbey Brewery 1866, both in Ock Street. Brewing was concentrated at the Abbey Brewery. Registered October 1887. Still independent 1990.

Walter Harry Tustin, *14 Ock Street*. Receiving order made May 1891.

Banbury

Zephaniah M.Brown & Co.Ltd, *Horse Shoe Brewery, 44a Parson Street*. Founded c.1875 at Fenny Compton, Warwickshire by Richard Guest Brown and was acquired by Z.M.Brown 1892. Registered January 1897 to acquire the business of Richard William Flick, Horse Shoe Brewery. Brewing was concentrated at Banbury in January 1898. Ceased brewing 1903 and was wound up in February 1906.
Edwin J.Crosby, *64 Fish Street* (1895)
Dunnell & Sons, *Old Brewery, 19 North Bar Street*. Acquired by Hunt, Edmunds & Co.Ltd January 1918 with 35 tied houses.
Hunt, Edmunds & Co.Ltd, *26 Bridge Street*. Founded 1840 by John Hunt. Registered September 1896. Acquired by Bass, Mitchells & Butlers Ltd 1965 with 187 public houses. Brewing ceased 1st May 1957.

Bicester

Frederick Blackman, *Sheep Street* (1914)
Shillingford & Co, *Causeway Street*. Established 1846. Acquired by Hall's Oxford Brewery Ltd 1898.

Bodicote

Bodicote Brewery, *Plough Inn, High Street*. Home brew house founded September 1982. Still in operation 1990.

Buckland

Hannah Walters. Acquired by W.G.Phillips & Sons Ltd 1899 and brewing ceased c.1905.

Burford

Garne & Sons Ltd, *Sheep Street*. Founded 1798. Registered May 1930. Acquired by Wadworth & Co.Ltd April 1969 with 9 tied houses. Brewing ceased and used as a depot until c.1991.

Chadlington

Henry Claridge (1892)

Chipping Norton

Hitchman & Co.Ltd. Founded 1796. Registered March 1890. Acquired by Hunt, Edmunds & Co.Ltd 1924 and brewing ceased May 1933. 36 public houses. Brewery demolished 1970 after being used as a mineral water factory.

Eynsham

Gibbons & Co.Ltd, *Eynsham Brewery* (1910)

Faringdon

Fairthorne & Co, *Eagle Brewery*. Founded *c.*1813. Acquired by W.G.Phillips & Sons Ltd in 1899.

Fringford

Ann & Thomas Gibbard (1939)

Goring

Gundry & Co. Acquired by Brakspear & Sons Ltd 1940 with 18 tied houses. Closed 1949.

Henley on Thames

W.H.Brakspear & Sons Ltd, *New Street*. Founded by Richard Hayward at Bell Street *c.*1779.and was acquired by Robert Brakspear 1803. Merged with Appleton & Shaw, New Street Brewery 1812. All brewing was concentrated at New Street. Registered January 1896. Still independent 1990.

Holmes & Steward, *Grey's Brewery, Friday Street*. Founded 1823. Operated as Byles & Co. until September 1874. Registered 1879 as Greys Brewery Ltd which was wound up in October 1884. Acquired by Frederick Holmes, brewer of Steyning, Sussex 1885. Acquired by Brakspear & Sons Ltd November 1898 with 54 public houses and brewing ceased in 1897.

Ive Brothers, *19/21 Market Place*. Acquired by John Lovibond & Sons Ltd May 1916.

Hook Norton

Hook Norton Brewery Co.Ltd. Founded by John Henry Harris 1856. Brewery built 1872. Registered July 1900 to acquire J.Harris & Co. Still independent 1990.

Oxford

Percy O.V.Hall, *St.Giles Brewery, Observatory Road*. Founded *c.*1830. Brewery and 4 public houses sold to the Northampton Brewery Co.Ltd August 1898.

Hall's Oxford Brewery Ltd, *Eagle Brewery, 32/34 Park End St.* Founded by 1646 as the Swan Brewery, Paradise Garden. Acquired by William Hall 1795. Registered December 1896 to acquire Hall & Co. From April 1899 all brewing was concentrated at the City Brewery. Acquired by Samuel Allsopp & Sons Ltd 1926 and brewing ceased. 300 tied houses. Name changed to Hall's Oxford & West Brewery Co.Ltd 1980. Buildings used as regional office and depot.

Hanley & Co.Ltd, *City Brewery, 20 Queen Street.* Founded in the 1840s. Registered April 1890. Acquired by Hall's Oxford Brewery Ltd with 100 public houses 1898. Brewery still standing.

Morrell's Brewery Ltd, *Lion Brewery, High Street.* Brewery acquired by Mark and James Morrell November 1782. Registered April 1943 to acquire the business from Morrell's trustees. Still independent 1990.

Oxford Brewery & Bakehouse, *2 Gloucester Street.* Home brew house in the former Red Lion. Founded by Halls Oxford & West November 1984. Still brewing 1990.

W.G.Phillips & Sons Ltd, *Tower Brewery, Park End Street.* Founded 1856. Registered November 1898 to acquire Phillips & Sons. Acquired by Hall's Oxford Brewery Ltd June 1910.

Queen's College Brewery. Founded in 1340-41. Brewing ceased 1940 because the vats had become warped with lack of use and it was decided not to renew them in wartime.

Weaving & Sons, *Eagle Steam Brewery, Park End Street.* Founded *c.*1871. Acquired by Hall's Oxford Brewery Ltd 1897 and was converted into a bottling plant.

Shutford

Arthur Vincent Cross (1940)

South Leigh

Mason's Arms. Home brew house founded 1974. Closed 1982.

Tadmarton

Henry Batterby Watts (1892)

Wallingford

Benjamin William Hilliard, *Anchor Brewery, St.Martin's Street.* Founded at Goldsmith Lane in 1830. Acquired by Hanley & Co, Oxford 1891. Premises now used as a laundry.

Wallingford Brewery Ltd, *Goldsmith Lane.* Founded 1720 by Edward Wells. Registered March 1896. Acquired by Hilliards *c.*1880. Brewery still standing.

Wantage

Frederick Henry Bennett, *Grove Street* (1921)

Lewis Rockwell Brewery Co.Ltd, *Rockwell Brewery.* Registered March 1902 to acquire Lewis, Collard & Lewis. Receiver appointed 5th January 1909 and was acquired by Belcher & Habgood Ltd on 5th March 1909.

Wantage Brewery Co.Ltd, *Back Street.* Registered October 1865. Wound up voluntarily March 1901 and a new company was registered in the same month. Acquired by Morland & Co.Ltd 1920 and brewing ceased 1939.

Watlington

Watlington Brewery Co.Ltd, *Brook Street.* Registered December 1893. Offered for sale 8th June 1902 with 47 public houses. Acquired by Hall's Oxford Brewery Ltd 1910. Brewery offered for sale again on 23rd July 1914 with 27 houses. Dissolved 30th November 1917.

Witney

Arthur Bateman, *Blanket Hall Brewery, High Street.* Founded *c.*1721 by William Smith. Acquired by W.G.Phillips & Sons Ltd 1898.

Clinch & Co.Ltd, *Eagle Brewery, Market Place.* Founded in 1840 by William Clinch. Registered April 1950. Acquired by Courage, Barclay & Simonds Ltd 1962 with 74 tied houses. Ceased brewing 1963 and the brewery was mainly demolished 1980/81.

Glenny Brewery, *Two Rivers Brewery, Station Lane.* Founded 1983 in Clinch's former maltings and moved to the above premises 1988. Still brewing 1990.

Woodstock

A.H.Haynes, *Marlborough Arms.* Home brew house. Brewing ceased 1917.

Wootton

Amelia Higgins (1920)

Royal Oak Brewery, Stockport

Recent view of Dale & Co.Ltd, Cambridge

McEwan's of Edinburgh, Front Yard in 1897

David William's, Taff Brewery, Merthr Tydfil

Wrexham Lager Brewery in 1920

Andrew Buchan's Rhymney Brewery in the 1930s

The Wallington Brewery of Boorne & Co.Ltd

Lonsdale & Adshead Ltd, Macclesfield, c.1950

Everard's Steam Waggon Fleet, Leicester Brewery

POWYS

Brecon

Brecon Brewery Ltd, *The Watton.* Founded by 1844 and was declared bankrupt by 1868. Ceased brewing until the 1890s. Registered May 1901. Acquired by the Hereford & Tredegar Brewery Ltd 1905 and brewing ceased on 1st July of that year.

Brecon Brewery, *Camden Arms, The Watton.* Founded 1979 reviving home brewing at the Camden Arms which had ceased in 1942. Closed later in same year.

James Durham, *Orchard Street* (1940)
John E.James, *Castle Street* (1921)
John Jones, *16 The Street* (1923)
Margaret Jones, (1895)
David Powell, *Brecon Old Brewery, 85 The Struet.* Founded by 1835. Ceased brewing 1939 as a subsidiary of the Anglo-Bavarian Brewery Co.Ltd, Somerset.

Frederick Wards, *Camden Arms* (1942) See also:- Brecon Brewery.

Bronllys

Talgarth Brewery & Bottling Co.Ltd. Registered 1924 to acquire the business of E.W.Davies. Ceased brewing 1935.

Builth Wells

Arthur Thomas Jones, *West Street* (1920)
Henry Thomas Price, *West Street* (1920)
Henry Thomas Price, junior, *Broad Street* (1923)
David Williams (Builth) Ltd, *19 Castle Street.* Founded 1866. Private company registered 1944. Acquired by Evan, Evans, Bevan Ltd 1952 with 33 public houses and was closed.
Thomas R.Worthington, *High Street* (1930)

Crickhowell

John Lewis, *Brecon Road* (1940)
William Henry Prosser, *Bridge Street* (1923)
John Rumsey, *Rumsey Place Brewery, Standard Street.* Acquired by the Brecon Brewery in 1900.
William Henry Burham Watkins, *New Street* (1930)
Anne Williams, *Bridge Street* (1920)

Hay-on-Wye

William S.Jones, *Church Street* (1935)
Thomas Stokoe, *Castle Street* (1906)

Knighton

Tom D.Henson, *Bridge Street* (1920)

Llanfair Caereinion

Jehu Brothers, *Vyrnwy Brewery, Bridge Street* (1915)

Llanfyllin

Mary Perry, *Bridge Street* (1910)

Llangattock

Rosetta Pugh, (1920)

Llanidloes

Mary M.Hamer, *Short Bridge Street* (1935)

Llansantffraid

Henry Jenks, *Vyrnwy Brewery.* Merged with the Ellesmere Brewery Co.Ltd, Shropshire 1897 to form Ellesmere & Vyrnwy Breweries Ltd. Closed 1914.

Montgomery

Evan Thomas Davies, (1930)
Richard Evans, *Broad Street* (1930)
Pleasure Jane Griffiths, (1935)
Hugh Garfield Powell, *Princes Street* (1926)
Henry Stanhope, *Pool Road* (1930)
S.Richards, *Buck Brewery, Princes Street* (1920)

Newtown

Barker, Halliwell & Co, *Cambrian Brewery, New Road* (1900). Acquired by Ind Coope by 1914.
Issard & Dawson, *Crown Brewery, Horse Market.* Founded 1831. Merged with David Roberts of Aberystwyth in March 1890 to form the Montgomeryshire Brewery Co.Ltd. Liquidated 1893.
Cornelius Morgan, *Angel Brewery, Market Street* (1890)
Samuel Powell Ltd, *Eagle Brewery, New Road.* Founded 1880. Ceased brewing 1956 and became a wholesale company.
Sam Powell Brewery, *Unit 14 Mochdre Industrial Estate.* Following the collapse of the Powys Brewery, premises bought by Samuel Powell Ltd and brewing restarted in 1983. 3 tied houses.
Powys Brewery, *Unit 14 Mochdre Industrial Estate.* Founded by Stuart Roberts 1981. Ceased brewing Autumn 1982.
Thomas Swift & Co, *Old Brewery, 30 Market Street.* Offered for sale 24th October 1924 due to the retirement of Thomas Swift. 17 public houses. Bought by the Wrekin Brewery Co.Ltd 1938 and was closed.

Old Church Stoke

David Evans, *Oak Inn* (1949)

Presteigne

William Burt, *Bull Brewery, St.David's Street* (1895)

Welshpool

John B.Davies, *28 High Street* (1926)
Thomas Davies, *Brookside Brewery, 5 Broad Street* (1930)
Mrs M.Gregory, *Raven Square* (1935)
Bertie L.Hughes, *8 High Street* (1920)
James Kirby, *Hall Street* (1921)
Charles J.Mytton, *29 Severn Street* (1940)
Stanley Mytton, *4 High Street* (1921)
Walter H.Mytton, *Berriew Street* (1926)
Fred Owen, *43 High Street* (1940)
George Owen, *16 High Street* (1940)
Levi Profit, *Salop Road* (1921)
Susan Pryce, *3 Severn Road* (1940)
Richard Pugh, *Salop Road* (1935)
Allen Thompson, *Salop Road* (1935)

SHROPSHIRE

Benthall

Richard Clinton (1921)

Bishops Castle

Charles M.Jones, *Church Street* (1920)
Richard Pugh, *Church Street* (1923)
Jim Wood, *Three Tuns Brewery, Salop Street.* Home brew house in existence 1642 and trading for many years as John Roberts & Son. Still brewing 1990.

Bridgnorth

Eliza Blakemore, *Listley Street* (1921)
William Bray, *St.John Street* (1921)
Thomas Browne, *4 Salop Street* (1920)
Sarah Coatman, *Friar Street* (1920)
Mary Cardwell Cooper, *Whitburn Street* (1920)
Charles Duffin, *2 Salop Street* (1921)
William Evans, *Railway Street* (1921)
Thomas Fryer, *Cartway* (1921)
Frederick Goodridge, *3 St.Mary's Street* (1940)
Thomas Head, *12 Listley Street* (1926)
Walter Heasman & Co, *Castle Brewery, Underhill Street.* Brewery to let 1913.
Sarah Hickman, *Bernard's Hill* (1920)
Hit or Miss Home Brewhouse, *Union Street.* Acquired by Trouncer & Co.Ltd 1913.
James Matthews, *38 Mill Street* (1920)
Benjamin T.Oliver, *St.John Street* (1923)
Mary Ann Oliver, *Mill Street* (1926)
John Pagett, *23 Underhill Street* (1921)
Emily Elizabeth Parker, *8 West Castle Street* (1920)
Thomas Rowley, *32 Salop Street* (1920)
Thomas Rutter, *Thomas Cartway* (1920)

Edward Bodenham Yates, *24 Northgate* (1940)

Broseley

Harriett Britton, *Church Street* (1920)
Emma Haughton & Son, *High Street* (1902)
John H.Matthews, *Workhouse Road* (1920)
Elizabeth Annie Powis, *Upper High Street.* (1920)

Chirbury

Robert White (1923)

Church Aston

Thomas Bott (1898)

1973 Charter Ale

J. ROBERTS & SON
THREE TUNS BREWERY
BISHOPS CASTLE
MINIMUM CONTENTS 9½ FL OZS

Church Stretton

Sarah Ann Lea (1920)

Cleobury Mortimer

Thomas Ball (1935)
Wiliam Preece Pratt (1923)
Eliza Price (1940)

Clun

Elizabeth Graves, *Market Square* (1921)
John Roberts, *Church Street* (1920)

Coalbrookdale

Michael Edwin Bailey (1940)
Henry Wilkes (1926)

Coalport

Mary Ann Jones (1923)

Dawley

William Bailey, *King Street* (1935)
Walter R.O.Harper, *Hinkshay* (1940)
Francis William Ketley, *Finger Lane* (1940)
Harry Plant, *Bush Hill* (1935)
Thomas William Plimmer, *Dawley Bank* (1926)
Stanley S.Poole, *Royal Exchange Inn, Burton Street.* A home brew house acquired by the Shrewsbury & Wem Brewery Co.Ltd 1946.
Thomas F.Roden, *Bank Road* (1940)
Traveller's Joy. Home brew house acquired by Trouncer & Co.Ltd 1913.

Donnington

James Lees (1923)

Ellesmere

Ellesmere & Vyrnwy Breweries Ltd, *Market Square.* Registered November 1889 as the Ellesmere Brewery Co.Ltd to acquire the business of the late George White Allinson. Name changed 4th March 1897 when they merged with Henry Jenks, Vyrnwy Brewery, Llansantffraid, Montgomeryshire. At least 5 tied houses. Dissolved 25th July 1922. Premises later used as a rennet factory.
George H.Townsend, *Scotland Street* (1921)

Ford

Thomas Barrett (1898)

Great Hanwood

Henry Edwards (1923)

Hadley

Elizabeth Gardner (1921)
Mark Sutton (1920)
John Woodfin (1923)

Hopton Wafers

John Whitehead (1906)

Horsehay

Harry Horler (1923)
Cecil Harry Machin, *Forrester's Arms* (1940)

Ironbridge

Ironbridge Brewery Co, *Bird in Hand, Waterloo Street.* Acquired by Southams c.1940 and was later in the hands of Wolverhampton & Dudley Breweries.
Other Breweries
George Bailey, *1 New Bridge Street* (1926)
Mrs J.Davies, *8 Wesley Road* (1920)
William Benjamin Dodd, *Lincoln Hill* (1940)
Nathaniel Fowler, *39 Madeley Road* (1940)
Edwin F.Groves, *Severn Brewery, High Street* (1914)
Thomas George Hayward, *21 Wharfage* (1940)
Eliza Heighway, *39 Newbridge Street* (1940)
Edwin Owen, *Waterloo Street* (1926)
James Potts, *Coalport Road* (1920)
Edward Richards, *High Street* (1920)
Holland E.Rowley, *Wharfage* (1940)

Jackfield

Adam Ball (1902)
William H.Harrison (1920)
Eliza J.Shinton (1940)

Ketley

John Grainger (1926)
Peter Hocking, *Unicorn Inn, Holyhead Road.* Home brew house founded 1987. Still brewing 1990.

Lawley

John E.Lane (1935)

Little Stretton

Charles Edward Davies (1935)

Ludlow

Ludlow & Craven Arms Brewery Co.Ltd, *45 Corve Street.* Registered 22nd November 1894. Acquired by Trouncer & Co.Ltd of Shrewsbury 1928 with 10 tied houses and brewing ceased.
Other Breweries
Samuel Bailey, *1 Corve Street* (1920)
William Simmonds Baker, *Old Street* (1920)
William George Beeston, *Upper Galdeford* (1920)
James Devey, *57 Lower Galdeford* (1920)
William Herbert Evans, *66 Corve Street* (1920)
Jack Hinksman, *Tower Street* (1923)
John Lamsdell, *89 Corve Street* (1920)
George Lunn, *3 Market Street* (1920)
William Joseph Perry, *3 Market Street* (1920)
Charles Raiswell, *85 Bull Ring* (1920)
Jane Rogers, *2 Lower Broad Street* (1940)
Edward Sheldon, *Oldgate Fee* (1926)
Alexander Whitbread, *13 Lower Galdeford* (1921)

Madeley

Keith Hardman, *All Nations, Coalport Road.* Home brew house founded 1789 and run for many years by members of the Lewis family. Still brewing 1990.
Other Breweries
George Bailey, *Madeley Green* (1920)
Thomas Biddulph, *Cuckoo Oak* (1920)
Arthur Bullock, *Aqueduct* (1935)
Edwin Bullock, *34 Park Street* (1926)
Nathaniel Fowler, *Madeley Wood* (1923)
William John Hill, *Park Lane* (1920)
Harry Lees, *Coalport Road* (1930) *& Court Street* (1926)
Joseph Morris, *11 High Street* (1940)
Richard B.Price, *58 Park Street* (1920)
Joseph Richards, *Park Street* (1920)
Agnes Annie Reeves, *Madeley Wood* (1923)

Market Drayton

Market Drayton Brewery Co.Ltd, *Royal Oak Hotel, Cheshire Street.* Registered March 1891. 5 public houses. Voluntary liquidation 18th March 1914.
Pearce's Crystal Fountain Brewery Co. Acquired by Marston, Thompson & Evershed Ltd 1925.
Wright's Crown Brewery Co.Ltd, *Station Road.* Registered June 1899. Acquired by J.Marston, Thompson & Co.Ltd 1904 with 6 tied houses.

Minsterley

William Henry Ray (1921)

Much Wenlock

Arthur R.Duckett, *Barrow Street* (1920)
Tryphena Annie S.Jervis, *High Street* (1940)
Selina Sankey, *Rock Hotel* (1935)
Martha Simpson, *Wilmore Street* (1923)
Wheatland Brewery Co.Ltd. Offered for auction 6th March 1922 with 5 public houses.
Frederick W.Yates, *High Street* (1940)

Newport

Benjamin Bellingham, *St.Mary Street* (1920)
Lucy Felton, *Upper Bar* (1920)
John Alfred Lees, *Lower Bar, High Street* (1920)
Newport (Salop) Brewery Co.Ltd, *Market Square.* Registered 1898 to acquire the business of C.Lewis at Newport and a similar concern carried on by G.Bouckley at Newport & Wellington. Public houses acquired by Marston, Thompson & Evershed Ltd 1927.

Daniel Stanworth, *High Street* (1920)
Harriett E.Tomlinson, *Upper Bar* (1923)

Norton

Phillips Brewery, *Hundred House Inn, Bridgnorth Road.* Founded 1981 at the Greyhound Inn, Marsh Gibbon, Bucks and moved to Shropshire 1986.

Oakengates

Henry Cadwalader (1910)
Samuel Edwards (1923)
Enoch Merrington (1923)
William Onions (1921)
Noel Stanley (1940)

Oswestry

Edwin Brown, *Oak Brewery, 47 Church Street* (1898)
George Henry Cooke, *Willow Street* (1920)
Dorsett, Owen & Co, *English Walls.* Formed part of Border Breweries (Wrexham) Ltd 1931.
John Evans, *Salop Road* (1920)
Thomas Hughes, *Upper Brook Street* (1892)
Fred T.Mines, *Willow Street* (1921)
Richard Pryce, *Willow Street* (1921)
Robert Richards & Sons, *Swan Brewery, Beatrice Street* (1895)

Pontesbury

Clara Davies (1923)

Priorslee

Thomas James Teague (1926)

Ruyton of the Eleven Towns

Edward Parry, *The Talbot.* A home brew house which also supplied 3 or 4 other houses. Sold to Southam's Brewery Ltd 1928.

Sheriff Hales

John Tomlinson, *Weston Heath Brewery* (1910)

Shifnal

Alfred Buttery, *Broadway* (1920)
George Meredith, *Currier's Lane* (1920)
George T.Molineux, *Shrewsbury Road* (1920)
Shifnal Brewery Ltd, *Hinnington Spring Brewery, Old Road.* Originally registered October 1897 as Hinckesman's Brewery Co.Ltd and the name was changed to the Shifnal Brewery Co.Ltd on 13th April 1899, this company being dissolved on 11th February 1910. A new company, the Broadway Brewery Ltd was registered December 1927 and was re-registered as above in October 1934. Acquired by Wolverhampton & Dudley Breweries Ltd 1960.

Benjamin Williams, *Park Street* (1906)

Shrewsbury

Shrewsbury & Wem Brewery Co.Ltd, *Circus Brewery, Bridge Street.* See also:- Wem.

Southam's Brewery Ltd, *Old Salop Brewery, Chester Street.* Registered November 1866 as the Salop Brewery Co.Ltd Ceased brewing 1880 and was acquired by Thomas Southam as a mineral water factory. Re-equipped as a brewery 1903. Registered as above February 1926. Acquired by Threlfall Chesters Ltd 1966 with 94 tied houses and brewing ceased. Demolished 1967.

Trouncer & Co.Ltd, *Old Brewery, Longden Coleham.* Founded 1807. Registered September 1894. Acquired by Ind Coope Ltd 1956 with 11 public houses and brewing ceased. Premises still in use as a warehouse by Rowlands & Co, fruit & vegetable merchants. 3 home brew houses acquired in 1913; Woolpack, Longden Coleham; Swan Inn, Frakwell and the Old Ship, Bridge Street.

Other Breweries

Amelia Cartwright, *17 Frankwell* (1921)
Horace Charlesworth, *90 New Street* (1920)
William Dorricott, *Coton Hill* (1920)
Pryce Francis Edwardes, *34 Wyle Cop* (1923)
Henry Edwards, *55 Wyle Cop* (1926)
John Edwards, *6 Butcher's Row* (1930)
John Evans, *Bridge Street* (1920), *Roushill* (1923)
Llewellyn William Everall, *28 Abbey Foregate* (1920)
Charles Farrall, *St.Julian's Friars* (1921)
Henry Gough, *98 Frankwell* (1920)
Richard Gough, *Smithfield Road* (1920)
Arthur Gwilliam, *Roushill* (1926), *23 Hill's Lane* (1921)
Ezra Hubbard, *53 Frankwell* (1923)
George Jones, *Bynner Street* (1920)
John William Lewis, *26 Barker Street* (1921)
William Owen, *85 Frankwell* (1920)
John Palmer, *8 Barker Street* (1923)
Arthur Parker, *38 Abbey Foregate* (1920)
Catherine Pinches, *14 New Street* (1923)
Edwin Price, *8 Frankwell* (1930)
Emily S.Price, *119 Frankwell* (1923)
Fred G.R.Revell, *2 St.Mary's Place* (1935)

Stirchley

Mary Elizabeth Roden (1921)

Stottesdon

Fox & Hounds. Home brew house founded 1979. Still brewing 1990.

Trench

James Cotterhill, *Furnace Lane* (1923)

Wellington

Potter & Cockburn, *Shropshire Brewery.* Brewery built 1851. Offered for auction March 1912 but was withdrawn at £20,000. 24 tied houses sold to W.Butler & Co.Ltd of Wolverhampton in the same year.

Red Lion Brewery Co, *King Street.* Acquired by the Wrekin Brewery Co.Ltd with 9 public houses for £20,020 April 1924.

Wrekin Brewery Co.Ltd, *Market Street.* Founded 1870. Registered November 1922. Acquired by Greenall Whitley & Co.Ltd 1951 with 94 tied houses. Brewing ceased September 1969.

Other Breweries

Mary Birks, *Park Street* (1920)
James Bramwell, *St.Georges* (1940)
A.H.Clarke. Acquired by Mitchells & Butlers Ltd 1945.
Robert Clayton, *St.Georges* (1920)
Mrs John Clemson, *St.Georges* (1923)
Cresswell Brothers, *Lion Street, Market Street & Laburnums Brewery, Hadley* (1951)
Mary Downes, *38 High Street* (1926)
Elizabeth Hiles, exors of, *Regent Street* (1910)
William Hiles, *Fox & Hounds, 7 Crown Street* (1910)
Morris Jones, *Crown Inn, 3 Crown Street* (1920)
Thomas Morris, *139 High Street* (1920)
Edward A.Murray, *Bell Street* (1926)
Samuel G.Partridge, *Bridge Road* (1921)
Herbert H.Picken, *High Street* (1921)
Elizabeth Pierce, *Market Street* (1923)
Thomas James Teague, *83 Market Street* (1940) & *Priorslee* (1926)
Union Brewery Co.Ltd, *Union Brewery, Walker Street* (1921)
Annie Weaver, *Albert Road* (1920)

Wem

Mary Brown, *High Street* (1920)

Charles Henry Kynaston, *Noble Street.* Acquired by the Shropshire Brewery Co.Ltd 1898 who then changed their name to the Shrewsbury & Wem Brewery Co.Ltd.

Shrewsbury & Wem Brewery Co.Ltd, *Circus Brewery, Bridge Street, Shrewsbury, Talbot Brewery, High Street and Noble Street, Wem.* Founded c.1860 at the Circus Brewery as Richards Brothers. Registered January 1898 as the Shropshire Brewery Co.Ltd to acquire William Hall & Co. with 2 breweries and 63 tied houses. Name changed as above later in 1898. Talbot Brewery closed 1900 and Circus Brewery 1912. Acquired by Greenall Whitley & Co.Ltd 1951 with 94 public houses. Brewing ceased February 1988.

Sarah E.Wilson, *High Street* (1920)

Weston Rhyn

James Edwards & Son, *Old Lodge Brewery.* Acquired by the Shifnal Brewery Ltd c.1934.

Whitchurch

G.F.A.Brown & Sons Ltd, *Alkington Road.* Founded 1747. Registered 20th August 1912 to acquire a wine & spirits merchants at Nantwich, Cheshire. Whitchurch brewery acquired 1920. Acquired by Greenall Whitley & Co.Ltd October 1930 with 6 tied houses.

Wistanstow

Wood Brewery Ltd, *Plough Inn.* Home brew house founded 1980. Still brewing 1990.

Wrockwardine

Norman Chilton (1940)
John Foster Wright (1940)

SOMERSET

J.J.Collings, *Cross.* Closed 1921. Some traces of the brewery still exist as part of a riding school.

Creech St.Michael

James H.Day (1914)

Crewkerne

Crewkerne United Breweries Co.Ltd, *Ashlands Brewery, North Street.* Registered 1880 to merge: Standfield & Co, Hermitage Brewery; Joliffe, Norman & Templeman and Samuel Merriott Pattemore. Acquired by Arnold & Hancock Ltd 1938.
Samuel Lawrence, *Merriott Steam Brewery* (1892)

Curry Rivel

Hambridge Brewery Ltd, *Hambridge.* Founded 1780 and was owned by the Lang family until 1938. Registered December 1933 as H.M.Lang & Co.Ltd and was re-registered as above March 1940. Acquired by Ind Coope Ltd 1958 and brewing ceased. Used as a regional depot. Their 58 tied houses were sold to Bristol Brewery Georges & Co.Ltd.

Dulverton

Petherick Bunt (1892)

Frome

Frome & Lamb Ltd, *Badcox Brewery, Vallis Way.* Registered March 1889 to amalgamate: Edmund Baily, Bath Arms Brewery, Palmer Street; Jonathan Drew Knight, Castle Brewery; Catherine Hill and Edward R.Trotman, Badcox Brewery as Frome United Breweries Co.Ltd. Brewing was concentrated at the Badcox Brewery. Name changed as above 1955 when they merged with the Lamb Brewery Ltd. Acquired jointly by the Stroud Brewery

Bishop's Lydeard

Bell Inn. Home brew house in operation 1980-82.

Bridgwater

Starkey, Knight & Ford Ltd, *Northgate Brewery, 54 High Street & Fore Street, Tiverton, Devon.* Founded by George Knight 1840. Registered November 1887 as Starkey, Knight & Co.Ltd to to acquire the businesses of Henry & George Knight, Northgate Brewery and Thomas Starkey, North Petherton and Taunton breweries with a total of 30 public houses. Name changed as above 1895 when Thomas Ford & Son of Tiverton was acquired with 40 tied houses. North Petherton and Taunton breweries closed 1906. Acquired by Whitbread & Co.Ltd 1962 with 400 tied houses. The Bridgwater brewery was closed in the same year. Business merged with Norman & Pring Ltd of Exeter 1964 and name changed to Whitbread Devon Ltd in the early 1970s.

Bruton

Jones & Sons, *Bath Arms Brewery.* Acquired by Frome United Breweries Co.Ltd 1905 and was closed.

Burnham on Sea

Berrow Brewery, *Coast Road, Berrow.* Founded 1982. Still brewing 1990.
Holt Brothers Ltd. Founded 1770. Registered 1895. Acquired by Starkey, Knight & Ford Ltd 1957 with 67 public houses and was closed.
Royal Clarence Hotel, *The Esplanade.* Founded 1982. Still brewing 1990.

Camerton

Charles Stone (1920)

Chard

Brutton, Mitchell & Toms Ltd, *Chard Brewery, High Street.* See also:- Yeovil.
Coling & Heasman, *Chard Steam Brewery, Silver Street.* Operated by John England & Co. until 1877 when it was acquired by Coling & Son. Brewing ceased 1892.
Sumner & Toms. Founded 1825. Brewery closed June 1937.

Cheddar

F.K.Parsloe (1900)

Compton Bishop

Co.Ltd and Usher's Wiltshire Brewery Co.Ltd 1957 with 300 public houses and was closed. The Badcox Brewery has been demolished.
Lamb Brewery Ltd, *Lamb Brewery, Christchurch Street.* Founded *c.*1850. Registered May 1893 to acquire the business of John & Thomas Baily with 82 tied houses. Merged with Frome United Breweries Co.Ltd 1955 to form Frome & Lamb Ltd.
Charles Stewart, *Queen's Head Brewery* (1902)

Hardington Mandeville

Hardington Brewery. See also:- Haselbury Plucknett.

Haselbury Plucknett

Hardington Brewery, *The Mill.* Founded 1979 at the Mandeville Arms, Hardington Mandeville and moved to the Brewer's Arms, South Petherton and finally to the present site in 1986. Still brewing 1990.

Holcombe

Holcombe Brewery Ltd. Registered September 1888 to acquire the business carried on by Arthur Green as John Ashman Green & Brothers. Bankrupt in the same year. Brewery acquired by George Henry Thatcher of Welton 1893. 7 tied houses. Brewing ceased 1904 but malting continued until after 1930. Remains of the brewery now used as a garage.

Ilminster

Joseph Paull & Son, *West Street.* Acquired by the Oakhill Brewery Co.Ltd 1936 with 14 public houses.

Limington

Witcomb Brothers (1906)

North Curry

James Tremlett (1930)

Norton Fitzwarren

Hewett & Co.Ltd, *Norton Brewery.* Operated by William Henry Hewett until 1887. Registered 25th July 1896 to acquire Hewett & Co. Acquired by S.W.Arnold & Sons Ltd of Taunton 1899 and brewing ceased in 1930.

Pilton

George Gloyne, *Pilton Brewery.* Acquired by Walter H.Baxter of Sherborne 1893.

Priddy

Miners Arms. See also:- Westbury-sub-Mendip.

Rode

Sidney Fussell & Sons Ltd, *Cross Keys Brewery.* Acquired by Bass, Mitchells & Butlers Ltd 1962 and was closed.

Shepton Mallet

Anglo-Bavarian Brewery Co.Ltd, *Wells Road.* Founded 1860 as an export brewery. Bought by Garton & Co. of Southampton 1870 for use a reserve brewery. The word "Bavarian" was dropped from the title during the First World War. Brewing ceased 1921 but recommenced on a smaller scale in 1934 to supply the domestic trade and finally ceased in September 1939. Buildings now used as a trading estate.

Charlton Brewery Co.Ltd, Operated by Francis Berryman from 1844. Registered as Berryman, Burnell & Co.Ltd July 1894 and name changed as above 1902. Acquired by Bristol United Breweries Ltd September 1937 and brewing ceased 1961 but was used as a Courage depot until the late 1970s.

Showerings Ltd, *Kilver Street.* Registered September 1932. Brewing ceased c.1951 when production was concentrated on Babycham, cider & perry drinks. Some of the original buildings still extant 1990. Subsidiary of Carlsberg-Tetley.

Somerton

Ord & Co. Offered for auction 28th April 1921 and was bought by Joseph Brutton & Sons Ltd.

South Petherton

Hardington Brewery. See also:- Haselbury Plucknett.

Stogumber

Stogumber Brewery Co.Ltd. Registered August 1900 to acquire the business of George Decimus Scutt. Brewing ceased c.1920 due to financial difficulties.

Stoney Stratton

Hill Brothers, *Evercreech Brewery* (1892)

Taunton

S.W.Arnold & Sons Ltd, *Rowbarton Brewery.* Founded 1876. Registered January 1898 to acquire S.W.Arnold & Sons and John Sloman, West Somerset Brewery Merged with William Hancock & Sons (Wiveliscombe) Ltd 1927 to form Arnold & Hancock Ltd. Brewing ceased 1960.

Hanbury & Cotching, *Cannon Street Brewery.* Founded before 1877. Due to the retirement of the owner the brewery was offered for auction on 14th December 1921 but was withdrawn. Closed January 1923 and the 78 public houses were sold to Starkey, Knight & Ford Ltd.

Hatch Brothers, *16 St.James Street* (1895)

Ross & Hill, *Fore Street Brewery* (1895)

John Sloman, *West Somerset Brewery.* Merged with S.W.Arnold & Sons 1898.

Thomas Starkey, *Taunton Brewery, Mill Lane.* See also:- Starkey, Knight & Ford Ltd, Bridgwater.

Trudoxhill

Bishop's Brewery, *White Hart.* Home brew house founded 1983 by Ted Bishop, formerly of the Cotleigh Brewery, Wellington. Business sold and moved to here 1988. Still brewing 1990.

Watchet

Matthew Mossman (1902)

Wedmore

James Mason Perrett. *Branch of Old Sodbury, Avon.*

Wellington

Bishop's Brewery. See also:- Trudoxhill.

Wemdon

Edward H.Churchill (1920)

Westbury-sub-Mendip

Miner's Arms Brewery, *Well House, Stoke Road.* Founded 1973 at Priddy by Paul Leyton. Businesss sold to Barry Haslam 1977 and moved to present site 1981. Still brewing 1990.

Wiveliscombe

Cotleigh Brewery, *Ford Road.* Founded by Ted Bishop 1979 at Cotleigh Farm, Washfield, Devon. Moved to here 1980. Business sold 1983 and Ted Bishop moved to Wellington.

Golden Hill Brewery. Founded June 1980 in part of Hancock's former brewery. Still brewing 1990.

William Hancock & Sons (Wiveliscombe) Ltd, *Wiveliscombe Brewery, Golden Hill.* Founded by William Hancock 1807. Registered December 1896 Merged with S.W.Arnold & Sons Ltd of Taunton 1927 to form Arnold & Hancock Ltd. Acquired by Ushers Wiltshire Brewery Ltd 1955 with 262 public houses. Brewing ceased in 1959. Buildings still standing 1990.

Yeovil

Brutton, Mitchell & Toms Ltd, *Yeovil Brewery.* Established in 1771. Founded at Chard 1825 as Sumner & Toms. Registered September 1891 as Mitchell, Toms & Co.Ltd to acquire Toms & Co. and F.Mitchell & Co, wine and spirit merchants. Took over Joseph Brutton & Sons Ltd of Yeovil April 1937 and was renamed as above. Acquired by Charrington & Co.Ltd 1960 and brewing ceased 1965.

J.D.Knight, *Royal Osborne Brewery.* Offered for auction 8th October 1907 with 18 public houses. Acquired by Baxter & Son of Sherborne 1912.

Mann & Co, *8/9 Wine Street.* Acquired by Mitchell, Toms & Co Ltd March 1925.

Bromley Hurst

John Bright Willis (1920)

Burton-on-Trent

Samuel Allsopp & Sons Ltd, *High Street.* Founded in the 1740s and was acquired by Samuel Allsopp 1807. Registered February 1887. In financial difficulties from 1900 and went into receivership 1913. Merged with Ind Coope & Co.Ltd June 1934 to form Ind Coope & Allsopp Ltd.

Bass, Ratcliff & Gretton Ltd, *137 High Street.* Founded 1777 by William Bass. Registered 1880 and was reconstructed 13th January 1888. Merged with Worthington & Co.Ltd 1926. Merged with Mitchells & Butlers Ltd 1961 to form Bass, Mitchells & Butlers Ltd. Still brewing 1990 as Bass (Brewing) Burton Ltd.

Beard, Hill & Co.Ltd, *Lichfield Street.* Founded before 1750. Registered 7th January 1893 to acquire Beard, Hill & Co. Acquired by J.Marston, Thompson & Co.Ltd 1900.

John Bell & Co.Ltd, *15 Lichfield Street.* Founded *c.*1840. Registered April 1897. Acquired by Thomas Salt & Co.Ltd 1902 and the brewery was sold to Magee, Marshall & Co.Ltd of Bolton who intended to brew here but failed to do so, water from the brewery being transported to Bolton.

Bindley & Co.Ltd, *New Street.* Founded 1873. Registered April 1888. Acquired by Ind Coope & Co.(1912) Ltd 1914 with 63 public houses and was closed.

Burton & Lincoln Breweries Ltd, *91 Moor Street.* Registered December 1889 to acquire E.P.Dawson, Burton and H.J.Buckmaster, Lincoln. 117 tied houses. Voluntary liquidation 2nd December 1898.

Burton Brewery Co.Ltd, *118 High Street.* Registered 1846 and was re-registered June 1888. Receiver appointed June 1907. Brewery sold to Worthington & Co.Ltd 1915. Acquired by Ind Coope & Co.Ltd 1927 with 75 tied houses.

Burton Bridge Brewery, *Bridge Street.* Founded June 1982 by Bruce Wilkinson & Geoffrey Mumford at the rear of a former Bass house. Still brewing 1990.

Charrington & Co.Ltd. *Abbey Brewery.* Founded 1872 and sold 1926.

James Eadie Ltd, *Cross Street.* Founded by James Eadie 1854. Registered 1893. In liquidation June 1896 and was reconstructed. 308 public houses. Acquired by Bass, Ratcliff & Gretton Ltd 1933 and brewing ceased.

Everard's Brewery Ltd, *Trent Brewery, Dale Street.* Founded 1849 when Thomas Hull and Thomas & William Everard leased the Southgate Brewery, Leicester, from Wilmot & Co. Acquired the Bridge Brewery, Burton from Henry Boddington & Co.Ltd 1893. Leased the Trent Brewery February 1898 and the Bridge Brewery was closed. Registered 1925 as W.Everard & Co.Ltd. Southgate Brewery closed 1931 and converted into a distribution centre. Registered as above October 1936. Trent Brewery renamed the Tiger Brewery *c.*1970 and was closed in 1983 being replaced by a new smaller brewery at Castle Acres, Narborough, Leicester. See also:- Heritage Brewery Ltd.

Sydney Evershed Ltd, *Bank Brewery, Bank Square.* Founded 1854. Registered March 1889. Acquired by J.Marston, Thompson & Co.Ltd 1905 with 86 public houses. Closed 1908.

Heritage Brewery Ltd, *Heritage Brewery, Anglesey Road.* Founded 1983 to continue brewing at Everard's former brewery and to preserve the brewery as a working museum controlled by a charitable trust.

Ind Coope Ltd, *High Street & Star Brewery, Romford.* Burton brewery opened 1856. Registered November 1886 as Ind Coope & Co.Ltd. In receivership January 1909 and was re-registered 1912 as Ind Coope & Co.(1912) Ltd. Name reverted to Ind Coope & Co.Ltd 1923. Merged with Samuel Allsopp & Sons Ltd 1934 and became Ind Coope & Allsopp Ltd. Name changed as above 1959. Now part of Carlsberg-Tetley.

Mann, Crossman & Paulin, Albion (Burton-on-Trent) Brewery Ltd, *Albion Brewery, Shobnall Road.* Brewery built 1875 by Mann, Crossman & Paulin and used by them until 1896. Registered March 1896 with 8 tied houses, a further 127 being acquired from the Gresley Brewery and Burton & Lincoln Breweries. In 1897 all the public houses were leased to Thomas Salt & Co.Ltd and in 1898 55 houses were acquired which were later leased to Ind Coope Ltd and others. Brewery sold to J.Marston, Thompson & Co.Ltd 1902. Voluntary liquidation 2nd March 1903.

Marston, Thompson & Evershed Ltd, *Shobnall Road.* Founded by John Marston 1834. Registered 1890 as John Marston & Son Ltd and was re-registered June 1896. Merged with John Thompson & Sons Ltd 1898 and the name was changed to J.Marston, Thompson & Son Ltd and as above in 1905 when Sydney Evershed Ltd was acquired. Still brewing 1990.

E.J.Miller & Co.Ltd, *Crescent Brewery, Victoria Crescent.* Registered July 1919 to acquire T.Cooper & Co. Acquired by Thomas Salt & Co.Ltd 1919 and was closed.

J.Nunnely & Co, *Bridge Brewery.* Founded 1720. Acquired by the Burton Brewery Co.Ltd 1895. Brewery used by Everards until 1901. Still extant having been converted to housing.

Thomas Salt & Co.Ltd, *119 High Street.* Founded as maltsters 1774. Registered November 1893. Acquired by Bass, Ratcliff & Gretton Ltd 1927 and brewing ceased.

Trent Brewery Co.Ltd, *Union Street.* Brewery built 1881 for Thomas Sykes of Liverpool. Registered 1889 as Sykes Brewery Co.Ltd. Name changed as above 1893. Voluntary liquidation June 1896. Brewery leased by Everard & Co. 1898.

Peter Walker & Co.Ltd, *Clarence Street Brewery.* Founded at the Willow Brewery, Wrexham, Clwyd 1860. Clarence Street Brewery opened 1883. Acquired by Atkinson's Brewery Ltd 1925.

Peter Walker & Son (Warrington & Burton) Ltd, *Shobnall Brewery.* Branch of Warrington. Also at the Midland Brewery, Victoria Road 1890-95. Shobnall Brewery closed 1923 and was sold to English Grains Ltd.

Worthington & Co.Ltd, *137 High Street.* Founded 1744. Registered January 1889. Merged with Bass, Ratcliff & Gretton Ltd 1927 but continued to operate as a separate concern until brewing ceased in 1967.

John Yeomans, *50 High Street.* Acquired by John Marston & Son Ltd 1890.

Other Breweries

Joseph & Thomas Bowler, *New Street* (1890)
Carter & Scattergood, *Victoria Street* (1902)
W.& G.R.Clarkson, *Victoria Street* (1895)
Clayton & Co, *Horninglow Road* (1895)
Frederick Heap, *Victoria Street* (1890)
Charles Hill & Son, *Lichfield Street* (1890)
James Porter & Son, *Dale Street* (1895)
Thomas Robinson & Co. See also:- Robinson's Brewery Ltd. Liverpool

Cannock

William Blencowe & Co.Ltd, *Also at Market Square, Brackley, Northants.* Registered May 1889. Brackley brewery founded before 1859. Cannock brewery and 32 tied houses acquired by W.Butler & Co.Ltd 1925. The Brackley brewery and 50 public houses was sold to Hall's Oxford Brewery Ltd October 1925.

Cannock Brewery Co.Ltd. Registered April 1880 to acquire the business of George Cotterell and Arthur Scattergood. Merged with William Blencowe 1889.

W.Webster, *Blackfords Brewery* (1930)

Cheddleton

Kent & Co, *Cheddleton Brewery.* Possibly acquired by Marston, Thompson & Evershed Ltd c.1920.

Cinder Hill

Richard Bates (1921)

Coven

Frederick Coleclough (1914)

Dawley Brook

Sidney Marsden (1930)

Essington

Hannah Giles, *Farm Brewery* (1898)

Fazeley

Amalgamated Clubs Brewery Co.Ltd, *Midland Brewery.* Registered May 1919 to acquire the business of Edward Freeland. Voluntary winding up 16th December 1922.

White & Coombe, *Original Brewery* (1917)

Great Chatwell

Susannah Parton (1920)

Great Haywood

Dabbs & Nicholson Ltd. Founded 1880 by B.Dabbs, mineral water manufacturer and beer bottler at 107 High Street, Coleshill, Warwickshire. Registered 1923. The brewery believed to have been closed c.1924 but the business was continued owning off-licences in Tamworth and Coleshill as well as bottling. Trading ceased at the end of the 1960s with the closure of the final off-licence at 124 Lichfield Street, Tamworth but the concern continued to exist as a family investment company until going into liquidation in 1991.

Hilderstone

Thomas Houldcroft Shelley, *Bird-in-Hand, Sharpley Heath.* Home brew house founded c.1750. Brewing ceased 20th December 1927.

Hixon

William Talbot (1902)

Leek

Ada Peach, *129 Mill Street* (1920)
George Walker, *25 Broad Street.* Acquired by Marston, Thompson & Evershed Ltd 1910 with 10 tied houses.

Lichfield

City Brewery Co.(Lichfield) Ltd, *Birmingham Road.* Registered April 1874. Acquired by Wolverhampton & Dudley Breweries Ltd 1917 with 200 public houses.

Dawes Brothers, *Old Brewery, 28/30 Sandford Street* (1917)

Lichfield Brewery Co.Ltd, *St.John's Street.* Registered July 1869 to acquire J.A.Griffith & Co, Lichfield Brewery and the Lichfield Malting Co.Ltd. Went into voluntary liquidation and was reconstructed in January 1890. Acquired by Samuel Allsopp & Sons Ltd 1930 with 182 public houses. Brewing ceased in 1935.

Trent Valley Brewery Co.Ltd, *Bird Street.* Registered December 1875. Acquired by the Lichfield Brewery Co.Ltd 1891 with 47 tied houses and brewing ceased.

Newcastle-under-Lyme

Frederick J.Ridgway & Sons, *Lower Street.* Acquired by the Burton Brewery Co.Ltd 1903 with 39 public houses and was sold to Parker's Burslem Brewery Co.Ltd 1915 with 24 tied houses.

Oakamoor

Samuel Mellor (1910)

Ruiton

John Meredith (1920)
William Nayler (1920)
Dan Marsh (1892)
James Morris (1920)

Salt

Lewis Foster, *Sandonbank* (1910)
John Tansley, *Lodge Farm* (1923)

Shebdon

John Ethell (1910)

Shenstone

Joseph Newey Dexter (1940)

Shirleywich

Henry Foster (1906)

Stafford

Catherine Corfield, *34 Friar Street* (1920)
Dawson's Princess Royal Brewery, *68 Sandon Road.* A home brew house founded c.1887. Acquired by Wolverhampton & Dudley Breweries Ltd 1952.
William Deakin, *Back Walls North* (1910)
Eley's Stafford Brewery Ltd, *Green Brewery, The Green.* Operated by John Bishop until 1877. Registered September 1899 to acquire the businesses of Eley, Tatham & Nesbit and Humby & Baillie. Acquired by W.Butler & Co.Ltd 1928 and was closed.
George Grattidge, *10 Eastgate Street* (1926)
Humby & Baillie, *Back Walls South.* Merged with Eley, Tatham & Nesbitt 1899.
Ada Jane Riley, *61 Greyfriars* (1920)

Stoke-on-Trent, Burslem

James Norris (Brewers) Ltd, *21 Market Place.* Acquired by John Joule & Sons Ltd 1965.
Parker's Burslem Brewery Co.Ltd, *Pitt Street East.* Founded c.1862. Acquired by Ind Coope & Allsopp Ltd 1948 with 468 tied houses. Brewing ceased 1963.

Stoke-on-Trent, Fenton

Thomas Cooper & Co, *Foley Place* (1904)

Stoke-on-Trent, Hanley

Joseph Edge, *High Street* (1898)
Five Towns Brewery, *Trent Trading Park, Botteshaw Street.* Founded January 1983 by Norman Turner. Closed 1987.
Edward Malam, *Trustees of, Hanley Brewery, Hope Street.* Founded 1872. Closed 1917.

Stoke-on-Trent, Longton

Standard Brewery Co.Ltd, *Caroline Street.* Registered February 1886 to acquire Steele & Co. Acquired by John Joule & Sons Ltd December 1887.
Steele's Longton Brewery Co.Ltd, *Crown Brewery, Market Street.* Registered November 1899 to acquire the business of Ralph Steele. Voluntary liquidation 21st October 1901.

Stoke-on-Trent, Middleport

Titanic Brewery, *1 Dain Street.* Home brew house founded October 1985. So named because Edward J.Smith, Captain of the Titanic, was a local man. Still brewing 1990.

Stoke-on-Trent, Shelton

Dix & Co.Ltd, *Shelton Brewery.* Registered December 1900. Acquired by Parker's Burslem Brewery Ltd 1921 with 31 public houses. Brewing ceased 1928.

Hedge's Brewery Co.Ltd, *Caledonian Road.* Acquired by Bindley & Co.Ltd 1897 but brewing continued until 1921.

Stoke-on-Trent, Shraleybrook

Rising Sun. Home brew house founded 1990.

Stoke-on-Trent, Town Centre

Brown Edge Brewery. Founded 1982 and closed 1983.

John Davies & Son Ltd, *John Street.* Registered 1926 to acquire the bottling business of J.H.Davies and to carry on the business of brewers & maltsters.

Olde Bull & Bush, *Potters Brew, 9 Hartshill Road.* Home brew house founded 1986. Still brewing 1990.

George Pim & Co.Ltd, *Copeland Street.* Registered July 1918 to acquire the business of J.W.Dunn carried on as G.Pim & Co. Acquired by Z.Smith & Co.of Shardlow in 1925, who were then a subsidiary of Marston, Thompson & Evershed Ltd. Brewery demolished 1970.

Stone

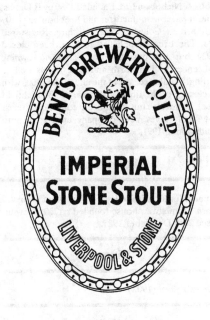

Bent's Brewery Co.Ltd. See also:- Liverpool.

John Joule & Sons Ltd, *High Street.* Founded 1780. Acquired by Harding & Parrington of Liverpool 1873. Registered December 1898. Acquired by Bass Charrington 1968 with 214 tied houses. Brewing ceased September 1972. Brewery mainly demolished but bottling stores still standing.

Montgomery & Co. Acquired by Bent's Brewery Co.Ltd 1889 with 23 tied houses. Brewery still standing.

Tamworth

Morgan & Co, *Castle Brewery.* Founded 1882. Acquired by Frederick Smith Ltd of Birmingham 1942.

Warwickshire Brewery. Founded 1985 but closed in the same year.

White & Combe, *Albert Road* (1914)

Uttoxeter

Charles Bunting Ltd, *Uttoxeter & Dove Valley Breweries, Church Street & High Street.* Registered June 1895 to acquire the assets of the Uttoxeter & Dove Valley Brewery Co.Ltd in liquidation, with 26 public houses. Acquired by Parker's Burslem Brewery Ltd 1929 but continued to trade until 1940.

George Gardner & Co, *New Brewery.* Acquired by Peter Walker & Son 1890 with 20 tied houses in Uttoxeter and 30 in Liverpool.

Wood Eaton

Samuel Barker (1902)

Woodseaves

Thomas Lees (1914)

STRATHCLYDE

Ayr

Turner's Ayr & Newton Breweries Ltd, *Ayr Brewery, Mill Street.* Founded by A.M.Turner at the Kyle Tavern, Ayr 1868. Newton Brewery acquired 1881. Registered March 1898 to acquire the business of James Watson & Co, Ayr Brewery. Ceased brewing at Ayr 1911/12 and at Newton in 1929 but the business was continued as mineral water manufacturers and bottlers. Name changed to Turner's (Ayr) Ltd c.1930. Associated with J.& R.Tennent Ltd from 1934 and were acquired by them in 1961.

Cambuslang

Wellshot Brewery Co.Ltd. Closed 1922 and was converted into an engineering works.

Catrine

Catrine Brewery Co. (1926)

Clydebank

Strathalbyn Brewery, *70 Beardmore Way, Clydebank Industrial Estate, Dalmuir.* Founded September 1982 by David Anderson & Stuart Turner. Went into liquidation 1987.

Dumbarton

Gillespie, Sons & Co.(Brewers) Ltd, *Crown Brewery, Brewery Road, High Street.* Registered October 1944. Closed 1953.

Glasgow

Hugh Baird & Co, *Great Canal Brewery, Possil Road* (1930)

Daniel Brown Ltd. Acquired by Steel, Coulson & Co.Ltd 1956.

Robert Brown, *17 Hope Street* (1892)

George Dalrymple & Co, *Home Brewery, 7 Invernairn Street, Parkhead.* Reputedly founded c.1556. Home Brewery built 1865/66. Acquired by Gordon & Blair Ltd 1904.

M.D.Dawson & Co, *Clydesdale Brewery, Victoria Road.* Recorded as the Tonbur Brewery Ltd in 1898 and the Clydesdale Brewery Co by 1906.

William Dawson, *Anderston Brewery, 60/66 Bishop Street* (1910)

Gillespie, Sons & Co.Ltd, *Crown Brewery, Slatefield Street* (1930)

Gray & Co, *Anchor Brewery, Davidson Street* (1914)

P.& T.Lynch Ltd, *Crownpoint Brewery, 796 Gallowgate.* Registered 1898. Closed 1902.

Maclachlans Ltd, *Castle Brewery, Maryhill.* See also:- Edinburgh

Robert Meiklejohn & Son, *27 St.Enoch Square.* Trading in 1887. Acquired by Maclachlans in 1923.

Oswald Paterson & Co, *Petershill Brewery, Springburn.* See also:- Edinburgh

P.& W.Brewery Ltd, *Pig & Whistle, McNeil Street, Gorbals.* Home brew house founded 1984. Closed 1986.

Steel, Coulson & Co.Ltd, *Greenhead Brewery, Cochrane Street.* See also:- Edinburgh

J.& R.Tennent Ltd, *Wellpark Brewery, Duke Street.* Founded c.1776. Registered 1890. Acquired by Charrington United Breweries Ltd 1963 with 240 public houses. Still brewing 1990.

Greenock

H.W.Armitage & Co, *Greenock Brewery* (1902)
Watt & Co, *Old Carr's Dyke Brewery*. Founded 1843. Acquired by Maclachlans Ltd of Edinburgh in 1948.

Hamilton

Bothwell Brewery, *Fullwood Foundry, Burnbank Road*. Founded August 1979 by Tom Abercrombie. Acquired in 1981 by Loudon Murray. Closed March 1982.

Kilmarnock

James Brown & Co, *Kilmarnock Brewery* (1920)
George Paxton & Sons, *Richardland Brewery* (1902)

Lanark

Thomas Gilroy & Co, *97 North Vennell* (1910)

Paisley

Sacell Brewery Co, *8 Sacell.* In operation *c.*1855-*c.*1921.

Stevenston

Ayrshire Brewers Ltd, *Stevenston Industrial Estate*. Founded December 1981 by David Wilson, Babriel Politakis & Tim Bailey. Brewing ceased 1982.

SUFFOLK

Aldeburgh

Flintham, Hall & Co.Ltd, *Albert Brewery, Station Road*. Registered January 1885. Acquired by Adnams & Co.Ltd 1924.

Bacton

Charles Wood, *The Bull*. Founded by 1885. Closed 1892.

Barking

Zacharias Southgate (1906)

Beccles

Harwood & Co, *Northgate Street*. See also:- Eye.

Boxford

John Moye, *White Hart*. Acquired by the Colchester Brewing Co.Ltd 1896 with 6 public houses.

Bures St.Mary

John Death (1922)

Bury St.Edmunds

Bishop & Co, *Saracen's Head Brewery, 65 Guildhall Street*. Founded by 1864. Bankrupt and the brewery and 5 tied houses were offered for auction on 9th December 1901.

Clarke Brothers, *Risbygate Brewery, 87 Risbygate Street*. Founded by 1844. Acquired by Greene King & Sons Ltd 1st May 1917 with 28 public houses and was closed.

Greene King & Sons Ltd, *Westgate Brewery*. Registered June 1887 to acquire E.Greene & Son, Westgate Brewery and F.W.King & Son, St.Edmund's Brewery, both in Westgate Street. Founded 1806 and 1868 respectively. Still independent 1990.

Other Breweries

Harry Colson, *Cannon Brewery, Cannon Street* (1916)
Thomas Simmonds, *Golden Lion, Guildhall Street* (1896)
Mrs M.A. Synett, *Southgate Brewery, 12 Southgate Street* (1892)
Charles Taylor, *Golden Fleece, 50 Churchgate Street* (1913)

Cavendish

Frederick Deaves, *George Hotel* (1910)
William Wallace, *Bull Inn* (1922)

Clare

David Farrance Glazin, *Cock Inn, Callis Street* (1900)
Nethergate Brewery, *11/13 High Street*. Founded 1986 by Ian Hornsey. Still brewing 1990.

Cranley Green

Jesse Rampling, *Langton Green* (1903)

Debenham

Devereux Jessop, *Red Lion* (1899)

Eye

Charles James Fisher & Co, *Church Street*. Founded 1874. Acquired by Adnams & Co.Ltd 1904 and was used as a depot until 1914 when it was sold to Steward & Patteson Ltd with 20 public houses.

Harwood & Co, *Eye Brewery, Lambseth Street & Northgate Street, Beccles*. See also:- Colchester Brewing Co.Ltd, Ipswich.

Flempton

Eliza Frost (1892)

Fornham St.Martin

Harry Brewster, *Woolpack* (1892)

Framlingham

John Page, *Castle Brewery, Castle Street* (1903)

Glemsford

Anna Game (1921)

Great Barton

Isaac Munns, *Bunbury Arms* (1900)

Great Cornard

George Baker, *Highbury Barn* (1906)
Uriah Cross, *King's Head* (1892)
Robert Parmenter, *Queen's Arms* (1922)

Great Thurlow

William Wootten, *Thurlow Brewery*. Founded by 1874. Brewery and 5 tied houses sold to F.C.Christmas & Co. January 1913 for £4,100.

Hadleigh

Woods & Co, *Angel Street* (1914)

Halesworth

J.C.Evans & Co, *Halesworth Brewery, 11 Market Place*. Founded 1770. Acquired by the Colchester Brewing Co.Ltd 1888 but brewing continued until 1925.

Frank Kendall Chapman, *Prince of Wales Brewery, Bungay Road*. Offered for auction 1st November 1906 but was withdrawn at £20,000.

Haverhill

John B. Ashard, *15 High Street* (1914)

SARACEN'S HEAD BREWERIES
A.C. & J.A. BISHOP
MILD ALE
WINE & SPIRIT MERCHANTS
BREWERS AND BOTTLERS
BURY ST. EDMUNDS

F.C.Christmas & Co, *Haverhill Brewery, Camps Road.* Founded by 1868 and acquired by Christmas in 1894. Acquired by Greene King & Sons Ltd 1918 with 49 public houses. Brewing ceased 1924.

Harry Pannell, *Chauntry Place.* Acquired by Ingold & Co. of Braintree c.1900.

William Ward & Son. Acquired by F.C.Christmas 1894.

Hawkedon

Adam Bacon, *Queen's Head* (1910)

Herringfleet

Mark Rushmere Mallett (1900)

Icklingham

Robert Hook, *Red Lion* (1900)

Ingham

Harry Smith, *Ingham Brewery, Griffin.* (1912)

Ipswich

Colchester Brewing Co.Ltd, *Falcon Brewery, 5 Falcon Street.* Founded c.1855 by Alfred Bowman. Acquired by Bridges, Cuthbert & Co.1864 and was registered June 1866 as Bridges, Cuthbert & Co.Ltd to acquire the Falcon Brewery and the Cross Keys Brewery, Culver Street, Colchester (closed 1880). Bankrupt 1868. Registered October 1886 as the Norfolk & Suffolk Brewery Co.Ltd to acquire Bridges, Cuthbert & Co.Ltd and Harwood & Co, Eye Brewery. Name changed to the Colchester Brewing Co.Ltd July 1887. Acquired by Ind Coope & Co.Ltd 1925 with 319 public houses and was closed.

Cobbold & Co.Ltd, *Cliff Brewery, Cliff Road.* Founded at Harwich 1723 by Thomas Cobbold and moved to Ipswich 1746. Registered March 1924. 236 tied houses. Merged with Tollemache's Breweries Ltd 1957 to form Tollemache & Cobbold Breweries Ltd owning 370 tied houses. Acquired by Ellerman Shipping Lines 1977 which was acquired by Barclay Brothers 1983. Brewing ceased 1989.

Tollemache's Breweries Ltd, *Brook Street Brewery, 39 Upper Brook Street.* Founded 1856 and was acquired by Tollemache Brothers from Charles Cullingham & Co.1888. Registered May 1896 as Tollemache's Ipswich Brewery Ltd. Name changed as above 4th August 1920 when Collier Brothers of Walthamstow were acquired. Merged with Cobbold & Co.Ltd 1957 and brewing ceased 1961.

Unicorn Brewery Co.Ltd, *Unicorn Brewery, Foundation Street.* Originally called Catchpole & Co. Registered June 1918. Wound up voluntarily 1923 and their 56 tied houses were divided equally between Tollemache and Cobbold.

Lavenham

Frederick Nunn, *Lion Hotel, High Street* (1892)

Long Melford

Charles Ashby & Sons, *Perseverance Hotel.* Brewing up to 1952 when acquired by Tollemache's Breweries Ltd. The last home brew house in Suffolk until the 1980s.

William Bixby, *Westgate Street* (1892)

Ann Claydon, *Crown Inn* (1892)

George Frederick Grice. Acquired by Ward & Son of Foxearth 1914 and was closed in 1920.

Peter Richold, *The Hare* (1892) Now a Greene King house.

Lowestoft

E.& G.Morse, *Crown Brewery, Crown Street.* Founded by Henry Morse at Bell Lane Brewery 1842 and moved to the Crown Brewery by 1868. Also at the Swaffham Brewery, Norfolk until 1895. Acquired by Morgan's Brewery Co.Ltd 1936 and brewing ceased. Premises now occupied by Windsor & Newton Ltd.

Scotties Brewery, *Crown Hotel.* Home brewery founded 1990.

Youngman & Preston, *Eagle Brewery, Rantscore.* Founded by 1844. Acquired by Lacon & Co.Ltd 1919 and brewing had ceased by 1922. Premises resold to Charrington & Co.Ltd and were acquired c.1960 by Birdseye Foods.

Melton

Melton Brewery, *Coach & Horses.* Founded by 1844. Brewing ceased c.1910. Coach & Horses later owned by Bullard & Sons Ltd.

Mildenhall

George Jeffrey, *White Hart Hotel, High Street* (1896)

Monks Eleigh

William Parr (1890)

Nayland

Thomas Cuddon, *Nayland Brewery.* Founded before 1844. Offered for auction 1918 with 10 public houses and was bought by the Colchester Brewing Co.Ltd.

Needham Market

George Clowes & Co, *High Street.* Brewery converted into a yeast factory 1899 and is still standing.

Newmarket

Edward Dean, *Saxon Street* (1898)

Newmarket Breweries & White Hart Hotel Co.Ltd, Registered June 1896 to acquire Benjamin Chennell, White Hart Brewery and Charles F.Moody, King's Head Brewery. Acquired by Greene King & Sons Ltd 1896.

Charles Stebbing, *Rutland Arms Hotel, High Street* (1892)

Christopher Turner, *Wellington Street* (1892)

Orford

Edward Rope, *Rope's Wharf.* Sold brewery and 2 tied houses to Flintham, Hall & Co.Ltd prior to 1912 and they were resold to Adnams & Co.Ltd 1922. Brewing ceased and brewery demolished.

Oulton Broad

Oulton Broad Brewery, *Harbour Road Industrial Estate.* Founded 1987. Still brewing 1990.

Polstead

Edward Lilley. Founded by 1885. Goodwill of business sold to Greene King & Sons Ltd 1925. Premises now the Brewery Farm.

Snape

Alde Brewery. Founded 1990 in Snape Maltings.

Southwold

Adnams & Co.Ltd, *Sole Bay Brewery, East Green.* Founded as a brew house attached to the Swan Hotel established by 1641. Acquired by George and Ernest Adnams of Newbury, Berkshire c.1870. Registered March 1890. Still independent 1990.

Southwold Old Brewery Co.Ltd. Registered 12th August 1888. Dissolved 8th December 1891.

Stoke-by-Clare

Edwin Deeks, *Red Lion* (1900)

Stowmarket

George Diaper, *Crown Brewery, Bridge Street* (1898)

Herbert Edward Miller, *Suffolk Brewery, Violet Hill* (1910)

Thomas Prentice & Co.Ltd, *Station Road.* Bought by Greene King & Sons Ltd 1934 for £1,250. No tied houses. Part of the brewery was still standing 1977.

Sudbury

William Bailey, *Four Swans, 10 North Street* (1892)

Grimwood & Co, *Phoenix Brewery, Church Walk* (1921)

J.C.Mauldon & Sons, *White Horse Brewery, Ballingdon.* Founded c.1793. Acquired by Greene King & Sons Ltd 1958 with 22 tied houses. Closed 1960.

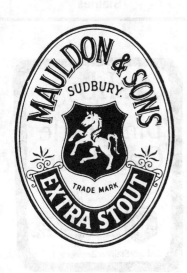

Mauldon's Brewery, *7 Addison Road, Chilton Industrial Estate*. Founded by Peter Mauldon December 1982, great grandson of the founder of the above brewery. Still brewing 1990.

Oliver Brothers, *Sudbury Brewery, Cornard Street*. Founded by 1874. Acquired by Greene King & Sons Ltd May 1919 with 51 public houses. Brewing ceased May 1932.

William Shelley, *Prince of Wales, 38 New Street* (1904)

Thomas Sillitoe, *92 East Street* (1892)

Harriett Theobald, *Plough Lane* (1920)

Waldringfield

John Hill (1904)

Wangford

Wangford Arms, *High Street*. Home brew house in operation 1985-86.

Westerfield

John Bird & Co.Ltd, *Westerfield Brewery*. Registered December 1902 to acquire the business of James P.Rann trading as John Bird & Co. Voluntary liquidation August 1908 but brewing appears to have continued until at least 1912. Brewery sold 1915.

Wickhambrook

Edward Mills (1916)

Wickham Market

William Rush (1900)

Woodbridge

John Baker, *North Hill Brewery, Bradfield Street* (1892)

Spencer Chaplin, *Bradfield Street* (1892)

Lockwood & Co. (Woodbridge) Ltd, *Castle Brewery, Castle Hill*. Owned by William Lockwood from at least 1844. Offered for auction 2nd May 1912 with 2 public houses. Registered as above 17th March 1914. Acquired by Steward & Patteson Ltd July 1932 with 3 tied houses.

Yoxford

William Spalding (1896)

SURREY

Addlestone

J.A.P.Clarke & Co. Acquired by Friary, Holroyd & Healy 1891.

Albury

John S.Beet, *Drummond Arms* (1910)

Ashtead

George Sayer, *The Street*. Founded by 1859. Merged with the Swan Brewery (Leatherhead) Ltd December 1912.

Beare Green

Henry Edward Turner (1892)

Betchworth

Frank Bridger, *Dolphin Brewery* (1923)

Bramley

William Smith. Founded by Charles Smith 1847. Acquired by Bruford & Co.Ltd August 1901 with 8 tied houses for £16,256.

Byfleet

George Barron Holroyd, *Byfleet Brewery*. Founded by Henry Dennett 1845 and became Dennett & Holroyd 1867. Merged with the Friary Brewery 1889 and was closed in 1909.

Chertsey

Healy & Co, *Guildford Street*. Founded *c*.1855 as Healy, Maddox & Wetton. Acquired by the Friary Brewery Co. January 1890.

Cobham

Ashby's Cobham Brewery Co.Ltd. Registered 1887 to acquire the business of Richard Wallis Ashby. Merged with Savill & Co.Ltd of Shalford 1913 to form Cobham United Breweries Ltd which was acquired by Watney, Combe, Reid & Co.Ltd 1922 with 33 public houses.

Cranleigh

Bruford & Co.Ltd, *Steam Brewery*. Registered September 1888 to acquire the business of George Bruford and Charles Bamford. Acquired by Savill & Co.Ltd 1912.

Dorking

Boxall & Son, *Sun Brewery, High Street*. Founded 1839. Acquired by the Swan Brewery (Leatherhead) Ltd March 1907 with 8 tied houses.

Wallace Breem & Co, *Red Lion Brewery, High Street*. Acquired by Lascelles, Tickner & Co. April 1888 with 5 public houses.

John Young & Son, *West Street*. Founded before 1832. Acquired by Friary, Holroyd & Healy's Breweries Ltd 1897.

East Molesey

Streets of London, *1 Bridge Road*. A Whitbread home brew house founded 1981. Closed 1984.

Epsom

William George Bradley & Son, *Ashley Road*. Acquired by Page & Overton's Brewery Ltd 1903 and was closed. Brewery (built 1900) demolished 1985 due to town centre redevelopment.

R.& F.Pagden Ltd, *Hope Brewery, Church Street*. Founded 1769 as Keeling's Brewery. Sold by William Cobbold, later of Colchester, to Trayton Peter Pagden on 23rd April 1824. Acquired by Barclay, Perkins & Co.Ltd September 1921 and was resold to Mellersh & Neale Ltd June 1931. Brewery since demolished.

Farnham

Thomas Bentall Barling, *Castle Brewery, East Street* (1926)

Farnham Brewery Co.Ltd, *Castle Street*. Registered 26th April 1888. Acquired by Reid's Brewery Co.Ltd 1896 with 12 tied houses.

Farnham United Breweries Ltd, *Lion Brewery, West Street*. Founded 1860. Registered October 1889 to acquire: G.Trimmer, Lion Brewery; R.T.& J.Barrett, Red Lion Brewery, Farnham and the Red Lion Brewery, Basingstoke. Acquired by Courage & Co.Ltd 1927 with 196 public houses. Brewing ceased 1928 but malting continued until 1956.

Thomas Matthews & Co, *West Street*. Bankrupt and brewery sold 1910.

Godalming

Agate & Son, *Sun Brewery, Bridge Street*. Founded before 1812. Acquired by Lascelles, Tickner & Co.Ltd 1891 with 12 public houses. Brewery offered for sale September 1923.

T.B.B.Baverstock, *(New) Sun Brewery, Bridge Street*. Built 1883. Acquired by Lascelles, Tickner & Co.Ltd 1892.

Frederick Blackman, *Stag Inn, Lower Eashing*. Home brew house acquired by Lascelles, Tickner & Co.Ltd 1894.

Thomas White, junior, *Bridge Brewery, Bridge Street*. Founded 1839. Acquired by Friary, Holroyd & Healy July 1890.

Gomshall

Reffell Brothers, *Black Horse Brewery.* Offered for auction 23rd March 1926 with 3 tied houses, 2 of which were bought by Young & Co's Brewery Ltd of Wandsworth, London.

Guildford

F.A.Crooke & Co.Ltd, *Guildford (or St.Nicholas) Brewery.* Founded *c.*1807 by James Crooke. Registered 1908. Offered for auction 10th June 1929 with 34 public houses and was bought by Hodgson's Kingston Brewery Co.Ltd for £152,150 and was closed.

Elkins & Co, *North Street Brewery.* Offered for auction 2nd August 1890 and was bought by Hodgson's Kingston Brewery Co.Ltd for £30,000.

Friary, Holroyd & Healy's Breweries Ltd, *Friary Brewery, Commercial Road.* Founded *c.*1868 by Thomas Taunton of the Cannon Brewery (founded 1844). Registered June 1895. Merged with Meux's Brewery Co.Ltd 1960 to form Friary Meux Ltd, now part of Carlsberg-Tetley. Brewing ceased 23rd January 1969 and the brewery has been demolished.

Lascelles, Tickner & Co.Ltd, *Castle Brewery, Bury Street.* Registered April 1889. Acquired by Friary, Holroyd & Healy's Breweries Ltd 1926 with 96 tied houses.

Haslemere

Walter Kiln, *Bell Vale Brewery* (1902)

Horley

Charles Dagnall & Co, *Horley Brewery.* Merged with Henry & Benjamin Holmes of Hornchurch, Essex to form the Hornchurch Brewery Co.Ltd, registered on 18th July 1890. Voluntary liquidation 19th December 1890.

Youell & Elkin, *Albert Brewery.* Acquired by Page & Overton's Brewery Co.Ltd 1903. Brewery still standing 1990.

Leatherhead

Swan Brewery (Leatherhead) Ltd, *Swan Brewery, High Street.* Founded before 1805. Swan Brewery built 1874 by George Moore. Registered October 1903. Acquired by Mellersh & Neale Ltd November 1921 with 21 public houses and was closed.

Milford

Lewis H.Luck, *Red Lion.* Home brew house acquired by Savill & Co.Ltd *c.*1900.

Newdigate

Butcher & Purton (1910)

Redhill

Bransbury, Stratton & Co, *Redhill Brewery, Station Road.* Acquired by Bushell, Watkins & Smith Ltd of Westerham, Kent 1914 with 10 tied houses.

Frank Waters & Co, *Roses Brewery, Mill Street.* Acquired by Stansfeld & Co. of Fulham, London 1895.

Reigate

Alfred Durrant & Sons, *56 Priory Road, South Park* (1910)

Mellersh & Neale Ltd, *19 High Street.* Founded in the 16th Century. Registered May 1899. Acquired by Meux's Brewery Co.Ltd June 1938 and brewing ceased. 44 public houses. Brewery demolished 1988.

Pilgrim Brewery, *11 West Street.* Founded by David Roberts at Woldingham 1982 and was moved to Reigate 1985. Still brewing 1990.

Reigate Brewery, *John Landregan off-licence, 46 Glovers Road.* Founded November 1983. Closed 1986.

Shalford

Jesse Boxall, *Star Brewery* (1898)

Savill & Co.Ltd, *Broadford Brewery.* Registered July 1904. Merged with Ashby's Cobham Brewery Co.Ltd August 1913 to form Cobham United Breweries Ltd. Closed 1922.

Staines

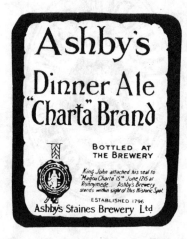

Ashby's Staines Brewery Ltd, *Church Street.* Founded by Thomas Ashby 1796. Registered 1887 as Charles Ashby & Co.Ltd. Re-registered as above June 1899. Acquired by H.& G.Simonds Ltd 1930 with 200/300 public houses. Brewing ceased 1931. Site now used as Courage headquarters.

Thomas Fladgate Harris, *Knowle Green Brewery, Kingston Road.* Founded by 1877. Acquired by Ashby's Staines Brewery Ltd July 1903 with 94 tied houses, half of which were sold to Watney, Combe, Reid & Co.Ltd. 1903/04. Brewing ceased 1914.

Thames Ditton

J.E.Dawes & Co, *Ditton Brewery, Gigg's Hill.* Acquired by Watney, Combe, Reid & Co.Ltd January 1906 and was converted into a bottling stores in 1914.

Walton-on-Thames

Jason, Gurney & Co, *Star Brewery.* Offered for auction 27th June 1891 with 22 public houses. Acquired by Brandon's Putney Brewery Ltd 1896.

Woking

Joseph Oldfield, *West Surrey Brewery, Town Street.* Acquired by Lascelles, Tickner & Co.Ltd 1889 with 15 tied houses.

John Stedman, *Brewery Road, Horsell.* Founded *c.*1867. Brewing ceased 1910.

Woldingham

Pilgrim Brewery. See also:- Reigate.

Battle

Bailey Brothers, *15 High Street*. Acquired by Ballard & Co.Ltd of Lewes November 1911 with 12 tied houses. Brewery was still standing 1987.

Brighton & Hove

Ashby & Co, *Bedford Brewery, Silwood Street & Castle Brewery, Castle Street*. Founded by 1864. Acquired by Smithers & Sons Ltd 1906.

Brighton Brewery. In operation 1986-87. See also:- Raven Brewery.

William Carter, *Station Brewery, 24 Vine Street* (1890)

M.P.Castle, *Albion Brewery, 10 Albion Street*. Founded c.1850. Acquired by Tamplin & Sons 1893.

Chapman & Co, *Black Lion Brewery, Black Lion Street*. Founded by Deryck Carver in 1545 although the brewery dates from the 18th Century. Acquired by the Rock Brewery (Brighton) Ltd 1902 and was later sold to Fremlins Ltd. Brewery demolished c.1970.

J.Dowling, *Gloucester Brewery, 121/22 Gloucester Road*. Originally a ginger beer manufacturer in 1856 but brewing 1864-99 when premises used for beer retailing.

Ellis, Wilson & Bacon, *36 Waterloo Street, Hove*. Registered 1933 to carry on the business of brewers.

Hodges & Ritchie, *College Brewery, 13,16/17 Montague Place*. Founded by North & Marshall 1854. Acquired by W.Willett & Son 1895. Brewing ceased 1900 and premises used by the Rock Brewery (Brighton) Ltd as stores. Demolished 1988.

Kemp Town Brewery (Brighton) Ltd, *6 Seymour Street*. Founded before 1833. Registered March 1933 to acquire Abbey's Kemp Town Brewery. Acquired by Charrington & Co.Ltd 1954 and brewery closed 1963.

Kemp Town Brewery, *Hand-in-Hand, 33 Upper St.James's Street*. Home brew house founded 1990.

Kidd & Hotblack Ltd, *Cannon Brewery, 16 Russell Street*. Founded by John Barnett c.1821 and was acquired by J.M.& F.J.Kidd 1872. Registered November 1906. Acquired by Tamplin & Sons June 1926. Brewing ceased c.1950 and the brewery was demolished May 1969.

H.B.Longhurst & Son, *Amber Ale Brewery, 72 London Road*. Founded by 1854. Acquired by Abbey's Kemp Town Brewery 1889. Brewery demolished 1901 for road widening but the malt house survives as the Duke of York cinema.

Raven Brewery, *35 Vine Street*. A new small brewery founded 1979 but liquidated 1982. Re-opened 1983 and closed 1986. In operation as the Brighton Brewery 1986-7.

E.Robins & Son Ltd, *Anchor Brewery, 57 Waterloo Street, Hove*. Founded 1789. Registered April 1894 to acquire the business of the late E.W.Robins. Acquired by Tamplin & Sons and Findlater, Mackie & Co.Ltd 1928 after brewing had ceased on 30th January 1924.

Rock Brewery (Brighton) Ltd, *61 St.James Street*. Founded c.1809 and was acquired by W.Willett & Son 1863. Registered April 1901 with 52 tied houses. Acquired by Portsmouth United Breweries Ltd 1927 who then became Portsmouth & Brighton United Breweries Ltd. Brewing ceased in 1928.

Smithers & Sons Ltd, *North Street Brewery, 89/90 North Street*. Registered July 1906. Brewing ceased 1923 having also been carried on at Dudney's Portslade Brewery since 1917. Acquired by Tamplin & Sons 1929. Brewery demolished 1984.

Tamplin & Sons Brewery, Brighton, Ltd, *Phoenix Brewery, Waterloo Street*. Founded 1821. Registered May 1889. Acquired by Watney Mann Ltd 1953 with 400 public houses. Brewing ceased in October 1973.

R.C.Weekes, *Brighton Brewery, Osborne Street, Hove*. Brewery built by George Gallard c.1852 and was acquired by Weekes 1870. Acquired by Tamplin & Sons March 1900 with 12 tied houses and was demolished.

West Street Brewery (Brighton) Ltd, *8 West Street*. Founded 1769. Registered September 1895 to acquire Vallance, Catt & Co. Acquired by Smithers & Sons Ltd 1913 with 32 public houses and brewing ceased.

Cooksbridge

George Norman & Co. Brewery destroyed by fire 7th August 1912 and the attached off-licence was sold to Southdown & East Grinstead Breweries Ltd.

Eastbourne

John Bignell, *Duke Street*. Founded by 1870. Closed 1914.

Martlet Brewery, *44 Hammonds Drive*. A new small brewery founded 1979. Closed 1983.

Star Brewery Co.Ltd, *Star Road, Old Town*. Founded 1777. Registered October 1886 to acquire the business of George Gates. Acquired by Courage, Barclay & Simonds Ltd 1965 with 43 tied houses. Brewing ceased 1967 and was demolished 1971.

Young & Rawley Ltd, *Lion Brewery, Pevensey Road*. Successor to Caleb Diplock brewing 1866/82. Registered September 1890. Became bankrupt and was acquired by Abbey's Kemp Town Brewery 1914. Premises are now the Southdown bus depot.

Etchingham

Old Oak Brewery, *De Etchingham Arms*. Founded November 1983 at the Ridgewood Inn, Uckfield and moved to here in the same year. Closed 1984.

Forest Row

Henry Beaman. Acquired by Ballard & Co.Ltd 1900.

Frant

George Ware & Sons Ltd, *Pale Ale Brewery*. Founded 1862. Registered February 1925. Acquired by E.& H.Kelsey Ltd 1950 with 12 tied houses and brewing ceased. Brewery still standing 1990.

Hailsham

|

141

Herbert Lynn, *Battle Road*. Founded 1808 and acquired by Lynn 1902. Merged with Molesworth's Poynings Brewery Ltd 1936 and brewing ceased 1940. Brewery was still standing 1985.

Hastings

Breeds & Co.Ltd, *Hastings Brewery, High Street*. Founded 1828. Registered October 1897 to acquire Thomas Breeds & Co. Acquired by George Beer & Rigden Ltd 1931 with about 32 public houses and brewing ceased.

J.C.Burfield & Co, *Phoenix Brewery, High Street*. Acquired by Smith & Co. of Lamberhurst 1908.

St.Clement's Brewery, *First In Last Out, 14 High Street*. Home brew house founded December 1985. Pub for sale 1988.

Herstmonceaux

Robert Wright, *Old Brewery, Gardner Street*. Founded by 1874. Ceased brewing 1911.

Lewes

Ballard & Co.Ltd, *Southover Brewery, High Street*. Founded 1878. Registered February 1898 to acquire Henry John Beaman carried on as Ballard & Co. 41 tied houses. Acquired by Page & Overton's Brewery Ltd 1924 and was closed in 1930. Brewery demolished 1980.

Beard & Co.(Lewes) Ltd, *Star Lane Brewery, Fisher Street.* Founded by 1741. Acquired by Thomas Beard 1811. Registered June 1936. Brewing ceased 1958 and beer is brewed for them by Harvey & Sons. Brewery retained as workshops. Still own 26 public houses. Company moved to Hailsham 1985.

M.H.Bishop & Sons, *South Malling Brewery, Malling Street.* Acquired by Tamplin & Sons 1900. Brewery destroyed by fire *c.*1966.

Harvey & Sons (Lewes) Ltd, *Bridge Wharf Brewery, 6 Cliffe High Street.* Founded by John Harvey 1790. Registered November 1898. Still operating independently 1990 with 33 tied houses.

Edward Monk & Sons, *Bear Yard, Cliffe High Street.* Acquired by Southdown & East Grinstead Breweries Ltd in 1898.

Southdown & East Grinstead Breweries Ltd, *Southdown Brewery, Thomas Street.* Hope Brewery, East Grinstead founded by Charles Absalom 1844 and Southdown Brewery established 1838. Registered July 1895 to acquire Dashwood & Co, Hope Brewery and A.G.S.& T.S.Manning, Southdown Brewery. Acquired by Tamplin & Sons 1923 with 90 public houses. Most of the buildings still standing.

Verrall & Sons, *Southover.* Founded in mid 18th Century by William Verrall. Brewery and 35 public houses sold to Page & Overton's Brewery Co.Ltd 1897. Brewery demolished 1905.

Newhaven

Arundel

G.S.Constable & Sons Ltd, *Swallow Brewery, Queen Street* and *Anchor Brewery, Littlehampton.* Littlehampton brewery founded 1845. Registered 1905. Merged with G.Henty & Sons Ltd of Chichester 1921 to form Henty & Constable (Brewers) Ltd. Brewing ceased at Arundel 1922 and Littlehampton 1926.

Lambert & Norris Ltd, *Eagle Brewery, Tarrant Street.* Founded before 1733. Registered November 1897. Acquired by Friary, Holroyd & Healy's Breweries Ltd 1910 with 81 public houses. Brewing continued until at least 1915.

Ashurstwood

Towner Brothers, *Tipper Ale Brewery.* Founded by Thomas Tipper in the mid-18th Century and was acquired by Thomas Stone *c.*1839 and Robert Towner *c.*1855. Offered for auction 8th August 1911 and was bought by the Rock Brewery (Brighton) Ltd.

Newick

Roberts & Co, *High Street.* Brewery built by Joseph Hammond 1882. Owned one off-licence but no tied houses. Brewing ceased *c.*1909. Most of the buildings remain.

Portslade

Alexandra Brewery, *19 North Street.* Founded November 1982. Owned 8 public houses. Later known as Beckets Brewery. Compulsory winding up January 1987.

J.Dudney, Sons & Co, *Southdown Brewery.* Founded 1849. Acquired by the Kemp Town Brewery 1919 and the brewery and several public houses were resold to Smithers & Sons Ltd. Later part of the brewery was operated as the Portslade Brewery Co but this venture failed. Brewery plant offered for auction 28th January 1930. The buildings remain intact.

WEST SUSSEX

Three Crowns, *Hammerwood Road.* Home brew house founded December 1983 by the Phoenix Brewery Co.(Watneys). Still brewing 1990.

Bognor

Richard Allen, *Victoria Brewery, Victoria Park.* Founded 1867. Brewing ceased *c.*1890.

Charles Percy Gibbons, *Upper Bognor Brewery.* Founded 1839 by Turner Brothers. Acquired by Gibbons 1882. Receiver appointed October 1893.

Burgess Hill

Railway Tavern, *Station Road.* A Whitbread home brew house founded 1983. Closed 1986.

Rye

John Bowen, *Landgate Brewery, King Street.* Brewery built by James Batchelor *c.*1852 and was acquired by Bowen 1878. Sold to Leney & Co. of Dover *c.*1900 and was used as a store. Still standing.

Chapman Brothers Ltd, *101 High Street & East Guldeford.* Registered December 1900. Brewing ceased *c.*1908 and brewery demolished 1911 but business continued as wine & spirit merchants until going into voluntary liquidation on 19th April 1920.

St.Leonards

Hewett & Co, *St.Leonards Brewery, Shepherd Street.* Founded 1840. Registered 1864. Went into voluntary liquidation on 6th April 1907 and was acquired by Breeds & Co.Ltd.

Mr Cherrys, *Marina Court, 42 Marina Street.* Home brew house founded February 1984. Closed 1985.

Seaford

Sexton & Sons, *Elm Brewery, Croft Lane.* Badly damaged by fire 1907. Acquired by Ballard & Co.Ltd *c.*1914. Still standing 1990.

Uckfield

Francis R.Bruce, *Lion Brewery, Framfield Road.* Brewery adjacent to Alma Arms. Brewing ceased *c.*1903. Now demolished.

Old Oak Brewery. See also:- Etchingham.

Sinden & Tasker, *High Street.* Brewery dated from 1793 rebuilt 1887. Brewing ceased *c.*1895.

Wadhurst

Four Keys, *Station Road.* Home brew house founded December 1982. Closed 1986.

Gregory Wright & Sons, *Holmesdale Brewery.* Founded 1874. Offered for auction 25th April 1913 after brewing had ceased in 1911.

Wellingham

A.W.Crosskey, *Wellingham Brewery.* Bankrupt 1913.

Thomas Saunders Stroud, *St.John's Brewery, London Road.* Founded by Thomas Charman *c.*1862 and acquired by Stroud *c.*1878. Sold to Harry Chapman of Worthing 1910 for use as a depot.

Bosham

Bosham Brewery, *Walton Lane.* Founded 1984 by Philip Turnbull. Closed 1986.

Chichester

George Henty & Sons Ltd, *Westgate Brewery, Westgate.* Registered 1893. Merged with Constable & Sons Ltd 1921 to form Henty & Constable (Brewers) Ltd. Acquired by Tamplin & Sons 1954, then a subsidiary of Watney Mann. 120 of their tied houses were sold to Friary, Holroyd & Healy's

Breweries Ltd.

Royds & Marsden, *East Walls Brewery*. Founded *c.*1839 by James Atkey and acquired by Royds & Marsden *c.*1882. Acquired by Lambert & Norris 1889.

Chidham

Old Chidham Brewery, *Old House at Home, Cot Lane*. Home brew house founded December 1979 by Ernest Scott. Closed 1983.

Crawley

Henry Holder, *New Town* (1892)
George Ockendon & Son, *New Road & Station Breweries*. Founded by 1862. Acquired by Southdown & East Grinstead Breweries Ltd 1907.

Cuckfield

Joseph Langton, *Dolphin Brewery, High Street*. Founded by Thomas Best 1855 and acquired by Langton *c.*1878. Acquired by Southdown & East Grinstead Breweries Ltd 1898.

East Grinstead

George Coomber, *North End Brewery* (1892)
Dashwood & Co, *Hope Brewery, London Road*. Merged with A.G.S.& T.S.Manning of Lewes 1895 to form Southdown & East Grinstead Breweries Ltd.
The East Grinstead Brewing Co.Ltd. *Dunnings Mill, Dunnings Road*. Home brew house founded July 1980 by George Spooner. Ceased brewing 1982 but reopened March 1985 but finally closed October 1985.

Edburton

Sussex Brewery, *Trileigh Manor Farm*. Founded January 1980. Closed 1983.

Hermitage

Sussex Brewery, *36 Main Road*. Founded November 1981 in a derelict former home brewery. Still brewing 1990.

Henfield

Frank Bowler, *Mockbridge*. Founded by J.A.Hughes *c.*1828. Closed *c.*1914 and is now a private house.

Horsham

G.H.Barnes & Co, *East Street Brewery*. Founded 1800. Merged with King & Sons Ltd 1906 to form King & Barnes Ltd. Still brewing independently 1990 with 65 public houses.
King & Sons Ltd, *North Street Brewery*. Founded 1850 as maltsters. Registered August 1893. Merged with G.H.Barnes & Co.1906.
H.Michell, *West Street Brewery*. Founded January 1835. Acquired by the Rock Brewery (Brighton) Ltd 1912 with about 12 tied houses and was closed.

Hurstpierpoint

John Edwin Couchman. Acquired by Smithers & Sons Ltd of Brighton *c.*1911. Brewery and malt house still remain as the Maxim Lamp Works.

Lindfield

Fanny Sarah Durrant, *Lindfield Brewery*. Founded *c.*1828. Brewing ceased 1906. Still standing at the rear of the Linden Tree public house.

Littlehampton

G.S.Constable & Sons Ltd. See also:- Arundel.

Midhurst

Ballards, *Elsted Marsh*. Founded by Mike Brown 1980. Brewery for sale 1987.
Parker & Popplewell, *Angel Brewery, North Street*. Acquired by Gale & Co.Ltd of Horndean 1923 with 5 tied houses and was closed in 1927.

Petworth

Manning Milton, *Stag Brewery, High Street*. Founded by James Milton *c.*1845 at rear of White Hart. 3 public houses sold to Friary, Holroyd & Healy 1900. Most of the brewery remains as a private house.

Poynings

Molesworth's Poynings Brewery Ltd. Founded *c.*1862 as Cutress & Sons. Registered June 1925. Brewing ceased 1940.

Shoreham

Albion Brewery, *Middle Street*. Founded *c.*1870 and brewing had ceased by 1895.

Sidlesham

Walter & Herbert Stevens (1902)

Steyning

John Banfield, *Church Street* (1898)
Steyning Breweries Ltd, *High Street*. Registered June 1898 to acquire the businesses of George Gates and George & Harriett Michell. Beer was brewed for them by the Rock Brewery (Brighton) Ltd for 2 years from 1st April 1920. Acquired by Portsmouth & Brighton United Breweries Ltd 1928. The remains of both breweries are still identifiable.

Walberton

Matilda Ellis. Acquired by Hoare & Co.Ltd of London 30th June, 1922 and the brewery and 4 tied houses were sold to the Rock Brewery (Brighton) Ltd on 25th January, 1926.

Worthing

Harry Chapman, *Tower Brewery, Warwick Road*. Acquired by Abbey's Kemp Town Brewery 1924 and was closed in 1926. Brewery tower still standing.

George Gravett, *39/43 Clifton Road* (1921)

George Pacey, *13 New Street*. Brewed draught beer mainly for their public house and the retail trade. Acquired by the Stockwell Brewery Ltd of London 1947 and the brewery was demolished and a public house built on the site.

Parsons & Sons, *Vine Brewery, High Street, West Tarring*. Home brew house acquired by Friary, Holroyd & Healy's Breweries Ltd 1940. Brewery still standing behind the Vine Inn.

Arbroath

McKinlay & Co, *Bell Rock Brewery* (1920)

Auchterarder

Carmichael & Co.Ltd (1902)

Blackford

Robert Eadie & Sons (1910)

W.B.Thomson Ltd, *Blackford Brewery*. Registered March 1890 to merge Alex Ferguson & Co, distillers, Glasgow and R.D.Sharp Ltd. as Ferguson, Sharp & Co.Ltd. Re-registered as above in 1898. Voluntary liquidation March 1915. Acquired by J.& A.Davidson of Coldstream 1916. Possibly the oldest brewery in Scotland reputed to date from 1488. The brewery is still standing 1990.

Blairgowrie

James Ogilvy, *11 Allan Street/Upper Mill Street*. Brewing ceased 1920 but the business was continued as bottlers until c.1930. The brewery dating from c.1780 is still standing 1990.

Brechin

Thomas Ireland, *North Port Brewery*. Acquired by James Aitken & Co.(Falkirk) Ltd 1910 and brewing ceased in 1914.

Broughty Ferry

William Gray & Son (1910)

Dundee

Ballingall & Sons Ltd, *Park & Pleasance Breweries*. Founded 1750 and was acquired by James Ballingall in 1844. Registered October 1897. Brewing ceased 1964 but they continued in business owning 7 tied houses supplied by Drybrough & Co.Ltd. Closed 12th February 1968 when Drybroughs acquired the public houses.

William Halley Brown, *Craigie Brewery, Lyon Street*. Founded 1865. Acquired by William Murray & Co.Ltd 1943 and was closed.

Hawkhill Brewery, *6 Midwynd Industrial Estate, Hawkhill*. Founded 1983 by John McDonald, Bob Welch & Burt Island. Closed 1985.

John Neave & Sons Ltd, *Victoria Brewery, 16/18 Victoria Road*. Registered 1899. Wound up 1909. Brewery sold for £2,450 in 1910.

M.& M.Whitton & Co, *King Street Brewery* (1900)

Forfar

W.A.J.Cameron & Co, *West Port Brewery* (1900)

Montrose

John Davidson & Son, *Montrose Brewery, 36 Ferry Street* (1902)

William Ross & Co, *Lochside Brewery, North Esk Road*. Acquired by James Deuchar Ltd 1926.

Monifieth

Buddon Brewery, *35 Adderley Avenue, Buddon*. Founded 1980 by Bob Welch but brewing ceased in July 1982.

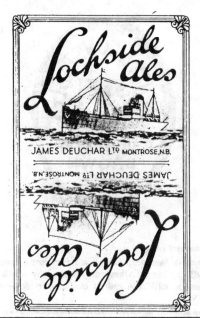

Orkney

Mrs Catherine Flett, *Dundas Street, Stromness* (1940)

Orkney Brewery, *Quoyloo*. Founded by Roger White April 1988. Still brewing 1990.

Perth

Muir & Martin, *South Inch Brewery, 121 Canal Street*. Founded 1815. Acquired by John Wright & Co.(Perth) Ltd in 1926.

John Wright & Co.(Perth) Ltd, *18 North Methven Street*. Founded c.1700. Registered 1925. Acquired by Vaux & Associated Breweries Ltd 1961

East Rainton

North of England Clubs Brewery Co.Ltd. Registered December 1905 to lease the Rainton Brewery. Dissolved 19th February, 1909.

Rainton Brewery Co.Ltd, *10 Norfolk Street*. Registered May 1904 to acquire the business of William James Cordner carried on as the Rainton Brewery Co. Acquired by Thomas Lamb (Hetton-le-Hole) Ltd 1909 with 9 public houses.

Gateshead

Thomas Garbutt & Co, *Mirk Lane* (1906)

Gateshead Breweries Corporation Ltd. Registered 1900. Acquired by John Rowell & Son Ltd 1920.

John Rowell & Son Ltd, *New Brewery, 143 High Street*. Founded by John Rowell 1840. Registered March 1894 to acquire: John Rowell & Sons, John M.Bruce, wine & spirit merchants, Newcastle; William Turnbull & Co, Ferry Brewery South Shields and Gilpin & Co, mineral water manufacturers, Newcastle. Acquired by Newcastle Breweries Ltd 1959.

John Stobart & Co, *19 Bottle Bank* (1890)

Swinburne & Co, Formed part of Newcastle Breweries Ltd 1890

Isaac Tucker & Co.Ltd, *Turk's Head Brewery, 3 West Street*. Founded 1790. Registered April 1929. Acquired by Whitbread & Co.Ltd 1967 with 50 tied houses.

Hetton-le-Hole

Thomas Lamb & Sons (Hetton-le-Hole) Ltd, *Barnes Street*. Founded by Thomas Lamb 1823. Registered March 1917 as Thomas Lamb & Sons Ltd, name changed as above in 1920. Acquired by Associated Breweries Ltd 1929 with 40 tied houses.

Houghton-le-Spring

Robinson Brothers (Brewers) Ltd, *City Brewery, Durham Road*. Founded 1754. Registered 1892 as Robinson Brothers Ltd, Name changed as above 1895. Acquired jointly by Vaux and James Calder & Co. (Brewers) Ltd of Alloa 1925 with 63 tied houses and was closed.

Howdon-on-Tyne

W.A.Falconar & Co, *Howdon Brewery*. Acquired by Newcastle Breweries Ltd c.1894.

Monkseaton

Northumberland Brewery Co. Private company registered May 1920 to acquire the Monkseaton Brewery, the Monkseaton Arms and the Ship Inn. Voluntary liquidation 6th March 1935.

Newcastle-upon-Tyne

Big Lamp Brewery, *1 Summerhill Street, Westgate Road*. Founded December 1982. Still brewing 1990 with 3 public houses.

John Buchanan, *Hanover Square*. Founded 1879 at South Street and moved to Hanover Square c.1890. Acquired by the Northern Clubs Federation Brewery Ltd 1929.

James Deuchar, *Ridley Arms Brewery, Pilgrim Street*. Founded in 1877 by Laurence Davison. Trading as Thomas Davison by 1880 and as above 1895.

Robert Deuchar Ltd, *Sandyford Brewery, Sandyford Road*. Founded 1869 when Robert Deuchar acquired the Chancellor's Head Inn, 114 Newgate Street. Took over J.S.Arnison's Sandyford Brewery 1890. Registered August 1897. Acquired Simson & McPherson Ltd of Edinburgh 1910 and all brewing was transferred to Edinburgh by 1920. Acquired by Newcastle Breweries Ltd 1954 with 360 public houses and brewing ceased in 1961.

Dog & Parrot, *Newcastle Brewhouse Co, Clayton Street West.* A Whitbread home brew house founded 1982. Still brewing 1990.

Dover & Newsome Baxter Ltd, *13 Mosley Street & Thornton-le-Moor, Yorks.* Registered July 1897 to acquire Newsome Baxter, brewers, Thornton-le-Moor and Dover & Co, ale & spirit merchants. The Newcastle business was acquired by Archibald Arrol & Sons Ltd 1901 and closed 1909. The Thornton brewery was sold to James Calder & Co.Ltd 1909 and closed.

Duncan & Daglish Ltd, *Westgate Hill Brewery, Westgate Road.* Founded 1898 when John Duncan and Jacob Daglish acquired Wilkinson & Co, Westgate Hill Brewery. Registered June 1899 to acquire J.Duncan & Co. with 33 tied houses. Acquired by Bass, Ratcliff & Gretton Ltd 1940 and brewing ceased.

Robert Emmerson & Sons Ltd, *Burton Brewery, 56 Sandyford Road.* Founded 1869 at the Flying Horse Brewery, Groat Market and acquired the Burton Brewery from the Burton Brewery Co.Ltd c.1880. Brewing ceased 1906.

Robert Emmerson junior, *1 George Street & 78 Scotswood Road.* Acquired by James Deuchar Ltd 1900.

J.H.Graham Ltd, *Oyster Shell Lane, Headley Street.* Registered November 1900. Receiver appointed 21st September, 1908. Under the control of Worthington & Co.Ltd from c.1910. Voluntary liquidation 21st September, 1920 and the brewery was bought by the Northern Clubs Federation Brewery Ltd 1921.

Hadrian Brewery, *7 Foundry Lane Industrial Estate, Byker.* Founded 1987. Still in operation 1990.

John Ewan McPherson. Merged with James Simson & Sons of Edinbrugh in 1896 to form Simson & McPherson Ltd.

Newcastle Breweries Ltd, *Tyne Brewery, Corporation Street.* Registered February 1890 to acquire: John Barras & Co.Ltd, Tyne Brewery; William Henry Allison & Co, High Brewery, Duke Street, North Shields and Monkwearmouth Brewery, Sunderland; Swinburne & Co, Gateshead and Carr Brothers & Carr, Low Lights, North Shields, with a total of 215 public houses. Merged with Scottish Brewers Ltd 1960 to form Scottish & Newcastle Breweries Ltd.

Robert Newton Ltd, *Victoria Brewery, Westmoreland Lane.* Founded 1843. Registered 1913. Acquired by J.W.Cameron 1919.

Northern Clubs Federation Brewery Ltd, *Federation Brewery, Lancaster Road, Dunston.* Founded at Alnwick 1919 when Smart's former brewery was acquired but this was found not to be in working order so brewing was transferred to Hedley Street, Newcastle where brewing began in March 1921. Moved to the Hanover Street Brewery 1931. New brewery opened at Dunston 1980.

Oubridge & Archibald, *1 West Blandford Street.* Founded 1879. Brewing ceased c.1900.

W.B.Reid & Co.Ltd, *Leazes Brewery, off Claremont Road.* Founded 1837. Registered May 1891 to acquire W.B.Reid & Co, Leazes Brewery; Reid Brothers & Co, wine and spirit merchants, Newcastle and the licensed houses belonging to the Tyne Brewery Co.Ltd. Acquired by William Younger & Co.Ltd 1956 with 154 tied houses.

Ridley, Cutter & Firth Ltd, *Manor Brewery, Stockbridge.* Founded 1845 as Samuel Ridley & Co. Registered January 1898. Acquired by Vaux & Associated Breweries Ltd in 1938 and brewing ceased.

John Sanderson & Sons, *Haymarket Brewery, 157 Northumberland Street.* Acquired by Newcastle Breweries Ltd 1898 and the site used as stores and offices which are now in use by the University.

Tyne Brewery Co.Ltd, *Bath Lane.* Registered May 1874 to acquire the business of Bells, Robson & Co. Acquired by W.B.Reid & Co.Ltd April 1891.

Wilkinson & Co, *Elswick Brewery, Pine Street.* Founded c.1890 by Edward John Wilkinson. Acquired by Hope & Anchor Breweries Ltd 1954.

Other Breweries

Robert Bridge, *16 Bell Street* (1894)
H.Davidson, *28 Cottenham Street* (1895)
John Meikle. Formed part of Archibald Arrol & Sons Ltd 1895.
Thomas Openshaw, *Crystal Palace Brewery, Palace Street* (1892).
Thomas Robinson & Partners, *Sandyford Road* (1890)
Robinson & Anderson Ltd, Acquired by Hammond's United Breweries Ltd 1948.
James Routledge. Acquired by Newcastle Breweries Ltd 1896.

North Shields

W.H.Allison & Co, *High Brewery, Duke Street.* Formed part of Newcastle Breweries Ltd February 1890.

Carr Brothers & Carr, *Low Lights.* Formed part of Newcastle Breweries Ltd 1890.

South Shields

R.S.& D.Crosthwaite, *Low Brewery, Faires Quay, Wapping Street.* Closed 1900.

John W.Pratt Ltd, *Pratts Bank, 34 East Holborn.* Previously known as the Licensed Victuallers Brewery. Also at Dean Road. Registered August 1913. Brewing ceased 1927 but the business was continued as wine & spirit merchants.

John Turnbull & Co.Ltd, *Victoria Brewery, James Mather Street.* Registered August 1918. In liquidation 1923 but the business was continued as the Victoria Bottling Co, which was bought by Hammonds United Breweries Ltd in the late 1950s.

William Turnbull & Co, *Ferry Brewery, Saltwell Lane & Tyne Street.* Acquired by John Rowell & Son Ltd 1896.

James Watt, *Rekendyke Brewery, Rekendyke Lane* (1930)

Westoe Breweries Ltd, *Dunelm Street.* Founded 1862. Operated by Robert Henderson until acquired by Joseph Johnson in 1907. Registered March 1917 as Joseph Johnson (Durham) Ltd to acquire the business and that of Joseph Johnson, City Brewery, Durham. City Brewery closed 1924 and the name was changed as above in 1938. Acquired by Hammonds United Breweries Ltd 1960 with 83 tied houses and brewing ceased.

Matthew Wood & Son Ltd, *Market Place Brewery, Spring Lane.* Registered August 1897. Acquired by Newcastle Breweries Ltd 1919

Stella

J.H.Dalton (1900)

Sunderland

T.E.Chapman & Son, *Lambton Brewery, 1/3 John Street.* Acquired by Cameron & Co.Ltd 1897 with 100 public houses.

James Deuchar Ltd, *Monkwearmouth Brewery.* Founded 1880 when James Deuchar acquired the Ridley Arms Brewery, Newcastle. Monkwearmouth Brewery acquired 1890. Registered July 1894 and was reconstructed in August 1898. Brewing ceased 1936 and was converted into a mineral water factory which was acquired by Newcastle Breweries Ltd in 1956.

R.Fenwick & Co.Ltd, *Sunderland Brewery, Low Street.* Founded 1770 by Robert Fenwick. Registered November 1896 with 63 tied houses. Acquired by George Younger & Son Ltd 1898 and was sold to J.W.Green Ltd 1952. Brewing ceased in April 1964.

North Eastern Breweries Ltd, *Wear Brewery, Westbourne Road.* Registered December 1896 to acquire: Bramwell & Co, Wear Brewery; William Story & Co, Moor Street Brewery, Sunderland; Richard Murray, wine, spirit and ale merchants and aerated water manufacturer, Consett; J.H.Graham, Middlesborough, wine & spirit merchant; P.B.Junor, Tower Brewery, Tudhoe Grange, Spennymoor and Thomas Elwen, Frederick Street, Sunderland, ale & porter merchants. Merged with C.Vaux & Sons Ltd 1927 to form Associated Breweries Ltd. The Wear Brewery was closed in 1942.

William Robson Ltd, *Central Brewery, Middle Street.* Brewing ceased 1941 after the brewery was bombed but the company is still in existence as bottlers.

Vaux Breweries Ltd, *Castle Street Brewery.* Founded by Cuthbert Vaux 1837 at Matlock Street Brewery. Moved to Castle Street 1875. Registered 1896 as C.Vaux & Sons Ltd. Merged with North Eastern Breweries Ltd 1927 to form Associated Breweries Ltd. Name changed as above 1985. Still independent 1990 with 450 tied houses.

Other Breweries

F.L.Jones & Co, *26 Bridge Street and 55 Moor Street.* (1902)
W.& A.St.John, *Queen Street Brewery* (1910)
Smurthwaite & Phillips, *100 Law Street* (1890)
Thomas Stone, *7 Hendon Street* (1890)

Swalwell

Matthew Taylor & Co. Founded 1765. Brewery demolished 1901.

Tynemouth

Openshaw Brothers, *7 Victoria Tynemouth Road.* Founded 1877. Ceased brewing c.1914.

Alcester

Alcester Brewery Ltd, *Church Street.* Brewery built 1886. Registered September 1889. Offered for auction 6th September 1899 with 18 tied houses but was withdrawn at £16,000. Receiver appointed 21st February 1911.

George Henry Woodfield, *Bell Inn Brewery* (1926)

Astley

Edwin Allen (1921)

Atherstone

Augustine J.Trivett (1923)

Bedworth

Thomas Dewis & Co, exors of, *Rye Piece, King Street.* Founded 1793. After the death of Thomas Dewis in August 1905 a second brewery, the Lion Brewery was built which is still standing as the Catholic club. Offered for auction on 16th September 1913 with one public house but brewing continued until 1924.

Brailes

P.& F.Taylor Brothers (1906)

Brandon

John Cave, junior, *Royal Oak Brewery.* Founded by 1868. Closed 1906. See also:- Wolston.

Claverdon

J.Aston, *Red Lion* (1892)

Colehill

Dabbs & Nicholson. See also:- Great Haywood, Staffs.
Robert E.B.Hextall, *Park Road* (1940)
John James Simms, *High Street* (1923)

Easenhall

Edward Moxon, *Trent Valley Brewery Co.* Founded by 1868. Possibly closed *c.*1921 but brewing may have continued until 1939.

Fenny Compton

Zeph.M.Brown. See also:- Banbury, Oxfordshire.

Kenilworth

The Wyandotte. A home brew house brewing until 1946. Now a Marston, Thompson & Evershed house.

Leamington Spa

Atkins & Bosley, *Clarendon Brewery, 59 Clarendon Street.* Brewing 1915-1919 but continued to trade as wine & spirit merchants.
Lucas & Co.Ltd, *130 The Parade.* Founded 1839. Registered July 1897 to acquire Lucas & Co with 124 tied houses. Acquired by Ansells Brewery Ltd November 1928 and brewing ceased in 1934.
A.W.Phillpotts, *26 Chandos Street* (1921)

THORNLEY'S
GOLD MEDAL
SUNBRIGHT
ALE
RADFORD BREWERY,
LEAMINGTON SPA.

H.E.Thornley Ltd, *Radford Hall Brewery, Radford Semele.* Founded 1900. Merged with Benjamin Kelsey Ltd of Birmingham 1933 to form Thornley Kelsey Ltd. Brewery closed October 1968 to allow concentration on the wine wholesaling business. Their 68 tied houses were sold, the majority to Davenports. The brewery has been demolished

Little Compton

Lardner & Sons, *Steam Brewery.* Founded by 1860. Acquired by Flower & Sons Ltd 1900.

Middle Tysoe

John Henry Middleton (1892)

Monks Kirby

The Bell. Home brew house in operation 1896-1912.
James Edward Lea, *Denbigh Arms.* Home brew house. Ceased brewing 1916.

Pailton

Cox, *The Fox.* Home brew house (1896)

Quinton

Thomas Green, *Moor Street* (1923)

Rugby

Liddington's Litchborough Brewery, *140 Wood Street.* The former Litchborough Brewery. See also:- Litchborough and Daventry, Northants. Brewing here from 1983 when Liddingtons acquired the business. Ceased brewing 1986.
Marcus Lowe, *Victoria Brewery, North Street.* In operation 1874-1892.

Stratford-upon-Avon

George E.Court, *21 Church Street* (1920)
William Eborall, *1 Mansell Street* (1926)
Flower & Sons Ltd, *Brewery Street.* Founded by Edward Fordham Flower 1831. Registered February 1888. Acquired by J.W.Green Ltd of Luton 1954 who then changed their name to Flowers Breweries Ltd. The brewery was closed in 1968 when Whitbread merged Flowers with West Country Breweries to form Whitbread Flowers Ltd. Brewery demolished.
William Gibbs, *1 Warwick Road* (1921)

Shipston-on-Stour

William Turner, *Caudlewell Brewery.* Founded 1884. Acquired by Flower & Sons Ltd 1896.

Snitterfield

Grant, *Snitterfield Brewery* (1896)

Studley

Studley Brewery, *Old Washford Mill, Icknield Street Drive.* Home brew house founded September 1978. Ceased brewing October 1982.
Thompson's Brewery Ltd, *Bell Brewery.* Founded 1880. Acquired by Mitchells & Butlers Ltd 1945 with 5 tied houses. Brewery demolished 1962.

Warwick

Dennis Aucott, *40 Brook Street* (1920)
Ernest John Barratt, *50 Friars Street* (1920)
Walter W.Clarke, *Coventry Road* (1906)
Dutton & Hudson, *Warwick Brewery, 4 Swan Street.* Founded February 1832. Acquired by Lucas & Co. of Leamington Spa 1896 with 12 public houses. Brewing ceased in 1928.
Thomas Enoch Iliffe, *1 Birmingham Road* (1920)
James B.McCartney, *Woodman Brewery, Priory Road.* Brewing 1896-1920.
William Job Power, *Saltisford* (1921)

Wolston

Cave's Brewery. See also:- Brandon.

Wolvey

William Bates (1892)

Isle of Lewis

R.A.Harper Ltd, *Hall Park Brewery.* Registered November 1916. Acquired by Eley's Stafford Brewery Ltd 1924 and brewing ceased in 1928.

Other Breweries
Mrs S.J.Brown, *92 High Street* (1935)
George Cox, *Broad Street* (1910)
William Darbey, *15 Coseley Street* (1921)
George Harbach, *55 Bridge Street* (1926)
Horace Henry Harbach, *20 Market Street* (1926)
Walter William Harbach, *12 Walsall Street* (1923)
Joseph W.Marsh, *Bilston Brewery, 128 Oxford Street* (1906)
George Meese, *11 Temple Street* (1921)

Bilston

Birmingham

E.T.Allen Ltd, *Dog & Duck Inn, 180 High Street, Aston.* Home brew house. Registered December 1918. Voluntary winding up 23rd September 1921.

Ansells Brewery Ltd, *Aston Brewery, Park Road, Aston Cross.* Founded by Joseph Ansell 1857. Registered 1889 as Joseph Ansell & Sons Ltd, re-registered as above June 1901. Now a subsidiary of Carlsberg-Tetley controlling 2,400 tied houses. Aston Brewery closed 1981.

Ashted Brewery Co.Ltd, *Ashted Row.* Registered April 1880 to acquire the business of George Wilkinson & Co. Ceased brewing 1890.

Aston Manor Brewery, *173 Thimblemill Lane, Aston.* Founded May 1983. Originally owned 3 public houses which were sold to allow concentration on the take home and supermarket trade. Still brewing 1990.

Atkinson's Brewery Ltd, *Aston Park Brewery, Aston.* Founded 1855 as Atkinson Brothers. Registered March 1898. Acquired by Mitchells & Butlers Ltd 1959. No longer brewing.

Borve House Hotel Brewery, *Borve, Lewis.* Established July 1983 by James & Gregory Hughes using plant from the defunct Penrhos Brewery, Herefordshire. Ceased brewing 1989. See also:-

M.V.Beard & Sons Ltd, *Greyhound Brewery, 89 Holloway Head.* Supplied 4 public houses. Closed January 1966 and is now a Bulmer's cider house.

Birmingham & North Wales Flagon Beer Co.Ltd. Registered December 1904 to supply the domestic trade. Voluntary liquidation 23rd August 1905.

Birmingham Breweries Ltd, *King's Heath Brewery.* Registered March 1896 to acquire: Frederick Everitt, trading as Isaac Bates, King's Heath Brewery; White & Lake, West End Brewery, Bristol Street, Edgbaston and Albert Henson, East End Brewery, Nechells, with a total of 136 public houses. Brewing ceased 1900.

Birmingham Star Brewery Co.Ltd, *58 Aston Road.* Registered 30th November 1888 as William Halford & Son Ltd to acquire the business of Frank Samuel Halford. Name changed as above 23rd May 1889. Wound up 24th July 1891.

Butler's Crown Brewery Ltd, *Crown Brewery, 36/37 Broad Street.* Registered January 1895. Merged with Henry Mitchell & Co.Ltd 1898 to form Mitchells & Butlers Ltd.

Castle Brewery (Birmingham) Ltd, *Castle Brewery, Prospect Row.* Registered 20th October 1893 to acquire the business of John Richard Downes. Voluntary liquidation 4th June 1894.

City Brewery Ltd, *20/21 Cato Street North, Nechells.* Registered February 1890 as Hutton's Brewery Ltd to acquire the business of Richard Bray Hutton. Voluntary liquidation 26th March 1891 and was registered as above 14th November 1894 to acquire Hutton's Brewery Ltd and George Jerrams, Pope's Lane, Oldbury. Receiver appointed 18th May 1899.

Dare's Brewery Ltd, *Southend Brewery, Belgrave Road.* Registered August 1927 to acquire William Dare & Son. Acquired by Davenports 1961 with with 30 public houses.

Ruthven, Grampian.

Davenport's Brewery Ltd, *Bath Row.* Founded 1739. Registered November 1896 as John Davenport & Sons Brewery Ltd with 57 public houses. Registered as above June 1929. Acquired by Greenall Whitley & Co.Ltd 1986 with 106 tied houses and brewing ceased.

Edgar Evans, *Well Head Brewery, 44 Aston Lane, Perry Barr.* Merged with James Evans 1899 to form Evans Brewery Ltd which was acquired by Mitchells & Butlers Ltd 1899 with 20 public houses.

James Evans, *Perry Barr.* Merged with Edgar Evans 1899.

Joseph Forrest & Son Ltd, *192 Winson Green Road, Winson Green.* Founded by 1877. Registered 1906. Acquired by the Holt Brewery Co.Ltd 1912.

Grigg & Brettell Ltd, *51 Kyrwicks Lane, Sparkbrook.* Operated by Edward Knight before 1895 after which it was acquired by Henry Grigg. Registered 1907. Acquired by Holt Brewery Co.Ltd 1912.

Holder's Brewery Ltd, *Midland Brewery, Nova Scotia Street.* Founded before 1872. Acquired by Mitchells & Butlers Ltd 1919 and was closed in 1923.

Holt Brewery Co.Ltd, *Holt Street.* Founded by Henry Fulford c.1872. Registered February 1887 to acquire the business of the late H.C.Fulford and was reconstructed on 19th March 1896. Acquired by Ansells Brewery Ltd 1934 with 250 public houses but was not closed until 1974.

Alfred Homer Ltd, *Vulcan Brewery, Tower Road, Aston.* Registered 1898. Acquired by Mitchells & Butlers Ltd 1899.

George Jones, *Kingston Brewery, Adderley Street, Bordesley.* Acquired by Mitchells & Butlers Ltd December 1917.

Benjamin Kelsey Ltd, *71a Ashted Row.* Founded 1859. Merged with H.E.Thornley Ltd of Leamington Spa 1933 to form Thornley Kelsey Ltd. Brewing was concentrated at Leamington before 1959.

George & John Kendrick, *Engine Brewery, Brearley Street.* Acquired by the Holt Brewery Co.Ltd 1919.

King & Barton, *West End Brewery, Wrentham Street.* Acquired by Rushton's Brewery Ltd October 1911.

James Lloyd, *32 Nova Scotia Street.* Acquired by Lichfield Brewery Co. 1892.

Meade & Co.Ltd, *Perry Barr Brewery, Wellhead Lane.* Registered April 1901 to acquire the business carried on by Charles Henry Thompson, Alfred Meade and Walter Meade. Acquired the Holt Brewery Co.Ltd 1919.

Moore & Simpson Ltd, *Priory Road, Aston.* Registered 1905. Wound up 1907.

Rushton's Brewery Ltd, *Lion Brewery, 69 Aston Road North, Aston.* Registered 1898. Acquired by Ansells Brewery Ltd 1923 with about 100 public houses.

Frederick Smith Ltd, *Aston Model Brewery, 249/251 Lichfield Road, Aston.* Founded 1875. Registered February 1895. Acquired by W.Butler & Co.Ltd 1955.

Standard Brewery Co.Ltd, *27/28 Duke Street.* Registered March 1905 to acquire the Standard Brewery Co. Dissolved 19th February 1909.

Vale of Evesham Brewery Ltd, *Cato Street North.* Registered 26th July 1904 to acquire the business of Charles William Herbert Smartt. Bankrupt 1905 and was wound up 12th February 1906.

Henry Charles While, *Central Brewery, Mott Street*. Acquired by Alfred Homer Ltd 1898.

Samuel White & Son, *Bellefield Brewery, 36/40 Winson Street, Winson Green*. Acquired by John Davenport & Sons Brewery Ltd 1928.

Other Breweries

George Allen, *162 Darwin Street* (1926)
James Attwood, *65 Emily Street* (1923)
Sarah Beardmore, *116 Irving Street* (1920)
Alfred Henry Bolton, *47 Arthur Street* (1914)
William C.Bott, *41 High Street, Deritend* (1914)
George Cammerer, *104 Liverpool Street, Bordesley* (1920)
Day Brothers, *1 Hurst Street* (1892)
Charles George Dimmer, *87 New Canal Street* (1921)
William Dulley & Sons, *9 Great Colmore Street* (1892)
Edkins & Guy, *Camp Hill, Bordesley* (1910)
James Foster, *28 Garrison Lane* (1921)
John Fulford & Son, *74 Victoria Road, Aston Park* (1898)
Platt S.Gollings, *278 Highgate Road* (1921)
Frederick P.Grove, *342 Arthur Street* (1921)
J.Hamilton-Day, *Handsworth Brewery, 2 Nineveh Road* (1910) & *Sparkbrook Brewery, Stoney Lane, Sparkbrook* (1902)
Hewitson & Co, *23/26 Lancaster Street* (1898)
Charles Hoare, *152/153 Grange Road* (1923)
Hollister & Chadwick, *Handsworth Brewery, Grosvenor Road* (1892)
Mary Ellen Johnson, *57 Staniforth Street* (1923)
George William Jones, *Watery Lane* (1914)
John Lea & Sons, *Highgate Brewery, 81 Highgate Lane* (1921)
George McKenzie, *170 Brighton Road* (1926)
Thomas & Miss A.M.Mansfield, *Mansfield Road, Acocks Green* (1923)
Carteret Maule, *Brewery Street, Handsworth* (1895)
Richard Mealings, *57 Angelina Street* (1923)
Edward Middleton, *New Oscott* (1902)
Charles Herbert Morley, *59 Ravenshurst Road* (1941)
Henry A.Morton, *163 Vaughton Street* (1923)
Patrick Nally, *238 Great Lister Street* (1921)
Walter Orme, *22 Garrison street* (1923)
Catherine Perks, *158 Bromsgrove Street* (1920)
Manasseh Phillips, *Middleton Road, King's Heath* (1920)
William Procter, *White Swan Brewery, 117 Edmund Street* (1923)
Mary Roberts, *12 Watery Lane* (1923)
T.Saxton & Co, *123 Balsall Heath Road* (1914)
George Edward Slater, *17 Lower Essex Street* (1920)
William Aubrey Slim, *22 Pershore Street* (1920)
James Smith, *School Road, Yardley Wood* (1914)

William Smith, *Bath Brewery, 55 Woodcock Street* (1890)
John Stone & Son, *Anchor Brewery, 92 Ryland Road* (1910)
Edward John Thornton, *24 Beliss Street, Ladywood* (1940)
G.E.Wetton & Sons, *51 Friston Street, Ladywood* (1914)
Arthur T.Wild, *215 Watery Lane* (1920)
James Williams, *Small Heath Brewery, 74 Prince Albert Street, Small Heath* (1904)

Blackheath

Garrard Brothers, *Rowley Brewery, Long Lane*. Formed part of North Worcestershire Breweries Ltd 1896.

Other Breweries

Mrs Richard Merris, *Mincing Lane* (1914)
Mrs Emily Parkes, *Olive Street* (1921)
Edward Sturman, *392 Long Lane* (1935)
William H.Taylor, *High Street* (1921)
Isaac Troman (1940)

Bloxwich

N.F.Bird, *Crown Brewery, 6 Leamore Lane*. Founded 1864. Brewing ceased 1965 but the business was continued as bottlers owning 4 public houses and an off-licence. Acquired by Ansells Brewery Ltd 1967.

Bloxwich Brewery Co.Ltd, *Bloxwich Brewery, Elmore Green Road*. Registered August 1898. Acquired by W.Butler & Co.Ltd 1923 with 42 tied houses.

Other Breweries

Alfred Marshall, *614 Bloxwich Road* (1923)
William Parkes, *13 Elmore Row* (1920)
John Smith, *Church Street* (1921)
Harry Tolley, *Portland Street* (1921)
Jane Tolley, *Field Street* (1920)
Frank Wilkes, *13 Wolverhampton Road* (1926)

Brierley Hill

Daniel Batham & Son Ltd, *Delph Brewery*. Founded 1877 at Netherton and acquired a second brewery at Cradley 1900. Both breweries were operated until the Delph brewery was built in 1905. Registered 1941. Still brewing independently 1990 with 8 tied houses but only brewing draught beer.

Benjamin Elwell, *33 Church Street*. Formed part of the Worcestershire Brewing & Malting Co.Ltd, Kidderminster 1896.

J.P.S.Breweries Ltd, *Dennis Brewery, Brettell Lane*. Founded by 1854. Acquired from Henry Bolton by J.P.Simpkiss on 26th August 1919. See also:- Home Brewery (Quarry Bank) Ltd. A new brewery was built on the site in 1934. Registered November 1938. Merged with Johnson & Phipps Ltd of Wolverhampton 1955. Acquired by Greenall Whitley & Co.Ltd July 1985 with 15 public houses and was closed.

Home Brewery (Quarry Bank) Ltd, *Evers Street*. Founded by 1857 and was originally known as the Swan Brewery. Registered December 1903 to acquire the business of J.P.Simpkiss. At least 23 public houses. Simpkiss lost control of the brewery after a lawsuit in 1916. Closed May 1921 and was demolished February 1959.

Smith & Williams, *Town Brewery, Round Oak*. Founded 1897 by W.H.Smith who had previously used the Delph Brewery. Acquired by Julia Hanson & Sons Ltd in 1934 with 60 tied houses.

Frederick Warren, *Plough Brewery, Church Street*. Founded by 1902. Offered for auction 23rd March 1926 after the death of the owner. The brewery was not sold but the 7 public houses realised £13,900.

Other Breweries

Sarah Ann Bailey, *Buckpool* (1920)
Thomas Banks, *139 Dudley Street* (1921)
Henry Bolton, *Brettell Lane* (1920)
Alfred Dunn, *Mount Pleasant* (1923)
Edward Fletcher, *Lower Delph* (1910)
Emma Gill, *Buckpool* (1930)
John Glover, *84 High Street* (1923)
William Henry Goring, *Mill Street* (1926)
Cornelius Gorton, *1 High Street* (1920)
Harry Jeavons, *Brettell Lane* (1935)
Thomas Jeffries, *Moor Lane* (1930)
Alice Kinsell, *92 Bank Street* (1926)
Nock & Co, *East Street, Quarry Bank* (1939)
George W.Pearson, *154/155 High Street* (1926)
J.Smith, *Buckpool* (1921)
Archibald Edward Vale, *Moor Lane* (1926)
Robert H.Wood, *91 Bank Street* (1940)

Brownhills

William Roberts Brewery Ltd, *Station Brewery, High Street*. Registered 1916. Acquired by Eley's Stafford Brewery Ltd 1925 and was closed in 1928.

Coseley

Joseph Adams, *Old Bush Inn, Skidmore Road* (1962)
Alice Allen, *Old Meeting Street* (1921)
Harry Bailey, *Walbrook* (1921)
Harry Baker, *Darkhouse Lane* (1921)
William T.Bayliss, *Wood Street* (1940)
Mary Ann Bryan, *Hollywell Street* (1940)
Job Butler, *Woodcross Inn Brewery* (1935)
Ed.S.Chesworth, *Biddings Lane* (1921)
William Clift, *Hurst Road* (1921)
Isaac Fellows, *Broad Lane* (1930)
Jack Flavell, *Druids Head Inn Brewery* (1971 due to the death of Flavell)
Michael Hanrahan, *Hall Lane* (1926)
Ernest Holcroft, *19 Ladymoor Road* (1940)
Thomas A.Holmes, *Sosom*.
Thomas W.H.Meddings, *Clifton Street* (1940)
Isaac Millard, *Deepfields* (1926)
John T.Naylor, *Hurst Hill* (1921)
Clara Jane Price, *37 Walbrook Street* (1940)
Joseph Richards, *Castle Street* (1921)
Daniel Rowley, *Dark Lane* (1921)
William Tranter, junior, *Hurst Road* (1940)
James Turley, *Webb Street, Deepfields* (1920)
Albert E.Williams, *Darkhouse Lane* (1921)
John Thomas Wilson, *Broad Street* (1940)

Coventry

Home Brewed (Coventry) Ltd, *Rock Brewery, Old Church Road, Foleshill*. Registered as Michael Spencer Ltd July 1896. Re-registered 1910 as above to acquire the business carried on by A.Blair. Closed June 1913.

William John Lynch, *White Friar Model Brewery, Much Park Street/White Friar Lane*. Brewing 1912-21 and possibly until 1935.

Phillips & Marriott Ltd, *Midland Brewery, 127 Much Park Street*. Registered January 1900 to acquire Phillips & Marriott and the business of the late William Ratcliff. Acquired by Bass, Ratcliff & Gretton Ltd 1924 and was closed.

William Ratcliff, *Coventry Brewery, Leicester Road*. Acquired by Phillips & Marriott 1900.

Other Breweries

Sarah Jane Athersuch, *Recruiting Sergeant, 14 Spon Street* (1928)

Thomas Bailey, *Samson & Lion, 15 Swanswell Place* (9.10.1967)

William Henry Batchelor, *Hop Pole, Leicester Row* (1920)

Joseph Bickley, *O Rare Ben Jonson, 18 New Street* (17.7.1959)

Mary Clara Brown, *Blue Bell, 60 Greyfriars Lane* (1920)

Frederick William Burr, *Fiveways Tavern, 61 Harnall Lane* (1920)

Henry Causer, *Malt Shovel, 93 Spon End* (1920)

Chouler & Co, Acquired by the Northampton Brewery Co.Ltd (1896)

Thomas Claridge, *Lamp Tavern, 13 Cook Street* (1930)

Joseph Cross, *10 Cross Cheaping* (1920)

Florence Duggins, *51 Yardley Street, Hill Fields* (1921)

Emma E.Faulconbridge, *19 Tower Street* (1920)

Lizzie Garbutt, *Globe, 23 Albion Street, Butts* (1920)

Alfred Hewitt, *60 Castle Street* (1923)

Annie Hewitt, *35 Smithford Street* (1920)

Frederick Hewitt, *Leopard, 33 Primrose Hill Street* (1914)

Thomas Kirby, *Livery Stables, 39 New Street* (1920)

John S.Mattock, *Golden Cup, 35 Far Gosford Street* (1920)

Lucy Overton, *49 East Street* (1923)

Thomas Paybody, *13 Radford Road* (1920)

William Sagar, *Meriden Tavern, 64 New Buildings* (1920)

Mary Ann Sidwell, *26 Cromwell Street, Red Lane* (1920)

Elijah Strong, *Woolston* (1921)

George Taylor, *Townwall Tavern, Bond Street* (1920)

James Thompson, *Hope & Anchor, 38 Sherbourne Streeet* (1920)

John Thomas Thorpe, *42 New Street* (1920)

Catherine E.Twyneham, *23 Spon Street* (1930)

Arthur Wareham, *Hope & Anchor, Whitefriars Lane* (1923)

Fred Watson, *Old Chase, 43 Gosford Street* (1920)

Cradley Heath

Thomas Darby & Sons Ltd, *High Street, Old Hill.* Registered 1916. Acquired by Mitchells & Butlers Ltd 1951.

Other Breweries

Alfred Aston, *Providence Street* (1926)

Harry Bellfield, *Grainger's Lane* (1920)

Arthur H.Cockin, *Halesowen Road, Old Hill* (1930)

Henry E.Foley, *Halesowen Road* (1923)

Arthur Ernest Hadley, *Reddall Hill Road, Old Hill* (1920)

Ernest Hall, *Cradley Road* (1920)

Thomas James, *Halesowen Road, Old Hill* (1920)

Arthur Ernest Jew, *High Street,, Old Hill* (1940)

George Johnson, *Halesowen Road* (1920)

Laura L.Perry, *Reddall Hill Road, Old Hill* (1940)

Benjamin Price, *Hollybush Street* (1926)

Llew Province, *Lomey Town* (1920)

Richard L.Province, *Grainger's Lane* (1940)

James E.Stafford, *Ridding Street, Old Hill* (1920)

Frank M.Tibbetts, *King Street* (1940)

John Thomas Webb, *High Street* (1940)

Thomas Williams, *Cherry Orchard, Old Hill* (1940)

Dudley, Town Centre

Joseph Henry Davies, *Wheelwright's Arms, Castle Street, Netherton.* Sold to Mitchells & Butlers Ltd with 11 public houses on 1st June 1942.

Jack Downing, *Black Horse Brewery, Greystone Street.* Originally at the Leopard home brew house and acquired the Black Horse from the Diamond Brewery, June 1901. Sold to W.Butler & Co.Ltd January 1923 with 20-30 tied houses.

Dudley District Breweries Ltd. Registered October 1896 to acquire: the High Street Brewery, Dudley; Salt's Brewery, Kate's Hill, Dudley; the Bull's Head Brewery, Netherton and the Talbot Brewery, Smethwick. Wound up 10th June 1897.

John Foley, *Kate's Hill Brewery, Kate's Hill.* Acquired by Foley 1902 after the failure of Dudley District Breweries. Sold to Thomas Plant 1910 and brewing ceased.

Julia Hanson & Sons Ltd, *89 High Street.* Founded 1847 as a wine & spirit business in Priory Street. Acquired the Peacock Brewery September 1895. Registered October 1897. Acquired by Wolverhampton & Dudley Breweries Ltd 1943 but the brewery is still in operation 1990.

Holden's Brewery Ltd, *Hopden Brewery, George Street, Woodsetton.* Registered 1964 with 11 public houses. Still brewing independently 1990.

J.F.C.Jackson Ltd, *Diamond Brewery, 19 Cromwell Street, Kate's Hill.* Originally registered 1899 as the Diamond Brewery Co.Ltd. Re-registered as above 1916. Acquired by Darby's Brewery Ltd of West Bromwich June 1937.

Harry Jones, *Cricketer's Arms, 10 King Street.* Originally a home brew house which expanded into a 10 quarter common brewery. The business was transferred to the Purity Bottling Stores, Claughton Road in 1917 and the brewery was leased to the Diamond Brewery.

Bert and Don Millard, *The Gypsies Tent, Steppingstone Street.* Founded 1867 by George Thomas Millard as the Jolly Collier. Name changed 1871-1881. Brewing ceased December 1961. The Gypsies Tent was closed in 1980.

William Onslow, *Netherton New Brewery, Hill Street.* Founded August 1875. Brewing 1901 and was later merged with John Rolinson & Son Ltd.

Doris C.Pardoe, *Old Swan Brewery, Halesowen Road, Netherton.* Home brew house founded c.1840. Acquired by Hoskins of Leicester 1987 and was sold to the Wiltshire Brewery, Tisbury.

Thomas Plant & Co.Ltd, *Steam Brewery, Netherton.* Founded by William Round 1837 and was acquired by Thomas Plant in 1875. Registered 1901. Acquired by the Hereford & Tredegar Brewery Ltd June 1912 and was closed. Re-opened 1915. Acquired by Ansells Brewery Ltd 1936 with 63 public houses and was finally closed in 1947.

John Rolinson & Son Ltd, *Five Ways Brewery, Five Ways, Netherton.* Founded as a home brew house c.1835 and was acquired by John Rolinson by 1877. Registered July 1896. Acquired by Wolverhampton & Dudley Breweries Ltd 1925 with 59 tied houses.

Matthew Smith, *Queen's Cross Brewery, Queen's Cross.* Brewery built c.1873. Sold to H.& B.Woodhouse 1917 and brewing ceased in 1934.

Smith & Williams, *Town Brewery, Round Oak.* Partnership dissolved 1923. Acquired by Julia Hanson & Sons Ltd 1934 with 60 public houses.

George Thompson & Sons, *Dudley & Victoria Breweries, Hall Street.* Formed part of Wolverhampton & Dudley Breweries 1890.

H.& B.Woodhouse, *Alma Brewery, Hall Street.* Founded as the Traveller's Rest beerhouse c.1830. Renamed the Alma Inn 1861. Acquired by Benjamin Woodhouse 1901. Moved to the Victoria Brewery 1914 which was then renamed the Alma Brewery and moved again 1917 to the Queen's Cross Brewery. 15 public houses. Ceased brewing 1934.

Other Breweries

Albion Inn, *15 Stone Street* (1925)

Angel, *9 Castle Street* (1918)

Barley Mow Inn, *36 Constitution Hill.*

Barrel Inn, *173 High Street* (1915)

Belle Vue Inn, *21 Dock Lane.*

Bird-in-Hand, *82 Chapel Street, Netherton.*

Blue Boar, *27 Stone Street* (1937)

Blue Gates Inn, *58 Church Street* (1960)

Thomas Booth, *Red Lion Brewery, Gornalwood.* To Julia Hanson 1953

Isaac Bradley, *Gornalwood.* Acquired by the Holt Brewery Co.Ltd 1930.

Brewer's Arms, *50 Birmingham Street.* To Peter Walker c.1900.

British Oak, *91 Sweet Turf, Netherton.* To Julia Hanson (1932)

Britannia, *18 Queen's Crosss* (1942)

Britannia Inn, *96 Hall Street* (1926) Bought by Frederick Smith Ltd.

Bull's Head, *Hall Street* (1902)

California Inn, *13 George Street, Kate's Hill.* To Wolverhampton & Dudley Breweries (1920)

Castle & Falcon Hotel, *207 Wolverhampton Street.*

Castle Hotel, *253 Castle Street* (1947)

Coach & Horses, *42 King Street* (1896)

Collier's Arms, *62 Chapel Street, Netherton* (1936)

Court House Tavern, *25 New Street.*

Cross Keys, *39 Oakywell Street* (1900)

Crown Inn, *29 Crown Street.*

Duke of Sussex, *78 Stafford Street* (1916)

Duke of York, *128 Wolverhampton Street.*

Eagle Inn, *14 Dock Lane.* To Wolverhampton & Dudley Breweries 1923.

Field House Cottage, *43 Oxford Street* (1940)

Four Ways Inn, *27 Brown Street, Kate's Hill.* Ceased brewing 1941 when acquired by Wolverhampton & Dudley Breweries.

Fountain Inn, *3 Dixon's Green.* To Mitchells & Butlers (1920)

Fox Inn, *502 Wolverhampton Street.* To Julia Hanson 1946.

Freebodie's Tavern, *69 St.John's Road, Kate's Hill* (1914)

Golden Fleece, *30 Oakywell Street* (1924)

Golden Lion, *5 Simms Lane, Netherton.* To Ansells (1920)

Green Dragon, *20 King Street* (1921)

Griffin, *8 Stone Street.* To Wolverhampton & Dudley Breweries.

Hammer Inn, *56 Stafford Street.* Sold to Ansells 1938.

Hearty Good Fellow, *9 The Square, Woodside* (1938)

Hearty Good Fellow, *8 Flood Street* (1935)

Horse Shoes, *93 Hall Street* (1900)

King William, *9 Cole Street, Darby End.* To Julia Hanson (1915)

Leopard Inn, *25 High Street, Kate's Hill.* To J.F.C.Jackson (1926)

Loving Lamb, *2 High Street, Kate's Hill.* Acquired by Darby's Brewery, June 1937.

Loyal Washington, *276 Washington Street* (1906)

Malt Shovel Inn, *191 High Street* (1920)

Malt Shovel, *46 Tower Street* (1940)

Miner's Arms, *98 Salop Street.* To W.Butler & Co.Ltd (1939)

Netherton Bottling Co, *Off-licence, 49 St.John Street* (1933)

New Cottage Spring, *45 Church Street.*

New Inn, *12 Flood Street.* To Julia Hanson 1922.

New Inn, *31 High Street, Netherton* (1890)

Old Cottage Inn, *24 Simms Lane, Netherton* (1930)

Old Priory Inn, *15 New Street* (1921)

Old Struggling Man, *95 Wolverhampton Street.*

Old Windmill, *13 St.James's Terrace* (1920)

Queen's Head, *45 St.John Street, Netherton* (1935)

Parrot Inn, *30 King Street* (1930)

Peacock Hotel, *161 Upper High Street* (1895)

Plume of Feathers, *148 Upper High Street.*

Railway Tavern, *The Croft, Woodside.* Bought by Julia Hanson 1934.

Red Lion, *31 Bath Street* (1954)
Reindeer, *21 Oakeywell Street* (1901)
Reindeer, *16 Cradley Road, Netherton* (1929)
Rose & Crown, *71 Spring's Mire* (1929)
Rose & Crown, *52 Withymoor Road.* Now Ansells. (1920)
Round House, *11 Dock Lane.*
Royal Exchange, *13 Church Street* (1935)
Royal Oak, *136 Salop Street.* To W.Butler & Co.Ltd (1945)
Royal Oak, *26 Martin Hill Street* (1957)
Shoulder of Mutton, *29 Dixon's Green Road.* To W.Butler & Co.Ltd (1939)
W.Simpson, *Off-licence, 96 Wolverhampton Street* (1916)
Sir Robert Peel, *35 Salop Street.* Bought by Wolverhampton & Dudley Breweries 1941.
Star & Garter, *71 High Street, Kate's Hill* (1902)
Struggling Man, *57 Salop Street.*
Trust in Providence, *7 Washington Street* (1912)
Unicorn Spirit Vaults, *124 Salop Street* (1925)
Victoria Inn, *23 Dudley Wood.* To W.Butler & Co.Ltd 1951.
Vine Inn, *23 Flood Street.* To Julia Hanson c.1900.
Vine Inn, *42 Wolverhampton Street.*
West End Hotel, *64 Wolverhampton Street.* To W.Butler & Co.Ltd (1951)
White Horse, *62 St.Thomas's Street, Netherton.* To Ansells (1938)
White Swan, *23 Baptist End, Netherton* (1939)
Why Not Inn, *23 Abberley Street* (1946)
Wonder Inn, *52 Church Street* (1928)
Woolpack, *15 Castle Street* (1960)

Dudley, Lower Gornal

Thomas Bailey (1926)
Samuel Bracknell (1926)
Elizabeth Evans (1926)
John Evans (1926)
Arthur Fieldhouse, *Ruiton Street* (1935)
David Hyde, *Lake Street* (1930)
Eli Jones, *New Street* (1935)
Matilda Jones, *New Street* (1923)
Joseph Jukes (1920)
Thomas Malpas, *Abbey Road* (1926)
Emily Marsh, *Himley Road* (1935)
Moses Marsh (1920)
Enoch Smart (1930)
William Wakelam (1930)
John Waterfield, *Five Ways* (1920)
William Willetts, *4 Church Street* (1923)

Dudley, Pensnett

George Dunn, *Bell Street* (1920)
John Fradgley, *Church Street* (1921)
Laban Hill, *Queen Street* (1921)
James Henry Parfitt, *Common Side* (1930)

Dudley, Quarry Bank

Roland Batham, *High Street* (1940)
Samuel Mobberley, *Sheffield Street* (1920)
Clara Stevens, *166 High Street* (1935)

Dudley, Roseville

John Arthur Grange, *Castle Street* (1940)
Ruth Millard, *Ward Street* (1926)
William Millard (1920)
Eder Porter, *Ebenezer Street* (1930)
James Richards, *Ward Street* (1920)
Samuel Timmins, *Ward Street* (1940)
James Henry Yates, *Castle Street* (1935)

Dudley, Round Oak

Annie Amphlett (1930)
Herbert Bissell (1921)
Charles Frederick Moore, *Wallows Street* (1940)

Dudley, Sedgley

Howard Darby (1921)
Mary Evans (1921)
Hugh Richard Fellows, *High Street* (1920)
Sarah Hughes, *Bilston Street* (1940)
Thomas A.Lisle, *Gospel End Street* (1923)
Ada P.Marsh, *Gate Street* (1940)
Harry Palmer, *47 Bilston Street* (1920)
William Henry Rollinson, *51 High Street* (1920)
Ellen Wallins, *Gospel End Street* (1920)

Dudley, Upper Gornal

Alfred Ernest Allen (1926)
Ada E.Cartwright, *Kent Street* (1923)
Mary E.Cole (1935)
William Richard Easthope (1940)
Thomas Fellows (1921)
James C.Guest (1935)
Harry Hammond (1935)
Bert Middleton (1930)
William Naylor (1940)
William Henry Westwood (1921)

Dudley, Woodsetton

Charles Box, *Regent Street* (1935)
Walter Foster (1920)
Evan Shaw, *9 Brook Street* (1921)
Charles Turley (1926)

William Willetts, *Brook Inn Brewery, Sedgley Road.* Closed 1940 and the public house was acquired by Julia Hanson & Sons Ltd.

Halesowen

Carr & Co. (Halesowen) Ltd, *Church Street.* Closed 1906. Brewery offered for sale July 1915 under a court order.

Other Breweries
Albert William Beale, *Hasbury* (1920)
J.Bloomer & Sons, *New Road Brewery* (1910)
William J.Cartwright, *Gorsty Hill* (1930)
J.Cooper & Co.Ltd, *Peckingham Street.* Registered 1900. Closed 1938.
Clifford Grainger, *Peckingham Street* (1920)
Henry Grainger, *Birmingham Street* (1935)
Lydia Hackett, *Islington* (1920)
John D.Harris, *High Street* (1930)
Ernest John Hollies, *Peckingham Street* (1935)
Mrs Harry Hollis, *Forge Lane* (1921)
Samuel Lowe, *Gorsty Hill* (1926)
Alice Marshall, *Birmingham Street* (1926)
Edith Moore, *Birmingham Street* (1921)
James Mynett, *Cornbow* (1914)
Hannah Rollason, *Cockhead Lane* (1921)
William Shuker, *Hasbury* (1920)
George Smith, *Birmingham Street* (1920)
Edward Sturman, *Long Lane* (1920)
Percy Withers, *Birmingham Street* (1940)

Hockley Heath

Laurence Lucas, *Bluebell Brewery, Wareings Green.* Home brew house bought by the Lucas family 1901. Brewing ceased late 1968 after the death of the owner. Now a Bulmer's cider house.

Kingswinford

Arthur Thomas Allen, *13 High Street* (1935)
Joseph Brettle, *High Street* (1940)
Dick Chambers, *Market Street* (1940)
Minnie Marsh, *Green's Forge* (1923)
William H.Morgan, *Mount Pleasant Brewery* (1910)
Florence Mary Penn, *Cot Lane* (1930)
William A.White, *Summer Street* (1930)

Kinver near Stourbridge

Susannah Gatti (1940)
Esther E.Keeley (1930)
Eli Millward (1935)
Leonard H.Turner (1926)
John Henry Yates (1926)

Oldbury

John Jordan & Co, *British Queen Brewery, Birmingham Road.* Brewery closed 1920 and tied houses sold to Mitchells & Butlers Ltd.

Charles King, *Arden Grove Brewery, Langley.* Acquired by J.Nunneley & Co.Ltd of Burton-on-Trent 1894.

Showell's Brewery Co.Ltd, *Crosswells Brewery.* Registered March 1887. Also at the Brookfield Brewery, Stockport which was formed into a separate company in 1896. The London public houses were sold to Reffell's Bexley Brewery Ltd 1899. Acquired by Samuel Allsopp Ltd 1914 with 194 tied houses.

Other Breweries
Joseph Evans, *Birchfield Lane* (1921)
Hannah Hadley, *Round's Green* (1926)
William Hadley, *exors of, Bath Row Brewery* (1914)
Maria Middleton, *Birchfield Lane* (1921)
Henry George Peers junior, *7 Talbot Street* (1935)
William Round, *Park Street* (1921)
Nathaniel Sadler, *Dingle Street* (1928)
Thomas A.Sadler, *Dingle Street, Round's Green* (1926)
Samuel Sherwood, *11 Church Bridge* (1940)
Henry Swain & Co, *Albion Brewery, Tatbank Road* (1921)
Frank Ward, *Tatbank Road* (1921)

George H.Williams, *Chapel Street, Round's Green* (1926)
John Yorke, *Birmingham Street* (1923)

Shire Oak near Brownhills

Thomas Boulter & Son, *Shire Oak Brewery* (1930)

Smethwick

Cheshire's Brewery Ltd, *Windmill Brewery, Windmill Lane*. Registered October 1896. Bought the Birmingham properties of Threlfall's Brewery Co.Ltd 1898. Acquired by Mitchells & Butlers Ltd 1913.

J.W.J.Kingstone Ltd, *Summit Brewery, Great Arthur Street*. Founded 1880. Registered 1923. Brewing ceased and the brewery and 20 tied houses were sold by auction on 16th February 1928.

Henry Mitchell & Co.Ltd, *Cape Hill Brewery*. Merged with Butler's Crown Brewery Ltd 1898 to form Mitchells & Butlers Ltd.

Other Breweries
Cresswell (Smethwick) Ltd. Founded 1960.
Edward Lewis, *296 High Street* (1926)
Charles Wheeler, *375 Oldbury Road* (1921)

Solihull

William Lines, *Solihull Brewery* (1930)

Springfield

Fred H.Mason (1926)
Thomas William Williams (1926)

Stourbridge

Rowland Hill, *Angel Brewery, 37 Coventry Street*. Under the name of H.& F.Kelley when the brewery and tied houses were offered for auction 10th November 1911. Closed 1923.

Herbert Newnam & Sons Ltd, *Pedmore Road, Lye*. Acquired by Wolverhampton & Dudley Breweries Ltd 1960.

Premier Midland Ales, *Stourbridge Industrial Estate*. Founded 1988. 7 tied houses. Merged with the Pitfield Brewery London 1990 to form Pitfield's Premier Brewing Co. concentrating their brewing at Stourbridge.

North Worcestershire Breweries Ltd, *Stourbridge Brewery*. Registered May 1896 to acquire and amalgamate: the Stourbridge Brewery; the Rowley Brewery, Blackheath; White Swan Brewery, Oldbury & the Round Oak Brewery, Brierley Hill with a total of 135 public houses. Brewing was concentrated at the Stourbridge & Round Oak Breweries. Acquired by Wolverhampton & Dudley Breweries Ltd 1910.

Other Breweries
Eliza Asbury, *19 Enville Street* (1923)
James Samuel Asbury, *77 Brettell Lane, Amblecote* (1920)
James Attwood, *Upper High Street, Lye* (1921)
James Charles Attwood, *Stourbridge Road, Lye* (1920)
John Auden, *Enville Street* (1923)
Aubrey O.Bache, *Mamble Road, Wollaston* (1926)
William J.Bache, *Cherry Street* (1921)
Frederick Barlow, *Mount Street* (1930)
Joseph Bate, *Wood Street, Wollaston* (1921)
Horace James Billingham, *145 Bridgnorth Road* (1940)
Maria Billingham, *Dudley Road* (1920)
John Bridgewater, *51 Stourbridge Road, Lye* (1926)
Francis Brooks, *Worcester Road, West Hagley* (1935)
Jeremiah Brooks, *Talbot Road, Lye* (1920)
Joseph Brooks, *New Road* (1923)
Mary Ann Brooks, *Pedmore Road, Lye* (1930)
Thomas Bywater, *King William Street, Amblecote* (1930)
Alfred Harry Cook, *Upper High Street, Lye* (1921)
Alfred Henry Cook, *Talbot Street, Lye* (1940)
Esther Cook, *Bromley Road, Lye* (1910)
James Cook, *Pedmore Road, Lye* (1926)
Samuel Cook, *Careless Green, Lye* (1940)
James Henry Cox, *Stourbridge Road, Lye* (1920)
Richard Cox, *56/57 Brettell Lane, Amblecote* (1920)
Charles Croxton, *14 Worcester Road* (1921)
Isaac T.Digger, *40 Enville Street* (1921)
Henrietta Evans, *Old Swinford* (1940)
Edward Fletcher, *High Street, Amblecote* (1926)
Isaac Fletcher, *Audnam* (1926)
Jeremiah Guest, *Upper High Street, Lye* (1920)
Daniel W.Hale, *49 Church Street* (1923)
James Higgs, *Coventry Street* (1940)
Benjamin Alfred Hill, *The Ridge, Wollaston* (1935)
Albert Hipkiss, *Queen's Brewery, Enville Street* (1933)
Frederick Hobson, *Belmont Road, Lye* (1921)
Isabella Hodgetts, *Careless Green, Lye* (1921)
William Hughes, *58 High Street* (1926)
Annie Jackson, *Stourbridge Road, Lye* (1921)
James Jeffries, *Hagley Road, Old Swinford* (1940)
George Johnson, *High Street, Lye* (1926)
Jesse Lashford, *24 Lion Street* (1926)
William Maiden, *Shepherd's Brook, Lye* (1921)
Frank J.Matthew, *Church Street* (1940)
Frank Matthews, *75 Enville Street* (1940)
Esther Maybury, *Orchard Lane, Lye* (1921)
Bert Middleton, *Stamber Mill* (1940)
William Miles, *27 & 49 Enville Street* (1940)
David Millward, *168 High Street* (1940)
Henrietta Moorcroft, *107 Worcester Street* (1940)
Thomas Newey, *2 Bald's Lane, Lye* (1940)
Edward Onions, *Birmingham Road* (1921)
Thomas Pagett, *27 High Street* (1923)
Thomas Pardoe, *113 Stourbridge Road, Lye* (1935)
Emily Parkes, *Heath* (1923)
Caleb Parrish, *Skeldings Lane, Lye* (1920)
Joseph Pearshouse, *Hayes Lane, Lye* (1921)
John & Horace G.Pearson, *36 Bridgnorth Street* (1921)
Mrs L.Penn, *Cross Walks Brewery, Cross Walk, Lye* (1956)
John Henry Perry, *Green Lane, Lye* (1921)

John N.Rhodes, *Pedmore Road, Lye* (1921)
John Thomas Roper, *Angel Street* (1926)
Thomas Sparrow, *91d Swinford* (1930)
John Henry Thornes, *Old Swinford* (1926)
U.Tromans, *Stourbridge Road, Lye* (1921)
James Thomas Walters, *Park Street, Lye* (1940)
Adam Wassell, *Heath Lane, Old Swinford* (1935)
Frederick Webster, *78 Brettell Lane, Amblecote* (1926)
Henry White, *Pedmore Road, Lye* (1920)
Walter H.Wooldridge, *14 New Road* (1930)
Esther Worrall, *79 Lower High Street, Amblecote* (1940)
Jabez Wylde, *Upper High Street, Lye* (1920)

Tipton

Old Lion Brewery Ltd, *140 Park Lane West*. Registered April 1895. Acquired by Peter Walker (Warrington & Bolton) Ltd. March 1898.

John Seedhouse & Sons Ltd, *Seven Stars Brewery, High Street, Prince's End*. Private company registered 1912. Ceased brewing after 1960.

Other Breweries
Alice Allsopp, *Groveland Road, Dudley Port* (1923) & *62 Park Lane West* (1920)
Arthur Bagnall, *28 Ocker Hill Road* (1923)
George Challinor, *186 Dudley Port* (1923)
Isaac Chater, *54 Wood Street* (1920)
Albert H.Clarke, *Star Brewery, 176 Horseley Heath* (1920)
William Henry Cox, *High Street* (1921)
Ernest Day, *12 Dudley Port* (1921)
Samuel Edwards, *6 Lock Side* (1920)
Arthur A.Fellows, *194 Bloomfield Road* (1923)
Robert Henry Fitzsimons, *Canal Street* (1923)
Benjamin Garbutt, *4 High Street, Prince's End* (1935)
William George, *45/46 Burnt Trees* (1940)
Sidney T.Gould, *49 Alexandra Road* (1940)
George Griffiths, *33 High Street* (1921)
Eliza Ann Hill, *81 Bloomfield Road* (1535)
Elizabeth Hunstone, *Upper Church Street* (1935)
Susan Hunt, *56 Owen Street* (1921)
Charles Jackson, *10/11 Waterloo Street East* (1920)
Samuel G.Jones, *Sedgley Road West* (1920)
Harry Lyndon, *18 Waterloo Street* (1920)
Alfred Mander, *13a Walton Street* (1940)
Elizabeth Middleton, *37 Bloomfield Road* (1923)
James Mills, *26 Hurst Lane* (1923)
Ann Morris, *Coneygree Road* (1930)
Harry Onions, *118 Horseley Heath* (1920)
Thomas Henry Palmer, *40 High Street, Prince's End* (1920)
Frederick Plant, *Upper Church Lane* (1921)
Alfred Purnell, *1 Lower Green* (1930)
Francis Rhodes, *54 Bloomfield Road* (1923)
William Rich, *51 High Street, Prince's End* (1935)
Thomas Henry Scriven, *74 Park Lane West* (1935)
A.& J.Sherwood, *Beehive Brewery, Lower Green* (1939)
Florence Sirrell, *Brown Lion Street* (1935)
Herbert Stanford, *29 Victoria Street* (1930)
Josiah James Stevenson, *Horseley Heath* (1921)
Mrs J.Summers, *116 High Street, Prince's End* (1940)
Thomas Taylor, *36 Union Street* (1920)
Albert E.Turner, *2 Sedgley Road East* (1921)
Ellen Walford, *7 Park Lane West* (1921)
Elizabeth Walker, *10 Canal Street* (1940)
John Thomas Walker, *38 Coppice Street* (1920)
John Whitehouse, *Park Lane West* (1902)
Charles Williams, *75 Union Street* (1923)

Wall Heath

William A.Kinsey, *Albion Street* (1930)
John Solari, *High Street* (1935)

Walsall

Arthur Beebee Ltd, *Malt Shovel Brewery, 130 Sandwell Street.* Registered January 1910. Acquired by the Highgate-Walsall Brewery Co.Ltd. 1924.

Butts Brewery Ltd, *46 Butts Street.* Registered February 1920 to acquire the Butts Inn with brewery attached and two other public houses. Voluntary liquidation October 1929.

Highgate-Walsall Brewery Co.Ltd, *Lodge Road.* Registered August 1898. Acquired by Mitchells & Butlers Ltd August 1939 with 30 pubs but the brewery is still in operation 1990.

John Lord, *Town Brewery, Shortacre Street.* Acquired by Mitchells & Butlers Ltd August 1939.

Rushall Brewery Ltd, *Rushall.* Registered March 1905 as the Old Rushall Brewery Ltd. New company registered as above April 1906. Ceased trading December 1915.

Twist's Brewery Ltd, *White Horse Brewery, 92 Wolverhampton St.* Private company registered April 1943. Acquired by Atkinson's Brewery Ltd 1950 with 20 public houses.

Walsall & District Clubs Brewery Ltd, *Daw End, Rushall.* Formed as the Walsall & District Clubs Co-operative Brewing Society c.1920 and was known as such until 1947. Acquired by Charrington & Co.Ltd 1960.

Other Breweries

Sarah Ann Allsopp, *33 Oxford Street* (1920)
William Annakin, *29 Hill Street* (1926)
Benjamin Baggott, *31 Dudley Street* (1926)
Henry Bateman, *Walsall Wood* (1921)
Richard J.Bayley, *126 Stafford Street* (1923)
Isaac Beebee, *38 Day Street* (1921)
Joseph Armitage Brook, *27 Butt Street* (1920)
J.W.Brooks, *17 Lysways Street* (1920)
Alfred Brown, *15 Caldmore Green* (1926)
Emma Brown, *58 New Street* (1926)
Rose Bull, *106 Stafford Street* (1940)
Walter Burgess, *4 High Street* (1926)
Sarah Ann Butler, *30 Newhall Street* (1923)
Edward Challinor, *26 Pleck Road* (1921), *17 Bank Street* (1920)
William Challinor, *87 Wisemore* (1920)
James Cleobury, *143 Portland Street* (1920)
David Cooper, *9 Green Lane, Birchills* (1921)
Norman S.Dawson, *Watering Trough Inn, 90 Ablewell Street* (195
Stephen Dawson, *1 Bottlane* (1920)
Charles W.Done, *3 Ryecroft Street* (1921)
Hannah Green, *19 Bridgeman Street* (1935)
Kate Hawley, *20 Pool Street* (1923)
Daniel Herbert & Edward Harrison, *Laburnums Brewery, Rushall* (1920)
John Hill, *54 Lower Rushall Street* (1920)
Horace Holmes, *193 Stafford Street* (1926)
Samuel E.Holmes, *Windmill Brewery, Bath Street* (1937)
Sydney John Holmes, *38 George Street* (1926)
William Lane, *84 Bloxwich Road* (1921)
William O.Letts, *101 Lichfield Street* (1930)
Thomas Burdett Lowe, *7 Windmill Street* (1920), *23 Lower Walhouse Street* (1940)
Arthur Marshall, *11/12 Windmill Street* (1930)
Lillian Marshall, *337 Green Lane* (1921)
Ada Mills, *44 Lower Hall Lane* (1930)
Charles Naylor, *8 Orlando Street* (1921)
David Noake, *30 Green Lane* (1921)
Joseph Pagett, *352 Pleck Road* (1920)
William Alfred Payner, *22 Tantarra Street* (1923)
George Place, *Blue Lane West* (1920)
Thomas Powell, *33 Lower Hall Lane* (1921)
Thomas Roberts, *269 Green Lane* (1926)
Arthur Shevyn, *16 Hill street* (1923)
George Sidwell, *37 Bridgeman Street* (1923)
Abraham Smith, *2 Regent Street, Pleck* (1920)
Emma Smith, *34 Queen Street* (1920)

Leonard Smith, *19 Stafford Street* (1935)
Ann Thomas, *109 Wolverhampton Street* (1921)
Frederick W.A.Thomas, *2 Green Lane, Birchills* (1935)
Edward Toon, *81 Lordstreet* (1921)
John Toon, *52 Dudley Street* (1923)
William Walkerdine, *36 Duncalfe Street* (1923)
J.Whitehouse & Son (1920)
Doris R.Wilcox, *173 Blue Lane West* (1935)
Albert E.Wood, *10 Paddock Lane* (1923)
Annie Yates, *39 Bank Street* (1923)

Wednesbury

Hickman & Pullen Ltd, *High Bullen.* Private company registered July 1918 to acquire the business of Bernard Thomas Hickman. 5 tied houses. Receiver appointed January 1927.

Other Breweries

Alfred Blakemore, *Darlaston Road, King's Hill* (1921)
Thomas Butler, *89 Mill Street, King's Hill* (1926)
Henry Williams Clifton, *King's Hill* (1920)
Arthur Darby, *Piercey Street, Newtown* (1930)
John Dayman, *Elwell Street* (1920)
Arthur Fieldhouse, *Wood Green Road* (1930)
Harry Hodgkiss, *Oxford Street* (1923)
Louisa Hughes, *139/140 Darlaston Road* (1923)
John Lacey, *11 Bilston Road* (1921)
Nicholas Edmund Lacey, *Portway Road* (1920)
Joseph Maloney, *Woods Bank, Moxley* (1921)
Millward Brothers, *Lea Brook* (1910)
Thomas William Nicholls, *Trouse Lane* (1920)
Sarah Onions, *14 Camp Street* (1940)
George Peters, *Dudley Street* (1921)
Edward Phillips, *Dale Street* (1906)
Isaiah Platts, *74 Darlaston Road, King's Hill* (1921)
Mary Ricketts, *100 Holyhead Road* (1923)
Emily Rogers, *King's Hill* (1920)
George W.Till, *New Street* (1920)
Fred Wheale, *Queen Street, Moxley* (1921)
Robert Whitehall, *Franchise Street* (1940)
Mary L.Whittaker, *56 Russell Street* (1920)
Harry Howard Wilkes, *Old Park Road* (1923)
William Winsper, *47 Foster Street* (1921)
Alfred Woodcock, *Elwell Street, Newtown* (1940)
Ernest Woodhall, *Holyhead Road* (1940)

Wednesfield

Joseph Beech, *Wood End* (1940)
Ernest John Gregory, *High Street* (1940)
Robert Thomas Griffiths, *Lichfield Road* (1923)
Wallace Johnson Gumbley, *Church Street* (1923)
James Howe, *High Street* (1930)
Richard T.Williams, *High Street* (1930)

West Bromwich

George Arnold & Co.Ltd, *Dartmouth Park Brewery, Dartmouth Street.* Registered 1919. Merged with Henry Bates 1924 to form Arnold & Bates Ltd. Acquired by Darby's Brewery Ltd 1928.

Henry Bates, *Sponwell Brewery, Spon Lane.* Merged with George Arnold & Co.Ltd 1924 to form Arnold & Bates Ltd.

William Bowen Ltd, *Cross Inn Brewery, 2 Oldbury Road, Greets Green.* Private company registered March 1927. Acquired by W.Butler & Co.Ltd 1945.

Darby's Brewery Ltd, *Dunkirk Brewery, 6 Whitehall Road, Greets Green.* Founded 1894. Registered 1923. Acquired by Mitchells & Butlers Ltd 1951 with over 100 public houses.

Thomas Oliver Ltd, *Sandwell Brewery, Walsall Street.* Acquired by W.Butler & Co.Ltd 1945.

Arthur James Price, exors of, *Lewisham Brewery, 43 High Street.* Acquired by Holder's Brewery Ltd May 1908 with about 40 tied houses.

Samuel Woodhall Ltd, *High Street Brewery, 140 High Street.* Founded 1874. Private company registered September 1904. Closed 1937.

Other Breweries

Frank Archer, *Hall Green* (1921)
Charles Bailey, *27 Dartmouth Street* (1926)
Emma Brain, *Great Bridge Street* (1920)
T.Brennand, *Malt House Brewery, Bratt Street* (1930)
Joseph Cox, *Albert Street* (1926)
Enoch Dabbs, *Harvills Hawthorn* (1914)
James Downing, *73 John Street* (1923)
Thomas Edwards, *29 All Saint's Street* (1926)
George Faulkner, *45 Lyndon Street* (1920)
Sarah Hale, *79 Moor Street* (1920)
Annie Hampson, *Holloway Bank* (1935)
Edwin Holden, *Swan Village* (1920)
William Hollyhead, *Union Street* (1920)
Susannah Hyde, *Swan Village* (1920)
Harry Jones, *Hill Top* (1921)
Joseph Jones, *Boat Inn Brewery, Gold's Hill* (1920)
Thomas Moorhouse, *Hargate Lane* (1921)
Joseph Arthur Parker, *58 Bull Street* (1935)
George Parkes, *Stoney Lane* (1920)
Frederick Ernest Perks, *62 Harvills Hawthorn* (1926)
Walter Randall, *Gold's Green* (1926)
Spencer's Phoenix Brewery
James Stanton, *Braybrook Street* (1935)
Florence Stockley, *Hill Top* (1921)
William Twist, *150 Union Street* (1920)
Joseph Whitehouse, *23/25 Ryder Street* (1920)
Thomas Wright, *Horton Street* (1920)

Willenhall

West Midlands Working Men's Club Brewery Co.Ltd, *150 Walsall Road.* Registered 1920 to acquire Henry Mills Old Oak Brewery. Closed 1931.

Other Breweries

Thomas Allen, *86 Walsall Street* (1926)
William Booker, *The Crescent* (1921)
John Brooks, *New Invention* (1921)
George Deans, *Lane Head, Short Heath* (1921)
Archibald Fenn, *Lane Head, Short Heath* (1921)
George Henry Harbach, *118 St.Ann's Road* (1920)
Randle Hobley, *57 Walsall Street* (1930)
Emily Lashford, *Temple Bar* (1926)
Sefus Lowbridge, *93 Coltham Road* (1923)
Frederick William Minors, *Cross Street* (1920)
Frederick Turberville, *Lane Head, Short Heath* (1923)
Elizabeth Watkins, *2 Wednesfield Road* (1920)
Samuel Whitehouse, *2 Water Glade* (1921)

Wolverhampton

William Butler & Co.Ltd, *Springfield Brewery.* Founded 1840. Registered April 1891. Acquired by Mitchells & Butlers Ltd 1960. Brewery scheduled for closure 1991.

James Cahill, *Swan Brewery, St.Matthew's Street, Heath Town.* Acquired by W.Butler & Co.Ltd 1919.

George Hill, *48 & 182 Park Street South, Blackenhall.* Acquired by Atkinson's Brewery Ltd 1919.

Johnson & Phipps Ltd, *Lichfield Street.* Merged with J.P.Simpkiss & Son Ltd 1946 to form J.P.S.Breweries Ltd. The brewery was closed due to redevelopment.

Lamsdale & Eccleston Ltd, *Retreat Street.* Registered May 1905 to acquire the business of Lamsdale & Eccleston with 8 public houses. Receiver appointed 23rd October 1908. Dissolved 14th December 1917.

Demolition of Taylor Walker's, Limehouse Brewery in the mid 1960s.

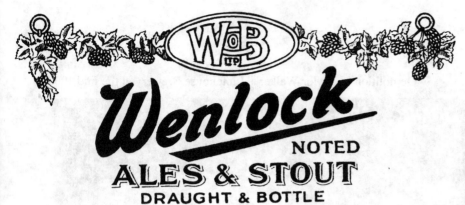
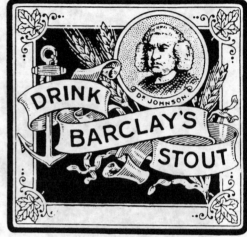

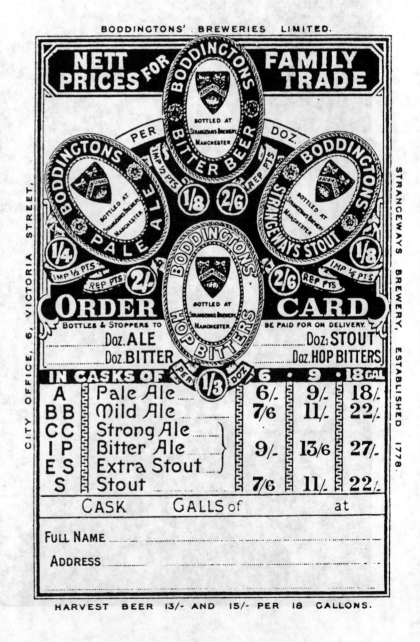

Frank Myatt Ltd, *West End Brewery, Raglan Street.* Founded 1900 at the Cross Keys public house by John Francis. Registered December 1900 as the Midland Home-Brewing Co.Ltd. The premises became too small and the Albany Brewery was acquired. Name changed to Frank Myatt & Co.Ltd August 1902. In 1909 the business was sold to Eley's (Stafford) Brewery Ltd. Myatt then founded another home brew house at the West End Inn and the Midlands public houses of the Manchester Brewery Co.Ltd were acquired. Took over Old Wolverhampton Breweries Ltd 1919 with 124 tied houses and was registered as above. Acquired by the Holt Brewery Co.Ltd 1927 with 94 public houses. Closed 1928.

Old Wolverhampton Breweries Ltd, *South Staffs Brewery, Market Street.* Registered 1910 to acquire J.& J.Yardley Ltd & I.Yardley & Sons of Bloxwich and Darlaston and the South Staffordshire Brewery Co.Ltd of Wolverhampton, with a total of 134 public houses. Acquired by Frank Myatt Ltd 1919.

Penn Brewery Co.Ltd, *Penn Wood Common Brewery.* Registered October 1887 to acquire the business of Williams & Empson. Acquired by the Burton Brewery Co.Ltd 1897. The brewery was sold to the Wolverhampton District Brewery Ltd August 1899.

Rogers & Calcutt Ltd, *70 Steelhouse Lane.* Registered 1920 to acquire the business of John Rogers. Acquired by Atkinson's Brewery Ltd 1923.

Thomas Russell Ltd, *Great Western Brewery, Great Western Street.* Founded 1877. Registered 1900. Acquired by W.Butler & Co.Ltd 1932 with 14 tied houses and was closed.

Shelton, *Queen's Arms, 10 Graizley Row.* Home brew house. Brewing ceased 1959 and was acquired by Ansells in 1964.

Staffordshire United Breweries Ltd, *Market Street.* Registered October 1896. Dissolved 22nd December 1903.

Wolverhampton & Dudley Breweries Ltd, *Victoria Brewery, Wesley Street, Bradley.* Registered May 1890 to amalgamate: Banks's & Co, Park Brewery; C.C.Smith, Fox Brewery, Wolverhampton, and George Thompson & Sons, Dudley & Victoria Breweries, Dudley, with a total of 193 public houses. Still independent 1990 with 800 tied houses.

Wolverhampton District Brewery Ltd, *Victoria Brewery, Wesley Street, Bradley.* Registered March 1898 as the Bradley Brewery Co.Ltd to acquire Peck & Kerrison. New company registered as above November 1898. Dissolved 18th November 1902.

Other Breweries

Joseph Adams, *Skidmore Road, Bradley* (1930)
Cyril T.Brewster, *15 Lewis Street* (1926)
William Howard Broome, *194 Wolverhampton Road, Heath town* (1926)
Richard Brown, *Grove Street, Heath Town* (1902)
Catherine Cartwright, *Tettenhall Wood* (1920)
Jacob Cartwright, *Tettenhall Wood New Brewery* (1920)
George William Chilton, *14 St.Mark's Street* (1921)
Louis Connolly, *Grapes Brewery, Chapel Ash* (1914)
George William Crane, *167 Horseley Fields* (1920)
John Ignatius Cunningham, *67/68 Moore Street* (1906)
Aubrey Cupiss, *325 All Saints Road* (1921)
Bernard Dagnan, *17 Inkerman Street* (1923)
Thomas Fieldhouse, *Wright Street, Bradley* (1920)

William Henry Garnett, *227 Coleman Street* (1920)
Arthur Edward George, *Salop Street, Bradley* (1920)
Henry George, *Cross Street, Bradley* (1921)
Francis Gill, *19 Piper's Row* (1923)
Joseph Griffiths, *Salop Street, Bradley* (1921)
Henry John Haddock, *58 Wulfrun Street* (1926)
Harmer & Co.(1912) Ltd, *Midland Brewery, Bilston Road* (1917)
William John Hawkes, *7 Cross Street, Bradley* (1940)
Harry Instone, *15 Bishop Street* (1923)
Betsy Jeavons, *Bank Street, Bradley* (1920)
Albert Henry Johnson, *1 Moor Street South* (1920)
George Jones, *Tettenhall Road* (1921)
Henry Kent, *28 Great Hampton Street* (1926)
Charlotte Lewis, *32 Eagle Street* (1923)
Anne E.Lockley, *40 Ash Street* (1935)
Joseph Martin, *21 Franchise Street* (1940)
John McDonald, *21 Stafford Street* (1923)
Meridale Brewery Co, *Meridale Street* (1914)
William Moseley, *132 Meridale Street* (1940)
Daniel Paul, *74 Hill Street, Bradley* (1930)
Alfred Richard Perry, *50 Salop Street* (1930)
Thomas Picken, *20 Wharf Street* (1920)
John E.Preston, *102 Lower Stafford Street* (1921)
Edward Shore, *10 Cartwright Street* (1935)
Elijah Stott, *17 Navigation Street* (1920)
Thomas Ward, *Skidmore Row, Bradley* (1926)
Charles Webberley, *8 Pearson Street* (1920)
Reuben Whitehouse, *88 Great Brick Kiln Street* (1923)
Samuel Richard Whitehouse, *20 Pountney Street* (1920)
F.Joe Zeller & Son, *434 Dudley Road* (1910)

Wombourn

William Jones (1920)

Wordsley

Wordsley Brewery Co.Ltd, *Brewery Street.* Registered March 1896. Ceased trading 4th December 1906.

Other Breweries

Thomas J.Banks, *Brewery Street* (1920)
Jane Dalrymple, *The Green* (1920)
Richard W.Griffin, *High Street* (1923)
William H.Morgan, *The Green* (1920)
William Nicholls, *High Street* (1926)
Albert E.Parrish (1940)
Joseph Price (1921)
Andrew Smart, *The Green* (1940)
William A.Thompson (1921)
William H.Walters, *Brierley Hill Road* (1921)

WILTSHIRE

Amesbury

Thomas Chivers, *Bell Inn* (1902)

Avebury

W.S.Butler, *West Kennett Brewery.* Acquired by the Stroud Brewery Co.Ltd 1922 with 16 tied houses.

Barford St.Martin

Alonso Scailes, *Dragon Brewery* (1935)

Box

David Milson, *Box Hill Brewery* (1926)
Edward S.Pinchin, *Box Brewery.* Sold to Usher's Wiltshire Brewery Ltd, with 6 public houses for £10,000 July 1924. Brewery converted into flats 1927.
Ralph Ponting (1920)

Bradford-on-Avon

William Robert Harding, *King's Arms Brewery* (1898)
S.Ruddle & Son, *Bravon Brewery, 6 Silver Street.* Acquired by Usher's Wiltshire Brewery Ltd 1924 with 12 tied houses.

G.& T.Spencer's Brewery Ltd, *Whitehead's Lane.* Registered April 1889. Acquired by Usher's Wiltshire Brewery Ltd 1913 with 58 public houses and closed.

Wilkins Brothers & Hudson Ltd, *Newtown Brewery.* Registered April 1897. Acquired by Usher's Wiltshire Brewery Ltd 1920 with 50 tied houses.

Broad Town

Samuel Hart, exors of (1910)

Bromham

F.A.Cripps, *Bromham Brewery.* Acquired by Wadworth & Co.Ltd 1896.

Bulkington

John Axford (1910)

Burbage

Henry Charles Norris (1920)

Calne

John Lindsay Duck, *Cherhill* (1921)
George Harris Holley & Sons, *London Road Brewery, 85 London Road* (1935)
Arthur Milton Portch, *Lansdowne Brewery* (1930)

Charlton

Stag Brewery. Acquired by Morgan & Bladworth of Warminster 1894.
Edward James Witchell (1920)

Chippenham

Dowding & Son, *Chippenham Brewery, Causeway/London Road*. Offered for auction 10th June 1913 and was bought by Wilkins Brothers & Hudson Ltd with 5 tied houses.
Job Franklin, *River Street* (1920)
Lion Brewery (Chippenham) Ltd, *Market Place*. Founded before 1884. Registered 6th June 1904. Receiver appointed 15th July 1908 and was acquired by Usher's Wiltshire Brewery Ltd. Wound up 31st December 1918.
Richard Slade & Sons, *Union Road*. Acquired by Bristol Brewery Georges & Co.Ltd 1926 and was closed.
Charles James Wilks, *New Road*. Acquired by Richard Slade & Sons 1906.

Corsham

Thomas P.Stevens, *Pickwick Brewery*. Acquired by Wilkins Brothers & Hudson Ltd 1896.

Devizes

Thomas A.Berry, *77 New Park Street* (1894)
J.F.& H.S.Humby, *Southbroom Brewery, The Green (also known as the Volunteer Arms Brewery)*. Acquired by Wadworth & Co.Ltd 1889.
Charles Jones, *Hare and Hounds Street* (1920)
Charles William Phipp, *Crown Brewery, Three Crowns, 25 Maryport Street*. A home brew house acquired by Wadworth & Co.Ltd 1919.
Wadworth & Co.Ltd, *Northgate Brewery, Northgate Street*. Founded 1875 when Henry Alfred Wadworth bought the Northgate Brewery founded 1837. Registered 1889. Still operating independently 1990 with 146 public houses.

East Dean

William Thomas Langridge (1910)

East Tytherton

Thomas Seager Rogers (1895)

Fonthill Gifford

Maurice Benjafield (1914)

Great Bedwyn

Charles Smallbones (1902)

Highworth

J.Wadley & Co, *Sun Brewery*. Acquired by Usher's Wiltshire Brewery Ltd 1918 with 17 tied houses.

Hilmarton

George Nelson Hobbs (1914)

Kington St.Michael

S.J.Perrett (1930)

Lacock

F.J.Kingsford. Acquired by J.H.& H.Blake Ltd of Trowbridge 1897. Brewery sold to a Melksham builder for £200 March 1924. Brewery still standing 1990.

Langley Burrell

Ralph Pearce, *Langley Brewery*. Acquired by Usher's Wiltshire Brewery Ltd November 1927. Brewery buildings still extant, situated behind the Brewery Arms public house.

Longbridge Deveril

William Henry Dufosee (1920)

Malmesbury

Duck & Co, *Cross Hayes Brewery, Silver Street*. Acquired by the Stroud Brewery Co.Ltd 1920 with 22 public houses.

Charles Richard Luce, *Mill & Abbey Breweries*. Acquired by the Stroud Brewery Co.Ltd 1912 with 42 tied houses and was closed. The Abbey Brewery is still standing, having being converted into offices 1989/90.
Joseph Moore, *Abbey Row* (1914)

Manningford Bohun

Rosa Peacock (1910)

Marden

George Herbert Hibberd (1902)

Market Lavington

Norman Neate (1923)

Marlborough

Arthur M.Adams, *Marlborough Brewery, High Street*. Brewery and 8 public houses offered for auction 19th September 1911 and were sold to Usher's Wiltshire Brewery Ltd.
Charles Henry Leader, *High Street* (1898)
Sarah Mansell, *111 High Street* (1902)

Melksham

James Arlcombe, *King's Arms Hotel* (1898)
Mole's Brewery (Wayward Ltd), *Merlin Way, Bowerhill*. Founded 1982. Still brewing 1990 with one tied house; the Rising Sun, Bowden Hill, Lacock.

Mere

Tom J.Norris (1923)

Netheravon

Bunce's Brewery, *The Old Mill, Mill Road*. Founded 1984 by Tony Bunce. Still brewing 1990 supplying the free trade.
T.W.Hussey & Son, *Netheravon Brewery*. Offered for auction 19th June 1913 with 23 tied houses. The brewery was withdrawn but the public houses were sold to Strong & Co.Ltd for £28,475.
John J.Sheppard (1920)

North Bradley

Edwin George Watts (1910)

Salisbury

W.Fawcett & Son, *35 Endless Street*. Acquired by the Lamb Brewery Co. of Frome in 1912 with 6 tied houses. Now the Salisbury Arms public house.
John Folliott & Sons, *Old George Steam Brewery, Rollestone Street*. Acquired by Usher's Wiltshire Brewery Ltd 1919. Brewhouse & site redeveloped 1989.

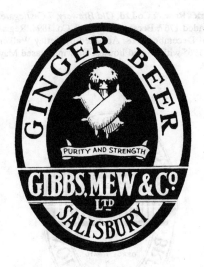

Gibbs, Mew & Co.Ltd, *Anchor Brewery, Milford Street.* Founded at the Swan, Haslemere, Surrey *c.*1750. George Bridger Gibbs became a partner in Facett's Brewery 1838 and moved to the Anchor Brewery in 1858. Registered May 1898 to acquire Bridger Gibbs & Son and Herbert Mew & Co. Still independent 1990 with 185 tied houses.

James Edward Holly, *Albion Brewery, Quidhampton.* Brewery for auction 29th September 1891 with the White Horse, Quidhampton; Victoria Arms, Wilton and the Ship Inn, Burcombe.

Hop-Back Brewery, *Wyndham Arms, Estcourt Road.* Home brew house founded by John Gilbert 1987. Still in operation 1990.

Other Breweries

Samuel Dear, *Three Crowns Brewery, West Harnham* (1902)

John Lovibond & Sons Ltd, *St.Anne's Brewery.* See also:- Greenwich, London.

James Millard, *Fisherton Street* (1892)

Harriett Norton, *7 Ivy Street* (1892)

William Henry Stanley, *Fisherton Street Brewery* (1906)

Alfred D.Stroyan, *King's Head Brewery.* Receiving order made December 1890.

Shaw

Taylor & Co, *Shaw Brewery.* Receiving order made 1911 against George Gingell Taylor trading as Taylor & Co. Now a private house 1990.

Shrewton

Thomas Herbert Knight (1892)

Slaughterford

Little & Sons, *Slaughterford Brewery.* Partnership dissolved 1917. Brewing ceased 1939.

Steeple Aston

Howard John Langley (1923)

Swindon

Archers Ales Ltd, *London Street.* Founded June 1979 by Mark Wallington. Still brewing 1990 with 3 tied houses.

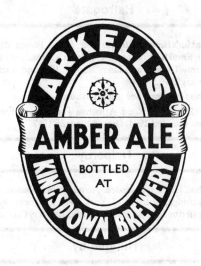

J.Arkell & Sons Ltd, *Kingsdown Brewery, Upper Stratton.* Founded 1843 by John Arkell at Lower Stratton. Present brewery built in 1861. Registered December 1927. Still brewing independently 1990 with 69 public houses.

R.B.Bowly & Co.Ltd, *North Wiltshire Brewery, 10/12 High Street.* Registered 1899. Acquired by H.& G.Simonds Ltd 1945 with 41 public houses and was closed.

Godwin Brothers Ltd, *Belmont Brewery, Devizes Road.* Registered October 1907. Acquired by Wadworth & Co. in 1938 and brewing ceased.

William Pound & Co, *Stratton St.Margaret.* Merged with Howard Horsell of Wootton Bassett in 1893 to form the Swindon & North Wilts Breweries Ltd which was dissolved on 24th December 1907.

Tisbury

F.H.S.& T.W.Styring, *Wiltshire Brewery & Marnhull, Dorset.* Founded 1868. Acquired by Eldridge, Pope & Co.Ltd in 1913 and the Marnhull brewery and 5 tied houses were sold to Hall & Woodhouse Ltd 1937.

Tisbury Brewery, *Old Brewery, Church Street.* Founded 1980. Closed April 1985. Occupied the premises formerly used by the concern above.

Wiltshire Brewery, *Stonehenge Brewery, Church Street.* Founded September 1985 as successors to to the above concern. Still brewing 1990 under the control of the United Breweries of India with 11 tied houses.

Trowbridge

J.H.& H.Blake Ltd, *Union Street.* Registered August 1897. Acquired by Usher's Wiltshire Brewery Ltd 1922 with 49 public houses and was closed.

Walter Pearce, *22 Silver Street.* Brewery and 2 public houses sold to Frome United Breweries 10th November 1905 for £5,850.

Usher's Wiltshire Brewery Ltd, *Wiltshire Brewery, Back Street.* Founded 1824. Registered April 1889. Merged with Watney Mann Ltd. May 1960 and was renamed Usher's Brewery Ltd 1964. Brewery still in operation 1990 following a management buy-out.

Warminster

Bartlett & Co.Ltd, *High Street.* Acquired by the Anglo-Bavarian Brewery Co.Ltd 1898 and was sold to Usher's Wiltshire Brewery Ltd 1920 with 44 tied houses and was closed.

Morgan & Bladworth, *Silver Street.* Acquired by the Anglo-Bavarian Brewery Co.Ltd 1898.

Charles Price, *West Street.* Offered for sale 20th August 1904 and was bought by Fussell & Sons Ltd 1912.

Other Breweries

Arthur Shepherd, *Deveril Road Common* (1921)

Warminster Brewery Co, *East Street* (1914)

West Dean

George Beauchamp (1892)

Westbury

Henry Mead, *Oak Brewery, Warminster Road.* Acquired by Fussell & Sons Ltd 1936 and was closed.

Edward Smallcombe, *George Inn, Warminster Road.* Acquired by Usher's Wiltshire Brewery Ltd 1914.

Wilsford

Robert Sharp (1892)

Wilton

Robert Beckett, *North Street* (1910)
Henry Street (1940)

Winsley

Florence K.Elms (1940)

Wootton Bassett

Howard Horsell, *Beaufort Brewery, Station Road.* Merged with William Pound & Co. of Swindon 1893 to form Swindon & North Wilts Breweries Ltd. From 1905-10 Marson, Owen & McNaught were listed at the Beaufort Brewery and it was offered for auction with 6 tied houses on 27th June 1916, some of which were sold.

Yarnbrook

Moody & Son (1898)

Zeals

Henry W.W.Hartgill (1920)

Aldborough

Ralph Jackson & Sons (1921)

Boroughbridge

Warwick & Co, *Anchor Brewery, Langthorpe.* Acquired by John Smith's Tadcaster Brewery Co.Ltd. April 1925 with 42 public houses.
York Brewery. See also:- Pocklington, Humberside.

Brompton-on-Swale

J.Fryer & Sons Ltd, *Crown Brewery.* Founded *c.*1880. Acquired by J.W.Cameron & Co.Ltd 1956 and brewing ceased in 1959.

Bubwith

Frederick Harper (1902)

Cropton

Cropton Brewery, *New Inn.* Founded by David Mullins September 1984. Sold to Michael and Sandra Lee January 1986. Still brewing 1990.

Easingwold

H.Haworth, *Uppleby Brewery.* Acquired by John Smith's Tadcaster Brewery Co.Ltd in 1887.

Elvington

Blossomward Brewery, *Elvington Industrial Estate.* Founded March 1983 in former Kingsley Brewery. Ceased brewing 1984.
Kingsley Brewery, *Elvington Industrial Estate.* Founded November 1981. Closed 1983.

Follifoot

Alfred Holmes (1902)

Gate Helmsley

Walter Turner (1895)

Harrogate

Franklin's Brewery, *Bilton Lane, Bilton.* Founded by Sean Franklin 1980 at the Gardener's Arms. Sold to Tommy Thomas and Jane Osborne 1985 and is still brewing 1990.
Nelson Brewery. See also:- Leyburn.
New Inn, *Otley Road.* A Joshua Tetley home brew house founded 1984. Ceased brewing 1987.

Helperby

Joshua Horner Ramsden. Acquired by Johnson & Bambridge, bottlers of York 1947 and beer was supplied by John Smith's Tadcaster Brewery Co.Ltd.

Hunmanby

James Kirk (1895)

Kearby with Netherby

Michael Stead (1914)

Kirbymoorside

Francis Edward Coverdale, *Market Place* (1906)

Kirkby Fleetham

David & John Linton (1923)

Knaresborough

William Ball, *Briggate* (1926)

Leeming

Plews & Sons Ltd, *Vale of Mowbray Brewery.* See also:- Darlington, Durham.

Leyburn

Golden Lion, *Market Square.* Founded at the Nelson Inn, Harrogate 1982 and moved to Leyburn 1984. Now closed.

Long Marston

Marston Moor Brewery, *Ashley, Tockwith Road.* Founded January 1984. Ceased brewing 1987.

Malton

Malton Brewery, *Crown Hotel, Wheelgate.* Founded 1984. Still brewing 1990.

Charles Rose & Co.Ltd, *Old Brewery, 7 Castlegate.* Founded 1767. Became C.Rose & Co. 1894. Registered December 1928. Acquired by Tetley Walker Ltd 1965 with 55 tied houses. Brewing ceased May 1969.

Russell & Wrangham Ltd, *Derwent Brewery, Castlegate.* Registered August 1897 to acquire James Russell & Son, Derwent Brewery and William Wrangham Ltd, Crystal Brewery, Malton. Founded in 1771 and 1843 respectively. Acquired by the Melbourne Brewery (Leeds) Ltd 1958 with 90 public houses and was sold to J.W.Cameron & Co.Ltd 1961.

Masham

T.Lightfoot, *Wellgarth Brewery.* Acquired by Theakstons 1919 with 7 tied houses and was closed.
T.& R.Theakston Ltd, *Red Lane.* Founded by Robert Theakston 1827. Present brewery built 1875. Registered March 1905. Acquired by Matthew Brown & Co.Ltd July 1984 and now controlled by Scottish & Newcastle Breweries Ltd. See also:- Carlisle, Cumbria and Blackburn, Lancashire.

Melmerby

John Wilkinson & Son, *Melmerby Brewery* (1940)

Monk Fryston

Thomas Berry. Founded *c.*1905 and mainly supplied the domestic trade. Acquired by Carter's Knottingley Brewery Co.Ltd 1926.

Naburn

Thomas Mason, *Blacksmith's Arms.* Home brew house bought by the Tadcaster Tower Brewery Co.Ltd 1905. Northallerton.
James Henry Ward (1902)

Osmotherly

Thomas Clarke (1906)

Pateley Bridge

John Metcalfe & Son Ltd, *Nidderdale Brewery*. Founded 1773 when Elizabeth Metcalfe inherited the George Inn. Registered October 1896. Acquired by John Smith's Tadcaster Brewery Co.Ltd June 1909 with 16 public houses. Brewing ceased 1930.

Pickering

F.H.& T.Stericker, *Castle Brewery, Westgate*. Acquired by Bentley's Yorkshire Breweries Ltd 1897.

Richmond

Alexander & William Young (1895)

Ripon

Hepworth & Co.Ltd, *Crown Steam Brewery, Bondgate*. Operated as Richard Lumley & Co. until 1887 when it was acquired by Hepworth & Co. Registered 1898. Acquired bv Vaux & Associated Breweries Ltd 1947 and brewing ceased.

Pearson's Brewery Co.Ltd, *7 Wellington Street*. Registered March 1896 to acquire the business carried on J.M.Tavernor as Richard Pearson. Never traded and was dissolved 4th October 1898. Succeeded by the concern below.

Wellington Brewery Co.Ltd, *7 Wellington Street*. Registered April 1900. No tied houses. Wound up 20th February 1906 and the brewery was sold to a builder on 21st January 1907.

Scarborough

E.H.Gawne & Co, *Old Brewery, St.Thomas Street*. Acquired by G.& H.Hudson & W.J.Hudson 1894.

E.D.Nesfield, *trustees of, Castle Road Brewery & Phoenix Brewery, King Street*. The earliest Yorkshire brewery founded 1691 by the Nesfield family. Acquired by Moors & Robsons Breweries Ltd 1919 with 33 public houses. Brewing ceased 23rd September 1932. The Phoenix Brewery is still standing.

North & East Riding Brewers, *The Highlander, 15 The Esplanade South Cliff*. Founded 1986 by Jamie Clark. Still brewing 1990.

Scarborough & Whitby Breweries Ltd, *North Street Brewery*. Registered October 1895 as the Scarborough Brewery Co.Ltd to acquire the businesses of G.& H.Hudson, North Street Brewery and W.J.Hudson, with a total of 61 tied houses. Name changed as above 1897 when the Whitby breweries were acquired. Acquired by John J.Hunt Ltd of York 1953 with 120 public houses.

Selby

James Oldridge & Son, *Griffin Brewery, Micklegate*. Acquired by Henry Bentley & Co.Ltd 1889.

John Richardson Ltd, *Oungate*. Acquired by Henry Bentley & Co.Ltd 1889.

Selby Brewing & Wine Co.Ltd, *Abbey Brewery, James Street*. Registered December 1882 to acquire the business of William Hawdon & Son. Voluntary liquidation 19th September 1889 and was acquired by Henry Bentley & Co.Ltd.

Selby (Middleborough) Brewery Ltd, *131 Millgate*. Founded c.1870 as maltsters. Registered September 1945 as J.N.& G.Middleborough Ltd. Brewing ceased in 1954 for economic reasons and a trading agreement was made with Dutton's Blackburn Brewery Ltd. Public houses sold to Dutton 1964 and the business was continued as beer bottlers and retailers. Brewing recommenced by Martin Sykes December 1972. Still brewing 1990 with one tied house.

Sherburn

James P.Kirk, *exors of, East Riding Brewery*. Brewery and 37 tied houses sold to Edmund Walker of York 14th July 1922 for £44,750. Brewery offered for sale again in 1923 by Scarborough & Whitby Breweries Ltd.

Sheriff Hutton

Arthur B.Everett. Acquired by J.H.Ramsden of Helperby c.1916.

Skipton

Scott & Co. (Skipton) Ltd, *Belle Vue Brewery, 45 High Street*. Brewery built 1816 for Christopher Scott. Registered August 1894 to acquire Scott & Co. Acquired by Bentley's Yorkshire Breweries Ltd 1912 with 32 public houses and was closed.

Stokesley.

J.Fryer & Sons Ltd. *Cleveland Brewery*. Founded at Brompton-on-Swale c.1880. Acquired from T.Wiggins in 1921.

Thirsk

William Barker, *Long Street* (1926)

Quintin Rhodes, *Kirkgate*. Founded before 1877. Acquired by John Smith's Tadcaster Brewery Co.Ltd 1897.

George Taylor, *exors of, Castle Brewery* (1906)

Thornton-le-Clay

Alexander Christie (1910)

Thornton-le-Moor

Newsome Baxter, *Thornton-le-Moor Brewery*. Merged with Dover & Co. of Newcastle-on-Tyne 1897 to form Dover & Newsome Baxter Ltd. Acquired by James Calder & Co. (Alloa) Ltd with 6 tied houses 1908.

John Metcalfe, *Star Brewery* (1935)

Thornton Watlass

Thomas Alton & Sons (1892)

Tockwith

Robert Brogden Sons & Co.Ltd, *Tockwith Street*. Registered January 1897. Acquired by John J.Hunt Ltd of York 1904 with about 60 public houses.

Wetherby

Wharfedale Brewery Co.Ltd. Registered July 1896 to merge the Wharfedale Brewery and the Eagle Brewery, Leeds. Acquired by Braime's Tadcaster Breweries Ltd. 1903 and the public houses were leased to the Leeds City Brewery Ltd from 1906-11.

Whitby

Corner & Readman, *Marine Parade Brewery, 2/3 Marine Parade & East Row*. Acquired by the Scarborough Brewery Ltd 1897 to form Scarborough & Whitby Breweries Ltd.

Robert Raine, *Esk Brewery, 16 Church Street*. Acquired by the Scarborough Brewery Ltd 1897 to form Scarborough & Whitby Breweries Ltd.

Whitby's Own Brewery Ltd, *St.Hilda's, The Ropery*. Founded by Duncan Evans June 1988. Still brewing 1990.

York

Brett Brothers, *City Brewery, Church Lane, Ousegate*. Acquired by John J.Hunt Ltd 1897.

John J.Hunt Ltd, *Ebor Brewery, Church Lane, Ousegate*. Founded by Joseph Hunt 1834. Registered March 1895. Acquired by Cameron & Co.Ltd 1954 with 102 tied houses. Brewery demolished 1972.

Rose & Crown, *Lawrence Street*. A Joshua Tetley home brew house founded March 1984. Ceased brewing 1987.

W.H.Thackwray & Co, *March's Brewery, 3 Ogleforth*. Founded 1805. Acquired by John Smith's Tadcaster Brewery Co.Ltd 23rd December 1929 with 3 tied houses. Brewing ceased 1940.

William Alexander Todd, *Crown Brewery, 94 Walmgate* (1898)

York Brewery. See also:- Pocklington, Humberside.

Yorkshire Clubs Brewery Ltd, *New Lane, Huntington*. Founded 1924 at Pocklington and moved to York 1933. Acquired by the Northern Clubs Federation Brewery Ltd in 1973.

Barnsley

Barnsley Brewery Ltd, *Oakwell Brewery, Pontefract Road.* Founded by Guy Senior 1857. Registered August 1888 to acquire Paul & Guy Senior. Acquired by John Smith's Tadcaster Brewery Co.Ltd 1961 with 250 public houses. Closed 27th March 1976.

Britannia Brewery Co.Ltd, *Britannia Street, Sheffield Road.* Registered October 1895 to acquire the business of William Tune. Acquired by the Barnsley Brewery Ltd 1907 with 5 tied houses.

Clarkson's Old Brewery (Barnsley) Ltd, *Duke Street.* Founded 1839. Registered December 1890 as Clarkson's Old Brewery Co.Ltd and the name was changed as above in 1902. Acquired by Tennant Brothers Ltd 1956 with 71 public houses. Ceased brewing 1960.

William Smith Flanders, *Townend Brewery, 83 Shambles Street.* Receiving order made February 1892.

Rockside Brewery, *Unit F, Beevor Industrial Estate, Pontefract Road.* Founded at Thurlstone 1984 and moved to Barnsley 1986.

Burton Salmon

John Davies (1898)

Thomas Elsworth, *Plough Inn Brewery* (1920)

Conisborough

Nicholson Brothers Ltd, *Holywell Brewery, Doncaster Road.* Founded by 1878. Registered August 1890. Acquired by Whitworth, Son & Nephew Ltd 1906 with 27 tied houses and 2 off-licences and brewing ceased.

Darton

Dransfield & Co, *Darton Brewery* (1921)

Doncaster

Alfred M. Eadon & Co.Ltd, *Plant Brewery, Sunny Bar.* Registered June 1894. Acquired by Warwicks & Richardsons Ltd 1897 with 16 public houses.

Edmund Fearnley Fisher, *Crown Brewery, Fitzwilliam Street.* Acquired by Thomas Windle c.1890.

Ream & Son, *Corporation Brewery, 133/35 Cleveland Street.* Bought by Samuel Smith's Old Brewery Co.Ltd 23rd February 1925 and 3 public houses were sold to Bass.

Stock's Doncaster Brewery, *The Hallcross, 33 Hallgate.* Founded by Cooplands (Doncaster) Ltd, a bakery chain, in 1981. Still brewing 1990 with 3 tied houses.

Thomas Windle, *Old Exchange Brewery, 42/46 Cleveland Street.* Acquired by Whitworth, Son & Nephew Ltd 1896 and was closed on 1st January 1915.

Other Breweries
Sarah Baxter, *West Laithgate* (1892)
Dickinson Brothers, *Old Brewery, Market Place* (1910)
Harry Earnshaw, *66 Cemetery Road* (1898)
Sarah Peters, *10 Market Place* (1921)
Frank Pickering, *Balby Brewery, Queen Street, Balby* (1914)
William James Sayles, *Frenchgate & East Laithgate* (1940)

Hatfield

Don Valley Brewery Co. (Hatfield) Ltd, *Don Valley Brewery.* Registered March 1920 to acquire W.Winder & Son, Artesian Well Brewery. Closed 1935.

Penistone

Brook & Co, *Cubley Brook Brewery.* Acquired by Stretton's Derby Brewery Ltd 1914.

Rotherham

Abbey Brewery, *Raw Lane, Stainton.* See also:- Torworth, Notts.

Bentley's Old Brewery (Rotherham) Ltd, *Old Brewery, Canklow Road.* Founded by Robert John Bentley 1820. Registered September 1949. Acquired by Hammond's United Breweries Ltd 1956 with 65 public houses and brewing ceased. See also:- Shaw & Bentley, Ashton-under-Lyne, Greater Manchester.

Mappin's Brewery Ltd, *Greasboro' Road.* Registered October 1885 as Mappin's Masbro' Old Brewery Ltd. Name changed as above in 1949. Acquired by William Stones Ltd 1954 and brewing ceased 1955.

Sheffield & Rotherham Brewery Ltd., *Effingham Brewery, Market Place.* Registered November 1900 as R.N.Hutchinson & Co.Ltd to acquire the Effingham Brewery Co.Ltd. New company registered as above April 1902. Acquired by Mappin's Masbro' Old Brewery Ltd 1914.

Sheffield

Thomas Berry & Co.Ltd, *Moorhead Brewery, Park Street.* Founded 1824 as the Ecclesall Brewery and was renamed the Moorhead Brewery 1874. Registered January 1874. Acquired by Tennant Brothers Ltd 1923 with 78 public houses and brewing ceased in 1983.

W.H.Birks & Co, *Lady's Bridge Brewery, 9 Bridge Street.* Founded 1791. Acquired by Duncan Gilmour & Co.Ltd 1900 but brewing continued until about 1954.

Robert Budd & Co, *Strong Arm Brewery, 236 Infirmary Road.* Founded 1860. Acquired by John Smith's Tadcaster Brewery Co.Ltd October 1893 with 14 tied houses.

Chambers & Co.Ltd, *Brunswick Brewery, Ellen Street.* Registered March 1898. Their 14 public houses were sold for £28,000 on September 1911. Wound up January 1913.

J.L.Cockayne & Son, *Owlerton Brewery, Chapel Street, Penistone Road.* Founded c.1845. Acquired by John Smith's Tadcaster Brewery Co.Ltd January 1914 with 27 public houses.

The Crown Brewery (Sheffield) Ltd, *Crown Brewery, Langsett Road.* Registered October 1906 to acquire the business carried on by William Bolsover as James Haynes & Co. Liquidator appointed 19th December 1911 and was wound up 1st July 1915.

Henry James Dearden, *High House Brewery, Penistone Road.* Founded 1833. Acquired by Duncan Gilmour & Co.Ltd 1901.

Frog & Parrot, *Division Street.* A Whitbread home brew house founded April 1982. Still brewing 1990.

Duncan Gilmour & Co.Ltd, *Dixon Lane.* Founded 1831 as wine & spirit merchants and were brewing by 1860. Registered October 1901 Acquired by Tetley & Sons Ltd 1954 and brewing ceased before 1964.

William Greaves & Co.Ltd, *Norfolk Brewery, South Park Street.* Founded 1860. Registered 1909. Acquired by Duncan Gilmour & Co.Ltd 1920 with 29 tied houses and brewing ceased.

Hooson & Co, *Park Brewery, Aston Street.* Acquired by Ind Coope & Co.(1912) Ltd in 1914 with 31 Public houses.

Hope & Anchor Breweries Ltd, *Hope Brewery, Claywheels Lane, Wadsley.* Founded 1892. Registered April 1899 as Carter, Milner & Bird Ltd. Merged with Henry Tomlinson Ltd 1942 and the name was changed as above. In 1959 Northern Breweries Ltd was formed to merge: Hammond's United Breweries Ltd, Hope & Anchor Breweries Ltd and John Jeffrey & Co.Ltd. The name was later changed to Northern Breweries of Great Britain Ltd and in October 1962 to United Breweries Ltd, now part of Bass Charrington.

Thomas Marrian & Co.Ltd, *Burton Weir Brewery.* Founded c.1830. Registered March 1882. Acquired by Whitworth, Son & Nephew Ltd 1903 and was closed.

Old Albion Brewery Ltd, *Albion Brewery, Ecclesall Road.* Founded c.1840. Registered July 1897. Acquired by the Worksop & Retford Brewery Co.Ltd 1939 with 52 public houses. Brewing ceased January 1950.

Thomas Rawson & Co.Ltd, *Pond Street Brewery.* Founded by Thomas Rawson 1758. The first provincial concern to brew porter. Registered September 1896. Brewery destroyed in an air raid 1940. Acquired by Duncan Gilmour & Co.Ltd 1946.

John Richdale & Co.Ltd, *Britannia Brewery, Brammall Lane.* Registered February 1898. Acquired by Hammond's United Breweries Ltd 1956 with 25 tied houses.

Sheffield Free Brewery Co.Ltd, *389 Queen's Road.* Founded 1900 as Rhoden, Freeman & Co. Registered November 1902 as Rhoden, Freeman & Co.Ltd. Voluntary liquidation 27th February 1905. A new company, the Queen's Road Brewery Ltd was registered in June 1905. Receiver appointed April 1911. Registered as above September 1911.

Acquired jointly by Tennant Brothers Ltd and William Stones Ltd 1954 and was controlled solely by Tennants from 1955. Brewing ceased 1954 and is now a cutlery works.

A.H.Smith & Co.Ltd, *Don Brewery, Penistone Road.* Founded 1832. Registered November 1900. Acquired by Tennant Brothers Ltd 1915 with about 108 public houses.

William Stones Ltd, *Cannon Brewery, Rutland Road.* Registered July 1895. Acquired by Bass Charrington Ltd 1968 with 257 tied houses. Still brewing 1990.

Strout's Brewery Co.Ltd, *Burton Road Brewery, Neepsend.* Registered December 1889. Acquired by Tennant Brothers Ltd March 1918 with 78 public houses.

Tennant Brothers Ltd, *Exchange Brewery, Bridge Street.* Founded 1820 and was acquired by Tennant Brothers 1840. Registered July 1882. Acquired by Whitbread & Co.Ltd 1962 with 700 tied houses.

Henry Tomlinson Ltd, *Anchor Brewery, Cherry Street.* Founded 1891. Registered November 1894. Brewery destroyed in an air raid 1940. Merged with Carter, Milner & Bird Ltd 1942 to form Hope & Anchor Breweries Ltd.

Trusswell's Brewery Co.Ltd, *Eyre Street.* Registered July 1865. Acquired by Hope & Anchor Breweries Ltd 1955 with about 50 public houses. The brewery has been demolished.

S.H.Ward & Co.Ltd, *Sheaf Brewery, Ecclesall Road.* Founded by John Kirby 1840 at the Sheaf Island Brewery, Effingham Street and was acquired by S.H.Ward 1871/2. Acquired the Soho Brewery and changed its name to the Sheaf Brewery. Registered February 1896. Acquired by Vaux 1972 with 102 tied houses. Still brewing 1990.

Whitmarsh, Watson & Co.Ltd, *South Street Brewery, Earl Street The Moor.* Founded before 1854. Registered October 1895 to acquire William Whitmarsh & Co, Earl Street and John Watson & Co, Spring Lane, with a total of 140 public houses. Acquired by Duncan Gilmour & Co.Ltd 1906.

Wilson's Parkside Brewery Co.Ltd, *Parkside Brewery, Sussex Street.* Registered May 1897 to acquire Wilson Brothers, Parkside Brewery and Benjamin Chapman, Effingham Mineral Works. Acquired by Whitmarsh, Watson & Co.Ltd 1906.

Thorne

W.M.Darley Ltd, *King Street.* Founded by 1837. Registered 1918 and was reconstructed in 1927. Acquired by Vaux 1978 with 61 public houses. Brewery closed September 1986.

Thurlstone

Rockside Brewery. See also:- Barnsley.

Wath-on-Dearne

Whitworth, Son & Nephew Ltd, *Wath Brewery, Moor Road.* Founded before 1872 and was acquired by Spedding Whitworth in 1880. Registered April 1891. Acquired by John Smith's Tadcaster Brewery Co.Ltd 1958 with 165 tied houses and brewing ceased.

WEST YORKSHIRE

Baildon

Thomas William Read, *Baildon Brewery, Wood Bottom* (1898)

Bardsey

Charles Edward Brenchley (1935)

Batley

Leeds & Batley Breweries Ltd, *Atlas Brewery, Warwick Road.* Registered April 1896 as R.H.Sykes & Co.Ltd to acquire R.H.Sykes, Soothill Brewery, Dewsbury and the Atlas Brewery. Went into liquidation April 1898 and was reconstructed as above when Cutler's Saville Green Brewery, Leeds was acquired. Acquired by Ind Coope & Co.Ltd 1900 and brewing ceased.

Bingley

J.R.Holmes & Sons. Acquired by Hammond's Bradford Brewery Co.Ltd 1919 with 52 public houses.

Richard Lightfoot, *Bellbank Brewery, Ireland Bridge* (1923)

Birstall

Clarkson & Wood, *Raikes Tower Brewery.* Acquired by Stretton's Derby Brewery Ltd 1896.

A.Lawson & Co, *Birstall Old Brewery* (1892)

Bradford

Crown Brewery Co, *Nesfield Street.* Acquired by Wheatley & Bates Ltd of Sheffield 1895.

Greenwood Brothers, *Caledonia Brewery, 133 Manchester Road.* Formed part of Boardman's United Breweries Ltd in 1903. Premises were in use by Stretton's Derby Brewery Ltd in 1906.

Hammond's United Breweries Ltd, *Fountain Brewery, 82 Manchester Road.* Founded 1840 by James Hammond. Registered November 1889 as Hammond's Bradford Brewery Co.Ltd. Name changed as above 30th December 1946. Acquired by Northern Breweries 1959 and is now a Bass Charrington subsidiary. The brewery has been demolished.

J.Hey & Co.Ltd, *Northbrook Brewery, Lumb Lane, Manningham.* Registered January 1897. Acquired by Samuel Webster & Sons Ltd 1966 with 94 tied houses.

Joseph & Henry Sagar Hirst, *Low House Brewery, Clayton Heights.* Merged with Henry Bentley & Co.Ltd 1892.

Horton Old Brewery Co.Ltd, *131 High Street, Horton.* Registered July 1914. Ceased brewing 1934.

Naylor Brothers, *Eastbrook Brewery, Burnett Street.* Partnership of F.& G.H.Naylor dissolved January 1893. Brewing ceased 1895.

J.& A.Orrell. Acquired by Leeds & Wakefield Breweries Ltd 1925.

Peel Park Brewery Co.Ltd, *Otley Road.* Registered August 1872 to acquire the business of Daniel Riddihough. Voluntary liquidation 18th April 1882. Daniel & William Riddihough were trading as the Yorkshire Brewery Co, Shipley in 1888. Acquired by Hammond's Bradford Brewery Ltd in 1891 with at least 5 public houses.

Joseph Spink & Sons Ltd, *Brown Royd Brewery, Rosse Street.* Registered October 1889. Acquired by J.Hey & Co.Ltd 1924.

Clement Taylor & Son, *Manningham Brewery, Wilson Square, Lumb Lane.* Merged with Henry Bentley & Co.Ltd 1892.

J.& S.Tordoff Ltd, *Devonshire Arms Brewery, 186 Thornton Road.* Registered 1900. Acquired by J.Hey & Co.Ltd April 1919 and was closed.

Trough Brewery, *Louisa Street, Idle.* Founded 1981. Still brewing 1990 with 5 tied houses.

Waller's Bradford Brewery Ltd, *Trafalgar Brewery, 24 Trafalgar Street, Manningham Lane.* Founded 1874. Registered September 1887 as Waller & Son Ltd. The brewery was sold to the Midland Railway in 1914 and brewing was transferred to Brear & Brown's Hipperholme Brewery. Re-registered as above in June 1925. Acquired by Leeds & Wakefield Breweries Ltd in 1935.

William Whittaker & Co.Ltd, *Old Brewery, Park Road.* Founded 1757. Registered November 1897. Brewing ceased 1928 and the brewery was demolished and replaced by a cinema. They continued to operate as bottlers, wine & spirit merchants and public house owners. Acquired by Joshua Tetley & Sons Ltd 1959.

Other Breweries
Briggs Brothers, *Thornton* (1902)
Joseph Hardy, *Albion Brewery, Low Lane, Clayton* (1923)
William F.Howard, *93 Barkerend Road* (1926)
David Smith, *95 Lumb Lane* (1890)
James Stephenson, *Ivy Hotel Brewery, 157 Barkerend* (1895)
Ferrand Swithinbank, *Bridge Street Brewery* (1906)
William Thorpe & Son, *Victoria Square* (1906)
Philip Wright, *Springhead Brewery, Thornton* (1906)

Brighouse

James Dyson, *33 Bradford Road* (1921)
H.& T.T.Ormerod, *Red Cross Brewery, Briggate.* Acquired by Samuel Webster & Sons Ltd 1890.
Prynn & Co, *Rastrick* (1902)
Richard Roberts, *Railway Brewery, Rastrick* (1902)

Cleckheaton

Spen Valley Brewery Co.Ltd, *Whitcliff Road.* Founded 1816. Registered 1901. Acquired by Thomas Ramsden & Son Ltd 1951 when they were operating only as bottlers and licensed house owners.

Crigglestone

John Garthwaite, *Calder Grove* (1930)
Herbert Glover, *Calder Grove Brewery* (1921)

Denholme

John Greenwood, *Denholme Gate Brewery.* Formed part of Boardman's United Breweries Ltd 1906.

Dewsbury

R.H.Sykes & Co.Ltd, *Soothill Brewery.* See also:- Batley.

Farnley Tyas

Edward Roberts & Sons. Acquired by Bentley's Yorkshire Breweries Ltd 1899.

Fenay Bridge

Phoebe Harrison (1900)

Guiseley

Station Brewery, *Main Street, Otley Road.* The first Joshua Tetley home brew house founded 1982. Ceased brewing 1987.

Halifax

James Alderson & Co.Ltd, *Warley Spring Brewery, Burnley Road, Northowram.* Registered 1900. Acquired by Thomas Ramsden & Son Ltd in 1919.

Crossley & Co, *Stump Cross Brewery.* Acquired by Bentley's Yorkshire Breweries Ltd 1896.

John Eastwood, *Crown Brewery, Northowram.* Acquired by Henry Bentley & Co.Ltd 1893. Closed 1900

John Naylor, *Albion Brewery, Fern Hill, Warley.* Acquired by the Halifax Brewery Co. (predecessors to James Alderson & Co.Ltd) 1897.

Thomas Ramsden & Son Ltd, *Stonetrough Brewery, Commercial St.* Founded by 1818 and acquired by Thomas Ramsden 1881. Registered January 1894. Acquired by Allied Breweries Ltd 1964 with 117 tied houses and was closed.

Joseph Stocks & Co.Ltd, *Shibden Head Brewery, Northowram.* Founded 1790. Registered November 1897. Acquired by Samuel Webster & Sons Ltd 1933 with 79 Public houses and brewing ceased.

Samuel Webster & Sons Ltd, *Fountain Head Brewery, Ovenden Wood.* Founded 1838 and was acquired by Samuel Webster 1860 Registered March 1890. Acquired by Watney Mann Ltd March 1972 with 288 public houses and was merged with Wilson's Brewery Ltd 1985. Still brewing 1990.

Richard Whittaker & Sons Ltd, *Seedlings Mount Brewery, 36 Corporation Street.* Founded 1849 as the Stannery Inn Brewery and moved to the Seedlings Mount Brewery in 1867. Registered April 1890. Acquired by Whitbread & Co.Ltd 1968 with 135 tied houses. Brewing ceased early in 1969.

Other Breweries

Harry Aspinall & Sons, *Mount Tabor* (1932)
Harvey & Co, *Pellon Brewery, New Pellon* (1900)
Benjamin Jackson & Sons, *Bradshaw Lane Brewery* (1910)
Jonathan Sheard, *Brackenbed Brewery, Ovenden* (1898)
Dick Swift, *Cross Keys Brewery, 73/75 King Cross Street* (1930)

Haworth

Ogden & Co.Ltd, *Fallwood Brewery.* Founded before 1878 and moved to the Fallwood Brewery 1889-93. Registered 1911. Acquired by Hammond's Bradford Brewery Ltd in 1933 with 7 tied houses.

E.Parker & Co.(Brewers) Ltd, *Clarendon Brewery, Clarendon Road.* Founded 1881. Registered July 1947. Voluntary liquidation 8th October 1966 and their 8 tied houses were sold, 7 being acquired by Timothy Taylor & Co.Ltd.

Heckmondwike

Heckmondwike Old Brewery Co.Ltd, *Albion Street.* Registered January 1895. Dissolved 23rd July 1901.
Springwell Brewery Co.Ltd, *Market Street.* Founded 1860 as Whitworth Brothers. Registered March 1888. Acquired by Hammond's Bradford Brewery Co.Ltd 1929 with 88 Public houses. Brewery closed 1930.

Hipperholme

Brear & Brown Ltd, *Hipperholme Steam Brewery.* Registered March 1894. Acquired by Waller's Bradford Brewery Ltd 1914 with 75 tied houses. Brewery closed 1935.

Huddersfield

Benjamin Ainley Ltd, *Royd Steam Brewery, Lindley Moor.* Founded 1853. Registered March 1896. Acquired by Bentley & Shaw Ltd in 1927 with 15 public houses.
John Ainley & Sons Ltd, *Wapping Spring Brewery, Lindley Moor.* Registered March 1899. Acquired by Samuel Webster & Sons Ltd 1957.

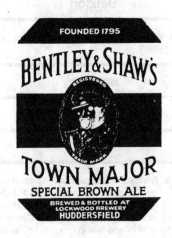

Bentley & Shaw Ltd, *Lockwood Brewery, Bridge Street.* Founded by Timothy Bentley 1795. Two of his sons established the breweries at Rotherham and Woodlesford. Registered October 1891. Acquired by Hammond's Bradford Brewery Co.Ltd in 1944 with 192 tied houses. Brewery closed 1963.

J.R.Bottomley Co.Ltd, *Aspley Old Brewery, Aspley Mill Lane.* Registered May 1897. Acquired by Bentley's Yorkshire Breweries Ltd 1899.

John Prance & Sons, *Hay Green Brewery, Marsden.* Partnership of J.F.France and J.Ward dissolved April 1892.

Linfit Brewery, *Sair Inn, Lane Top, Linthwaite.* Home brew house founded 1982. Still brewing 1990.

P.Marsland & Sons, *Watergate Brewery, Watergate.* Registered 1899. Acquired by Wilson's Brewery Ltd September 1930 with 30 public houses and was closed.

Seth Senior & Sons Ltd, *Highfield Brewery, Shepley.* Registered January 1910. Acquired by Hammond's United Breweries Ltd 1947 with 99 tied houses.

Other Breweries

Joseph Marshall, *Spring Mill Brewery, Milnsbridge* (1894)

George Netherwood & Sons, *Lindley* (1900)

Shaw & Sykes, *Brook Street Brewery.* Acquired by J.R.Bottomley & Co. 1892.

Abraham Spivey, *Globe Brewery, 45/49 King Street* (1895)

West Riding Brewery, *Bradley Mills, Bradley Mills Road.* See also:- Meltham.

Ilkley

Ilkley Brewery & Aerated Water Co.Ltd, *Brewery Road.* Registered March 1873. Acquired by Hammond's Bradford Brewery Co.Ltd 1923 with 37 tied houses.

James Weatherill, *Ilkley Wells Brewery, Skipton Road* (1892)

Ingrow

Frederick Binns, *White Horse Brewery.* Acquired by Scott & Co. (Skipton) Ltd 1897.

Keighley

William W.Cattle, *Eastwood Brewery, Brewery Street.* Offered for sale 1903 with 13 public houses.

Aaron King & Co, *Old Brewery, Cook Lane.* Founded by Timothy Taylor 1858 before moving to the Knowle Spring Brewery in 1863. Ceased brewing 1946 and the public houses were bought by Timothy Taylor & Co.Ltd.

John Shuttleworth, *Black Horse Brewery, Low Street* (1898)

STRONG ALE

KNOWLE SPRING BREWERY
KEIGHLEY

Timothy Taylor & Co.Ltd, *Knowle Spring Brewery, Belina Street, South Street.* Founded 1858. Registered November 1929. Still brewing independently 1990 with 29 tied houses.

Knottingley

Carter's Knottingley Brewery Co.Ltd, *Hilltop.* Founded c.1800. Registered April 1892 to acquire John Carter & Co. Acquired by Bentley's Yorkshire Breweries Ltd 1935 with 66 public houses and was closed.

Steam Packet Inn. Home brew house founded 1989.

Leeds

Albion Brewery (Leeds) Ltd, *50 Woodhouse Lane.* Founded 1852 as John Young & Co. Registered April 1897 with 70 public houses. Acquired by the Kirkstall Brewery Co.Ltd in 1927 and brewing ceased in October 1935.

Ale House, *79 Raglan Road.* Off-licence home brew founded December 1987.

Armley Brewery Ltd, *73 Commercial Street, Armley.* Founded c.1820 and was under the control of John William Wright from at least 1871. Registered February 1898 to amalgamate T.E.T.Wright, Borough Brewery and J.S.Tempest, maltsters. Acquired by Thomas Ramsden & Son Ltd 1929 and brewing ceased in the same year.

Bentley's Yorkshire Breweries Ltd, *Eshaldwell Brewery, Woodlesford.* Founded by Henry Bentley 1828 as the Oulton Brewery. Registered 1880 as Henry Bentley & Co.Ltd. Re-registered 1892 as Henry Bentley & Co.Yorkshire Breweries Ltd and the name was changed as above March 1893. Acquired by Whitbread & Co.Ltd 1968 with 380 tied houses and brewing ceased in October 1972.

Cowbrough & Co.Ltd, *63/65 Boar Lane.* Registered October 1896. Closed 1902.

Findlay's Brewery Ltd, *24 Nippet Lane, Burmantofts.* Registered July 1895 as the Burmantofts Brewery Ltd to acquire the business of George Henry Finlay. Name changed as above 31st August 1897. Receiver appointed 19th March 1912 and was dissolved 30th January 1922.

J.W.Hemingway Ltd, *York Road.* Founded 1866. Registered September 1949. Acquired by Tetley Walker Ltd 1967 with 5 tied houses.

Kirkstall Brewery Co.Ltd, *Kirkstall.* Operated by Thomas Walker from before 1834. Acquired by Benjamin Dawson c.1845. Registered June 1871 to acquire Benjamin Dawson & Co. Reconstructed company registered January 1899. Acquired by Dutton's Blackburn Brewery Ltd 1936 with 83 public houses. Brewery bought by Whitbread & Co.Ltd 1957 and was closed in January 1983.

Samuel Ledgard, *Nelson Brewery, Nelson Hotel, Armley Road.* Home brew house possibly brewing until the death of the owner in 1952. Now a free house.

Leeds & Batley Breweries Ltd. See also:- Batley.

Leeds & District Clubs Brewery Ltd, *Woodhouse Street.* Registered August 1914 and occupied the premises of the former Leeds & District Liberal Clubs Brewery Co.Ltd. Merged with Yorkshire Clubs Brewery Ltd 1939.

Leeds & District Liberal Clubs Brewery Ltd, *Woodhouse Street.* Formed 1911. Voluntary liquidation 1913. Brewery offered for sale 1914 for £1,250 and was bought by the Leeds & District Clubs Brewery Ltd.

Leeds Brewhouse Company, *Fox & Newt, Burley Road.* A Whitbread home brew house founded 1982. Still brewing 1990.

Leeds City Brewery Ltd, *Durham Street, Kirkstall Road.* Operated by Wright Brothers from 1884. Registered March 1897 with 19 tied houses. Acquired by Ind Coope Ltd 1931 and was closed.

McQuat Ltd, *29 Meadow Lane.* Founded 1871. Registered October 1924. Acquired by Samuel Smith Ltd 1947 with 7 public houses. Now demolished.

Melbourne Brewery (Leeds) Ltd, *Melbourne Brewery, Plum Street.* Registered December 1889 as the Leeds & Wakefield Breweries Ltd to amalgamate Kirk, Matthews, Melbourne Brewery and Carter & Sons, Victoria Brewery, Wakefield. Name changed as above December 1957. Acquired by Tetley & Sons Ltd 1960 and brewing ceased. 245 public houses.

Musgrave & Sagar Ltd, *Rutland Brewery, 13 Marlborough Street.* Registered 1907. Brewing ceased 1958 but still operating as bottlers.

Rilot's Brewery Ltd, *Lavender Walk, Accomodation Road.* Private company registered February 1926. Voluntary liquidation 17th February 1930. One tied house - Weaver's Arms, 1 Upper Cross Street.

John Thomas Rothwell, *Pointer Inn, 132 Beckett Street.* Acquired by John Smith's Tadcaster Brewery Co.Ltd c.1924.

Round Oak Brewery Co.Ltd, *1 Ivory Street, Hunslet.* Registered 22nd May 1895. Voluntary winding up 2nd May 1896. Dissolved 5th November 1907.

J.Spencer, *Waterloo Brewery, Kidacre Street, Hunslet Lane & 69 East Street.* Founded 1824. Closed 1929.

Joshua Tetley & Sons Ltd, *21 Hunslet Road.* Founded before October 1822 when Joshua Tetley acquired William Sykes' brewery. Registered July 1897. Merged with Walker Cain Ltd 1960 to form Tetley Walker Ltd. Became part of Allied-Lyons but in January 1993 was renamed Carlsberg-Tetley as a result of an amalgamation with the Carlsberg Brewery.

Willow Brewery Co.Ltd, *Willow Place, Kirkstall Road.* Founded 1836. Acquired by the Kirkstall Brewery Co.Ltd 1928 and was closed in 1934.

Other Breweries

Benjamin Adams, *17 Moseley Street* (1906)

Adelaide Aldred, *79 Richmond Road* (1920)

Thomas Armitage, *10 Mill Street, Marsh Lane* (1923)

Joseph W.Atkinson, *259 Dewsbury Road, Hunslet* (1926)

John Banks, *16 Wade Lane* (1920)

Harry Barber, *2 Shakespeare Street* (1920)

Alfred Bellhouse, *133 Hunslet Road* (1914)

William Bennett, *Barley Mow Inn, 37 Town Street*

(1910)

Arthur Benson, *26 Lowerhead Row* (1920)

Harold Best, *42 Wortley Road, Armley* (1930)

Mary Ann Best, *22 Trinity Street* (1930)

Bickerdike Home Brewed Beer Co, *Bickerdike Road* (1921)

Arthur Blades, *10 Ellerby Road* (1920)

John William Blades junior, *9 Church Street, Hunslet* (1923)

George Henry Bonner, *127 Hyde Park Road* (1920)

Harry Bosomworth, *30 Wheat Street, York Road* (1920)

John William Bosomworth, *44 Catherine Street* (1914)

Joe Briggs, *17 Robson Street* (1926)

John Broadbent, *86 Top Moor Side, Holbeck* (1920)

Ethel Brown, *3 Lloyd Street, Burley Road* (1923)

Henry Brown, *19 Rigg Street, Beeston Hill* (1920)

Ernest Brownfoot, *57 Moor End, Hunslet* (1921)

John William Buckle, *48 Beckett Street* (1921)

Albert Edward Buckley, *10 Crossfield Street* (1920)

Richard Burrows, *1 Waterloo Road & 2 Low Road, Hunslet* (1921)

Emanuel Calvert, *12 Somerby Street* (1926)

Charles Abraham Castelow, *Palace Inn, 1 East Street* (1910)

Kezia Castelow, *4a Camp Road* (1940)

Joseph H.Cawood, *20 St.Matthew's Street, Holbeck* (1921)

William Mitchell Charlton, *Cardigan Arms, 350 Kirkstall Road*

Matthew Clarkson, *2 Garland Fold, Marsh Lane* (1920)

Mary E.Cliff, *50 York Road* (1921)

Joseph Cockshott, *122 Church Street, Hunslet* (1923)

Walter Cordingley, *101 Whitehall Road* (1920)

Ted Cowburn & Thomas Upton, *30 Mill Street* (1935)

Charles Cracknell, *67 Tong Road, New Wortley* (1920)

Eleanor Crowther, *7 Rigg Street, Lady Pitt Lane* (1920)

Harriett Crowther, *81 York Road* (1921)

Jim Crowther, *77 Dewsbury Road* (1920)

John Crowther, *95 Green Road* (1923)

Wilfred Crowther, *44 Goodman Street, Hunslet* (1920)

Joseph Cudworth, *46 Elland Road* (1920)

John H.Daniels, *104 Otley Road, Headingley* (1926)

George Dennell, *Seacroft* (1930)

Philemon Denton, *44 West Street* (1920)

Job Dixon, *1 George Street* (1920)

John Thomas Dixon, *33 West Street* (1920)

Fred Duxberry, *10 Ainsley Street* (1921)

James Ellam, *2 Tong Road, New Wortley* (1920) & *Burley Road Brewery* (1910)

Elizabeth Evans, *137 Dewsbury Road* (1920)

Sutcliffe Farrar, *134 Armley Road* (1920)

Joseph Henry Fishburn, *7 Ward's Fold, Mabgate* (1935)

Thomas N.Foxcroft, *17 Vicar Lane* (1923)

Mary Frisby, *32 Great Garden Street* (1923)

William Garbutt. Receiving order made 22nd February 1895.

Emmanuel Gaunt, *88 Regent Street* (1920)

Patrick Grady, *13 High Markland Street* (1930)

Jane Elizabeth Grant, *35 Great Garden Street* (1923)

Arthur Greenwood, *36/38 Domestic Street, Holbeck* (1920)

Sarah Hambleton, *85 South Accommodation Road, Hunslet* (1920)

Charles F.T.Hargrave, *135 Grape Street* (1920)

Annie E.Hartley, *67 Hillidge Road, Hunslet* (1921)

George Hatton, *7 Cross Stamford Street* (1920)

Thomas Hawkhead, *95 North Street* (1920)

Sarah Ann Hawksworth, *5 Granville Terrace, Beckett Street* (1940)

William Henry Heaney, *6 Tonbridge Street* (1930)

Arthur Heathfield, *30 Great Garden Street* (1926)

Charles Hebden, *15 Edgar Street* (1920)

George Hepplestall, *1 Holbeck Lane, Holbeck* (1914)

Charles Hepworth & Son, *81/83 Hall Lane* (1930)

William Herson, *90 Pollard Street, Beckett Street* (1940)

Frank Hollings, *Upper Carr Place, Hunslet* (1923)

Agnes Hunt, *23 Middle Row, Holbeck* (1923)

Jeremiah Jagger, *8 Roundhay Street* (1921)

Lily Johnson, *205 Tong Road, Wortley* (1923)

Edmund Jowett, *1 York Road* (1920)

Thomas Jowitt *18 Stocks Hill, Holbeck* (1921)

Arthur Kershaw, *42 Dolly Lane* (1926)

Robert Kitchen, *7/9 Whitelock Street* (1926)

Lengthorn's Chemic Tavern Brewery (1914)

Henry Lister, *5 Bridge Street, Kirkstall* (1930)

George Gommersall Longbottom, *61 Thwaitegate, Hunslet* (1923)

John Mallinson, *48 Somerby Streeet* (1926)

Joseph Mann, *30 Catherine Street* (1923)

Anthony McCarmick & Co, *124 Vicar Lane* (1926) & *34 North Street*

Harold Edward Middleton, *4 St.James' Street* (1926)

Tom Mills, *23/25 Benson Street* (1920)

Thomas Morton, *75 Theaker Lane, Armley* (1926)

John Edwin Mosley, *74 York Roasd* (1920)

Elvira Naylor, *31 Wheeler Street* (1921)

John L.Naylor, *77 Accomodation Road* (1940)

Mary Hannah Park, *Skinner Lane Brewery, 81 Skinner Lane* (1923)

Jesse Peel, *Stone House Inn Brewery, Thornthwaite* (1910)

Arthur L.Pence, *79 Meadow Street* (1926)

William Priestley, *124/26 Town Street* (1921)

Benjamin Pullan, *North Tavern Brewery, 106 North Street* (1920)

William Pyrah, *47 Wordsworth Street* (1920)

Elizabeth H.Rathbone, *64 Mabgate* (1940)

Benjamin Rhodes, *86 Kirkstall Road* (1926)

Fountain Rider, *90 Wellington Road, New Wortley* (1926)

George Roberts, *Seacroft* (1923)

Harriett Roberts, *1 Cross Princess Street, Holbeck* (1920)

Jane Roberts, *18 Speedwell Street* (1940)

Joseph William Robertshaw, *3 Dewsbury Road, Hunslet* (1923)

Lewis Robinson, *Black Dog Fold, East Street* (1920)

Herbert Robinson, *49 Thwaitegate, Hunslet* (1920)

Baron Rothschild, *86 Camp Road* (1923)

Sarah E.Rourke, *1/3 Carver Street* (1940)

Ralph Rowark, *87 Town Street, Armley* (1926)

Mary Ellen Rushworth, *106 Wellington Road, New Wortley* (1914)

Anetta Ryder, *Crossgate* (1921)

John George Saddington, *North Hall Terrace* (1914)

John Scholes, *39 Carlton Street* (1910)

Arthur Silcock, *Victoria Brewery, 11/12 Hills Yard* (1910)

Emma Simpson, *Old George Hotel Brewery, 174 Briggate* (1920)

Arthur Smith, *8 Tong Road, New Wortley* (1921)

Robert Smith, *97 New Church Place* (1935)

Frank Smithson, *11 Grove Street* (1921)

Arthur Sowry, *196 Armley Road* (1923)

Frederick Sowry, *136 Upper Wortley Road* (1920)

George Sowry, *4 West Street* (1920)

John Spencer, *56 Lady Lane* (1930)

Samuel Heaton Spencer, *2 Ellerby Lane* (1926)

William Standheaven, *85 Regent Street* (1921)

Edwin Stead, *32 Call Street* (1926)

Joseph Stead, *54 Cross Green Lane* (1926)

Sarah Kitchin Taylor, *25 Galway Street* (1923)

Amy Teale, *1/2 Dolly Lane, New Town* (1940)

Gertrude Van Den Daele, *44 North Street* (1923)

Mary Ann Wainwright, *166 Glasshouse Street, Hunslet* (1926)

John Louis Walton, *92 Sheepscar Street* (1923)

James Dean Waterhouse, *20 Cromwell Street* (1920)

Walter Dring Watkin, *Silver Cross Hotel, Dewsbury Road* (1923) & *16 Pearson Street, Hunslet* (1920)

Ernest Webster, *70a Langham Street* (1923)

William Henry Webster, *8 Robson Street* (1920)

Rowland Welbourn, *2 Balm Walk, Holbeck* (1940)

Charles Herbert Wood, *61 Town Street, Beeston* (1920)

Stephen Wood, *Union Cross Brewery, Armley* (1902)

John Kendrick Wooding, *Harrison Street* (1914)

Luddendenfoot

George Bedford Whitaker, *Grove Brewery, Brearley*. Acquired by Richard Whitaker & Sons Ltd of Halifax 1905 with 20 public houses. Brewery converted into a public house.

Meltham

West Riding Brewery, *New Bridge Road*. Founded at Huddersfield 1980 and moved to Meltham after a fire in 1983. Following another fire in January 1986 brewing ceased and beer is now brewed for them by the Oak Brewery, Ellesmere Port, Cheshire.

Otley

George Arthur Robinson, *Westgate* (1921)

Pontefract

W.Pickersgill & Co.Ltd, *Old Castle Brewery, South Baileygate*. Registered 1907. Acquired by Bentley's Yorkshire Breweries Ltd 1932 with 14 tied houses.

Queensbury

Daniel Fielding & Sons, *White Castle Brewery*. Acquired by Samuel Webster & Sons Ltd of Halifax in 1962 and was closed.

Ripponden

Ripponden Free Brewery Co.Ltd, *Hanging Lane*. Registered March 1900 as the Sowerby Bridge & District Clubs Brewery Co.Ltd. Wound up 17th November 1923 and a new company was registered as above in 1924.

Shipley

Yorkshire Brewery Co. See also:- Peel Park Brewery Co.Ltd, Bradford.

Sowerby Bridge

Edwin Cotton, *Bank Brewery, Tuel Lane* (1895)

Lydia H.Platt, *Puzzlehall Brewery, Hollins Mill Lane*. A home brew house bought by S.H.Ward & Co.Ltd of Sheffield 1935.

Tadcaster

Braime's Tadcaster Breweries Ltd, *Victoria Brewery, Chapel Street*. Registered September 1895 to acquire Benjamin Braime, Victoria Brewery and Wilson & Cundall, New Brewery, Tadcaster. Amalgamated with the Leeds City Brewery Ltd 1903.

John Smith's Tadcaster Brewery Co.Ltd, *High Street.* Founded 1757 and was acquired by John Smith 1847. Present brewery built 1884. Registered August 1892. Acquired by Courage, Barclay & Simonds Ltd 1970. Brewery still in operation 1990.

Samuel Smith Old Brewery (Tadcaster) Ltd, *Old Brewery, High Street.* Samuel Smith was the nephew of John Smith of the concern above and being excluded from the family business, he acquired the Old Brewery after John Smith's new brewery was built in 1884. Registered 1923. Still brewing independently in 1990 with 300 tied houses.

Tadcaster Tower Brewery Co.Ltd, *Wetherby Road.* Brewery built 1882. Registered June 1894. Acquired by Hammond's Bradford Brewery Co.Ltd August 1946 with 247 tied houses. Brewery still in operation 1990.

Todmorden

John Bulcock, *Rock Spring Brewery, Gauxholme.* Acquired by J.Grimshaw Ltd of Burnley, Lancs 1914.

Towton

Daniel Stoker, *Towton Brewery.* Acquired by John Smith's Tadcaster Brewery Co.Ltd in 1910.

Wakefield

Beverley Brothers Ltd, *Eagle Brewery, Harrison Street.* Founded 1861. Registered June 1888. Acquired by Watney Mann Ltd March 1967 with 173 public houses and brewing ceased October 1968.

Carter & Sons, *Victoria Brewery, Fairground Road.* Founded 1830. Merged with Kirk, Matthews & Co. of Leeds 1889 to form Leeds & Wakefield Breweries Ltd. 67 tied houses.

H.B.Clark & Co.(Successors) Ltd, *Westgate Brewery, Parliament Street.* Founded 1906. The brewery was in operation until 1960 supplying the free trade only and not brewing continuously, only to meet demand. Brewing recommenced July 1982 in a new brewhouse. Still brewing 1990 with 4 tied houses.

Clubs Breweries (Wakefield) Ltd. Formed 1920 and went into voluntary liquidation in February 1925.

N.L.Fernandes & Co, *Old Bridge Brewery, Doncaster Road.* Founded before 1877. Brewery and 42 public houses offered for auction 1st October 1919 and were acquired by John Smith's Tadcaster Brewery Co.Ltd.

Wakefield Spring Brewery Co.Ltd, *Wild's Yard.* Registered August 1894. Voluntary liquidation 10th September 1897 and was dissolved 22nd May 1908.

Walker & Co.Ltd, *Crown Brewery, Providence Place, Kirkgate.* Founded 1854 when George Newton purchased the Phoenix Brewery, York Street. Moved to the Crown Brewery in the early 1870s. Acquired by George Walker & Co. 1884. Registered 1886. 19 public houses sold by auction on 3rd November 1922 and brewing ceased.

Other Breweries

John Garthwaite, *Calder Row* (1936)
Minnie & Laura Harrison, *65 Northgate* (1921)
John McGuinn, *5/7 Silver Street* (1906)
Frederick William Walsh, *Duke of York Hotel, Westgate* (1923)

IRELAND

Bandon, County Cork

Allman, Dowden & Co, *Watergate Street.* Founded c.1800 and acquired by Allman, Dowden 1865. Acquired by Beamish & Crawford Ltd 1914.

James D'Arcy (1900)

Belfast

McConnell's Brewery Ltd, *Cromac Brewery, Ravenhill Road.* In operation 1890-c.1930.

Ulster Brewery Co.Ltd, *Mountain Brewery, Glen Road.* Registered December 1925 as Thomas R.Caffrey & Son Ltd. Public company formed January 1951. Renamed as above in 1947. Acquired by Charrington United Breweries 1964. Now operated as Bass Ireland. No tied houses.

Blessington, Wicklow

Harty's Brewery, *Industrial Estate.* Established in September 1983 by Liam Hartlake, Patrick Murray and Oliver Hughes. After 1984 traded as Dublin Real Ale Ltd. Ceased production 1985.

Carrick on Suir, Tipperary

Richard Feehan & Son, *Castle Street.* Founded 1820. Acquired by James Sullivan & Co. of Kilkenny 1911.

Castlebellingham, Louth

John Woolsey & Co.Ltd, *Castle Brewery.* Founded 1772. Merged with William Cairnes & Son Ltd of Drogheda 1890 to form Castlebellingham & Drogheda Breweries Ltd. Brewing ceased 1923.

Clonakilty, Cork

Deasy & Co.Ltd, *Emmett Square.* Founded by Richard Deasy 1800. Acquired by Travers, Canty & Wright 1880. Brewing ceased 31st January 1940 and porter was supplied by Guinness. Later used as a broiler chicken factory.

Clonmel, Tipperary

Thomas Murphy & Co.Ltd, *Nelson Street Brewery.* Founded 1798. Brewery for sale 1925 and was acquired by Bulmers Cider. Brewery still standing and used by Showerings.

Coleraine, Derry

Herald Old Traditional Brewery Ltd, *Old Stables, Millburn Road.* Established by Michael Herald in July 1982

Cork

J.A.Arnott & Co.Ltd, *St.Finbarr's Brewery.* A porter brewery. Acquired by James J.Murphy & Co.Ltd in 1901.

Beamish & Crawford Ltd, *Cork Porter Brewery, South Main Street.* Founded before 1715 when it was under the name of Edward Allen. Acquired by Beamish & Crawford 1792. For many years the largest brewery in Ireland until overtaken by Guinness. Registered October 1901. Acquired by Canadian Breweries 1962. Brewery still in operation 1990.

Lane & Co.Ltd, *Southgate Brewery, South Main Street.* Founded 1758. Acquired by Beamish & Crawford 1901 to whom they were adjacent.

James J.Murphy & Co.Ltd, *Ladyswell Brewery, Leitrim Street.* Founded 1856. Premises originally a foundling hospital. Registered December 1883. Acquired by Watney Mann Ltd 1966 but in 1971 the Irish government bought Watney's holding. In 1974 the brewery was bought by Licensed Vintners Holdings a consortium of independent publicans.

Riverstown Brewery Co, *Riverstown.* Acquired by James J.Murphy & Co.Ltd 1901 and was closed.

Drogheda, Meath

Cairnes Ltd. Founded 1828 by William Cairnes. Registered April 1890 as the Castlebellingham & Drogheda Breweries Ltd to acquire John Woolsey & Co.Ltd, Castlebellingham and William Cairnes & Son Ltd. Name changed as above in November 1933. Acquired by Guinness and ceased brewing in 1959.

-109-

Casey's Drogheda Brewery Co.Ltd, *Mell Brewery, West Street*. Founded 1840. Registered 1889 to acquire the business of Patrick Casey-Connolly. Closed 1920.

Dublin

John D'Arcy & Son Ltd, *Anchor Brewery, Usher Street*. Founded 1740. Registered 1896. Acquired by Watkins, Jameson, Pim & Co. 1926 and was closed.

Dartry Brewing Co, *Dublin South City*. A lager brewery founded by John Stoer 1892 but closed in 1897.

Dempsey's Brewery Ltd, *James Town Industrial Estate, Inchicore*. Established in July 1982 by Brian Herlely and Liam O'Duyer. Ceased brewing in 1986.

Foxes Brewery, *James Town Industrial Estate, Inchicore*. Established in Dempsey's old premises 1987.

Arthur Guinness, Son & Co.Ltd, *St.James's Gate*. Founded 1759. Registered October 1886. Park Royal Brewery, London opened 1936. Still brewing 1990.

Jameson, Pim & Co, *North Anne Street Brewery*. Founded *c.*1715. Merged with Joseph Watkins & Co. 1904 to form Watkins, Jameson Pim & Co.Ltd.

Robert Manders & Co, *New Brewery, 113 James Street*. Acquired by the Phoenix Brewery (Dublin) Ltd 1897 and was closed in 1900.

Mountjoy Brewery Ltd, *Russell Street*. Founded 1852. Known as Findlater & Co. until June 1891. Closed 1957.

Phoenix Brewery (Dublin) Ltd, *89 James's Street*. Founded 1778 and was later known as the Phoenix Porter Brewery Co. Registered January 1897. Acquired by John D'Arcy & Son 1906.

Sweetman & Co, *Francis Court Brewery, Francis Street*. Closed 1895. See also:- S.R.Conron, Hornchurch, London.

Joseph Watkins & Co, *Ardee Street*. The oldest Dublin brewery, reputed to date back to 1536. Merged with Jameson, Pim & Co. 1904. Closed 1937.

Dundalk, Louth

Great Northern Brewery Ltd, *Carrick Road*. Founded 1897. Acquired by Guinness 1959 for the production of Harp Lager. Still brewing 1990.

MacArdle, Moore & Co.Ltd, *Cambricville*. Founded *c.*1850. A Guinness subsidiary.

Dungarvan, Waterford

St.Brigid's Well Brewery. Founded before 1890. Ceased trading *c.*1905.

Enniscorthy, Wexford

G.H.Lett & Co.Ltd, *Millpark Brewery, Millpark Road*. Founded by the Pounder family 1832 and acquired by Lett 1864. Only Irish brewery to adopt Burton Union system. Brewery powered by a water wheel. Ceased brewing 1956. The French brewery, Pelforth acquired the rights to brew Lett's ales.

Enniskillen, Fermanagh

W.& J.Downes & Co.Ltd, *Anne Street*. Founded 1852. Registered 1905. Brewery and plant offered for sale April 1916 but possibly not closed until 1924.

Kells, Meath

Regal Lager Brewery Ltd. Founded 1937. Private company registered 1947. Closed 1954.

Kilkenny

E.Smithwick & Sons Ltd, *St.Francis Abbey Brewery*. Founded 1710. Registered 1899. A Guinness subsidiary through Irish Ale Brewers.

James Sullivan & Co, *St.James's Street*. Founded 1702 and acquired by the Sullivan family in 1810. 6 public houses. Acquired by Smithwicks 1914.

Lisburn, Antrim

Down Royal Brewery, *Down Royal Inn, Balinderry Road*. Home brew house established June 1982 by Paul Hont. Name changed to Foyle Brewery by 1988.

Hilden Brewery, *Hilden House*. Established October 1982 by Seamus Scullion.

Londonderry

Maiden Oak Brewery, *Ballymagroarty Industrial Estate*. Established July 1985 by Pat Doherty and Matt Bradley.

Lurgan, Armagh

James Johnstone. In operation *c.*1890-1915.

Monasterevan, Kildare

Cassidy & Co.(Monasterevan) Ltd. Founded 1860. Registered 1921. Also distillers. Closed 1925.

New Ross, Wexford

Cherry Brothers Ltd, *Greywell Brewery*. Founded 1828. Acquired by Irish Ale Brewers 1954.

Offaly

Shinrone Brewery Co. Never actual brewed beer as all their ales were produced by Harty's Brewery, Blessington.

Rathdowney, Laois

Robert Perry & Son Ltd. Founded 1800. Registered 1877. A Guinness subsidiary, closed 1967.

Sligo

Foley & Co.Ltd, *Lough Gill Brewery*. Founded 1842. Ceased brewing in the 1920s but bottling continued until 1972.

Strabane, Tyrone

Smyth-Holmes. Closed *c.*1895.

Tralee, Kerry

Lawrence Malone & Co. Closed *c.*1905.

Tullamore, Offaly

P.& H.Egan Ltd. Founded 1852. Registered 1896. Brewing ceased in 1926 but they continued to bottle until about 1980

Waterford

Davis-Strangman & Co.Ltd, *Mary Street Brewery*. Founded 1792. Registered 1888. Closed 1948 but was reopened 1954 by Guinness.

Patrick Keily & Sons Ltd, *St.Stephen's Brewery, New Street*. Founded 1798 and was acquired by Patrick Keily 1858. Registered October 1926. Closed 1946.

Westport, Mayo

William Livingstone Ltd, *Bridge Street*. Founded 1799. Registered 1907. Brewery closed 1920 but the business may have continued until *c.*1930 as ale & stout merchants and bottlers under the name of Livingstone Traders (Westport) Ltd.

Wexford

Michael Wickham, *Wexford Brewery*. Founded *c.*1800. Closed 1930.

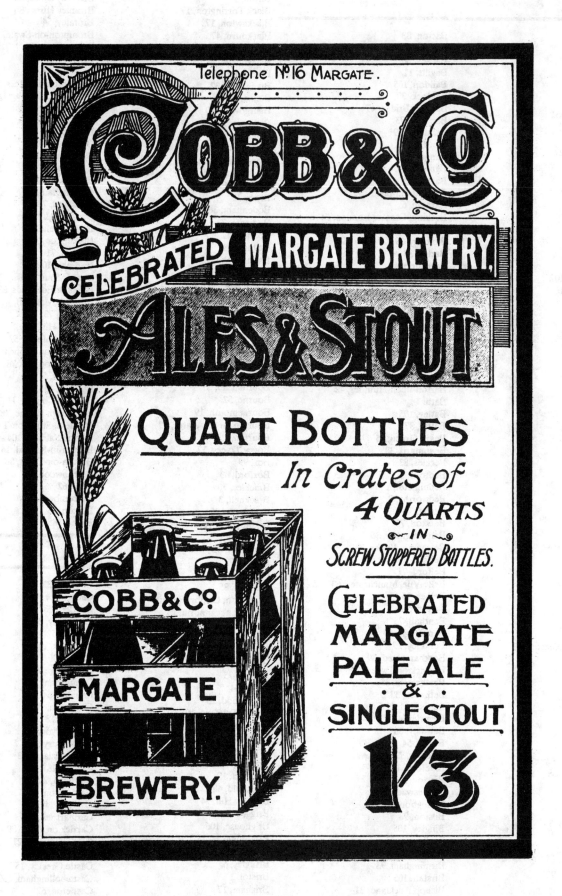

INDEX OF TOWNS

INDEX OF BREWERIES

Lacock Priory, Wilts, Brewing Copper, 16th C

The minnow amongst the Burton giants

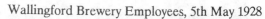

Wallingford Brewery Employees, 5th May 1928

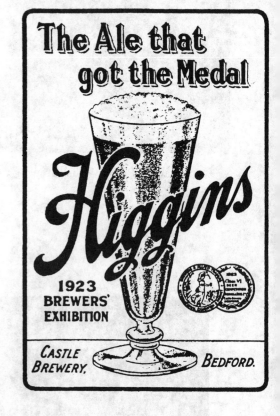

Penrhos Brewery, 38
Pentland Brewery, 60
Pentre Brewery, 27
Perry Barr Brewery, 93
Peterhead Brewery, 31
Petershill Brewery:-
 Edinburgh, 60
 Glasgow, 82
Phillips Brewery, 77
Phoenix Brewery:-
 Andover, 33
 Bedford, 3
 Boston, 52
 Brighton, 87
 Cardiff, 28
 Dorchester, 19
 Dover, 44
 Hastings, 87
 Horncastle, 52
 Kensington, 57
 Liverpool, 67
 Llantrisant, 26
 Luton, 3
 Margate, 45
 Newbury, 4
 Northampton, 70
 Peterborough, 8
 Portsmouth, 34
 Scarborough, 103
 Sleaford, 53
 Southwark, 58
 St.Helens, 68
 Sudbury, 84
 Wakefield, 109
 Wateringbury, 47
 West Bromwich, 98
Pickwick Brewery, 100
Picton Brewery, 26
Pilgrim Brewery, 86
Pilton Brewery, 79
Pinfold Brewery, 11
Pioneer Brewery, 54
Pitfield Brewery, 55
Plant Brewery, 104
Plassey Brewery, 11
Plasterer's Arms Brewery, 22
Pleasance Brewery, 90
Plough Brewery:-
 Adlington, 47
 Brierley Hill, 94
 Ledbury, 38
 Wandsworth, 59
Plough Inn Brewery, 104
Plympton Brewery, 18
Pockthorpe Brewery, 69
Pointings Brewery, 1
Pokesdown Brewery, 19
Pond Street Brewery, 105
Poole Brewery, 20
Poolstock Brewery, 66
Portcullis Brewery, 2
Portsmouth Brewery:-
 Brickwood, 34
 Tessier, 35
Powys Brewery, 75
Prince Arthur Brewery, 62
Prince of Wales Brewery:-
 Cambridge, 7
 Finchingfield, 24
 Halesworth, 83
 Llangollen, 11
 Nottingham, 72
Princess Royal Brewery, 81
Prior Well Brewery, 73
Priory Brewery:-
 Cambridge, 6

Neots, 8
Pritchard's Arms Brewery, 22
Prowse's Brewery, 19
Puzzlehall Brewery, 108

Q

Quarry Burn Brewery, 21
Quarry Hill Brewery, 46
Quay Brewery, 7
Queen Street Brewery:-
 Castle Douglas, 21
 King's Lynn, 68
 Sunderland, 91
Queen's Brewery:-
 Birkenhead, 66
 Blackpool, 48
 Carlisle, 14
 Macclesfield, 10
 Moss Side, 64
 Stourbridge, 97
Queen's College Brewery, 74
Queen's Cross Brewery, 95
Queen's Head Brewery, 78

R

Rabbit Brewery, 6
Radford Hall Brewery, 92
Radstock Brewery, 2
Raikes Tower Brewery, 105
Railway Brewery:-
 Bath, 1
 Brighouse, 106
Railway Inn Brewery, 38
Rainford Brewery, 68
Rainton Brewery, 90
Ram Brewery:-
 Bath, 1
 Wandsworth, 59
Raven Brewery, 87
Reciprocity Brewery, 67
Red Cross Brewery, 106
Red Kite Brewery, 22
Red Lion Brewery:-
 Alford, 52
 Basingstoke, 85
 Cardigan, 22
 Dorking, 85
 Dudley, 95
 Farnham, 85
 Greater London, 58
 Pwllheli, 33
Redbrook Brewery, 32
Redcliffe Brewery, 1
Redcliffe Mead Brewery, 1
Redcross Brewery, 1
Reddish Brewery, 66
Redhill Brewery, 86
Reepham Brewery, 69
Regent Brewery:-
 Plymouth, 18
 Ramsgate, 46
Regent Road Brewery, 65
Reigate Brewery, 86
Reindeer Brewery, 69
Rekendyke Brewery, 91
Rhadegund Brewery, 6
Richardland Brewery, 83
Richmond Brewery:-
 Liverpool, 67
 Plymouth, 18

Rickmansworth Brewery, 40
Ridley Arms Brewery, 90
Ringwood Brewery, 35
Risbygate Brewery, 83
Risca Brewery, 32
River View Brewery, 33
Roath Brewery, 28
Robin Hood Brewery:-
 Great Staughton, 7
 Tottington, 66
Rock & Fountain Brewery, 27
Rock Brewery, 94
Rock House Brewery, 66
Rock Spring Brewery, 109, 48
Rockside Brewery:-
 Barnsley, 104
 Thurlstone, 105
Rockwell Brewery, 74
Rodney Brewery, 7
Rose & Crown Brewery, 61
Rose Brewery, 67
Rose Street Brewery, 60
Roses Brewery, 86
Rossendale Brewery, 47
Rothbury Brewery, 71
Rothwell Street Tavern Brewery, 61
Round Oak Brewery, 97
Rout Green Brewery, 52
Rowbarton Brewery, 79
Rowland's Brewery, 37
Rowley Brewery:-
 Blackheath, 94
 Stourbridge, 97
Royal Albert Brewery, 4
Royal Arms Brewery, 33
Royal Brewery:-
 Brentford, 56
 Moss Side, 64
 Newport, 43
 Upton Snodsbury, 38
 Windsor, 4
Royal Forest of Dean Brewery, 30
Royal George Brewery, 37
Royal Oak Brewery:-
 Bath, 1
 Brandon, 92
 Croydon, 55
 Ledbury, 38
 Macclesfield, 10
 Stockport, 66
Royal Stag Brewery, 6
Royal Victoria Brewery, 46
Royal Well Brewery, 38
Royd Steam Brewery, 106
Rumsey Place Brewery, 75
Rutland Brewery:-
 Ketton, 50
 Leeds, 107
 Newark on Trent, 72
 Oakham, 51

S

Saddler's Arms Brewery, 22
Sailor's Home Brewery, 27
Salem Bridge Brewery, 54
Salford Brewery, 47
Salford New Brewery, 47
Salmon Springs Brewery, 30
Salt's Brewery, 95
Saltash Brewery:-
 Plymouth, 18
 Saltash, 13
Sam Powell Brewery, 75
Sandwell Brewery, 98
Sandyford Brewery, 90
Sandywell Brewery, 65
Santa Clara Brewery, 23

Saracen's Head Brewery:-
 Bury St.Edmunds, 83
 Margate, 45
Sark Brewery, 9
Saville Green Brewery, 105
Saxon Cross Brewery, 15
Scotties Brewery, 84
Sea Horse Brewery, 34
Seedlings Mount Brewery, 106
Serjeant-at-Arms Brewery, 64
Setch Bridge Brewery, 69
Seven Stars Brewery:-
 Kendal, 14
 Tipton, 97
Sevenoaks Brewery, 46
Severn Brewery, 76
Severn Side Brewery, 27
Shakespeare Brewery:-
 Cambridge, 7
 Redditch, 38
Shaw Brewery, 101
Sheaf Brewery, 105
Sheaf Island Brewery, 105
Sheering Hall Brewery, 25
Shelton Brewery, 82
Shernold Brewery, 45
Shibden Head Brewery, 106
Ship & Bell Brewery, 26
Ship Brewery:-
 Hereford, 37
 Lytham St.Annes, 49
 Merthyr Tydfil, 26
Shire Oak Brewery, 97
Shirley Brewery, 55
Shobnall Brewery, 81
Shore Brewery, 9
Shropshire Brewery, 77
Sidegate Brewery, 61
Sileby Brewery, 51
Six Bells Brewery, 26
Skinner Lane Brewery, 108
Slaughterford Brewery, 101
Small Heath Brewery, 94
Smithy Bank Brewery, 66
Snig Brewery, 47
Snig's Foot Brewery, 49
Snitterfield Brewery, 92
Soho Brewery:-
 Liverpool, 67
 Sheffield, 105
Sole Bay Brewery, 84
Solent Brewery, 34
Solihull Brewery, 97
Somerset Brewery, 29
Soothill Brewery, 106
South Cheshire Brewery, 10
South Cross Street Brewery, 34
South Devon Brewery, 18
South Devon Steam Brewery, 17
South Durham Brewery, 21
South Inch Brewery, 90
South Malling Brewery, 88
South Staffs Brewery, 99
South Stoke Brewery, 2
South Street Brewery, 105
South Wales Brewery, 28
South Western Brewery, 59
Southbroom Brewery, 100
Southdown Brewery:-
 Lewes, 88
 Portslade, 88
Southend Brewery, 93
Southgate Brewery:-
 Bury St.Edmunds, 83
 Cork, 109
 Leicester, 51
Southover Brewery, 87

INDEX OF BREWERIES

INDEX OF BREWERS

INDEX OF BREWERS

Hewitt Brothers Ltd, 42
Hewitt, Alfred, 95
Hewitt, Annie, 95
Hewitt, Frederick, 95
Hewitt, H & Co Ltd, 4
Hewitt, Robert & Son, 4
Hewitt, William, 6
Hextall, Robert E.B, 92
Hey, Edmund, 65
Hey, J. & Co.Ltd, 105
Heyes, Thomas, 67
Hibbard's Anchor Brewery, 32
Hibberd, George Herbert, 100
Hibbert, William, 73
Hickman & Pullen Ltd, 98
Hickman, Bernard Thomas, 98
Hickman, Charles, 3
Hickman, Sarah, 75
Hicks & Co, 18
Hicks, Walter & Co.Ltd, 13
Hickson, Giles, 65
Higgens, Frank & Co Ltd, 5
Higgins & Sons Ltd, 3
Higgins, Amelia, 74
Higgs, James, 97
Higgs, S H Ltd, 4
Highbury Brewery Ltd, 56
Higher Eanam Brewery Co.Ltd, 47
Highgate-Walsall Brewery Co.Ltd, 98
Highland Brewery Co.Ltd, 41
Higson's Brewery Ltd, 67
Hilden Brewery, 110
Hiles, Elizabeth, 77
Hiles, William, 77
Hill & Sons, 2
Hill Brothers, 79
Hill's Cromford Brewery Co.Ltd, 15
Hill, Augustus, 68
Hill, Benjamin Alfred, 97
Hill, Caroline, 13
Hill, Catherine, 78
Hill, Charles & Son, 81
Hill, Eliza Ann, 97
Hill, George, 72
Hill, George, 98
Hill, J & Co.Ltd, 23
Hill, James & Henry, 30
Hill, John, 85
Hill, John, 98
Hill, Laban, 96
Hill, Matthew, 15
Hill, Rowland, 97
Hill, Thomas, 37
Hill, William John, 76
Hilliard, Benjamin William, 74
Hills, W & Sons, 44
Hilton & Sons, 18
Hilton Brewery, 45, 46
Hilton, Alice, 48
Hilton, Henry, 62
Hilton, Ian, 45, 46
Hilton, John, 16
Hinckesman's Brewery Co.Ltd, 77
Hinde, T M & E W, 21
Hine Brothers, 35
Hinksman, Jack, 76
Hipkiss, Albert, 97
Hipwell & Co, 6
Hirst, John, 16
Hirst, Joseph & Henry Sagar, 105
Hit or Miss Home Brewhouse, 75
Hitch, Caleb, 41
Hitchman & Co.Ltd, 73
Hitherly, Edward A, 51
Hoar, Barrie & Robert, 51
Hoare & Co.Ltd, 58
Hoare, Charles, 94

Hoare, Herbert, 43
Hobbins, Thomas Harry, 72
Hobbins, Tom Harry, 71
Hobbs & Co, 34
Hobbs, George Nelson, 100
Hobley, Randle, 98
Hobson, Frederick, 97
Hockaday, Frederick James, 37
Hockaday, William, 27
Hocking, Peter, 76
Hoddinott, Benjamin, 29
Hodges & Ritchie, 87
Hodges, Cornelius W, 25
Hodgetts, Isabella, 97
Hodgkinson, Frank, 49
Hodgkinson, Joseph, 49
Hodgkiss, Harry, 98
Hodgson's Kingston
  Brewery Co.Ltd, 57
Hodgson, Mary C, 15
Hodgson, William, 14
Hodson, Thomas, 62
Hoe, Sarah, 72
Hogg, Mary Anne, 65
Hoggarth, George, 14
Hogge & Seppings Ltd, 69
Hoile, John, 46
Holben's Brewery, 7
Holcombe Brewery Ltd, 78
Holcroft, Ernest, 94
Holden's Brewery Ltd, 95
Holden, Edwin, 98
Holden, Henry, 44
Holden, John, 3
Holden, Richard Ltd, 47
Holden, William, 49
Holder's Brewery Ltd, 93
Holder, Henry, 89
Holdon, Edmund, 5
Hole, James & Co.Ltd, 72
Hole, Samuel, 66
Holehouse, Annie, 72
Holland, Albert, 72
Holland, John, 49
Holland, Joseph S, 6
Hollerton, William, 37
Holley, George Harris & Sons, 100
Hollies, Ernest John, 96
Hollings, Frank, 108
Hollingworth, A, 15
Hollingworth, Tom, 72
Hollinwood Brewery
  & Bottling Co.Ltd, 64
Hollis, Ellen, 16
Hollis, Frederick I, 73
Hollis, Mrs.Harry, 96
Hollister & Chadwick, 94
Holloway, Mrs, 35
Holly, James Edward, 101
Hollybush, 16
Hollyhead, William, 98
Holmes & Steward, 74
Holmes, Alfred, 102
Holmes, Harper & Neame, 30
Holmes, Herbert, 51
Holmes, Horace, 98
Holmes, J.R. & Sons, 105
Holmes, James & Co, 14
Holmes, Samuel E, 98
Holmes, Sydney John, 98
Holmes, Thomas A, 94
Holroyd, George Barron, 85
Holsten Brewery Ltd, 59
Holt & Co, 57
Holt Brewery Co.Ltd, 93

Holt Brothers Ltd, 78
Holt, Joseph Ltd, 63
Holtby, Thomas, 42
Home Brewed (Coventry) Ltd, 94
Home Brewed Ale Co.Ltd, 15
Home Brewery (Quarry Bank) Ltd, 94
Home Brewery Co, 8, 61, 71
Homer, Alfred Ltd, 93
Homes, Henry & Benjamin, 56
Homfray's Brewery Ltd, 38
Hont, Paul, 110
Hook Norton Brewery Co.Ltd, 74
Hook, Robert, 84
Hooley, Albert Arthur, 73
Hooley, George Ltd, 72
Hooley, John, 73
Hooper, Harold, 37
Hooson & Co, 104
Hop-Back Brewery, 101
Hopcraft & Norris Ltd, 70
Hope & Anchor Breweries Ltd, 104
Hopkins, Ernest Hambler, 38
Hopkins, Garlick & Co.Ltd, 37
Hopkins, Henry, 17
Hopper, George & Son, 3
Hordern, C.A. & Co, 10
Horler, Harry, 76
Hornby, Elizabeth, 49
Horncastle & Kirkstead
  Brewery Co.Ltd, 52
Hornchurch Brewery Co.Ltd, 56, 86
Horner, William Samuel, 2
Hornsey & Co, 40
Hornsey, Ian, 83
Horry, W.& Sons Ltd, 52
Horse Shoes, 95
Horsell, Howard, 101
Horsfall, Thomas, 48
Horton Old Brewery Co.Ltd, 105
Horton, Arthur Speller, 39
Horton, George Henry, 53
Hosking, Simon, 58
Hoskins & Oldfield Brewery Ltd, 51
Hoskins, Philip, 51
Hoskins, Stephen, 51
Hoskins, T. Ltd, 51
Hothersall, Henry, 49
Hough, Samuel, 10
Hought, William, 42
Houghton, Agnes, 49
Houghton, G G, 67
Houlding's Brewery Co.Ltd, 67
Hounslow Brewery Co.Ltd, 56
House family, 39
How & Son, 8
How, Sarah & Sons, 5
Howard, John, 73
Howard, Thomas Harry, 38
Howard, William F, 106
Howard, William Henry, 73
Howarth, Mary E, 49
Howarth, William H, 49
Howcroft's Brewery Ltd, 61
Howcroft, John, 73
Howden, Elizabeth, 54
Howe, James, 98
Howe, John, 21
Howell, Isaac B, 30
Howitt, Samuel, 8
Howland, William, 1
Hoxton Brewery Ltd, 55
Hubbard, Ezra, 77
Hubbard, Jennie, 73
Hubbard, John Henry, 52
Hubbert, William Henry, 52
Hucker, Henry Charles, 38
Hudson's (Cambridge &
  Pampisford) Brewery Ltd, 6
Hudson, G.& H, 103

Hudson, Philip Llewellyn, 8
Hufford, M, 6
Huggins & Co.Ltd, 59
Huggins, Mrs.S.A, 26
Hughes, Annie M, 37
Hughes, Arthur, 49
Hughes, Bertie L, 75
Hughes, Edward, 11
Hughes, Henry Gwynne, 38
Hughes, J.A, 89
Hughes, James & Gregory, 93
Hughes, Louisa, 98
Hughes, Mary Alice, 11
Hughes, Oliver, 109
Hughes, Sarah, 96
Hughes, Thomas, 77
Hughes, William, 97
Hull & Co, 37
Hull Brewery Co Ltd, 42
Hull Brewery Company, 42
Hull United Breweries Ltd, 42
Hull's Brewery Ltd, 49
Hull, James & Sons, 49
Hull, John J, 51
Hull, Thomas, 51, 80
Humby & Baillie, 81
Humby, J.F. & H.S, 100
Hundleby Brewery Ltd, 53
Hunstone, Elizabeth, 97
Hunt & Co, 33
Hunt & Son, 42
Hunt, Agnes, 108
Hunt, Edmunds & Co.Ltd, 73
Hunt, Frederick Walter, 2
Hunt, G.& H.R, 53
Hunt, John J.Ltd, 103
Hunt, M.P, 17
Hunt, Martha, 25
Hunt, Susan, 97
Hunt, W.J, 36
Hunter, John, 31
Hunter, Thomas Herbert, 37
Huntley, F.O.J, 12
Huntly Brewery Co, 31
Hurdle & Co, 25
Hurdle & Wileman, 23
Hurman, Robert, 56
Hurnard, Robert, 23
Hurst, Alex & Co, 34
Hurst, John L, 51
Hurst, Maureen, 3, 12
Hussey, T.W. & Son, 100
Hutchins, George, 34
Hutchinson Leisure Group, 48
Hutchinson, R.N. & Co.Ltd, 104
Hutchinson, W.H. & Sons Ltd, 72
Hutton's Brewery Ltd, 93
Hyde's Anvil Brewery Ltd, 64
Hyde, C.F, 65
Hyde, David, 96
Hyde, Susannah, 98
Hyslop, Stuart, 61
Hythe Brewery Co, 34

I

Iliffe, Thomas Enoch, 92
Ilkeston Brewery Co.Ltd, 16
Ilkley Brewery & Aerated
  Water Co.Ltd, 107
Imperial Lager Brewery Ltd, 56
Impett & Gardner, 46
Ind Coope Alloa Brewery Ltd, 9

Maiden Oak Brewery, 110
Maiden, William, 97
Mainwaring, Richard, 13
Major, Lucas & Co, 70
Major, Mary Ann, 37
Major, William, 73
Malam, Edward, 81
Malden, Aubrey C E, 8
Mallett's Brewery, 13
Mallett, Mark Rushmere, 84
Mallinson, John, 108
Malone, Lawrence & Co, 110
Maloney, Joseph, 98
Malpas, Thomas, 96
Malt & Hop Brewery, 70
Malt Shovel, 16, 95
Maltby & Co, 52
Maltby, Frederick Thomas, 53
Malton Brewery, 102
Malvern Chase Brewery Ltd, 38
Manchester Brewery Co.Ltd, 63
Mander, Alfred, 97
Manders, Robert & Co, 110
Manley, Thomas, 12
Mann & Co, 79
Mann, Crossman & Paulin Ltd, 59, 80
Mann, Joseph, 108
Manning, A.G.S.& T.S, 88
Manning, T & Co Ltd, 70
Mansell, Sarah, 100
Mansfield Brewery Co.Ltd, 72
Mansfield, Thomas & Miss A.M, 94
Maple Leaf, 72
Mappin's Brewery Ltd, 104
Mardell, James, 39
Marisco Tavern, 18
Market Brewery, 58
Market Drayton Brewery Co.Ltd, 76
Market Rasen Brewery Co.Ltd, 53
Markland, Ben, 50
Marlet Brewery, 87
Marrian, Thomas & Co.Ltd, 105
Marsden, Sidney, 81
Marsh, Ada P, 96
Marsh, Dan, 81
Marsh, Emily, 96
Marsh, J.L. & Sons Ltd, 19
Marsh, Joseph W, 93
Marsh, Minnie, 96
Marsh, Moses, 96
Marsh, Richard, 44
Marshall & Elvet Ltd, 30
Marshall Brothers
  (Huntingdon) Ltd, 7
Marshall, Alfred, 94
Marshall, Alice, 96
Marshall, Arthur, 98
Marshall, David & Co, 61
Marshall, George, 37
Marshall, John, 16
Marshall, Joseph, 107
Marshall, Lillian, 98
Marshall, William, 51
Marsland, P. & Sons, 107
Marsland, Sarah, 66
Marson, Owen & McNaught, 101
Marston Moor Brewery, 102
Marston's Dolphin Brewery Ltd, 20
Marston, John Taylor, 53
Marston, Thompson
  & Evershed Ltd, 80
Martin Ales, 44
Martin, Christopher, 53
Martin, Francis, 37
Martin, Frederick, 36
Martin, J, 36
Martin, John Henry, 37
Martin, John, 49
Martin, Joseph, 13, 99

Martin, Thomas, 50
Martin, William Henry, 45
Martin, William, 13
Marton Brewery Co.Ltd, 48
Maryport Brewery Ltd, 14
Mason Brothers, 71
Mason's Arms, 74
Mason, E. & Co.Ltd, 45
Mason, Fred H, 97
Mason, Henry Paul, 14
Mason, Thomas, 102
Massey's Burnley Brewery Ltd, 48
Massey, Dorothy May, 37
Massey, Stanley E, 37
Matcham & Hussey, 19
Mather, William Henry, 63
Matheson, W.A, 67
Matley, John W, 65
Matley, Levi, 65
Matthew, Frank J, 97
Matthews & Canning, 57
Matthews & Co, 20
Matthews, Ambrose, 12
Matthews, Frank, 64, 97
Matthews, James, 75
Matthews, John H, 75
Matthews, Leyshon, 29
Matthews, Thomas & Co, 85
Mattock, John S, 95
Mattock, Samuel, 38
Mauldon's Brewery, 85
Mauldon, J.C. & Sons, 84
Mauldon, Peter, 85
Maule, Carteret, 94
Maurice, F.W. & Co, 10
Mawdesley, Alan, 50
Mawson, Thomas, 56
May, Sydney, 17
Maybury, Esther, 97
McAdam & Co, 31
McArdle, John, 29
McBride, Roger, 46
McCarmick, Anthony & Co, 108
McCartney, Fred, 50
McCartney, James B, 92
McCauley, Hugh & Co, 31
McConnell's Brewery Ltd, 109
McDonald, John, 90, 99
McDonnell's, 55
McDonnell, John, 55
McEwan, William & Co.Ltd, 60
McFarale, George, 1
McGeorge & Heppenstalls Ltd, 72
McGregor, John, 68
McGuinn, John, 109
McGuinness, Thomas, 50
McIver, S.D, 51
McKee, Charles Frederick, 70
McKenna, B & J Ltd, 63
McKenzie, George, 94
McKerney, Hugh, 50
McKinlay & Co, 90
McLean & Co, 21
McLennon & Urquhart Ltd, 60
McLeod, Charles Campbell, 52
McLocklin, Albert, 16
McMillan, Robert & Co, 60
McMullen & Son, 40, 54
McNellan, John, 9
McNish, Alexander, 38
McPherson, John Ewan, 91
McQuat Ltd, 107
Meacher, Thomas, 5
Mead, Henry, 101
Mead, Walter, 23
Meade & Co.Ltd, 93
Meade, Alfred, 93

Meades, Mrs Julia, 37
Mealings, Richard, 94
Mears, Francis D'Oyley, 29
Meddings, Thomas W.H, 94
Medway Federation
  of Clubs Brewery Ltd, 44
Meek, Charles Lyon, 59
Meek, George, 29
Meese, George, 93
Meikle, Ian, 61
Meikle, J, 9
Meikle, John, 91
Meiklejohn, Robert, & Son, 9, 82
Meiklejohn, William, 26
Melborne Arms, 16
Melborne Brewery (Leeds) Ltd, 107
Melbourns Brewery Ltd, 53
Melcombe Horsey Brewery, 20
Mellersh & Neale Ltd, 86
Mellor, James & Sons Ltd, 67
Mellor, Samuel, 81
Melton Brewery, 84
Melvin, Alexander & Co, 60
Mendip Brewing Co Ltd, 2
Mendip United Breweries Ltd, 2
Mercer & Sons, 56
Mercer, John Ltd, 47
Mercer, Mr, 43
Mercer, Nicholas, 50
Mercer, T, 48
Meredith, George, 77
Meredith, John, 27, 81
Meridale Brewery Co, 99
Merrington, Enoch, 77
Merris, Mrs. Richard, 94
Metcalfe, John & Son Ltd, 103
Metcalfe, John, 103
Metropolitan & Home
  Counties Clubs Bry, 43
Meux's Brewery Ltd, 60
Meux, Richard, 54
Mew, Herbert & Co, 101
Mew, Langton & Co.Ltd, 43
Meyer, P A, 8, 40
Michell & Aldous, 54
Michell, George & Harriett, 89
Michell, Goodman,
  Young & Co.Ltd, 55
Michell, H, 89
Michie, J. & Sons Ltd, 31
Mickles Brewery, 40, 41
Middleborough, J.N. & G. Ltd, 103
Middleton, Bert, 96, 97
Middleton, Edward, 94
Middleton, Elizabeth, 97
Middleton, George, 51
Middleton, Harold Edward, 108
Middleton, Harry, 37
Middleton, John Henry, 92
Middleton, Maria, 96
Midgley, William, 65
Midland Brewery Co.Ltd, 51
Midland Home Brewing Co.Ltd, 99
Midlands Clubs Brewery Ltd, 51
Miles, John, 35
Miles, William, 97
Milford, James, 2
Mill Brewery, 18
Mill's Brewery (Wisbech) Ltd, 8
Millar, Robert, 26
Millard, Bert & Don, 95
Millard, Isaac, 94
Millard, James, 101
Millard, Ruth, 96
Millard, William, 96
Miller & Aldworth Ltd, 44
Miller, Daniel Herbert, 7

Miller, E.J. & Co.Ltd, 80
Miller, Frederick, 23
Miller, Herbert Edward, 84
Miller, J.& J, 9
Miller, Jane, 6
Miller, John, 29
Miller, R W & Co Ltd, 1
Miller, R.W. & Co, 37
Millington, Randolph Kemp, 73
Mills & Co, 29
Mills Brothers, 18
Mills, Ada, 98
Mills, Edward, 85
Mills, Frank, 65, 68
Mills, Henry, 98
Mills, James, 97
Mills, Tom, 108
Millward Brothers, 98
Millward, David, 97
Millward, Eli, 96
Milne, James & Co, 31
Milson, David, 99
Milton, Manning, 89
Min Pin Inn, 13
Miner's Arms Brewery, 79
Miner's Arms, 79, 95
Minera Brewery, 11
Minerva Brewery, 42
Mines, Fred T, 77
Minkley, Joseph, 15
Minors, Frederick William, 98
Miskin Arms, 27
Miskin, William, 44
Mitcham & Cheam
  Brewery Co.Ltd, 57
Mitchell, Charles R, 37
Mitchell, F.& Co, 79
Mitchell, Henry & Co.Ltd, 97
Mitchell, R.& J, 26
Mitchell, Robert, 71
Mitchell, William, 17, 48
Mitchells & Butlers Ltd, 93
Mitchells of Lancaster
  (Brewers) Ltd, 48
Mobberley, Samuel, 96
Moffat, Jim, 31
Moffatt, William, 52
Mole's Brewery (Wayward Ltd), 100
Molesworth & Bean, 50
Molesworth's Poynings Brewery Ltd,
89
Molineux, George T, 77
Molyneux, Thomas, 67
Mona Brewery Co.Ltd, 33
Money, Benjamin, 53
Monger, James, 58
Monk, Edward & Sons, 88
Monkswear Brewery, 91
Monmouth Fine Ales, 32
Monson, G.J.& Co, 3
Montgomery & Co, 82
Montgomery's Brewery, 67
Montgomery, Harris & Co, 70
Montgomery, Thomas, 10
Montgomeryshire
  Brewery Co.Ltd, 22, 75
Moody & Son, 101
Moody, Charles F, 84
Moor Park Brewery Co, 49
Moor, Henry & Charles, 42
Moorcroft, Henrietta, 97
Moore & Simpson Ltd, 93
Moore, Charles Frederick, 96
Moore, Edith, 96

INDEX OF BREWERS

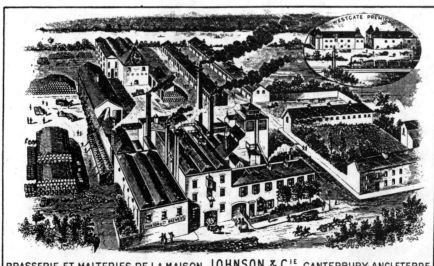

BRASSERIE ET MALTERIES DE LA MAISON JOHNSON & Cⁱᵉ CANTERBURY, ANGLETERRE

THE BREWERY HISTORY SOCIETY

The Brewery History Society was founded in April 1972 to bring together people with a common interest in the history of brewing, to stimulate research and to encourage the interchange of information. To this end members receive a quarterly Journal - Brewery History - which contains articles about brewers and breweries from as early a date as possible as well as more up-to-date news of mergers, takeovers and new small breweries.

Meetings are held in different parts of the country at which members can get together for a chat and a pint or two and occasional visits to breweries are arranged.

The Society has an Archivist whose responsibility it is to safeguard the books and research material acquired by the Society. He will endeavour to answer specific enquiries from both members and the general public, or will pass them on to the appropriate County Archivist. These are volunteers who take responsibility for correlating research within their own area whilst liaising with the Archivist. A Photographic Collection is maintained to which members are encouraged to donate copies of their own photographs. Copies of photographs in the collection may be purchased. The Society also maintains a Book Shop which holds a large stock of new and second-hand books on beer and brewing.

Upon joining, new members will receive a copy of the Journal, membership card, a list of fellow members and their interests, a copy of the Rules and Constitution and current Book Shop list.

Further details may be obtained from:-
THE MEMBERSHIP SECRETARY
Brewery History Society
Manor Side East
Mill Lane
Byfleet, Weybridge
Surrey KT14 7RS

Also published by the Brewery History Society

JUSTLY CELEBRATED ALES

A Directory of Norfolk Brewers, by Andrew P Davison

ISBN 1-873966-01-6 - A4 Paperback

WESTERHAM ALES

A Brief History of the Black Eagle Brewery, Westerham,

by Peter Moynihan and K R Goodley

ISBN 1-873966-00-8 - A5 Paperback

For more information on these and other brewing related publications please write to:

The Sales Manager

Brewery History Society,

6 Pine Close,

Biggleswade,

Bedfordshire SG18 OEF

THIS SPACE HAS BEEN PROVIDED FOR YOUR OWN RESEARCH NOTES

c/o 102 AYELANDS, NEW ASH GREEN, LONGFIELD, KENT DA3 8JW

PLEASE DO NOT FORGET TO NOTIFY THE AUTHOR OF ANY NEW FINDINGS
c/o 102 AYELANDS, NEW ASH GREEN, LONGFIELD, KENT DA3 8JW

THIS SPACE HAS BEEN PROVIDED FOR YOUR OWN RESEARCH NOTES

PLEASE DO NOT FORGET TO NOTIFY THE AUTHOR OF ANY NEW FINDINGS
c/o 102 AYELANDS, NEW ASH GREEN, LONGFIELD, KENT DA3 8JW